THE HORIZON BOOK OF
LOST WORLDS

The
*c*HORIZON
Book of

LOST WORLDS

By the Editors of

HORIZON MAGAZINE

Editor in Charge

MARSHALL B. DAVIDSON

Narrative by

LEONARD COTTRELL

Published by AMERICAN HERITAGE PUBLISHING CO., INC., NEW YORK

Book Trade Distribution by DOUBLEDAY & COMPANY, INC.

Horizon

PUBLISHER
James Parton

EDITORIAL DIRECTOR
Joseph J. Thorndike, Jr.

EDITOR
William Harlan Hale

MANAGING EDITOR
Eric Larrabee

EDITOR, BOOK DIVISION
Richard M. Ketchum

Staff for this Book

EDITOR
Marshall B. Davidson

ASSISTANT EDITORS
Norman Kotker
Dale Haven

PICTURE EDITORS
Mary Sherman Parsons
Phyllis Tremaine Iselin

COPY EDITORS
Jane Ferguson Hoover
Miriam R. Koren

EUROPEAN BUREAU
Gertrudis Feliu, *Chief*
Claire de Forbin
Timothy Green
Maureen Green
Maria Todorow
Ann Natanson

ART DIRECTOR
Irwin Glusker

DESIGNER
Joel Szasz

HORIZON Magazine is published by American Heritage Publishing Co., Inc., 551 Fifth Avenue, New York 17, N.Y.

FRONTISPIECE: *This row of portraits from the ancient past summons up the spirit of four vanished nations. Bearded and stern, the bronze visage at left portrays an Elamite priest or ruler, whose people had settled in southwestern Iran by the second millennium* B.C. *The next portrait, carved in highly polished stone, is of Gudea, the pious and powerful governor of Lagash. The third, a faintly smiling face, crowns a statue called the Apollo of Veii, a god of the Etruscans. The last portrait, in stone, is of the remarkable Queen Hatshepsut who ruled Egypt as the pharaoh; to secure her role as god-king, she was frequently pictured as a man, and here wears "the beard of the Gods," which was a pharaonic insigne.*

COVER IMPRINT: *The Egyptian hieroglyphs are from an inscription upon the Great Girdle Wall of the Temple of Horus at Edfu. Dating from around 100* B.C., *the text records the amount of land that could be tilled in certain sections of the Nile Valley.*

CONTENTS

INTRODUCTION

Between five and six thousand years ago, in a few favored areas of the world, man firmly mastered the formulas that released him from an immeasurably long past of savagery, barbarism, and nomadism. He took root as he had never done before, and he flourished. Millenniums before the classic age of Greece he had learned to adventure with "language and wind-swift thoughts and city-dwelling habits." For the first time in his history on earth he became aware of his humanity. He had become civilized.

At different times, in diverse places, and amid varying circumstances—independently or encouraged by helpful exchanges of ideas and practices—a number of major civilizations emerged from the dim obscurity of the Stone Age. Each developed distinctive and complex patterns and each made a rich contribution to human experience. Most of them endured for many centuries, a few for a longer time than separates our own world from that of Christ and Caesar. But they all faded and withered away, and their remarkable achievements were practically forgotten for ages to come. Even as early as the fifth century B.C., Thucydides, the most reliable of ancient historians, confidently observed that nothing of importance had happened before his time.

Vague memories of some of these "lost worlds" lingered throughout the centuries in the form of legends from an improbable, remote past. Others were recalled in resounding but tantalizing passages of the Old Testament. Some left imperishable monuments whose meaning, however, remained inscrutable to later ages. Still others vanished under mounds of dust, desert sands, or silt from floods, or were covered by the overwhelming growth of tropical jungles, and were all but gone from the sight and mind of man.

The recovery of these long-forgotten episodes in human history has been an astonishing performance—as remarkable in its way, and as rewarding, as weighing the stars or reaching the moon. As a result of an immense amount of research that has been carried out in the field, the study, and the laboratory, our own generation is aware of more aspects of the distant past than were dreamed of by our great-grandfathers and their fathers. Much that was long accepted as implausible myth or poetic allegory has been substantiated. The great Tower of Babel, the labyrinthine palace of Ariadne's father, King Minos, the fabulous Hanging Gardens of Babylon, and other wonders and curiosities of the ancient world have taken the shape of historical reality. The worlds of the all-conquering Sargon and Hammurabi the lawgiver, of Sennacherib and Assurnasirpal, "the great king, king of Assyria," of Abraham and Moses, of Agamemnon, Priam, and the wise King Nestor, and of the mighty Egyptian pharaohs Tuthmosis III and Ramesses II have come alive again before our eyes.

So too, without any warning from history, the virtually forgotten civilizations, which once had flourished in and about the Indus River Valley in what is now northern India and Pakistan, in the Cambodian realm of the Khmers, and in the land of the American Maya, have been recovered from their long oblivion and their story has been in part retold.

In some instances the languages of these ancient peoples have not been deciphered, or their written literature not discovered. But in every case they left images of themselves and of the world about them and we can visualize them as they chose to see themselves—in wall paintings and reliefs, in carved and sculptured portraits, in votive figures and talismans that gave some descriptive form to the forces that shaped their lives and that reflect the nature of life as they knew it. It is an indication of the growing awareness of our past that these images, which when first discovered often seemed incomprehensibly archaic, alien, and grotesque, have taken their places in the history of art as significant and, as often as not, beautiful objects.

There are times, to be sure, when our picture of this remote past seems kaleidoscopic. Fragments of fact and conjecture fall into attractive patterns that brighten the imagination; then, with new discoveries and further studies, the pattern shifts and suggests new meanings. For all that has been done and learned only a tiny fraction of the full record has been unearthed and deciphered. The site of Sargon's capital at Akkad, one of the most crucially important cities of third-millennium Mesopotamia, has not yet been identified, much less excavated. We still do not know the exact location of Arzawa, the ancient kingdom which contested the authority of the formidable Hittites a thousand years later; or of Wassukkanni, capital of the Mitanni empire which also challenged the Hittites and which fought as well against the great Tuthmosis III, "the Napoleon of ancient Egypt." Archaeologists are still searching around the temple centers in the jungles of Guatemala and Yucatan for aggregations of dwellings that would provide evidence of truly urban life among the Maya; every other high civilization ultimately produced cities, and if the Maya did not we would like to know the reason. And with the mention of cities we are led to wonder if the sites of Sodom and Gomorrah will ever be excavated and, perhaps, the legend of their wickedness confirmed.

Time may tell, but it will not tell all. What is continually being revealed to us from the record of the past cannot ever be more than a bare outline of the complete story. Yet what has already been learned is enough to remind us that the more we recover of the lost worlds of history, the more fully we realize that they have never really been lost. As Herbert Muller has observed, time the great destroyer is also the great preserver. More of the past has been preserved than we can ever be conscious of—"the immense accumulation of products, skills, styles, customs, institutions, and ideas that make the man on the American street indebted to all the

More importantly than any other single factor, the Rosetta Stone (above) led to the understanding of Egyptian writing. On this basalt slab the same message is inscribed in hieroglyphs (top register), demotic (a cursive Egyptian script; middle register), and Greek (bottom register). With the aid of the familiar Greek the other two were deciphered.

peoples of history, including some who never saw a street."

When we look back over the millenniums to the earliest of the major civilizations that developed on our planet, our distant view tends to foreshorten the course of events. What seems from our perspective a sudden, miraculous flowering was in fact a relatively slow growth. The first transition from nomadic and predatory life to a settled and orderly existence took thousands of years. The beginnings of the process can be discerned in the well-watered uplands bordering the Arabian, Syrian, and Iranian deserts somewhere between 8000 and 7000 B.C., when men tentatively left their caves and provisional shelters and gathered together in more or less fixed communities. By learning to domesticate plants and animals he spared himself the burdensome task of searching them out, of collecting them, and hunting them. In his patch of barley or wheat he captured and tamed a small part of the wilderness world. He learned to breed goats and pigs and cattle and he thereby converted a similarly small part of the animal kingdom into "living larders and walking wardrobes" that were at his constant service.

It was a more abundant and secure life than his long line of forebears had known. By about 4000 B.C. or earlier some communities had by such means so increased their production of food that their arable fields could support a burgeoning urban population, and "city-dwelling habits" with all their complexities were in the making. Within three or four thousand years the conditions of life had changed more radically than they had over the preceding quarter of a million years. Placed against this longer perspective it was indeed a sudden and miraculous flowering.

Yet the next thousand years witnessed an even more spectacular revolution in the condition of man. With the elementary problems of agriculture and stock breeding solved, human energies were released for countless untried experiments and enterprises that need not be concerned with the procurement of food. The period between about 4000 and 3000 B.C. has been judged more fertile in fruitful inventions and discoveries than any other period in human history before the sixteenth century A.D. During this span of years were mastered the basic mechanical principles on which the higher life we call civilization would depend—weaving, metallurgy, the plow, and the wheel both for transportation and for turning pottery. The technique of molding bricks was invented, draft animals were harnessed for new sources of motive power, sails were devised to capture the force of the winds, and seals were created to distinguish and protect private property—first evidence of the incipient capitalism that tempered the essential communalism of most early societies. Rudimentary as many of these mechanical developments may seem to us, they were nevertheless foundation stones on which the structure of a civilized world could rise.

An unprecedented pooling of human experience, skill, and effort attended both the birth of civilization and the rise of cities wherein it first took discernible form. More was involved than increased wealth and advanced technology, although both were required; life at a civilized level called for new relationships between human beings—economic organization, political controls, and social attitudes that, like the wheel and the plow, had to be invented and tried in practice. And it entailed new relationships as well with the gods who controlled human destinies—a more elaborate formulation of religious beliefs and observances to match the increasingly complex problems of society.

Above all the rise of civilization depended upon a meeting of minds, and it was in the cities with their market places, temples, and palaces—and their side streets—that such meetings more readily took place. The very word *civilization* literally means the making of cities and urban life. And it was to serve the busy traffic of the city that the Sumerians created the art of writing, the clearest indication of all that man was civilized. Now as never before he could share his experience, record his old traditions, project his thoughts over distances, and bequeath them to the future.

The text and pictures of this book describe nine different early worlds in which a human society adopted the innovations, mastered the inventions, and developed the institutions that led to high civilization. They have been selected because their notable achievements are now a story that can be told with some adequate measure of completeness. In some cases the record is rich and detailed. In others it remains a broad outline to be filled in, we may hope, by work in progress and by discoveries yet to be made. With increasing knowledge we can more clearly retrace the complex currents that have fed the main stream of our civilization from many directions and from distant sources. The enormous debt of the Western world to the cultures of ancient Greece and Rome has been so continually obvious that it has obscured what lay beyond—the sizable debt these people in turn owed to still more ancient people. As the earlier quoted remark of Thucydides suggests, the Greeks and Romans themselves were little enough aware of it.

We are no more intelligent than the Greeks and Romans, but we are better informed about the distant past than they were. We can see well beyond the time of their own rude beginnings, and we can trace the shifting course of our Western tradition back to the earliest of all civilizations in Mesopotamia—the land of Sumer—and in Egypt.

No one knows who the Sumerians were, that is, what their racial origins may have been or what was the source of their language; but virtually everyone agrees that these brown-skinned, dark-haired people who came down from the mountains of Iran to settle the marshy lands of the Tigris-

Euphrates Valley were the first people in history to develop the arts and practices that constitute civilized life. During the course of the fourth millennium B.C. they had already raised proud cities with monumental temples, converted the capricious bounty of the Twin Rivers into a regulated system of irrigation, invented a system of writing, and created a literature, learned to use copper and then cast bronze for tools and weapons, and by a score of other successful trials and experiments evolved a culture that endured in its essentials for thousands of years and radiated influences in all directions. To the east, Sumerian influence may have played some part in the growth of a civilization in the valley of the Indus River that can be traced back at least to 2500 B.C.

Almost simultaneously with the rise of Sumer, in a comparable outburst of human creativity, another civilization rose along the banks of the Nile. How much this efflorescence owed to the light of earlier Sumerian experience cannot be accurately measured, although some debt is apparent. However, the rapid development of Egyptian culture took its own distinctive and tenacious form and found its principal strength in purely native forces of mind and spirit—and, it should be added, without the friction and ferment of urban life. The fabulous capital of Memphis, where ten successive dynasties of early pharaohs built their temples and their palaces, was indeed a venerable center, and the authority that emanated from it reached far up the length of the Nile Valley. Someone has referred to ancient Egypt as one long suburbia; many centuries passed before the valley could boast of true cities.

If we push back in time beyond Sumer and Egypt we reach universal primitivism. In these two instances, perhaps the only instances in history, the transition from a rudimentary level of subsistence to the conditions of highly civilized life was achieved independently and spontaneously. These, in any case, are the only instances in which we can witness such a transition, and we might consider this the birth of civilization in a general sense. In the Far East and in Middle America man also created new worlds but, fascinating as these are, their origins remain obscure, at least for the present.

For the rest, civilization has been acquired by people of primitive ways from their more advanced fellows by peaceful inheritance or by violent appropriation. It has spread with the drift of men about the earth—along the routes of migrations, invasions, and trading enterprises. Both Sumer and Egypt—and the Indus Valley as well—enjoyed the advantages of great rivers that replenished and watered their lands and that served as major highways for the transit of men with thoughts and goods to exchange.

The ancient Near East, athwart the international highways that link the three continents of Africa, Europe, and Asia, has played the most prominent role in the diffusion of cultures. From the very beginning the populous centers of Sumer were magnets that attracted the motley who lived beyond the pale of civilization. In the nearby Arabian Desert and on the fringe of the highlands to the north, east, and west roamed barbarian nomads who were scorned by the city sophisticates, but who were feared as well, for they were ever poised to swoop down into the fertile valley or slowly infiltrate its precincts. They traded and fought with the valley dwellers, and in the process themselves took on the complexion of civilization.

The Arabian Desert was, so far as history reveals, the original home of the tribes that comprised the Semitic peoples. On the steppes far to the north were other tribes whose language was Indo-European. In one of the great continuing movements of history, for millennium after millennium, nomadic people erupted out of these two great, relatively barren regions and descended upon the civilized areas of the Near East and the Mediterranean world.

At a very early date Semitic tribesmen had intermingled with the nations of the Nile Valley to prepare the way for the development of Egyptian civilization, and in later times, years of famine in their own lands led wandering Semites from the east and north to the greener pastures bordering the Nile Delta, as later in the times when the wondering Shepherd Kings—the Semitic Hyksos—moved in and even usurped the authority of Pharaoh. (The children of Israel arrived in their train.) Other Semites had overwhelmed the previous inhabitants of Canaan and took over such ancient sites as Jericho and Byblos and built other cities throughout the hills overlooking the eastern Mediterranean coast.

Another wave of Semites had rolled eastward into the Tigris-Euphrates Valley and by 2300 B.C. usurped the control of its city-states from the native Sumerians. They assimilated the indigenous culture of Sumer and ruling from their capital at Akkad—the Akkad of Sargon—reinvigorated a civilization that survived almost two thousand years more through the leadership of Babylonia and Assyria.

These settlers were in turn subjected to further invasions of Semitic nomads from the desert. About the turn of the second millennium B.C. Babylonian reports complained of aggressive "westerners," who were the Amorites and whose princes left their names everywhere from the coastline of Syria to the highlands of Iran. Centuries later the Hebrews pushed westward to seize Canaan from other Semites, and many centuries still later the greatest Semitic wave of all, the great migration of the Arabs, swept across the lands and shaped an empire that stretched from Spain to India.

The first Indo-Europeans to appear on the world stage were the Hittites, who thrust westward out of the uplands of central Asia and shortly after 2000 B.C. asserted their rule over a large part of Asia Minor, shouldering aside or subjugating the earlier inhabitants and, as their power waxed, challenging the authority of Babylonia to the east and Egypt to the south. At the same time another stream of Indo-Europeans coursed into Greece and imposed their Greek language upon the earlier inhabitants of that peninsula. In close association with the brilliant contemporary civilization on the island of Crete, these so-called Mycenaeans developed an aggressive civilization of their own that is vividly recalled in the great epics of Homer. Earlier, kinsmen of the Mycenaeans had settled at Troy, overlooking the Hellespont—a citadel that stood at the crossroads of two continents and that was sacked and rebuilt time and again before the days of Agamemnon, Achilles, and the fair Helen.

Farther to the east Indo-European contemporaries of the Hittites and the Mycenaeans threatened to engulf the ancient world of Mesopotamia, the kingdom now ruled from Babylon; but the Babylonians suffered their intrusions and, in time, absorbed them into their own deep-rooted civilization. Still other warrior tribes filtered down through the Caucasus and drifted over the higher land northeast of Mesopotamia and settled there. The Greeks and Romans referred to this plateau country as Ariana; today we know it as Iran. Both words were derived from the name that the nomads used for themselves, a name akin to the term *Aryan*. The Iranians included peoples known to history as the Medes and the Persians, who in the sixth century B.C. swarmed over ancient Mesopotamia and brought the long continuity of its culture to an end. And in the more distant Orient divergent expeditions of Indo-Europeans fell upon the hapless people of the Indus River Valley and almost completely obliterated the civilization that had been nurtured there for more than a thousand years; but on its neglected ruins these invaders laid the grounds for the long and rich development of Indian culture.

Toward the end of the thirteenth century B.C., a great convulsion of wandering people shook the ancient world; established patterns were shattered as tumultuous hordes of migrants poured into Asia Minor and the Aegean world and down the Syrian and Palestine coast. Some of these barbarians, storming across Anatolia and overthrowing the mighty Hittites who had held sway there for seven centuries past, proceeded to sack the cities of Canaan. In several great waves other tribes of wanderers, including the Philistines and people with strange names who are collectively known to us as the Sea Peoples, mounted crippling but unsuccessful attacks on Egypt. Under the leadership of the Philistines, some of these restless tribes settled among the Semites along the coastal plains of the Levant. And into this rich land, so long a crossroads of empire and now free of Egyptian and Hittite domination, a confederation of tribes who called themselves Hebrews, after years of wandering in the desert wilderness, were finally able to settle uneasily in the neighborhood of the more powerful Philistines.

On the western coast of Asia Minor there was soon formed another new confederacy, led by the people of Troy. But Troy had powerful rivals and, probably sometime in the thirteenth century B.C., Homer's heroes, the Mycenaeans, laid siege to the city. After ten years, they entered and sacked this often-beset citadel. Then, within decades, the Mycenaeans were themselves overcome and dispersed by more roving tribes, the Greek-speaking Dorians, who poured down into Hellas from regions to the north.

By about 1100 B.C. high civilization was once again confined mainly to its original homes in Egypt and Mesopotamia. Asia Minor was thrown into darkness, in Greece even the art of writing was forgotten, and the glories of Crete and of Mycenae vanished into legend. But during this Dark Age other civilizations were seeded and slowly matured. The Hebrews enjoyed a brief period of ascendancy under their great kings Saul, David, and Solomon, a thousand years or so before the time of Christ. To their north the Phoenician cities of Tyre and Sidon took over from the wreckage of the Mycenaean maritime empire the trade routes of the Mediterranean Sea. Along with freight, Phoenician ships also carried colonists who, about 800 B.C., founded Carthage. With these merchants and settlers went the alphabet that the Phoenicians had evolved and that the illiterate Greeks learned to use and to shape into forms of classic beauty. In time the Greeks rivaled the Phoenicians as traders in the east, and in the west Greek colonists joined in a three-cornered contest for control of the Mediterranean trade with the Carthaginians and a new people, the Etruscans, whose development in Italy may have been a by-product of the great disruption caused by the migrating waves of Sea Peoples.

On the Asiatic mainland new empires arose. In the centuries between about 900 and 331 B.C. the Assyrians, the Babylonians, and the Persians in turn took control over the old world of Mesopotamia and went on to conquer Syria, kingdom of the Hebrews, and the tottering realm of the pharaohs. After the fall of Babylon to the Persians in 539 B.C. Mesopotamia and Egypt became provinces of new empires and their old civilizations faded into the evolving patterns of the future. It had taken long centuries for the Persians, the Greeks, and the Romans to rise from semibarbarism and take over the mantle of civilization. But now it was these descendants of migrant hordes who would define its terms and pass on its traditions, forgetful of the ultimate sources of their own great cultures.

As the ancient Mesopotamian and Egyptian worlds slowly lost their identities and drifted into obscurity, a new world of astonishing complexity was forming beyond the unknown limits of the western sea. The Maya of Middle America evolved a classic culture that was rooted in the mysterious depths of the jungle and that flourished while medieval

Europe, set upon by still more wandering tribes from the barbarian world, was passing through its own Dark Ages. Preoccupied with the passage of time, the society of these strangely gifted people seems to have suddenly disappeared, as all the other societies had waned and in turn were lost to time. As the Maya reached the summit of their achievement and started their decline, the Khmers on the other side of the world were building their great capital of Angkor Thom in the jungles of Cambodia—jungles that relentlessly grew back over these high achievements and obscured them from the rest of the world for centuries to come.

Civilization is a relative condition; it implies an advance from a state of barbarism. We might say it involves the pursuit of happiness. But, as in the case of happiness, we have no satisfactory way of measuring degrees of civilization. Because our own age has such a highly developed sense of the past, such a broad historical perspective, we can realize the unique quality of modern civilization better than any earlier societies were able to assay their age in comparison with what had gone before. Yet man has always lived in "modern" times, even if in ages past this obvious fact has not impressed him so deeply as it does us in our own day. And as we explore the dead civilizations of history we find, amid much that seems strange and even grotesque, human values, human achievements, and human situations that are commensurable with our own.

It would be a rash critic who claimed, for instance, that our contemporary art shows any significant advance from the finest work of the ancient Egyptians or of the Khmers of early Cambodia; or that our present civilization has achieved a greater harmony of individual and society and of society and nature than characterized the civilization of those same Egyptians or of the so-called Minoans of ancient Crete. As we recognize the term, civilization has always been attended by surplus wealth, advanced technology, and specialization of human effort within a community. But it is not reasonable to define the term by equating the progress of civilization with the increase of material well-being. The conversion of more and more luxuries into more and more necessities has not in our present world, at least, always speeded the pursuit of happiness.

The more we ponder the term the more elusive its real meaning appears to be, although we continue to use it confidently enough. Alfred North Whitehead has claimed that adventure is the true key to civilization. In sharing the adventures of the human beings who developed the "forgotten" worlds of the past we may hope to reach a better understanding of what civilization essentially amounts to. As we enlarge the awareness of our heritage from these remote societies we can only add to the meaning of our own experience.

The Editors

NAMES AND DATES

The long road back to the pioneering past of Sumer and Egypt leads us to places with strange names and introduces us to people whose names are even stranger. In many cases there is no general agreement, even among scholars, as to how these should be spelled. The spelling used in these pages follows what seemed to be the most common usage and the simplest forms, with every effort to maintain reasonable consistency. So too there is often disagreement among the most knowledgeable authorities in the matter of dates. The chronology of the ancient world is in a constant state of flux; dates are more frequently than not interdependent, and when one is changed in the light of new discoveries, in time—sometimes slowly and erratically through the medium of scholarly publications— scores of others are dislocated from their tentatively established positions. Here again, in the chart on pages 12 and 13 and throughout the text, a reasonable consistency in relation to the most generally accepted and qualified opinion has been aimed at, but in a great many cases, the dates that are indicated must still be considered only approximate.

CHRONOLOGY

EGYPT		MESOPOTAMIA		CRETE AND MAINLAND
PREDYNASTIC PERIOD				
OLD KINGDOM	**3100–2160**	**JEMDET NASR PERIOD**	**3200–3000**	
Union of Egypt	3100	Rise of Sumerian city-states	before 3000	
		EARLY DYNASTIC PERIOD	**3000–2370**	**RISE OF CRETAN CIVILIZATION**
				Neolithic settlement at Dimini
Third Dynasty	2670–2600			
Step Pyramid	2650			
Cheops' Pyramid	2575	Royal Tombs at Ur	2500	
		Sargon	c. 2370	
Period of Anarchy	2160–2133	**SUMERIAN REVIVAL**	**2230–2000**	
		Building of great Ur ziggurat	2100	
MIDDLE KINGDOM	**2133–1625**	**OLD BABYLONIAN PERIOD**	**2000–1595**	**MYCENAEANS ENTER GREECE**
		Age of Mari	c. 1800	
		Hammurabi	1792–1750	**HEIGHT OF CRETAN CULTURE**
Rise of Osiris cult				Building of great palaces
				Minoan domination of the sea
Hyksos Domination	1700–1567			Development of Linear A script
NEW KINGDOM	**1567–1085**	Hittites sack Babylon	1595	Grave circles at Mycenae
Eighteenth Dynasty	1567–1320	**MIDDLE BABYLONIAN PERIOD**	**after 1595**	
				Development of Linear B script
Empire of Tuthmosis III	1482–1450			**MYCENAEANS RULE IN CRETE**
		Kassites rule Babylon		Destruction of palaces
				and fall of Minoan civilization
Akhenaten	1379–1361			Mycenaean maritime supremacy
Tutankhamen	1361–1352			
Ramesses II	1304–1237			
Temples of Karnak and Abu Simbel				Trojan War
Exodus of the Hebrews	1240			Fall of Mycenaean centers
Great Invasion of Sea Peoples	1191			
		ASSYRIAN PERIOD	**1115–612**	**DORIAN INVASION**
LATE PERIOD	**1085–525**	Conquests of Tiglath-pileser I	1115–1077	Final destruction of Mycenae
				DARK AGE
Assyrians conquer Egypt	671	Height of Assyrian power	875–630	
Saite Period	664–525	Fall of Nineveh	612	Homer
		NEO-BABYLONIAN PERIOD	**612–538**	
		Nebuchadnezzar II	c. 600	**CLASSICAL AGE OF GREECE**
PERSIAN DOMINATION	**525–404**	**PERSIAN RULE**	**538–331**	Persians invade Greece
Herodotus visits Egypt	c. 450	Herodotus visits Babylon	c. 450	Herodotus
Alexander the Great conquers Egypt	332	Alexander conquers Babylon	331	Alexander the Great
PTOLEMAIC PERIOD	**323–30**			
Cleopatra	69–30			

GREECE	ANATOLIA AND THE LEVANT		OTHERS		
					3000
3000–1900					
2700	Egypt trades with Byblos	2600			
	Troy II	2500–2250	**INDUS VALLEY CIVILIZATION**	**2500–1500**	
	Alaja Huyuk	2400–2200			
					2000
2000–1700	**HITTITES ENTER ANATOLIA**	**c. 1900**			
	Assyrian traders at Kultepe	1900			
after 1700					
c. 1750					
1600–1500	Mursilis I	1620–1590			
after 1500	**RISE OF MITANNI**	**c. 1500**			
after 1500	Phoenicians develop alphabet	c. 1500			
	HITTITE EMPIRE	**1460–1200**			
1400?					
1400–1200	Suppiluliumas I	1380–1340			
	Battle of Kadesh	1300			
	Collapse of Hittites	1200			1250
1200	**PHRYGIAN OCCUPATION OF ANATOLIA**	**1200–700**			
c. 1200	Invasions of Sea Peoples	c. 1200			
	Hebrews invade Canaan	c. 1200			
c. 1150					
1100	Neo-Hittite kingdoms in northern Syria	after 1100			1000
	RISE OF SIDON AND TYRE	**c. 1000**	**VILLANOVAN CULTURE IN ITALY**	**1000**	
	ASSYRIANS DOMINATE LEVANT	**875–630**	**HEIGHT OF ETRUSCAN CIVILIZATION**	**800–500**	
775?	Phoenicians found Carthage	814?	Founding of Rome	753	
492–479	**PERSIAN CONQUEST OF ANATOLIA AND LEVANT**	**540–538**	Rome expels Tarquins	510	
c. 450			**DECLINE OF ETRUSCANS**	**400–200**	
c. 330			Gauls invade Italy	400–300	
			Rome conquers Veii	396	
					B.C. / A.D.
			MAYA CLASSIC AGE	**300–900**	
			HEIGHT OF KHMER CIVILIZATION	**802–1215**	

BRONZE AGE

IRON AGE

MYTH
AND
REALITY

During the course of the first millennium B.C. the fall of old empires and the spreading influence of new cultures transformed the face of the ancient world. The continuity of human experience was shattered, and by the dawn of the Christian era the historical realities of the more distant past had already dwindled to dim and uncertain memories. Babylon "of the beautiful towers and the great wall" was desolate and abandoned; Nineveh, capital of the great Assyrian empire, was little more than a mound of rubble; and the venerable cities of Sumer, which so long before had nurtured the early advances of civilization, had faded into obscurity.

Alien rulers had taken over the land of the pharaohs, and traditions that had endured for thousands of years along the banks of the Nile were gradually degenerating into mysteries that would take much more than another thousand years to unfold. A prophecy that foretold this sad decline remains one of the most deeply moving documents that has survived from dying antiquity: "Egypt will be forsaken, and the land which was once the home of religion will be left desolate, bereft of the presence of its deities . . . There is worse to come. Egypt will have yet more to suffer . . . O Egypt, Egypt, of thy religion nothing will remain but an empty tale, which thine own children in time to come will not believe; nothing will be left but graven words, and only the stones will tell of thy piety."

And so in time it actually happened.

With the Dorian invasions dark shadows fell over the Aegean world. The gracious culture that had flourished in Crete during the Bronze Age and the rugged civilization of the Mycenaeans on the Greek mainland yielded to a more barbaric form of life; they were, in effect, lost. Over several centuries of turbulence the arts declined to a rudimentary level; trade among the Greek people all but vanished; writing was forgotten.

Yet here, as in other and later dark ages, the past was not completely obliterated. During those days of rudeness waning memories of what had gone before were handed down from generation to generation in the songs of wandering minstrels, whose lays blended wonder and fiction with what was recalled of the facts. Time was telescoped—and the immediate and the remote past were inextricably confused. Here as elsewhere, the earlier times were peopled with fabulous heroes and giants, some of whose exploits summarized the long-endured trials of whole peoples.

From this slow accumulation of traditional lore there emerged legends of such universal interest that they remain one of the most treasured legacies of our western world. Many of these stories were ancient long before the time of Homer and Hesiod, who first gave them some comprehensive and systematic form. They reached back to the "primitive underworld of folklore" and to distant places—to Egypt, Babylon, Crete, Palestine, and elsewhere. They carried the wisdom of long-distilled experience.

The classical world went to school to Homer. Contemporaries of Plato and Aristotle accepted the story of Troy as real, and it remained real to the generations that followed.

When Alexander crossed the Hellespont on his way to war with the Persians, he viewed the site of the Trojan War as hallowed ground, and in a spirit of homage he ran naked and oiled around the tomb of Achilles—as did Caracalla, who remembered this performance and who in his madness imagined himself to be Achilles. Caesar too, when he passed the meandering stream that crosses the plains of ancient Troy, paid homage before its ruins and burned incense to the gods. Centuries later Constantine thought of building the new eastern capital of the Roman empire on the site of Troy, but he settled instead upon the old fortress town of Byzantium.

As early as ancient Roman times the defeated Trojans of Homer's epics had been remodeled into virtuous heroes whose glory survived the fall of their citadel. Homer himself said that the might of Aeneas, younger member of the Trojan royal family, "shall reign among the Trojans, and his children's children who shall be born in the aftertime." Vergil made Aeneas the hero of his great epic, written to celebrate the glory of imperial Rome, recounting how he had escaped the disaster that befell Troy and sailed to Italy, to become the true founder of the Roman people.

Five centuries later, when that grandeur was visibly fading, the Roman statesman Cassiodorus prepared a Trojan family tree for his impressive client Theodoric the Great, king of the Ostrogoths. And in the years that followed, as Helen Waddell has observed, the Norman kings of England sat more firmly on their throne after they had, with industry worthy of the College of Arms, traced out their common Trojan ancestry with Arthur and the Britons.

From Homer's own time the stories in his great epics have been told and retold with myriad variations. Every age down to our own has added to their store and given them fresh emphasis and new meanings. For a while, during the dark days that followed the decline of the classical world, they lay neglected; but they were never entirely forgotten. They were revived by the storytellers and the artists of the later Middle Ages and the Renaissance, who passed them on, reinvigorated, to the modern world. From whatever sources were available, including the most entertaining inventions, medieval chroniclers and jongleurs wove their own romances of Troy, transforming the epic heroes into armored knights and their Homeric exploits into shining deeds of chivalry. Troy was a living city, no less real because it had to be imagined. The greatest of these fabricated romances, *The Romance of Troy,* written in France in the twelfth century, was taken from the story of an "eyewitness" who had, the forgery claimed, been an actual combatant in the war.

In such variegated legends, built upon other legends that had been adapted from late Greek romances, Boccaccio found materials for his poem *Filostrato,* yet another version of the Trojan War, and from this, in turn, Chaucer took what he wanted for his own poem *Troylus and Criseyde,* introducing the tale of Troy into the literature of England where it took new root and flourished.

The rediscovery during the Renaissance of more ancient classical texts replenished the stock of historical lore and mythology with a wealth of material upon which artists and authors for all time could draw for their themes and their inspirations. There were accounts other than those given by Homer—some from sources similar to those he used, some from later writers who reported and speculated upon the actual remains of civilizations older than their own.

The story of Theseus and the Minotaur came from the writings of men who had reason to believe its historical truth. For centuries the Athenians treasured the ship in which, it was said, Theseus had voyaged to Crete; they kept it in repair and used it as a vessel for annual journeys of a sacred embassy to the feast of Apollo on the island of Delos, as their ancestors had vowed to do if the gods favored Theseus' mission. A Delphic oracle in the fifth century B.C. had commanded the Athenians to recover the mortal remains of Theseus from the rocky and barren island of Scyros, and in a grave of the Bronze Age the bold and ambitious Cimon found the bones of a warrior of imposing stature, his weapons at his side. He brought them back to Athens where they were reverently interred as those of Theseus.

It was in Crete, according to legend, that Daedalus fashioned wings of wax for himself and Icarus to escape confinement in King Minos' labyrinth. In the second century B.C. Pausanias, "father of all Baedekers," told of a marble relief of Ariadne that Daedalus himself had created—a story that would be more easily dismissed as pure legend if the experience of such archaeologists as Sir Arthur Evans, who excavated the labyrinthine palace of Minos at Knossos, had not warned us to be skeptical of our own skepticism in these matters.

Other early Greek and Roman authors wrote stories of distant lands. Some were pure romances, such as Ovid's tale of the Babylonian lovers Pyramus and Thisbe, which Chaucer drew upon for his *Legend of Good Women,* and much later Shakespeare incorporated in a "tedious brief scene" played by Nick Bottom and his companions in *A Midsummer Night's Dream.* Still others purported to be authentic history and description, and from some of these came mixtures of fact and fable that have not yet been altogether separated.

The legend of the famous Assyrian princess Semiramis, whose deeds included the founding of Babylon and the building of dikes to confine the Euphrates, reached the Middle Ages through the progressively garbled accounts of ancient writers and later romancers. The prototype of this wondrous being may have been Sammuramat, the female regent of Assyria late in the ninth century B.C., who was celebrated on a monument discovered in our own century—a woman obviously of great influence and worthy to be remembered. She was, in fact, included among the female "worthies" who were selected from history in the fourteenth century as counterparts of the nine male heroes of yore—three pagans, three Christians, and three Hebrews—whose claims to fame were widely celebrated in the arts and literature of the Middle Ages.

But throughout the ages, the most constant reminder of the ancient traditions of the Near East was provided in passages of the Hebrew Bible. When this was included in the Christian canon in the fourth century A.D. the stories of the

Old Testament traveled with the spread of Christianity to all corners of the western world. It was not an altogether sympathetic record; the Hebrews, who remembered their bondage in Egypt, the exile of their brethren by the cruel Assyrians, and the destruction of their Temple and their captivity by the Babylonians, could not view these more powerful contemporaries with friendly understanding. In later times Christian apologists treated the accounts of the Old Testament as allegories of the future church; as such they were widely accepted, even though St. Augustine warned Christians to believe them as facts and to remember that "Abraham really lived and he really had a son by Sarah his wife."

Within the last fifty years Abraham's biblical home, Ur of the Chaldees, has been excavated and studied, and bits of the rediscovered law code of Hammurabi, the great Babylonian contemporary of Abraham, have revealed accounts that are almost exactly duplicated in Exodus. A vast body of long-forgotten literature, and other archaeological evidence have been unearthed that bring the stories of the Old Testament close to ancient traditions shared by other tribes and peoples who lived in the land of the Bible—and in numerous instances also bring these stories close to what has been learned of the historical realities.

During the waning days of classical antiquity, as the Scriptures made their way about the western world in Greek and Latin translations, a stony silence settled over Egypt. As it had been prophesied, the graven hieroglyphs that covered temple walls and obelisks remained for all to see, but their meaning was lost. Down through the centuries both men of learning and charlatans sought to find in those curious pictorial symbols some clue to an occult wisdom that would explain the mystery of life. For it was widely believed that the hieroglyphic script was a divinely inspired Egyptian invention, and that properly understood it would provide an insight into the very essence of things.

The early years of the Christian era witnessed the spreading influence of an Egyptian "fashion" that influenced art and decoration throughout Roman Italy. Augustus imported the first obelisk to Rome, a precedent so admired that at one time the city was said to have more than two score of these alien monuments. When the supply of original obelisks was exhausted, new ones were quarried and duly inscribed with pictures that bore an imagined and specious resemblance to actual hieroglyphs.

Centuries later even Erasmus was taken in by similar curious misunderstandings of the Egyptian language; and in 1517 the great Albrecht Dürer added to the confusion by designing for Emperor Maximilian a triumphal arch inscribed with allegorical pictures that represented "a mystery in sacred Egyptian letters," and that he had adapted from a strangely contorted version of early Egyptian documents. Egypt's mysterious past remained veiled until 1821 when the gifted French linguist and cryptographer Jean François Champollion deciphered the hieroglyphs and inaugurated an age that was to witness the recovery of so many ancient stories from the realm of myth.

Even in its earliest known forms the tale of ancient Troy was a confused mixture of hearsay, myth, and invention. Since Homer's day artists in every medium have improvised on its themes and adapted them to their own times. A medieval French miniature (right) depicts the abduction of Helen, legendary cause of the Trojan War. Against a fantastic late Gothic architectural stage, the not-unwilling beauty is led away by Paris, whose "knights" fight off the opposition. In a detail from an earlier French miniature (below) the Achaeans emerge from their wooden horse to end the long siege of Troy. In the seventeenth century Rubens portrayed the wrath of Achilles, the theme of Homer's Iliad, *in a cartoon designed for a tapestry (above).*

Until the discoveries of modern archaeology, virtually all that was known of the heroic age of Greece and the golden age of Crete was contained in legends that survived from that distant past. For more than twenty-five centuries historians, romancers, and artists turned to these accounts for materials that would serve their separate purposes. According to various myths, Zeus, in the guise of a magnificent snow-white bull, abducted the beautiful Europa, princess of Tyre, and swam with her on his back to Crete where she bore him three sons. The first-born, Minos, became ruler of the island kingdom. Titian's large canvas at right is one of the most memorable representations of that abduction scene. Other legends, referred to in Homer as well as in the works of Herodotus, Thucydides, and later historians, preserve vague recollections of the civilization that we now know flourished on Crete between three and four thousand years ago—and whose glory was obliterated centuries before the time of Homer.

At the siege of Troy, as Homer tells the story, the wise King Nestor harked back to an even earlier time when men lived who were "the strongest men that Earth has bred . . . men whom not a soul on earth today could face in battle." Among those giants of the past he numbered the hero Theseus, who is shown (right) on a sixth-century B.C. Attic vase slaying the formidable Minotaur to deliver the youths and maidens of Athens from death. Other forms of paintings in which Greeks of the classical period pictured history as they understood it have almost entirely disappeared. However, Athenian pottery decorated with such scenes was distributed by traders to widely distant places, where it served —beyond its practical purposes—as a pictorial supplement to the literature of legend and as a carrier of tradition.

In a painted panel by the Renaissance artist Piero di Cosimo (reproduced above) Theseus' adventures are presented as a running narrative depicted in "modern" dress and in a "modern" setting. Distinctions of time and place are blended into a continuous story of contemporary interest. In the center foreground the heroic Athenian, fully armed in Renaissance fashion, strides from his ship toward the labyrinth designed by the architect Daedalus to house the monstrous step-son, half man and half bull, of King Minos. At the left Ariadne, attended by her nurse, proffers Theseus the ball of thread that will help him retrace his way from the maze. In the right foreground, as Theseus struggles with the grim hybrid the two women await the outcome. Beyond the labyrinth, to the left, Theseus leads them to his waiting ship which, in the upper right, departs with its black sails raised for Naxos and Athens, whose towers rise on the horizon.

The civilization of the ancient Etruscans had all but disappeared two centuries before our era, although these mysterious people once ruled over most of the Italian peninsula. According to a legend that was recorded at least as early as the third century B.C., the advance of their armed forces was stopped on one occasion at the banks of the Tiber only by the individual bravery of the Roman warrior Horatius. The actual occasion that may be recalled in this story had long before receded into a mythical past, but tradition relates that Horatius alone withstood the Etruscan army while his companions destroyed the wooden bridge that gave access to Rome. Thus he is shown above in a sixteenth-century engraving by Georg Pencz and again, at left, in another, contemporary engraving by Marcantonio.

Another old legend recounts that the Etruscan kings of Rome—the Tarquins—were expelled as a result of the suicide of Lucretia. This virtuous Roman matron was raped by the son of King Tarquin and, after telling her husband and asking for vengeance, she stabbed herself. The story has been elaborated in many retellings. A medieval illumination of Boccaccio's version of the story (above) and a Mannerist painting (right) depict her suicide. Tarquin's fateful visit to Lucretia's bedchamber (below) is reproduced from a seventeenth-century canvas.

Comcon edifia la tour de babiloune. et le languege fule mue en lxxii. langueques. et les anges la deffruirut:

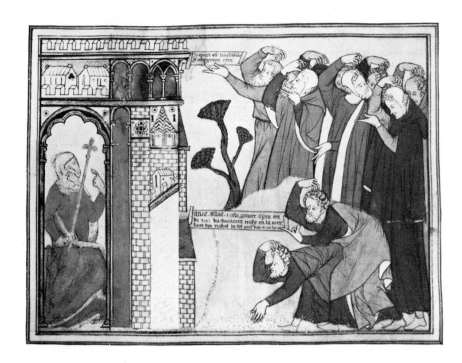

Since the adoption of the Old Testament as part of Christian Scriptures, the events and scenes referred to in the books of the Hebrew Bible have been abundantly pictured as allegories or as imagined historical reconstructions. At left, a reproduction from the Book of Hours of the Duke of Bedford reveals a medieval conception of the building of the Tower of Babel. As construction proceeds at the lower levels, angels of the Lord descend from on high to disperse the workmen. From the Book of Daniel the English artist William Blake drew his image of the great Babylonian king, Nebuchadnezzar, gone mad and ranging in the grass like an animal (below). A thirteenth-century illumination (above) depicts Babylonians lamenting the final destruction of their notorious city, as told in the Revelations of St. John the Divine.

In Mesopotamian history, as recounted by ancient Greek writers, legends of fabulous variety clustered about the memory of Queen Semiramis. Virtually every stupendous work of the ancient Near East was ascribed to her. Her fame survived the Dark Ages of Europe, and in later medieval times she was recalled as one of the great heroines of the past. The tapestry reproduced above shows her as Queen of Babylon. It was she, the legend above her figure reads, who conquered the barbarians, Indians, and Syrians and who killed the king of Ethiopia. Under the arch at the left in the painting opposite appears the handwriting on the wall that confounded the revelers at Belshazzar's great feast and that foretold the doom of Babylonia. In his canvas the Bolognese artist V. M. Bigari staged the biblical story in a magnificently ornate architectural setting in the style of the eighteenth century.

MANE THECEL
PHARES

At an early point of their history the children of Israel were commanded to make for themselves no graven images, nor "any likeness of anything that is in heaven above, or that is in the earth beneath, or that is in the water under the earth." The illustration of their history, their traditions, and their legends was left almost entirely to later people of other faiths. By the time the oral traditions of the Hebrews were committed to writing and accepted as authoritative many of the events they recorded belonged to a more or less remote past. In contrast to the days of their bondage, as told in the Bible, Egypt had become an old and feeble giant. Little in its surviving literature adds to the biblical story of the long sojourn and deliverance, although the Hebrew accounts of their years in the land of the pharaohs may incorporate elements of Egyptian folklore. But Egypt remained a land of vast legend, which over the centuries to come continued to excite interest in the stories of the Hebrews' experiences.

A carved ivory plaque from the sixth century (top left) depicts Joseph as a figure of importance supervising the distribution of corn. He is seated before a scribe who makes notes of the transactions. In a panel from Ghiberti's famous doors at the Baptistery in Florence (bottom left), episodes in Joseph's life as revealed in Genesis are recreated as a narrative. At the top right of the panel Joseph is sold to the Ishmaelites; in the center, within a circular structure, he gathers the corn he later sold, "as the sand of the sea, very much, until he left numbering"; on the left is depicted the story of Benjamin; and at the right stands a group of Egyptians. A fourth-century ivory relief (left center) shows the indignant Moses slaying an Egyptian who had smitten a Hebrew.

Centuries elapsed between the time of Joseph and the miraculous release of the Hebrews from their bondage in Egypt. The story of the exodus remains one of the greatest epics of mankind. The illumination reproduced opposite depicts their grim sojourn in the desert near Mount Sinai (with a very Red Sea beyond) where Moses received the sacred tablets from the Lord. It illustrates the story as told by the first-century chronicler of the Hebrews, Flavius Josephus, in a manuscript prepared in the early fifteenth century for the Duke of Berry, one of the greatest patrons of the arts in history. The version of the Hebrew history written by Josephus was very popular during the Middle Ages.

puis ce que les hebreux
furent donez de tel salut.
Adonc soudainement
il: furent courouciez
quant on les menoit en la montai
gne de synay pour ce que estoit une

region moult deserte et souffraiteuse
des necessaires nourrissemens. et le
aue y estoit fort a auoir. en tant que
non pas tant seulement on neu po
uoit trouuer pour les hommes. ma
is aussi elle nestoit pas couueriable

The humanists of the Renaissance were fascinated by the hidden wisdom they detected in
Egyptian thought and religion. By the most
elaborate fabrications the confidential secretary of the Borgia pope Alexander VI traced
the ancestry of his patron directly back to the
son of the Egyptian god Osiris. This heroic
version of the family genealogy was used by
Pinturicchio in decorating the ceiling of the
Borgia apartments in the Vatican. A detail at
left shows the death of Osiris, an aspect of
the Egyptian myth then widely considered a
prefiguration of the death of Christ. Another
fanciful version of Egyptian motifs (above)
was adopted by Bernini in 1667 for his
monument erected in the Piazza della Minerva
in Rome. The inscribed "hieroglyphs" are
cryptic symbols invented for the occasion.

THE

FLOWERING

OF

EGYPT

Kingdom of the Pharaohs • I

There is no landscape in the world quite like that of Egypt. Its strangeness, its uniqueness, have intrigued men from before the time of Herodotus, who visited Egypt almost twenty-five hundred years ago; and it continues to fascinate jet-age travelers who see more countries in a month than the "Father of History" saw in a lifetime.

Yet the natural scene offers no spectacular variety. There are the immense margins of desert that hem in the valley of the Nile. But even in the valley there are no sky-reflecting lakes and fjords, no woods and meadows such as excite interest in other landscapes. One Egyptian village looks exactly like another, and the pattern of vegetation hardly changes from the Sudanese border in the south to the Mediterranean in the north. Nearly all the valley is cultivated; cotton, wheat, clover, beans, rice, barley, sugar cane grow in fields of monotonous flatness, varied only by the darker green of date palms, by mud-brick villages, occasionally displaying the domed shrine of the local holy man, and here and there are towns with mosques and ornate nineteenth-century villas.

Thus described, Egypt sounds dull enough. But it is not. There is the astonishing contrast between the dry, powdery desert sand and the fecund green of the valley, a demarcation so precise and uncompromising that in places one can stand with a foot on sand and the other on soil. There is also the contrast between both these elements and the age-worn, fissured cliffs of golden limestone from which the ancient Egyptians quarried their building blocks and in which they tunneled their tombs. Third and most important there is the sudden, heart-stopping impact of man-made stone moun-

tains reaching into the sky; of soaring columns, exceeding the girth of forest trees, crowned by capitals which gigantically reproduce the papyrus and lotus buds with which the valley proliferated in pharaonic times.

Even without the monuments of its mighty past the lure of Egypt would not disappear. The Nile itself, rolling inexorably through a thousand miles of arid desert, the only source of fertility in an almost rainless land, is wonder enough. On either bank the strip of rich green vegetation, varying in width from a few hundred yards to several miles, supports some twenty million people. Egypt, as Herodotus remarked, is truly the gift of the Nile.

However, the remote origins of Egyptian civilization are to be found not in the river valley itself, but in the deserts that flank it on east and west. There, in the limestone cliffs and in the nearby wadis, or valleys, have been found stone implements and sometimes cave-shelters containing the bones of creatures such as the hippopotamus and buffalo, gazelle and wild ass, aurochs and ostrich. For the earliest ancestors of the ancient Egyptians were not cultivators but hunters who pursued these animals over twelve thousand years ago, when Egypt still received enough rain to provide prairie-like country such as exists today in the Sudan and East Africa.

As the European glaciers receded toward the end of the last Ice Age, the climate slowly changed throughout the Near and Middle East. Over countless millenniums there was a gradual drying up, and men were forced to move close to the remaining sources of the water without which they could not survive. As the Nile slowly shrank into its present bed, it left behind a series of eight terraces; and it is on the lower four of these that the worked flint tools and weapons, such as hand axes and spearheads, and the bones of slaughtered animals have been discovered. In some regions this progressive

The Sphinx portrays the early pharaoh Chephren as a powerful lion. In later centuries, the Egyptians forgot its original significance, and worshiped it as a representation of the sun god.

desiccation killed the rivers. But even after the rain failed in Egypt and the tributary streams which once fed it vanished, leaving only dried-up wadis to mark their former courses, still the Nile survived.

Far to the south there are in fact two Niles, the White and the Blue. The former, the main stream, rises in the great lakes Victoria and Albert in equatorial Africa. The Blue Nile, with its tributary the Atbara, flows down from the Abyssinian plateau. For a while these mountain rivers, swollen by spring rains and melted snows, and carrying a heavy burden of fertile silt, hold back the waters of the White Nile where they meet south of Khartum. Then, as their flood subsides, the White Nile is released. Thus it is those gigantic reservoirs, the lakes of central Africa, that provide the impetus that drives the waters of the Nile through a thousand miles of desert during the dry season; it is the soil scoured from the far-off highlands of Abyssinia, borne on the summer torrents of the Blue Nile and the Atbara, that provides the land with its miraculous fertility. And it is this combination of geographical circumstances that endowed Egypt with its unique heritage.

The mere existence of a large river providing a perpetual water supply and easy transport would not in itself have ensured the development of civilization. As the prairies turned to desert, animals as well as men would tend to move nearer the river valley, so that hunting would be even easier. There would be no need for men to change their nomadic life for one of permanent settlement.

For millennium after millennium the rich bounty of the Nile was ignored, while the valley dwellers continued to hunt for their food, as their ancestors had done, unaware of the potential wealth which lay beneath the marshy pools where they fished and snared wildfowl. We are dealing with

a period thousands of years before the invention of written records, and no one knows who first thought of planting the seeds of wild grasses in the fertile mud and reaping the crop. Possibly the notion was brought to Egypt by immigrants from Palestine and Syria, who in turn had learned the techniques of primitive agriculture from other inhabitants of western Asia. Or, equally conceivable, the early Africans who dwelt along the Nile may have developed these elementary procedures independently.

Precise dating is impossible, but from an examination of relics found at various points along the valley, it can be established that about 5000 B.C. there were people living in Egypt who had reached a neolithic stage of development; that is to say they were using finely worked stone tools and lived mainly by hunting, which they had begun to combine with agriculture and stock raising. They buried their dead in shallow pit graves in the sand; the corpses were laid on their sides in a crouching, embryonic position, as if awaiting a second birth, and were accompanied by a few pots containing food offerings, suggesting a belief in an afterlife. Their dwellings were probably mere shelters of reeds, or mud huts.

It would be easy to dismiss the prehistoric period of Egypt, about which so tantalizingly little is known, in a few lines and to proceed quickly to the epoch of high civilization that is so much better understood. But these early centuries of effort, adaptation, and change provide the background of Egyptian culture and it is worthwhile to consider what may have happened.

Egypt falls naturally into two divisions, Upper (southern) and Lower (northern), with the dividing point where the narrow Nile Valley broadens out into the Delta. The character of the two regions is strongly contrasted. Upper Egypt comprises the long, tortuous river valley, coiling like a green

Memphis was the earliest capital of a united Egypt; nearby rose the great pyramids of Giza, shown on the facing page. The largest one, built by Cheops, appears at right; next to it is that of Chephren, his son. New Kingdom pharaohs built extensively throughout Egypt. The immense temple of Abu Simbel, deep in Nubia, dates from their time. Much of the tribute that they brought back from conquests in Asia and Nubia went to adorn their capital, Thebes. Ruins of the great temple of Amen can still be seen there, but little remains of the city that the heretic king Akhenaten founded at el Amarna, or of the capitals which later pharaohs built in the Delta.

CYPRUS

LEBANON •Kadesh

Byblos•

MEDITERRANEAN

SYRIA

Sidon•

SEA

Damascus•

ISRAEL •Jerusalem

JORDAN

Megiddo•

Alexandria• •Buto

Sais•

Busiris• •Tanis

LOWER
EGYPT

Cairo•

Giza•

Memphis•

Saqqara•

SINAI

Gerza•

FAYUM

el Amarna•

NILE

Deir Tasa•

Badari•

UPPER
EGYPT

N

Thinis•

Abydos•

Dendera•

RED

WADI HAMMAMAT

VALLEY OF
THE KINGS →

Thebes → •Karnak

SEA

Luxor•

Hierakonpolis•

Edfu•

First Cataract •Aswan

Abu Simbel•

Scale

Second Cataract

NUBIA

0   25   50   75 Miles

In Egyptian art and ritual the bull often symbolized Pharaoh. This was an outgrowth of a primitive cattle cult which is still widespread among African tribes whose ancestors were culturally akin to the ancient Egyptians. The fragment above, which shows a royal bull goring an enemy, is part of a slate palette which may commemorate a victory over desert nomads, or perhaps the subjugation of the Delta by Narmer, the king who unified Egypt. Below the bull a lion stands within a walled fortress; it represents a captured town that has not yet been identified.

snake between desert cliffs from the First Cataract down to Cairo; from there on Lower Egypt, like a huge fan, extends north, east, and west in a broad plain, through which the Nile branches out and continues on to the Mediterranean.

Archaeologists have long disputed in which area Egyptian civilization first struck its roots. Some have suggested that it was in the Delta, arguing that such a richly fertile area would be bound to attract settlers from an early period, once the possibilities of agriculture were understood. Another point in the Delta's favor was its nearness to the sea, to Palestine, Syria, and the Sinai Peninsula, through which influences might filter from the early Mesopotamian civilizations. Against this theory others argue with equal force that it would have been easier to colonize the southern valley of the Nile. The truth of the matter remains obscure. It might be observed in passing, however, that throughout historical times the great movements of conquest and consolidation of the "Two Lands" came from the South.

All we know for certain is that between 5000 and 4000 B.C., perhaps even earlier, the descendants of the folk who had lived on the fringes of the Nile Valley began to move down into it. At that time the river, bordered by reeds and swamps, was still prolific in game; crocodiles and hippopotamuses basked with snouts just above the muddy water; wildfowl rose in clouds from the forest of papyrus reeds where the light skiffs of the hunters darted; harpoons and throwing sticks flashed in the sunlight; nets were lowered from frail boats of papyrus to bring up rich catches. This abundance of game persisted into historic times, and was remembered in tomb paintings and reliefs picturing life along the river in later centuries.

The primitive Egyptian lived perpetually among animals; he studied their habits in order to trap and kill them for

food, and to protect himself from predators. But he also revered them, because they possessed powers superior to his own. So in time, the flying falcon became one of the insignia of royalty; the crocodile, lion, and hippopotamus were hybridized into the infernal monster that devours guilty souls; the lion, given a regal human head, became the sphinx, symbolizing kingly majesty; and the ibis with its thoughtful, knowing appearance became Thoth, the god of wisdom (and of writing).

The groups of people who early settled along the great length of the Nile Valley developed at different paces and in different ways. Scholars have given their separate, roughly consecutive cultures various impressive-sounding names, such as Tasian, Badarian, Amratian, Merimdian; but these are merely labels of convenience, derived from the modern Arabic names of the sites where evidence of these phases was first found. Although such cultures differed markedly from one another, we should not view them as separate civilizations. From stage to stage these developments reveal a significant over-all continuity and a progressive evolution.

The funerary deposits of the fifth millennium B.C. and the early part of the fourth show that these peoples, who still lived mainly by hunting and fishing, learned to depend more heavily upon primitive agriculture and stock breeding. They grew barley and wheat, which were stored in mat-lined pits. They made clothes of animal skins, using bone needles, and already the Egyptian love of personal adornment shows itself in the form of bracelets of shell and ivory, beads of pierced stone, ivory and bone combs, and other jewelry. They also made green eye paint by grinding malachite on slate palettes which were often carved in the shape of animals, birds, or fish. Their tools and weapons continued to be made of flint, though a few copper objects came into use in Ba-

In Egypt, the greed of the hippopotamus was proverbial. Coming out of the swamps, the beasts trampled cultivated fields and devoured the crops. Crocodiles were even more dangerous; the relief below shows one about to dine on a newborn hippopotamus calf which has not yet completely emerged from its mother's body. The fisherman at right uses a handline to catch his dinner. Fish formed a major part of the Egyptian diet, although certain species were taboo in some areas, and kings were forbidden to eat any at all.

darian times. They used arrows tipped with flint or bone, and a certain type of mace with a pear-shaped head is often found in Amratian graves. Without benefit of the potter's wheel they fashioned earthenware vessels of excellent workmanship; and they also made vases hollowed out of stone, which was plentiful in the cliffs bordering the Nile and in the adjoining deserts. This early acquaintance with stone-working was to have tremendous consequences in later times.

Just how long this so-called Predynastic Period lasted can only be surmised. However, it culminated in one of those startling leaps forward which mankind is capable of making from time to time. Before the middle of the fourth millennium the social organization of the Egyptians seems hardly to have advanced beyond that of the primitive Dinka and Shilluk tribes who today inhabit the farther reaches of the upper Nile in the Sudan. Three hundred years later (about 3200 B.C.) the entire valley, stretching seven hundred and fifty miles from the First Cataract to the Mediterranean, was an integrated state and most of the lineaments of Egyptian civilization were already apparent. These early people had achieved a written language of a very complex nature, they could fashion beautiful objects of the hardest stone, they had undertaken a monumental architecture, their craftsmanship in copper, wood, and ivory was irreproachable. Five centuries later their descendants were raising gigantic pyramids, nearly five hundred feet high, meticulously planned and of exquisite workmanship.

Something happened that in a remarkably short time transformed this conglomeration of semi-barbaric Nilotic tribesmen into a highly civilized state that lasted for almost three thousand years. What that something was we can only guess, but the archaeological evidence gives us several clues, and it is hoped that future discoveries will fill the gaps in

the story. Several facts are certain. The Badarian, Amratian, Merimdian, and other neolithic cultures left nothing to compare with the mighty structures of historic times. Flinders Petrie, who made some of the greatest discoveries in Egyptian archaeology, refused at first to believe that these primitive hunter-farmers could have had any direct connection with the builders of the great pyramids. He sought a clue in the appearance, about 3600 B.C., of a new culture, the so-called Gerzean, evidences of which have been found at Gerza and other sites in Lower Egypt, and which gradually replaced the earlier Amratian cultures at certain Upper Egyptian sites. Petrie called them the New Race and suggested that they belonged to some desert tribe whom the "true" Egyptians permitted to live on the fringe of their territory when they themselves had become civilized. But he changed his mind when discoveries elsewhere in Egypt revealed a continuous chain of cultural development connecting all these early peoples with the Egyptians of historical times.

There have been suggestions by other Egyptologists that the impetus to civilization came from an influx of peoples, probably from the East. The inhabitants of Upper Egypt were generally longheaded and of small stature, and occasionally their skulls show signs of Negroid admixture. But in the north, archaeologists discovered the bodies of a fairly tall people with a different skull formation. Even so, the fact that they are confined mainly to the north, and not in impressively large numbers, rules out any suggestion of a complete foreign infiltration of the Nile Valley. Egypt's culture remained predominantly indigenous, although it may have been fertilized by influences from outside. Oriental influences, or interrelationships, in any case, are clearly evident.

On Gerzean pottery and later in scenes painted on mud-covered walls appear lively pictures of boats of considerable

The herdsmen shown below, attempting to lead their cattle across a crocodile-infested stream, support one calf that is unable to swim by itself. One of the men in the boat carries a waterbird that has probably just been captured. At right, stalks of papyrus bend beneath the weight of a cat, specially trained for hunting, as it retrieves waterfowl downed by its master's throwstick.

size. Since no timber suitable for such vessels was to be found in Egypt (particularly for tall masts) there must have been contact with the nearest timber-producing country—Lebanon, famous for its cedars. Indeed we can be certain of this, for such wood has been found lining tombs of the Predynastic Period. Eastern influence is again obvious, among other instances, in a knife found at Gebel el Araq, on whose ivory handle appear carved representations of ships with vertical prows and sterns and with standards, each crowned with a crescent-shaped symbol, which was a typical feature of Mesopotamian vessels. On the reverse side of the handle a bearded figure is depicted standing between two rampant lions, a motif that frequently appears in early Mesopotamian seals.

Writing was developed slightly earlier in Mesopotamia than in Egypt, and some scholars believe that the idea of writing may have passed from the former land to the Nile Valley. From its earliest stages, however, the Egyptian writing system used its own distinctive signs and advanced along its own native lines. This new "tool" had an enormously important influence on the early development of civilization in the Nile Valley.

A number of other features of predynastic Egypt clearly reveal Mesopotamian influence. One of the most striking is a type of mud-brick building with a paneled façade. Such architecture was known slightly earlier in ancient Sumer, a land where stone was almost unobtainable, and where brick construction continued to be used even in the most monumental forms. Remains of some of these early Egyptian structures may still be seen in the region of Memphis as well as in cemeteries in the South. This method of building soon developed into a characteristic Egyptian practice that was continued into historical times, and its stylistic features were

copied in the great stone monuments of the early dynastic pharaohs of the succeeding centuries.

Meanwhile other techniques were introduced into Egypt. The valley dwellers still made tools and weapons of exquisitely worked flint and continued to do so until well into historical times. But they were also learning to fashion knives, axes, and spearheads of copper; they may have learned the mystery of metalworking from smiths who brought the craft from the east.

In spite of these innovations, however, the basic pattern of culture remained the same. They still worshiped the animal gods of their forefathers. Although they now had learned to live in one place, to grow crops in the Nile mud, and to store grain, their young men still stalked the wild beasts in the wadis as their ancestors had done. They lived in tribal areas scattered along the banks of the river, occasionally waging war on their neighbors or, from time to time, joining with them in a temporary alliance against a powerful enemy. At an early date each separate group adopted a certain cult sign, very roughly corresponding to a national emblem of today. Each of these provinces, or *nomes* as the Greeks later termed them, had its guardian deity, usually but not always in the form of an animal. Some of these survived throughout the entire history of ancient Egypt, such as the falcon god Horus of Hierakonpolis in Upper Egypt and the cobra goddess Wadjet of Buto in Lower Egypt.

It was a small and circumscribed world. If a man lived in the Delta, he worshiped Wadjet, knew the wide-spreading marshes of the Delta and the "Great Green Sea" beyond. If he was a southerner, hemmed in his narrow valley, he knew the First Cataract and the water sliding over the black rocks, and must have seen the dark men who lived still farther south, and who brought the gleaming white ivory

from which the craftsmen made their carved knife hilts. And his temple was that of the "White One" of Nekheb.

Before 3200 B.C., powerful chieftains had arisen who made war on each other and celebrated their conquests on carved palettes of schist—elaborate, greatly enlarged versions of the simple slate palettes buried in the little pit graves of earlier centuries. The discovery of these commemorative palettes, together with decoratively carved knife handles and fine stone vessels, provided unmistakable links between the primitive valley dwellers and the sophisticated Egyptians who lived under the rule of the great pharaohs.

One palette shows a group of roughly square shapes with serrated edges, each containing a number of crude symbols in which are plant and animal forms. Standing on top of the squares are various animals—including a lion, a scorpion, and a falcon—apparently attacking the squares with picks. Egyptologists have interpreted this design as follows. Each of the squares represents a fortified city (the serrations are the projecting towers or bastions of a city wall). The plant or animal figures inside are the cult signs or emblems of the cities; the triumphant figures above with their picks represent the successful attackers of the stricken towns. Similar indications of the turbulence that preceded the unification of Egypt can be seen in warring figures on the Gebel el Araq knife handle, where combatants attack one another with clubs and sticks.

The most dramatic of all these discoveries was made in 1898 in the temple at Hierakonpolis in Upper Egypt. There was unearthed a magnificent example of the large palettes, in perfect condition, one of the most important historical documents ever found in Egypt. Dominating the scene on one side is a figure wearing the Egyptian kilt that is so familiar from innumerable later representations; on his head is the

The palette of Narmer (right) shows the king who unified the Nile Valley wearing the white crown of Upper Egypt. At left, in a detail from the reverse side of the palette, Narmer wears the red crown of the North. The king towers above the vizier and standard bearers who walk in procession with him; stretched out before him are the decapitated bodies of his enemies. In both war and peace, all of Egypt's achievements were credited to Pharaoh. Opposite, the prehistoric ruler known as the "Scorpion King" holds a hoe in his hand, to mark the opening of an irrigation canal.

tall crown of Upper Egypt and his right hand grasps a mace, while his left is entwined in the hair of a kneeling bearded figure obviously representing an enemy. On the other side of the palette the same dominant figure wears the crown of Lower Egypt, and on each side, at the top in a central position, is a hieroglyphic inscription that reads "Narmer." Each of these inscriptions is contained within a *serekh*, a symbolic design representing the paneled façade of the royal palace.

The significance of this discovery was tremendous, because here, for the first time, archaeological evidence could be linked with written records. For according to the later historian Manetho, Upper and Lower Egypt were unified by a conqueror from the South who first brought the entire country under one rule about 3200 B.C. His name, in Greek, was Menes, whom scholars have identified with the first Egyptian pharaoh, Narmer.

Manetho lived in the third century B.C. when Egypt was ruled by the Ptolemies. He compiled a list of Egyptian kings from the earliest known pharaohs, dividing it into thirty-one dynasties, each representing the period during which successive generations of one family ruled the land. The list has survived only in copies which are manifestly inadequate and in part inaccurate, but for lack of a better, Egyptologists continue to use this framework, modifying it from time to time in the light of new archaeological and philological research. Until the last decade of the past century no trace of the twenty-six pharaohs listed by Manetho as having ruled during the first three dynasties, a period that he claimed covered several centuries, had been unearthed. In the 1894 edition of his history of Egypt, Petrie unequivocally stated that the chronicle of those early dynasties could only be regarded as "a series of statements made by a state chronographer, about three thousand years after that date, concerning a period of

which he had no contemporary material." Yet the Fourth Dynasty was magnificently represented by the Great Pyramid of Cheops and all it implied concerning the development of technology and civilization. What had happened that could explain this almost miraculous flowering? Could this gap ever be filled?

The answers came in a series of dramatic discoveries, all made within a decade. Narmer's palette proved beyond doubt that the first king of the First Dynasty was no myth. Two years earlier a French scholar, E. Amélineau, had made an even more sensational discovery near Abydos, in Upper Egypt. West of the well-known temple of Sethi I, a mile beyond the cultivated area, rose a desert mound called by the Arabs Umm el Gaab, Mother of Pots. It was littered with potsherds, fragments of votive offerings brought there by ancient Egyptian worshipers who believed it to be the burial place of Osiris, the god of death and resurrection. Ruthlessly searching for salable antiquities, and thus doing considerable damage to the remains, Amélineau came upon a large number of mud-brick tombs or *mastabas* (an Arabic word for the rectangular mud benches which still may be seen outside Arab houses and which such tombs resemble). These structures were already in a disastrous state of ruin before Amélineau got at them; but on jar sealings, bits of inscribed ivory, and other fragmentary relics there were the names of a number of early Egyptian kings.

A little later Petrie made a much more thorough and scientific excavation of the site. After months of patient effort he was able to plan the layout of each tomb, and to recover a considerable number of the inscribed stone vessels, jar sealings, ivory and ebony tablets; he also found several large carved stelae. Meanwhile other scholars had applied themselves to the study of the royal names discovered by Améli-

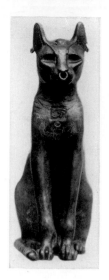

neau. It was a dramatic moment, and a landmark in the history of Egyptology, when it was announced that here undoubtedly were tangible records of some of Manetho's kings of the First and Second Dynasties, monarchs who had ruled Egypt at the dawn of her dynastic history.

At first the mastabas found at Abydos were regarded as the tombs of these early pharaohs, which had been rifled in antiquity so that not a fragment of their bodies remained. Since then, however, fourteen large, impressive mastabas of the First Dynasty have been excavated at Saqqara, near ancient Memphis, at the junction of Upper and Lower Egypt. We are told by Manetho that after his conquest of the country Narmer moved his capital to this point, so it has been argued that the real tombs were at Saqqara, and that those at Abydos were cenotaphs, probably built there because the First and Second Dynasty kings came from the town of Thinis nearby; Manetho called them the "Thinite Kings." The matter is still being warmly discussed, and the final answer may be slow in coming.

However, as a consequence of all this, whereas the 1894 edition of Petrie's history covered the whole of predynastic Egyptian history in eight pages, that of 1902 contained concrete historical information concerning most of the kings who ruled before Snofru, first king of the Fourth Dynasty, with an account of their tombs, inscriptions, furniture, and art.

The discoveries by Petrie and V. E. Quibbell of the predynastic cemeteries at Naqada and Ballas helped to complete the story, and from a careful examination of the contents of these tombs and the Abydos mastabas, it was possible to trace a continuous development from the primitive hunter-farmers who moved down from the desert into the Nile Valley, some seven thousand years ago, to the later Egyptians whose colossal monuments can still awe us in the twentieth century.

We might pause to reconsider why one of the earliest and longest-lived civilizations in the world should have burgeoned in Egypt. We surmise that it was the result of a geographical accident and of the political unity that was at first imposed by force (and thereafter maintained by intelligent, far-seeing rulers) on a population that might have continued at a primitive level of culture for a long period of time. One essential to the creation of civilization is easy communication, which in Egypt was provided by the Nile. A second is fertile soil, in this case ensured by the annual flooding of the river. A third vital element is some directing intelligence. Since early Egyptian historical records are as scanty and incomplete as they are, we cannot know what kind of men ruled the country during the first three dynasties; but among them, surely, there must have been men of genius. Only men of high intellectual caliber and forceful character could have transformed a congeries of independent tribes, each with its own insular traditions, into a homogeneous state. Narmer may have been such a man.

When he put an end to centuries of intertribal strife and brought the entire country under his rule, Narmer became the master of a land that required only the organized effort of its inhabitants to realize its ample resources. The Egyptian year was divided into three seasons beginning with the rise of the Nile, the "inundation," followed by the "emergence of the fields from the waters" (cultivation), and then the "deficiency of water," the drought (harvest). From early times the swollen river spread out across the valley, drowning the fields and leaving only occasional reedy mudbanks showing above a waste of brown water. When the waters went down they left behind the mud, and then came the time

Before a table laden with offerings, a worshiper adores Re-Harakhte, a composite god characteristically shown with the hawk's head of Horus and Re's solar crown. From the sun disk atop the god's head, rays of flowers stream down upon the devotee. According to one theogony, Re had created the world. This was not a unique distinction; most Egyptian temples claimed that accomplishment for the god to which they were dedicated. But the chroniclers who compiled the king lists generally assigned the credit to Re, by recording him as the first king of Egypt.

of sowing. Deep plowing and fertilizing were not necessary. All that was required was to hoe or plow shallow channels in the rich silt, plant crops, and wait for them to ripen. But if Egypt was the "gift of the Nile," sometimes that gift was withheld. There would be a "bad Nile" when the flood was unusually low; then famine would follow. Or at other times the great river roared down the valley in an uncontrollable torrent, sweeping away men and beasts along with the frail mud-brick buildings in its path. The Nile could bring life or death, prosperity or disaster. It was to this vital problem that the Egyptian intellectual class, its priest-technicians, applied their minds.

Over the centuries the Egyptians learned how to control the flood waters, to conserve and channel them during the long dry season, and to preserve the precious top soil, with a complex system of canals, dikes, and catchments. Such a system of irrigation could only be accomplished by large bodies of people working together, and this called for organization and discipline. The development of this intelligently directed communal effort marked an important step in the advance of Egyptian civilization. The necessity of redefining land boundaries after floods had washed them away led to the development of an accurate system of surveying; the necessity of keeping records of crop yield encouraged the Egyptians to develop their writing system without which, in turn, the administration of the state would not have been possible.

The Third Dynasty started about 2670 B.C., and ushered in what is known as the Old Kingdom, Egypt's first golden age. The era lasted through the Sixth Dynasty, or for about five hundred years. The pharaohs of this epoch enjoyed a concentration of power which, once lost, was never fully recovered. Their sculptured portraits reflect this majesty and

are among the highest achievements of Egyptian art. It was during this period that Egyptian architecture developed its most familiar and lasting forms, the great pyramids, those almost incredible masses of masonry whose construction demanded such an enormous expenditure of wealth, labor, and skilled direction.

Manetho tersely notes that it was one Imhotep who first taught the Egyptians to build in stone, and the ancient chronicler adds, "he also improved the writing." This is all he has to tell us about the architect who lived some twenty-three hundred or more years earlier—a man who must have been one of the great geniuses of Egypt. Imhotep was the vizier (or prime minister) of Djoser, second pharaoh of the Third Dynasty. The Greeks knew him, at least by reputation, under the name Imouthes, and identified him with their god of medicine, Aesculapius. At the time when Greek traders settled in Egypt, scribes poured out a libation to him before beginning their work. His name and his titles appear on the base of a statue of Djoser found at Saqqara. Such an honor was rare when all great works were routinely ascribed to the pharaoh; so we are justified is assuming that it was Imhotep, not Djoser, who was responsible for raising the first great stone building on earth, the Step Pyramid at Saqqara. It is the oldest, most awe-inspiring, monumental stone structure in the world.

The Step Pyramid was begun as a large stone mastaba; later Imhotep enlarged it in stages, superimposing a number of progressively smaller mastabas on top of one another. But here we are looking not only at a royal tomb. Djoser's "House of Eternity" was surrounded by various dummy buildings and courts that almost certainly reproduced the mud-brick palace and temples and the enclosures that once served the pharaoh in his earthly capital at Memphis. The

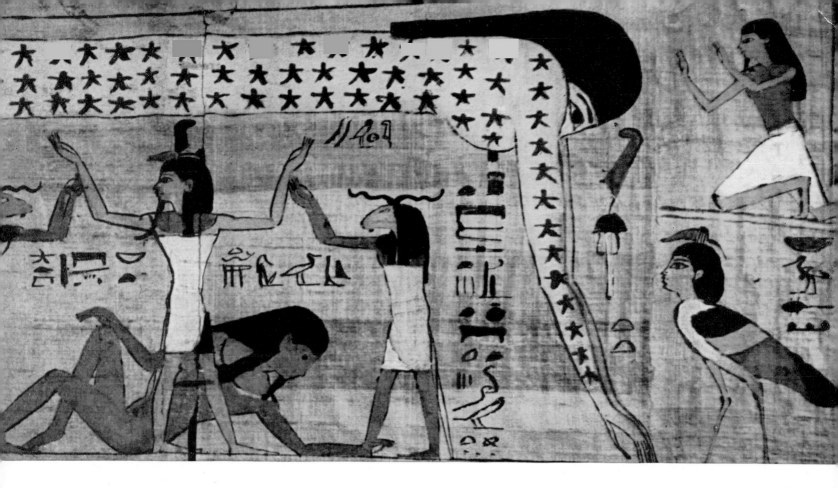

entire complex, which has been partly restored, was once enclosed by a thirty-four-foot wall of paneled design whose perimeter extended for more than a mile.

One enters the pyramid on its north side, descends a long, sloping corridor, and eventually looks down into a pit ninety feet deep. At the bottom lies the granite burial chamber with a hole in the top to admit the royal body, sealed by a granite plug weighing several tons. About this chamber are rooms cut out of the solid rock, one hundred feet beneath the surface of the desert, one of them still lined with green-blue glazed tile panels imitating reed mats which may once have adorned the rooms of Djoser's palace. Similarly, the engaged, fluted columns of the entrance colonnade are reproductions in stone of the bundled reeds that supported the roof of public and domestic buildings; the ponderous stone doors, perpetually ajar, reproduce down to the last detail the wooden doors of early palace architecture.

Djoser's pyramid was built of small stone blocks, little bigger than the mud bricks that were their prototypes. But within less than a century such uneconomic building methods were abandoned. Instead, accurately cut blocks of white limestone weighing several tons each were used. Some of the larger granite monoliths used for burial chambers weighed as much as fifty tons. The Great Pyramid built for Pharaoh Cheops shortly after 2600 B.C. incorporated more than two million stone blocks averaging two-and-a-half tons in weight in the main structure, which was over seven hundred and fifty feet along each base line and rose to a height of nearly five hundred feet. (When he laid eyes on this stupendous monument, Napoleon estimated that it contained enough building material to make a wall ten feet high around most of France.) The structure is oriented to within one-twentieth of a degree to the true north. The stone blocks

A papyrus discovered in the tomb of a priest illustrates one Egyptian view of the universe. It shows the god of the air, Shu, separating the earth from the sky, while ram-headed deities assist him. Above Shu's head is the sky goddess, Nut, her body covered with stars, and the hieroglyphic sign for west written in front of her face. One Egyptian interpretation of nightfall held that the sun was swallowed up by Nut when it disappeared in the west each evening. It traveled through her body at night, and was born again in the morning. Like the sun, the dead also disappeared into the west, but they too would be reborn, and scenes such as this were often placed in tombs as a token of their reascent into life. Here, a bird, representing the soul of the priest for whom the papyrus was made, is shown riding along the circuit of the sun in a small boat. The sky goddess touches the level of the earth only with her fingers and toes. Far beneath her, her husband, Geb, the earth god, lies exhausted after struggling against Shu's efforts to separate him from the sky. His bent knees and elbows represent the mountains and valleys on the surface of the earth.

were cut with such precision that the blade of a knife could not be inserted between them when they were laid in place. Moreover, the giant granite elements had been quarried in far-off Aswan and brought by boat or raft along the six-hundred-mile length of the river. And the entire building was originally sheathed in a skin of smoothly finished white limestone. All this was achieved almost five thousand years ago by a people whose only mechanical devices were the lever, the roller, and the inclined plane. They did not even know the wheel or the block and tackle—they had only simple tools.

When Djoser was put to rest beneath his Step Pyramid so long ago, recorded Egyptian history had barely begun; over twenty-six hundred years were to pass before the last pharaoh ruled the land. Yet the pattern of Egyptian civilization had already been set. The features of Egyptian culture had become fixed in a rigid mold, and it changed very little in character throughout the long course of ancient Egyptian history.

Why did this civilization assume the pattern it did? Why did they bury one frail mortal, a pharaoh though he be, so richly bedizened, under millions of tons of precisely cut stone? What conviction could have persuaded them to expend untold man-hours in raising innumerable tombs, richer than the houses their owners occupied in life, adorned with elaborate and beautifully executed sculpture and painting which no human being was intended to see? Why did they worship and make sacrifices to fantastic gods with human bodies and animal heads?

The answer is not easy to give. The theological system of the Egyptians remains somewhat puzzling to us, as indeed it probably was to most Egyptians. They inherited what seems to us a hodgepodge of widely varying customs and beliefs,

many of them mutually inconsistent, and stemming back to those far-distant times when their ancestors lived in tribal communities along the Nile Valley, each with its local deity. As one scholar has written: "The impression made on the modern mind is that of a people searching in the dark for a key to truth and, having found not one but many keys resembling the pattern of the lock, retaining all lest perchance the appropriate one should be discarded."

The two principal religious cults which helped to shape Egypt's culture throughout her long history were those of Re, the sun god, and Osiris, god of death and resurrection. They originated independently, and there was never any logical connection between them, except that both can be taken to symbolize birth, death, and renewal. The sun is an omnipresent force in Egypt. Every day, in that hot, cloudless sky, the fiery disk is seen rising behind the eastern hills, arching across the valley, and descending below the rim of the western desert. It is easy to see why the Egyptians adored the sun as the giver of life and saw in its progress the pattern of life perpetually renewed. Every night Re died in the west and every morning he was reborn in the east. It was doubtless for this reason that the Egyptians buried their dead in the west; indeed one of the names for the dead was the "Westerners." The center of the Re cult was at Heliopolis not far from the city of Memphis which Narmer made his capital after the unification of Egypt. This would help to account for the predominance of the sun god from the early dynastic period to the end of the Old Kingdom.

The cult of Osiris, his wife and sister Isis, and their son Horus involves a myth that according to one version may be summarized as follows. In the beginning there was only a waste of waters, the primeval ocean, on which appeared an egg from which was born Re, the sun god. He had four

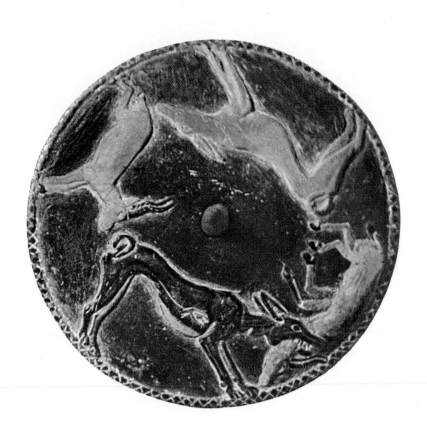

children, Geb, the earth god, Shu and Tefnut, gods of the atmosphere, and Nut, the sky goddess. Shu and Tefnut, planting their feet on Geb, raised Nut to the heavens. In some later Egyptian tombs, a painting on the ceiling or under the lid of the sarcophagus, represents Nut as a woman whose body is arched across the sky.

This is certainly a primitive creation myth with which the cult of Osiris was later integrated. Osiris was the son of Geb and Nut, who had three other children, Isis, Nephthys, and Seth. Osiris married his sister Isis (within the Egyptian royal family brother-sister marriages became common practice), and subsequently succeeded to the throne of Egypt, which he governed wisely and humanely. He persuaded the Egyptians to give up cannibalism, and introduced them to useful arts and crafts. (Surely the prototype of Osiris was an earthly ruler who was later deified or became identified with an already existing god.) His wicked brother Seth was jealous and plotted against him. Eventually Seth succeeded in killing Osiris by treachery, later dissecting the body and burying the pieces in various parts of Egypt, all except the penis that he threw into the river at Oxyrhyncus. The head was buried at Abydos, later an important cult center to which pilgrimages were made.

Isis, the faithful wife, recovered the parts of her husband's body (all save the organ of generation) and, with the help of the god Anubis, reassembled and reanimated the corpse. But since Osiris had now lost his reproductive powers he could no longer rule over the living. He therefore became god of the dead and judge of souls.

That was the first part of the myth. The resurrection of Osiris bears resemblances to myths underlying the fertility cults practiced by other peoples. The second part concerns Horus, the devoted and loyal son of Osiris, who sought out

Seth and eventually slew him, though in the fight Seth plucked out his nephew's eye, which was later restored to him by the god Thoth. (The "eye of Horus" figures prominently in many Egyptian religious monuments and inscriptions as a symbol of sacrifice.) Thus, after revenging his father, Horus himself ascended the throne of Egypt.

That the Osiris-Isis-Horus myth took such a hold on the Egyptian's imagination, that it survived for more than thirty centuries was due, surely, to its humanity. The cult of the sun god and his sacred bark into which only the king could enter was an austere conception, the product of an intellectual priestly class. But every wife could identify herself with the faithful Isis, every son with Horus, every father with Osiris. As for the second part of the story, the revenge of Horus, it may be significant that Europe's greatest psychological drama closely parallels this ancient myth. Claudius treacherously kills his royal brother to gain the throne; Hamlet, his nephew, kills Claudius to avenge his father.

It is important to outline these myths, for from an early date Pharaoh was considered both god and king. He proclaimed himself Horus, who became Osiris on death. Later he became the divine son of the sun god Re. This title, which probably originated when the pharaohs ruled from Memphis, near the Heliopolitan center of the sun cult, was retained down to the last dynasty, even when, with the rise of the Theban kings, the Theban god Amen had come to be associated with the sun god as Amen-Re.

In very early times the king may have been sacrificed after a certain number of years to propitiate the gods and to renew the fertility of the soil. This sacrificial role was not forgotten in later times. Among the reliefs that have survived in the Step Pyramid complex we see Djoser in a running posture, wearing the crowns of Upper and Lower Egypt, but other-

wise almost naked. And in the great courtyard to the south of his pyramid, archaeologists have discovered the remains of two posts, like those of a racecourse. It has been suggested that the reliefs depict part of the *heb-sed,* a festival in which the monarch had to prove his vitality by sprinting around a set course. Once he would have been killed when his powers started to wane, but in these later times his strength could be magically renewed by a ritualistic formula that represented him passing this test of vigor.

This tenacity of ancient religious beliefs is further disclosed by inscriptions on the walls of pyramid chambers of the Fifth and Sixth Dynasties. These so-called Pyramid Texts, a large body of magic formulas that ensured the happiness and fulfillment of Pharaoh in the next world, include a description of the dead king sallying forth to lasso and kill the gods for his cooking pot. This cannibalistic spell is obviously a relic of that far-off time when the ancestors of the pyramid builders were ruled by a king who feasted ritually on the bodies of his foes in order to bring the rain—a custom that has been practiced by barbarous tribes until fairly recent days.

Throughout historic times it was the function of the king to perform the necessary sacrifices to the principal gods. In this way he protected his subjects by acting as intermediary between them and the unseen, unknown powers that governed men's lives. The prosperity of the land, the fertility of the soil, and the survival of his people depended ultimately upon the king. In their eyes he was divinity incarnate, and after his earthly death he would continue to watch over Egypt's welfare as he had done in life.

Unless we accept the fact that these and other religious beliefs were valid to the Egyptians, the pyramids, rock-cut tombs, gigantic temples, and all the rest of their funerary art will appear only as curiosities, perversions of the human mind. But they were in fact practical devices that grew out of the conditions of human life as the Egyptians lived it and as they understood the meaning of existence. They provide insights into customs and beliefs that have long since vanished.

It is difficult to penetrate the minds of people who lived at a time so remote from our own. Certainly the ancient Egyptians believed in what we call the soul. In fact they recognized two souls, the *ba* and the *ka.* The former they represented in hieroglyphs by a figure of a little, bearded, human-headed bird. The hieroglyph for the *ka* consisted of two human arms bent at the elbow, to which was sometimes added a bearded human figure wearing them as a crown. Neither of these entities could survive into afterlife unless the body of the deceased was preserved and protected from violation, and it was for this reason that the Egyptians practiced mummification.

In predynastic times when the dead were buried in shallow pits, the dry sand preserved them to such an astonishing degree that even today there are corpses, interred without embalming, which still retain their skin and hair. Such graves could be robbed; once the Egyptians began to protect them by sinking shafts into the rock, and covering these with mud-brick or stone superstructures, the bodies tended to decompose unless preventive measures were taken. This led the Egyptians to develop the technique of artificial preservation at least as early as the Second Dynasty. There was nothing mysterious about the embalming process, which could probably be improved upon today. The most ancient mummy known was found by Petrie at Medum and dates from the Fifth Dynasty. Long before, however, attempts were made to make the corpse appear lifelike by

Taxes were usually paid in kind with hides, labor, or agricultural produce. Having failed to fulfill their tax assessment, the overseers at left kneel before an official for judgment. While seated scribes record their cases, one delinquent villager is punished with a whipping.

wrapping each limb separately and even inserting resin-soaked pads under the wrappings to give the body the appropriate contours.

As time passed this method was refined until there grew a large corps of skilled embalmers who even had a tariff of charges; the price varied according to the complexity of the process and the work involved. The de luxe method, reserved for royalty and high officials, took several months. First the embalmers made an incision and removed the viscera: heart, liver, lungs, intestines—all the most decomposable parts. These were installed separately in a set of stone vessels, later called canopic jars, each consigned to the protection of a particular god. The heart, however, was re-inserted within the body, probably because the Egyptians regarded the heart and not the brain as the seat of intelligence.

Meanwhile the eviscerated corpse was allowed to soak for about seventy days in a bath of niter, after which it was removed, dried, and wrapped in resinous strips of linen. But it was in the process preceding this that the embalmer exhibited his greatest skill. By placing linen pads under the skin he was able to fill out the sunken cheeks and give an appearance of firmness to the limbs which, before wrapping, were adorned with fine jewelry and ornaments.

This, of course, represents the ultimate in embalming technique, as practiced a thousand years after the end of the Old Kingdom. The bodies of the pyramid builders may not have been so skillfully preserved, though we cannot be sure, since none have survived. However, even in the age of Cheops, the embalming process took several months, as we know from written evidence. We are told that 272 days passed between the death and burial of his grandchild Queen Meresankh III. Again, when the American archaeologist George Reisner discovered the tomb of Cheops' mother, Queen

The emaciated herdsman above has led his cattle in from the marshes. There was famine in the years when the Nile failed to rise high enough; then "grain was scant, fruits were dried up." But during years of plenty, grain supplies were so ample that some could be used to fatten fowl, like those shown in the relief below, being force-fed.

One of the most individualized portraits surviving from the time of the
Old Kingdom is that of Prince
Ankhhaf, at right. He was probably
a son of King Cheops, and served
as vizier under King Chephren.
These pharaohs, along with Mycerinus, built the three great pyramids
at Giza. Mycerinus' tomb is the
smallest and latest of the three; it
may have remained unfinished because Egypt could no longer afford
to pay for such monumental building. The statue below shows Mycerinus standing alongside his queen.

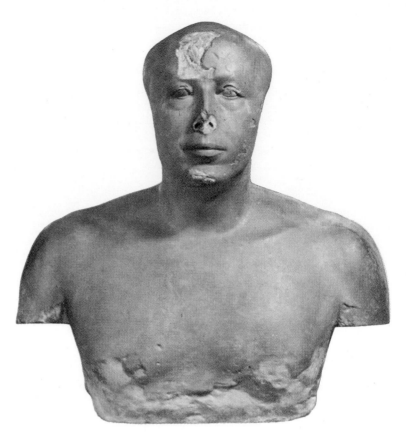

Hetepheres, though the body was missing the alabaster vessel
containing her viscera was still in place and in one of the
canopic compartments liquid embalming fluid was still preserved. These internal organs together with the queen's gold
throne, silver anklets, make-up box, and other equipment can
still be inspected in the Cairo Museum—an intriguing juxta-
position of mortality and vanity.

As additional protection the form of the deceased was
reproduced in sculptures and in paintings to provide other
substitute refuges for the spirits. These likenesses, buried
in the silent chambers of the dead, were not intended to be
seen by human eyes. They were in effect a supplementary form
of afterlife insurance. The main point was to preserve the
appearance of the body so that the *ba* or *ka* would recognize
it even if the mortal remains that they represented were destroyed. The dead also had to be provided with food, drink,
and other material needs of a living body. In early days these
were stockpiled in royal tombs in enormous quantities and
later supplemented by regular offerings. Actual physical remains of these tomb offerings have been found. One such,
discovered by W. B. Emery in a Second Dynasty mastaba,
consisted of soup, ribs of beef, kidneys, pigeon, quail, fish,
fruit, bread, and cake.

Other peoples to our own day have also believed devoutly
in an afterlife, but none have taken such elaborate precautions to assure life beyond death. Future generations
would gain little understanding of our Western way of life
from our somewhat nebulous picture of heaven. "You can't
take it with you," we say. Not so the Egyptians. They believed
they could, and their picture of the hereafter was of a life
lived much as it had been known on earth. There was nothing morbid about their concept of death. Rather it projected
the industrious, cheerful, and plentiful life that the Egyptian,

with reasonable expectation, wished to enjoy everlastingly.

They attached a magical value to representations of their possessions—their families and servants as well as their houses, gardens, flocks, and herds—whereby these models, paintings, and reliefs were invested with all the attributes of the real thing, throughout eternity.

In representing the world about him the ancient Egyptian artist observed relatively fixed conventions that were accepted and understood by his contemporary audience. Human figures are scaled according to their importance in the Egyptian social and hierarchical scheme. The pharaoh or a high official is depicted much larger than the servants or commoners who attend him at the banquet table or who swarm about him in the fields and in the marshes. Perspective as we understand it was not attempted. The various elements of a scene are arranged in a series of horizontal registers, nearer objects being indicated in the lower panels, and in ascending order, the more distant ones shown above. To represent the human figure the Egyptian painter selected the most characteristic and easily recognizable aspects of his subjects and combined them in an image that never meets normal vision. The head is shown in profile, but the eye within it appears in front view; the torso is also shown as seen from the front, but the arms and legs in profile. Rigid and unnatural as the conventions may seem by the traditional standards of Western art, to the Egyptian they conveyed an impression of the complete and enduring power of the human body.

When the king died the chambers of his sepulcher were filled with rich furniture—beds, couches, and chairs inlaid with ivory and gold, his chests of clothing—as well as weapons, ornaments, food, and wine, to serve his every need in the hereafter. More than eighty pyramids, many of them extremely large although only one rivaled Cheops' pyramid in size, were built to protect the mortal remains of the god-kings and their possessions. And every one of these bodies was stripped, destroyed, and robbed of its precious equipment thousands of years ago. All that survives are the empty shells of the sacred tombs. The bodies of the royal dead have disappeared, as have those of the countless hordes who labored to build for the great ones their eternal homes.

Yet, ironically, while the personalities and achievements of the god-kings have been reduced to mere names, those of their noble servants—and of even servants of those servants—have more substance for us. From the Fourth Dynasty on it was customary for the great officials to build mastabas near Pharaoh's pyramid. Whole streets of these tombs have survived, and in some of the larger examples there are brilliant reliefs depicting the aspects of the dead man's earthly life which he particularly wished to be perpetuated in the hereafter. These often follow set patterns; there are scenes of hunting with the nobleman harpooning hippopotamuses or hurling a throwing stick at wildfowl while delicately poised in a light skiff of papyrus reeds; sometimes his wife or daughter is shown holding his leg in a companionable spirit, and a servant crouches in the bow of the boat to pick up the game. There are also feasting scenes. In these we see the great man and his wife seated on stately chairs and receiving their guests; tables are spread with delicacies, servants pour wine, and dancing girls perform to the sound of flutes, harps, and drums. The food served at such banquets can be recognized from these sculptured and painted representations. The tomb of the vizier Kagemni contains a pillared hall with adjoining rooms, one of which is adorned with reliefs showing ducks in a duckpond and fishermen coming home with their catch. More extraordinary is a scene showing hyenas being

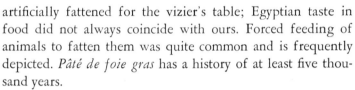

At right, two traders haggle with each other, while a water carrier, still a feature of the Egyptian market place, stands nearby. Most trading was in kind, but sometimes copper, gold, or silver rings were used for exchange. Those shown above are being measured against standard weights, which were often given animal shapes. "Do not lean on the scales nor falsify the weights," Egyptians were warned; the gods watched as closely as the customers did to ensure fair dealings.

artificially fattened for the vizier's table; Egyptian taste in food did not always coincide with ours. Forced feeding of animals to fatten them was quite common and is frequently depicted. *Pâté de foie gras* has a history of at least five thousand years.

The fact that women are shown sharing these social pleasures with men distinguishes the ancient Egyptians from some other Oriental civilizations; the wife of an official is given equal prominence with her husband, and frequently the couple are shown in an affectionate posture, with her arm around his waist—as occasionally, indeed, are a pharaoh and his spouse. These ladies of so long ago have an elegance and sophistication which appeal strongly to an age in which the slim, svelte line is again fashionable. Even their make-up is not too exotic to us; they reddened their lips, painted their fingernails and toenails, and used heavy eye shadow. Writers on ancient Egypt often call attention to the fact that a set of workman's tools—say those of a carpenter—would be immediately familiar to his modern counterpart. This is true; but it is equally true that a modern Western woman, faced with a set of ancient Egyptian cosmetics in their elegant alabaster jars and other beautifying paraphernalia, would know what to do with most of them.

Other tomb scenes show very clearly the sources of wealth that supported this luxury. It came from the land. We see farm hands working in the fields, sowing and harvesting the grain; we see lines of fat cattle being driven to slaughter, and butchers with knives cutting up the carcasses; other men carry haunches of beef to the burial chamber, so that the *ka* would never lack sustenance, even if the descendants of the dead man or the priests appointed by them ceased to make real food offerings at the tomb. The intimate details often depicted in these scenes take us back into the immediate

presence of these long-dead people. Sometimes hieroglyphic inscriptions introduce a line or two of comment or dialogue. One highborn lady at a noble banquet cries out, "I want to drink till I'm drunk; my inside is like a straw," while a servant refills her goblet. In the mastaba of Mereruka, vizier of the first king of the Sixth Dynasty, one field worker calls to another, "Where are you now, you loafer?" and the foreman exclaims, "This barley is very good, fellow!"

On the walls of the tomb of Vizier Ptahhotep we see boys playing games. Some are trying their skill at a feat which small boys still attempt today, to rise from a sitting position while holding their toes. Another boy kneels on the ground, trying to confuse his playmates by catching their feet. They in turn attack him, amid cries of "Look, you've kicked me!" and "I've got you!" All this dialogue is faithfully recorded in the inscriptions, as for instance in a scene where fish are drying in the sun and a boy and an old man are making ropes for boat building. "O strong youth, bring me ropes," asks the old fellow; and the boy replies, "O my father, here is the rope."

Among the most amazing Old Kingdom reliefs are those in the mastaba of Ankhmahor, a high official under the pharaoh, Teti (Sixth Dynasty). It is often called "The Physicians' Tomb" because one room contains representations of surgical operations, including circumcision and an operation on a man's toe. Although such scenes have no special reference to Ankhmahor, these and other reliefs give this tomb a particular interest. In one of them a line of dancing girls is executing a concerted high kick which would do credit to any modern chorus line. The big toe of each barefoot dancer exactly touches the line dividing this scene from the one above; heads are thrown back, at exactly the same angle; each girl's hair is tied in a pigtail with a pompon at the end, and

Thoth was the god of just measure, and it was his sacred animal, the ape, who sat beside the balance according to Egyptian tradition. Appropriately enough monkeys were trained to guard against pilfering in the market. The one shown above has just apprehended a thief, and holds on to him by the leg.

their arms are rhythmically raised, caught, almost photographically, in a "frozen moment" of time.

These tomb paintings and reliefs are like windows through which we may peer into the Egyptian past. Humble men and women are often depicted with compassion and humor, as indeed are the domestic animals. One has the feeling that life for a workman or peasant on a nobleman's estate was no worse, or better, than it was, let us say, on a great estate in nineteenth-century England. There is no positive proof, but it is permissible to believe that, on the whole, Egypt was humanely and wisely governed.

The pharaohs were both divine rulers and temporal governors. Some of these men played an extremely active, creative role in the administration of the state; they appointed and supervised officials, instituted reforms, and initiated great public works. Some became capable, even brilliant, generals who led their armies in person.

Immediately beneath the pharaoh, at the second stage of the social pyramid, were large numbers of high officials, the "senior civil servants" representing the upper echelons of the Egyptian administrative system. (Particularly in the Old Kingdom, this ruling group included the progeny of the pharaoh and his wife or his concubines, and other royal relatives, sometimes numbering hundreds.) Some were the *nomarchs* who governed the nomes or provinces. Many had purely honorary functions, such as the "Fanbearer on the King's Right Hand," or supervised the palace staff including, of course, the royal harem. Others were priests whose function was more than sacerdotal; they not only performed rites of propitiation and sacrifice, but administered the gods' vast estates and temples. They also largely controlled the educational system. Not infrequently, and not surprisingly, court and priesthood were in conflict.

Beneath the great officers in descending order of rank and responsibility came other, lesser officials, all of whom would have been scribes, for literacy was the the first prerequisite of office. Writing was taught in the temple schools, which might also be regarded as training colleges for the innumerable officials who administered Egypt. Being a scribe had many attractions, not the least of which was exemption from manual work. The ordinary Egyptian peasant or laborer was liable to be conscripted for large-scale public works such as digging ditches and repairing embankments after the annual inundation. But not the scribe. An Egyptian school exercise of a much later period contains the refrain, "Be a scribe, who is freed from forced labor, and protected from all work"; that is, manual work. The same document gives a vivid and probably exaggerated picture of the plight of the poor peasant who cannot pay his taxes:

"And now the scribe landeth on the embankment and will register the harvest. The porters carry sticks, and the negroes palm-ribs. They say: 'Give corn.' 'There is none here' [says the peasant]. He is stretched out and beaten; he is bound and thrown into the canal. His wife is bound in his presence, his children are put in fetters. His neighbors leave them, they take to flight, and look after their corn. But the scribe, he directeth the work of all people. For him there are no taxes, for he payeth tribute in writing, and there are no dues for him. Prithee, know that."

Admittedly this comes from a prejudiced source, but there is little doubt that the laboring masses were sometimes treated with severity, even with cruelty. However there is little or no evidence that the ordinary Egyptian felt he suffered from social injustice; he did not question the established order of things. There were apparently no codified laws. Law was the word of Pharaoh, and as god Pharaoh was the personification

of justice as the Egyptians understood it. He interpreted the inevitable, divine order of the world—and to the early Egyptians, at least, Egypt *was* the world—in terms of what was good, right, and equitable. This concept of the established "rightness" of things, of what was good as opposed to what was bad, was broadly covered by the Egyptian word *maat*, a word that has no equivalent in our language.

Much that we know of the ancient Egyptians is derived from those of their own accounts that have survived. The beginnings of a written language can be found in the signs on predynastic commemorative palettes. By about 2500 B.C. the Egyptians had already a burgeoning literature. What had begun as a method of keeping records had developed into a subtle and flexible instrument of communication. Pictographs had long ceased to be merely symbols of things—heads of cattle, measures of land, wheat, wine, and oil. They had come to represent the sounds of the Egyptians' spoken language, with all its grammatical complexities, variations of meaning, and rhythm. There were, at this time, two methods of writing the language: the fully formed hieroglyphs which were usually carved in stone; and the flowing, cursive style with abbreviated symbols which, like our modern handwriting, were easier to write, and which the Greeks later called hieratic. By extracting the pith from the papyrus reed that grew in the marshes along the Nile, gluing the reed strips together, and drying them, the ancient Egyptians produced a light, portable, and convenient writing material on which they wrote with fine brushes or rush pens. Our modern word *paper* is derived from *papyrus*, just as the word *Bible*, originally meaning *book*, reminds us of the port of Byblos in Lebanon, which later was the main port for the export of papyrus scrolls.

Many examples of scribes' writing materials have been found in Egyptian tombs, and a considerable number of inscribed papyri, though these represent only a minute fraction of the quantity that must once have existed. They include the earliest known medical textbooks; also letters, state records, school exercise books, religious texts, stories, and poems. Some of these documents date back to the Old Kingdom, and include tales of fantasy and wonder of which the Egyptians were very fond.

One of the latter concerns the pharaoh, Snofru, father of Cheops. In a fit of very deep depression the king asked his court magician, Djadjamankh, to devise some sort of entertainment that would distract his mind, dispel his mood. In a free version of a standard translation the popular story proceeds as follows:

". . . And Djadjamankh said to him: 'If your majesty would but go to the lake of the palace. Man a boat with all fair damsels from the inner apartments. Then will your heart be diverted when you watch them row to and fro.' . . . And his majesty replied: 'I will do this. . . . Bring me twenty paddles of ebony inlaid with gold. . . . and twenty women with the fairest limbs, and with beauteous breasts and braided tresses, such as have not yet given birth, and moreover bring me twenty nets, and give these to the women instead of their clothes.' And it was done according to all that his majesty commanded. And they rowed to and fro, and the heart of his majesty was glad when he saw them row.

"Then a leader became entangled with her braided hair, and her hair ornament of new malachite in the form of a fish-pendant fell into the water. And she became silent and stopped rowing, and the girls on her side became silent and stopped rowing. Then his majesty asked: 'Why do you not row?' . . . She said: 'My new fish-pendant has fallen into the water.' He had another brought to her and said: 'I give you this instead.' But she said: 'I like my own better.'"

This is perhaps the most fascinating episode in the tale, for the mighty pharaoh obeyed her whim. He recalled his magician Djadjamankh, and explained his difficult position. Fortunately the magician was equal to the difficulties of the occasion. He performed the same miracle that Moses accomplished on the Red Sea a thousand years later. He parted the waters of the lake.

"Then Djadjamankh said his say of magic, and he placed the one side of the water of the lake upon the other, and found the fish-pendant lying on a piece of pottery. And he brought it and gave it to its mistress. . . . Then he said his say of magic, and he brought the waters of the lake to their place."

Admittedly this is merely a folk tale, yet it must have been drawn to some degree from observed experience. The testimony of the Hebrews and tales of oppression under the pyramid builders repeated by dragomen to Greek travelers in much later times cannot be accepted at face value. In spite of old legends of slave-driving autocrats, it would seem that the affairs of the royal family attracted general interest and that Pharaoh, certainly Snofru, enjoyed the affection of his people. And it is also part of the record that when the Israelites came to Egypt at a time of famine, they received corn—probably at a fair price—from the hands of one of their own race who had won the confidence of the king.

One of the most remarkable documents that have survived is the so-called Edwin Smith Papyrus, a later copy of what was probably the earliest treatise on surgery. As the anatomist Warren Dawson has pointed out, this papyrus indicates that at an early date the Egyptians made serious attempts to understand the structure of the human body. They had studied the brain, observed that its hemispheres were patterned with convolutions, and understood that injury to it would affect other parts of the body; although in spite of their ample experience in dissection through embalming, they apparently did not discover that the brain was the seat of intelligence. They knew that the heart "speaks" in other parts of the body, but they did not grasp the concept of the circulation of the blood, a concept, we might add, that was only defined a few hundred years ago.

They knew that certain injuries could be repaired and that others were hopeless. Ancient skulls have been found showing loose teeth fastened together with gold wire and, in at least one case, evidence of a successful operation to drain an abscess at the root of a molar. There were obviously specialists. We read of eye doctors, also "those who know the secret and specialize in the body fluids," those who could prescribe for diseases of the lungs, bladder, stomach, and even for falling or graying hair; and bowel specialists, splendidly entitled Guardians of the Anus.

Among the drugs recommended by ancient Egyptian doctors there are a number that are still used by the modern medical profession, including acacia, anise, cassia, castor beans, wormwood, coriander, and saffron. Among the mineral substances are sodium bicarbonate, arsenic, and niter (of which the very name is Egyptian), alum, and sulphur.

Despite such impressive testimony it would be unrealistic to regard this medical knowledge as being based on anything remotely resembling a scientific approach to medicine. Whatever was practical and efficacious in their methods was the result of a long process of trial and error. They owed it less to their own inquiring minds than to the experience of generations of ancestors who had tried out certain remedies in the past and discovered that some were effective and others less so. The same is true of their other achievements; in the field of mathematics, for instance, there exists a famous mathematical document called the Rhind Papyrus, which among other things deals with the problem of triangles. It is a highly practical and useful document, but it would be false to compare it to the productions of Euclid and Pythagoras over two thousand years later. The Greeks were more interested in pure knowledge than in its practical application. Not so the ancient Egyptians. Given the task of healing a wound, curing a disease, drawing a boundary, measuring the rise of the Nile or the movement of the stars, or leveling a site for a pyramid, they faced the problem and solved it to the best of their ability and then got on with the job. And that was as far as they went.

In the elaborate hierarchical society that so early developed in Egypt, every man and woman, from Pharaoh down, had a definite place and function; albeit people of drive and ability could and did rise from the ranks. All wealth was in kind; it was derived almost entirely from the land; and all land was, nominally, owned by the pharaoh. Using units of grain and copper as a measure of value, the Egyptian held markets, lent on interest, and developed an elaborate system of taxation. There was some internal trade although, at least in the early period, each nome was virtually self-sufficient and every royal or priestly estate had its own group of tradesmen, craftsmen, and field workers.

Foreign commerce was nominally the province of Pharaoh. Even in the Old Kingdom, Egypt traded with Lebanon, Asia Minor, the Aegean Islands, and with the Land of Punt (probably Somaliland) from which were imported perfumes and incense. From Nubia (directly to the south) Egyptians brought back, by trade or conquest, ivory, ebony, gold, ostrich feathers (for fans), myrrh (for incense), and such exotic beasts as giraffes and monkeys.

Protected by the natural barriers of barren wastelands and sea, Egypt had the advantage of developing and maintaining its unique culture, undisturbed by major foreign invasion, over a period of some two thousand years. In this comfortable isolation there was room and, except in bad times, food for everyone. On the whole the evidence suggests that the Egyptian way of life seemed good to all concerned. As we have seen, the basic pattern of civilization was established at an early date, and the Egyptians clung to this pattern with remarkable resourcefulness and with relatively minor changes throughout their long, remarkable history. We who tend to equate change with progress and revolution with historical evolution may be reminded that a static condition of harmony in the social body has, or has had, much to recommend it.

THE RELIGION
OF EGYPT

To awaken Pharaoh each morning, his courtiers sang a hymn to the sun, greeting the king with the same adoring words chanted at dawn in the temple of Re, the sun god. For the Egyptians worshiped Pharaoh as a god, as the link between earth and heaven and the focus around which their religion revolved. He was the living son of Re, and the incarnation of the divine falcon who ruled the heavens, the god Horus who is shown above protectively enfolding Pharaoh Chephren in his wings. There was a Nile god and a fertility god, but Pharaoh also brought the grain, and his participation in the annual harvest festival was required to maintain the prosperity of the land. Famine, rebellion, or defeat never called his divine omnipotence into question. His victory was certain; his supremacy as unchallengeable as that triumphant system of order, or *maat,* which ruled the universe according to Egyptian belief. This righteous order was innate in the universe and inherent in the nature of Pharaoh. Any wrongdoer was out of harmony with it and it was inevitable that he be destroyed.

THE GODS

Daily in every temple throughout Egypt, the images of the gods were unveiled at sunrise. To the sound of chanting, the high priest broke open the seal which had closed the sanctuary the day before, and offered food, drink, and flowers to the idol within. He reverently washed its body and anointed its brow with oil, and once or twice a week changed its clothing as well. Every four or five days, the images were taken from their temples and carried in procession through the towns, in wooden ships borne on the shoulders of priests. During these processions, worshipers were allowed to consult the gods for advice; their answers were determined by the direction in which the divine boat lurched. No matter which god the temple served, ritual practices rarely changed, for despite grotesque variations in their outer forms, Egypt's major deities were remarkably similar in character. Re, Atum, or Khnum might be incarnate in the falcon, the serpent, or the ram, but to their devotees, each was a supreme god. Their celestial power might wax or wane with the political importance of their cult center, but if they were threatened with oblivion, they could survive by merging their identities with those of different, more favored gods. Priests contrived ingenious and complex theologies to impose some unity on the pantheon; but these attempts at rationalizing their religion (the Egyptian word for it can best be translated as *magic*) had little hold on the great mass of people, who worshiped dozens of minor deities as well as Pharaoh and the universal gods. There was Heqet, the frog goddess; there was Merseger, the cobra goddess who guarded against snakes; and Toueris, the pregnant hippopotamus who watched over childbirth. Although animals themselves were not worshiped until very late in Egyptian history, the relationship between gods and beasts was a close and mysterious one. For beasts shared the divine knowledge of nature's inscrutable laws; they represented fecundity and power and cunning; their ways were unchanging, as Egypt itself hoped to be.

The bird-headed terra-cotta figure at right may represent a dead woman's soul. The Egyptians were not the only primitive race to imagine the dead as birds, but they, more than others, attributed animal characteristics to their gods. In the painting opposite, the funerary deity, Anubis, is shown with a jackal head. Next to him are Re, the sun god, and Osiris, the king of the dead, who is seated upon the throne of Egypt.

Tearing their garments and strewing dust upon their heads, bare-breasted professional mourners wail a noisy farewell to the dead.

ENTERING THE AFTERWORLD

Once the embalmers had finished preparing a corpse for eternity, the mummy was dispatched on a journey to Abydos, the sacred city of the dead. Only the very rich could afford to be buried in its great necropolis, next to Osiris, the king of the afterlife, but many could purchase a posthumous visit to the city, and funeral boats ranged up and down the Nile transporting dead passengers there. Originally, the privilege of joining Osiris in death had belonged only to kings; later it was assumed by nobles too, and eventually every dead Egyptian became identified with the god. Mummification had been first used to preserve the god's body from corruption; to become an "Osiris" in the hereafter, Egyptians also imitated the other funeral rites that had once restored him to life. Daily offerings of food and incense were provided for the dead man, as they were for the gods in their temples. But because mummies were hidden far within the tomb for safety, these sacrifices had to be placed in an antechamber, in front of an effigy. Before this statue could accept sacrifices, it had to be brought to life, and for this purpose rituals that had revived Osiris were celebrated over it too. The dead man and his image were installed in the tomb while his widow stood wailing outside. The statue within would survive even if the mummy itself failed to heed the fervent prayer of the funerary priest: "O flesh . . . decay not, perish not, let not thy odor be evil."

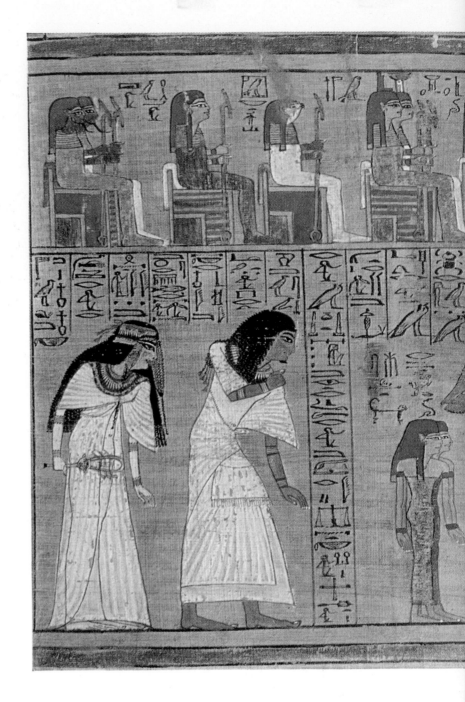

With the deceased and his wife looking on, the funeral god Anubis weighs the heart of the scribe Ani, in an illustration from a papyrus Book of the Dead found in a New Kingdom tomb. The ceremony took place before the throne of Osiris, in the Hall of Double Justice, while a fierce hybrid monster called the Devourer waited nearby, ready to consume the dead man's heart if it failed to balance with a feather (symbolizing truth) placed on the other scalepan. Such illustrations invariably showed the scales in equilibrium as a token of favorable judgment. After the ibis-headed god Thoth recorded the results and Osiris pronounced his judgment, the deceased enjoyed eternal happiness, like the royal harem lady, Kawit, who is shown below, contentedly sniffing a lotus blossom and dipping her finger into an ointment jar.

THE
BOOK
OF
THE
DEAD

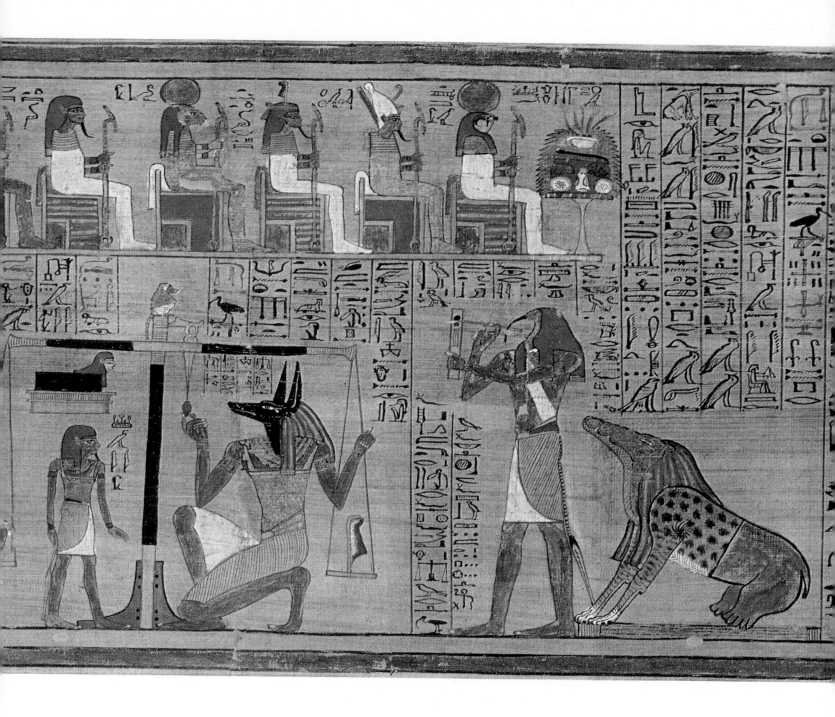

"Behold me—I have come to you without sin, without guilt, without evil . . . I have given bread to the hungry, water to the thirsty, clothing to the naked . . . Rescue me; protect me . . ." Pleading for eternal life in the judgment hall of Osiris, the dead stood trembling before the forty-two frightful gods who aided the king of the afterlife in the weighing of souls. One was called the Breaker-of-Bones; among his comrades were the Swallower-of-Shadows and the Eater-of-Blood. Before them, it was not enough for a man merely to proclaim his own virtue, or to rely on the scarab which had been placed on his heart to keep it from bearing evil witness against him. He had to know their secret names as well, or else he would be destroyed; he had to be equipped with spells to drive off the snakes and crocodiles who were as dangerous in the afterlife as they were on earth. The proper magic was required to avoid eviction from the sun

bark of the god Re, in which the dead journeyed across the sky; to keep from drinking urine, or forgetting one's own name, or worst of all, dying again in the hereafter. It was to prepare for these dreadful eventualities that each corpse, usurping a burial custom which once only kings had been privileged to follow, was furnished with a collection of spells, known as the Book of the Dead. Once his tomb contained them, a man was safe, for the spells usually worked; no matter how wicked he actually had been on earth he was promised the rewards of a righteous life. If the gods decided against him, the book's magic was so powerful that they might even be punished themselves. The journey there was perilous, but if the deceased finally entered the Field of Rushes, life went on as pleasantly as it had in the Nile Valley. Safe in the abode of the blessed, he "plows there and harvests there and drinks there and loves there, and does everything he had done upon earth."

ANARCHY
AND
RECOVERY

Kingdom of the Pharaohs · II

The pattern of Egyptian civilization, which had been set at such an early date, and which retained its basic character over such an immense span of time, was never completely rigid. Various forces—political, economic, religious—impinged upon the valley dwellers, bringing about changes that called for adaptations within the established system. We can see this develop during the middle years of the third millennium B.C. and culminate in the Sixth Dynasty, with which the Old Kingdom came to an end. The pyramids of this and the preceding dynasty are smaller than those of the Fourth Dynasty and less carefully constructed. They suggest a decline of the royal power; and when the absolute authority exercised by the early Memphite kings diminished, anarchy ensued, at least in some parts of the land.

"Plunderers are everywhere . . . the Nile is in flood, yet none ploweth . . . Every man saith: 'We know not what hath happened throughout the land.' . . . Plague stalketh through the land and blood is everywhere . . . Men do not sail to Byblos today. What can we do to get cedars for our mummies? Priests are buried with their produce, and princes are embalmed with their resin as far as the land of Keftiu [Crete?], and now they come no more . . . laughter hath perished and is no longer made. It is grief that walketh through the land, mingled with lamentations . . . The land is left over to its weariness, as when one hath pulled up the flax . . . corn hath perished everywhere. People are stripped of clothing, perfume, and oil. Every one saith: 'There is no more.' . . . The storehouse is bare, and he that kept it lieth stretched out on the ground . . . A thing hath been done,

The Sixth Dynasty ruler, Pepi II, was the last great pharaoh of the Old Kingdom. During the ninety-four years of his reign, royal power declined, and Egypt fell prey to anarchy at his death.

that happened not aforetime; it is come to this that the king hath been taken away by poor men [the royal sepulcher had been plundered] . . . he that was buried as a hawk lieth on a bier. What the pyramid hid will become empty."

This lament, excerpted from what is called "The Admonitions of the Prophet Ipuwer," criticizes an unnamed pharaoh of the Sixth Dynasty for allowing his country to fall into such a state of unrest and confusion. Though probably exaggerated, its tone makes clear the disorganization that was besetting Egypt at the time. There appear to have been civil uprisings, and we know that the pyramid tombs of Cheops, Chephren, and Mycerinus were rifled and their statues left to neglect and destruction. This occurs time and again in Egyptian history; we have noticed how the First Dynasty mastabas at Abydos and Saqqara had been plundered. Perhaps this was not the work of thieves, but the acts of contending and usurping forces within the kingdom.

How did it happen that the mighty pharaohs lost their accustomed supreme control over the land? What accounts for the disturbances that moved Ipuwer to his long and bitter lament? The kings of the later dynasties of the Old Kingdom probably overreached themselves by endeavoring to extend their power beyond its permissible limits. They could have been forced to do this by external circumstances. It was necessary to exercise some kind of control over the southern frontier, partly for purposes of security and partly for purposes of trade. Carved inscriptions on the rocky cliffs overlooking the Nile beyond the First Cataract bear the names of First and Second Dynasty kings, proving that even in that remote age royal expeditions were sent to the area. Similarly, in the northeast, in the Sinai peninsula where the Egyptians mined copper and malachite, there are rock-cut figures of the pharaohs who sent expeditions there; even as early a king as

Holding their offerings out before them, three men who are probably priests present Meketre with a censer, a leg of beef, and a papyrus roll, which he will use in the afterworld. Written on the roll is a record of Meketre's funerary supplies: "a thousand of bread and beer, a thousand of beef and fowl."

Sekhemkhet, successor to Djoser, is represented. The desert Bedouins who threatened these expeditions had to be held back; and in the west as well the warlike Libyans of the Western Desert were ever a thorn in Egypt's side.

On the southern frontier of Egypt, which was governed by powerful border lords, conditions were especially turbulent. Besides keeping watch on the Nubians to the south, these great officials conducted lucrative trading ventures across the Arabian Desert and beyond the sea to the mysterious Land of Punt, where the Egyptians obtained their supplies of incense for temple rituals. No doubt the provincial rulers and their associates made fat profits from these deals.

Extension of power meant delegation of authority. Possibly there was the traditional conflict between the "man on the spot"—the efficient frontier soldier who knew local conditions—and the well-cushioned civil servants who issued the king's orders from his luxurious capital hundreds of miles away. So in time the provincial governors, the nomarchs, assumed greater independence. When their power could no longer be effectively restrained by a central authority it inevitably grew, until a time came when the nomarchs ruled almost as little kings—or, indeed, when the king was himself little more than another nomarch. It is significant that after a time these provincial officials no longer built their tombs alongside the royal pyramid as their forefathers had done, but in their own nomes.

In addition, these men of lesser rank more and more assumed for themselves the privilege, once reserved exclusively for Pharaoh, of joining the gods in afterlife, of becoming an Osiris in the next world. From royal tombs they adopted the painted offerings and magic spells that guaranteed this blessed eternity. The belief that any man who could afford the necessary tomb trappings might take a favored place in the here-

after was never renounced; subsequently, indeed, all Egyptians assumed this comforting privilege. The cult of Osiris had to do largely with life after death and its rising popularity in no way challenged that of other deities. The "democratization" of religion in which this resulted, however, marked a profound change in the Egyptian outlook.

It was in association with the growth of this cult of the god of the dead that, during these years, there were introduced statuettes known as shawabtys, which represented the deceased in miniature, not as he appeared in life, but as a wrapped mummy. Osiris and his wife Isis play a prominent part in the offering formulas with which these little mummiform figures were inscribed. Their original and primary function was to provide an alternative haven for the spirit in the event the actual mummy were by some chance destroyed. In time, however, this conception was expanded and the shawabty gradually assumed the nature of a magical servant who took over for the deceased all the arduous and distasteful chores that might be demanded of him by the gods in the hereafter. Ultimately these statuettes almost completely replaced the representations of real servants that were such a common feature of earlier tombs; they enjoyed a widespread popularity that endured throughout the remainder of ancient Egyptian history.

Under the conditions described above, enterprising upstarts could flourish and grow rich, threatening the authority of those who owed their positions to birth and succession. This would account for Ipuwer's sour comment, "He who had nothing is now rich, and the high official must court the parvenu." His warning to the pharaoh evidently was to no avail, for the great Memphite kingdom founded by Narmer went down in ruin, never to rise again. The Heliopolitan priests of Re—who for more than five hundred years had so

influenced the Memphite kings that many of them, such as Sahure and Niuserre, incorporated the god's name in their own—had to accept an amalgamation of their god with a minor deity named Amen, whose center was the hitherto obscure town of Thebes in Upper Egypt.

For it was from Thebes (then called No-Amen) that there arose a new dynastic line of pharaohs, originally provincial nomarchs who by prowess in battle won the right to rule a reunited Egypt. Thus began Egypt's Second Golden Age, which historians call the Middle Kingdom (2133–1625 B.C.), ruled by the kings of the Eleventh and Twelfth Dynasties. It was during the long reign of Mentuhotep II, one of Egypt's great kings, that Thebes was firmly established as the seat of royal power. On the walls of a chapel at Dendera an inscription tells of him "clubbing the eastern lands, striking down the hill countries, trampling the deserts, enslaving the Nubians . . . the Medjay and Wawat, the Libyans, and the (Asiatics)." Mentuhotep was followed by such pharaohs as Sesostris I, Sesostris II, Sesostris III, and Ammenemes III, all men of force who maintained the supremacy of Thebes over the centuries to come.

The portrait sculptures of Middle Kingdom rulers present some striking differences from the royal portraiture of the Old Kingdom. Such Old Kingdom masterpieces as the figures of Chephren in the museum in Cairo and those of Mycerinus and his queen in the Boston Museum of Fine Arts have an aloof and imperturbable majesty that sets them above and apart from ordinary mortals. They are sure of their absolute authority. They are still men and women, but they have been idealized as muscular, ever-youthful figures beyond the touch of time. Some of the finest royal sculptures of the Middle Kingdom, particularly those of the Twelfth Dynasty, reflect more human concern. Sometimes they show the marks

of age and suffering, notably in the case of Sesostris III. The likenesses of Ammenemes III show a hard, bitter, almost tortured face.

There were grim times as pharaohs of these dynasties struggled to re-establish the royal supremacy over rebellious nobles. As has been suggested, such sculptures may be "evoking the angry spirits of these reformist kings." Some of the writings of the period have a comparable bitterness. There is a document called "The Teaching of King Ammenemes" (the first king of that name), who was apparently murdered by his court officers. In this work the dead king is made to advise his son, Sesostris I, "Be on guard against subordinates . . . Trust not a brother, know not a friend, and make not for thyself intimates."

From these and other writings we can learn something about the achievements of the rulers of the Middle Kingdom. Some of them were remarkable men. The Ammenemes referred to above was an Upper Egyptian nobleman who seized power and overcame the hostile factions that were contending within the country at the close of the Eleventh Dynasty. The son to whom the cynical advice was addressed pushed the Egyptian frontier southward into Nubia. Ammenemes II was active in Sinai, where he reopened and exploited the gold mines. Sesostris III, he of the careworn likeness, completely broke the resistance of the landed nobility. It was he who cut a vast channel for his war galleys through the granite of the First Cataract and completely subjugated Nubia. Egypt was beginning to thrust out beyond her traditional frontiers and even to invade Syria for the first time.

We have only fragments from the literature that was produced during these centuries of trial and achievement. Among them, fortunately, is a minor masterpiece. It is not a work of fantasy, like the story of Snofru and his rowing girls; nor is

it a historical work, although it may contain elements of history. It is a novel, one of the earliest examples of this art form, that tells the story of an official, Sinuhe, "Prince and Count," who was serving in Libya with the army of the young prince, Sesostris. When news reached the camp that the prince's father, the great Ammenemes I, had died, the heir to the throne "flew" to the capital to protect his interests. Sinuhe, either because he feared that civil war would break out, or because he suspected a plot directed against him, decided to flee from the camp.

The army was operating against the Tehenu in the Western Desert where the Allied Armies fought in World War II. On hearing the news of the king's death, Sinuhe writes: ". . . was mine heart distraught . . . trembling fell on all my limbs. I betook me thence leaping, to seek me a hiding place; I placed me between two bushes so as to sunder the road from its traveller."

Then he set off southward, following a route which anyone who knows Egypt north of Cairo can still follow today. He reached the Nile above the point where it branches out through the Delta, and there "crossed over in a barge without a rudder." Sinuhe evidently made the crossing near modern Cairo, for the manuscript mentions the Red Mountain which is not far from that city and contained quarries which are still worked today. From this point he made his way toward the frontier of Palestine.

"I gave a road to my feet northwards, and attained the Wall of the Prince [a frontier fortress] which had been made to repel the Asiatics. I bowed me down in a thicket lest the watcher for the day on the wall should espy me.

"At eventide I passed on, and when day dawned I reached Petny and halted on an island [in the Bitter Lake]. There . . . I fell down for thirst, I was parched, my throat burned,

Even those ornaments that were not designed specifically as amulets often incorporated religious symbols. The inlaid golden pectoral shown at left, part of the treasure of a Middle Kingdom princess, displays a figure of the god of years, promising her father, the king, hundreds of thousands of years of life. The jeweled collar at right dates from a later period. The hawk decorations on it, like those on the pectoral, derive from the solar cult. Wigs were made of human hair, sometimes mixed with plant fibers. The one opposite, carved of wood like the female portrait it adorns, is covered with gilt to represent the gold rings and jewelry which Egyptian women fixed in their hair.

and I said: 'This is the taste of death.' Then I lifted up mine heart and gathered up my body, for I heard the sound of the lowing of cattle and descried Bedouins. The sheik among them, who had been in Egypt, recognized me. He gave me water and cooked milk for me, and I went with him to his tribe and they treated me kindly."

Through Sinuhe's eyes, or those of the unknown author of this tale, we see the refugee official fleeing northward into Syria. "Land gave me to land," he writes. "I set forth from Byblos and I drew near to Kedemi and spent a year and a half there." Eventually he met a Syrian chieftain, Amunenshy, one of the despised desert nomads who, after asking him the reason for the flight from Egypt and receiving a noncommittal reply, persuaded Sinuhe to join his tribe. Then follows the most intriguing part of the tale. The Egyptian official, a highly civilized man, educated at the court of the pharaoh, "goes native"; he becomes one of the scorned barbarians, and even marries the chief's daughter and has children by her. He rises to high rank and serves Amunenshy in peace and war.

One of the most dramatic episodes describes how Sinuhe fights "a mighty man of Retenu" and defeats him. Sinuhe's description of his single combat with his adversary is not marred by understatement; it concludes: ". . . I avoided his arrows, one closely following the other, to the last arrow. Then he charged me, and I shot him, my arrow sticking in his neck. He cried out and fell on his nose. I laid him low with his own axe, and raised my shout of victory on his back. . . ."

As the years pass Sinuhe is seized with longing to return to his own land and finally plucks up courage to write to Sesostris, formerly the prince whom he had served, whose camp he had deserted, and who had for many years occupied the throne of Egypt. The pharaoh, now a man advanced in years

and presumably willing to forget and forgive former injuries, real or imagined, replies to Sinuhe's letter in kindly fashion, and the long-absent "Prince and Count" makes the journey back to his distant homeland, dirty, and still wearing the dress of the desert tribes. He fearfully prostrates himself before the king, who calls out to his queen and the royal children: " 'See, this is Sinuhe, who has come back as an Asiatic, a real son of the Bedouins.' She uttered an exceedingly loud cry, and the royal children shrieked out all together. They said unto his majesty: 'Is it not he in sooth?' [And] his majesty said: 'It is he . . .' "

The story has a happy ending. "Years were made to pass away from my body," Sinuhe remarks. "I was shaved, my hair was combed. A load of vermin was given over to the desert, and the [filthy] clothes of the nomads. And I was arrayed in finest linen and anointed with the best oil. I slept on a bed, and gave up the sand to those who live there, and the olive oil to him that smeareth himself therewith."

Sinuhe was given a house and servants, but, even more important to an Egyptian, a fine tomb was prepared for him: "The chief architect began the building of it, the painter designed in it, the master sculptor carved in it, then superintendents of the necropolis busied themselves with it. All the glistening gear that is placed in a tomb-chamber, care was taken to place them into mine . . . It was his majesty who caused it to be made. . . . And so live I, rewarded by the king, until the day of my death cometh."

No one has found Sinuhe's tomb, if indeed it ever existed. Aside from the works of the "master painter" and the "master sculptor" so generously provided by Sesostris, its equipment might well have included a collection of small, painted wood models of Sinuhe and of his servants busy at their various tasks. Such miniature figures, carved and colored in the

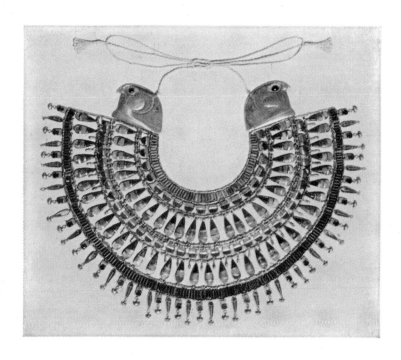

most realistic manner to represent the details of daily life as a favored noble would have known it, were made in profusion during the Middle Kingdom. They were, like the paintings and reliefs earlier described, magical substitutes for the real thing, designed to serve the needs of the dead man in the life to come. Many of them have survived and may be seen in museums throughout the world. The finest assemblage of all was discovered by Herbert Winlock in 1920 when he was conducting for the Metropolitan Museum excavations in the necropolis at Thebes.

The tomb with which Winlock was concerned was that of a Middle Kingdom noble Meketre; it had been thoroughly plundered in antiquity and nothing remained of the body and its furniture. Winlock, an experienced Egyptologist, was well aware of this fact, so that he was unimpressed when one of his excited workmen overtook him with the words: "The headman Hamid says I must tell no one, but Your Honor will see something up there."

The same night, however, he was persuaded to return to the lonely tomb, hollowed in the hillside, and there saw something which few men have ever seen. Shining his torch into a hole in the rock he started back in astonishment and wonder. "The beam of light," he wrote, "shot into a little world of four thousand years ago, and I was gazing down into the midst of a myriad of brightly painted little men going this way and that. A tall slender girl gazed across at me perfectly composed; a gang of little men with sticks in their upraised hands drove spotted oxen; rowers tugged at their oars on a fleet of boats, while one ship seemed foundering right in front of me with its bow balanced precariously in the air. And all of this busy going and coming was in uncanny silence, as though the distance back over the forty centuries I looked across was too great for even an echo to reach my ears."

One of Tutankhamen's treasures, the bracelet below is decorated with scarabs, or beetles, symbolizing birth and the sun. Egyptians imagined that a beetle pushed the sun across the sky the way the dung beetle on earth rolls its eggs along in front of it as it crawls.

By one of those miracles that happen all too infrequently, this distinguished American Egyptologist came upon an intact cache of models, made for the tomb of a high official, which chanced to have been overlooked by the robbers who plundered the tomb thousands of years ago. "He himself," writes Winlock, "had been buried in a gilded coffin and a sarcophagus of stone in a mortuary chamber deep down under the back of the corridor, where the thieves had destroyed everything ages before our day. Only this little chamber had escaped and it was turning out to be a sort of secret closet where the provision was stored for the future life of the great man."

The little rock-cut chamber was crammed with models, all carefully made and proportioned; there were models of ships, ranging from a traveling boat with the model crew raising and trimming the sail and another with oars laid up in the oarlocks, to smaller craft with cooks at work which Winlock called kitchen tenders. These evidently followed the bigger craft and their function was to provide meals for the great man and his staff on their journey along the Nile. Then there were several models of fast yachts for less formal occasions; sporting boats for hunting, and fishing canoes.

There were models of Meketre's residence, with its pillared courtyard and trees surrounding an ornamental pool. Another model showed Meketre inspecting his cattle, which were being driven past him as he sat beneath a pillared pavilion. There was a model stable for his cattle, a butcher's shop, a granary, a brewery, and a bakery, a weaving shop, a carpenter's shop—all teeming with tiny figures of the men and women who had served Meketre in life.

By several lucky accidents there have also survived from the Middle Kingdom superb examples of the jewelry that was lavished by the pharaohs on their female relatives. The discovery of these long-buried treasures was doubly fortunate, for the court jewelers of the Twelfth Dynasty brought this ancient craft to an unsurpassed height of excellence.

The pyramid-building kings of both the Old and Middle Kingdoms constructed smaller pyramids for their wives alongside their own great buildings. In 1894–1895 the archaeologist Jacques de Morgan, excavating near the pyramid of Sesostris III at Dashur, came upon a rock-cut gallery entered from a pit at the northeast corner of the main pyramid. This had belonged to one of the small subsidiary pyramids, and though it had been robbed of its main contents— the body and its furniture—de Morgan found a rectangular cavity at the foot of the sarcophagus. In this box, overlooked by the robbers, were jewelry and treasures of gold, silver, and semiprecious stones, mingled with fragments of the casket that had once enclosed them.

Not long afterward de Morgan came upon other royal treasures belonging to royal ladies of the Twelfth Dynasty— Princess Merit, Princess Nubhotep, and the Princesses Ita and Khnumit. There were diadems, one with a naturalistic design of tendrils held together with florets of gold with hearts of carnelian, petals and berries of lapis lazuli; there were pectorals, or breast ornaments, of gold, one with the car-

touche of Sesostris II and another with that of Sesostris III.

Nineteen years later Petrie, excavating near the ruined pyramid of Sesostris II, found an equally wonderful cache. In one of the smaller royal tombs a recess at the side of the ransacked sarcophagus chamber had been choked by dried mud left by floodwater in very ancient times, and under this cover the jewelry had escaped detection. These objects, among the finest known examples of ancient Egyptian goldwork, had belonged to Princess Sathathorynet, daughter of one pharaoh, sister of another, and aunt of a third.

Among these treasures were a silver mirror, toilet vases containing perfumed ointments, and even small copper razors. There was a girdle made of hollow golden shells in the form of lion heads, and joined by double rows of amethyst beads, a girdle so small that only a very slim woman could have worn it; and—an intriguing detail—the little golden shells of which it was composed contained pellets which would make a tinkling sound when the princess walked.

From the tombs of the royal masters whose bounty provided such precious gifts, little has survived. In emulation of past monarchs they too built pyramids, at Dashur, Hawara, and Lisht; magnificent buildings in themselves, though inferior to those of the Fourth Dynasty. The over-all design of these tombs was the same, but the architects had thought of new devices to confuse their eternal enemy, the tomb robber. Mere masses of masonry were no longer enough. Deep shafts in the rock had failed, as had the chambers within Cheops' Great Pyramid, built within the main structure and sealed by ponderous portcullis blocks of granite. The architects of the Middle Kingdom tried these and still other methods. One of the two pyramids built for Ammenemes III incorporated puzzle passages of elaborate intricacy designed to outwit plunderers; blind alleys that led in various directions; trap doors that opened the way to other dead ends; and, concealed in the roof of one passage, a twenty-ton block of stone that could slide sideways, leading on to other chambers and corridors and eventually to still another dead end.

All this ingenuity, skill, knowledge, and labor were wasted. As usual, intruders found the true sepulcher, robbed it, took away its most valuable contents, and destroyed the rest. When Petrie tunneled his way in some four thousand years later, he found only an empty water-logged room choked with mud and debris.

Among the pharaohs of the Middle Kingdom there were, as we have seen, men of great stature. But the most powerful of them never enjoyed the absolute authority that had been exercised by Old Kingdom rulers. With the end of the reign of Ammenemes III this second great period of Egyptian history showed signs of disintegration. The traditional life of the land went on as before. The great river rose and then fell, the crops were gathered, laborers and craftsmen went about their accustomed tasks in the ways of their ancestors. But there were indications of new turmoil in the Delta. This, the richest area in Egypt, lay nearest the several foreign lands whose inhabitants, in times of unrest, were ever tempted to move in and settle on this good earth.

EGYPTIAN
SOCIETY

Ranked between the officials and the laboring class of peasants and craftsmen, the scribe despised any trade but his own. Gardeners had to awaken early, and builders got "dirtier than pigs." Embalmers had foul-smelling hands, and fishermen worked "on the river, mingled with the crocodiles." But the scribe's job was clean and safe; the literate man was his own master, and sometimes the ruler of others. Although many scribes remained humble letter-writers, Old Kingdom society made it possible for others to advance and earn noble rank and great estates for themselves. In time, Egyptian society became too free, however; nobles eroded Pharaoh's power and brought the Old Kingdom to an end. It was Sesostris III (above) who finally crushed the last of these feudal nobles, to ensure once more the centralization of royal power. In the centuries which followed, as a new class of petty officials arose to govern Egypt, the New Kingdom instituted more rigid class barriers than the valley of the Nile had ever known before.

Both the priest Ka-aper, standing with his staff at right, and the seated scribe shown on the facing page, lived at the beginning of the Fifth Dynasty, after high government positions had been opened to men from outside the royal family for the first time. The dwarf Seneb, shown above with his wife and children, was an official in charge of a weaving workshop in Lower Egypt. Although not of royal blood himself, Seneb married a woman who was related to the king, after having worked his way up through the ranks of Pharaoh's service.

OFFICIALS

"Offices have no children," one Egyptian writer advised ambitious officials who planned to bequeath their own high government positions to their descendants. Yet it was customary in Egypt to pass jobs on from generation to generation, although government appointments still required the approval of the king. The men who administered Pharaoh's kingdom were chosen from among the scribes and landowners. They were charged with measuring the height of the inundation and the growth of the grain in the fields; they judged village disputes, officiated at religious rites, and supervised the construction of roads, canals, and monuments. Above them stood the vizier, or minister of state, who was installed in office by the king with the admonition: "Forget not to judge justice. It is an abomination of the god to show partiality." Often enough, however, gold persuaded him and the officials beneath him to disregard this high-minded advice—a breach made easier by the absence of any comprehensive system of written law. There were general edicts which dealt with matters of taxation, however. Officials paid a tax to the palace for their position, but they often got it back by appropriating for themselves part of the money which they had collected for the king. If a farm under their control failed to deliver its tax assessment, its overseer might be whipped. But the avarice of officials and landowners was held in check by the fact that the workmen might flee from the land if they were driven too hard, leaving their master still liable for his own tax to the royal treasury.

Princes such as Rehotep, shown above with his wife, served as Pharaoh's advisers and were given command of the royal army. These statues date from the beginning of the Fourth Dynasty. OVERLEAF: *The Middle Kingdom noble, Meketre, served as Overseer of the Chancellery, Great Steward, and Governor of the Six Great Tribunals. Models discovered in his tomb show him watching estate workmen driving cattle past during an annual tax inspection. Seated within the pavilion, Meketre and his scribes have close-cropped hair as a sign of rank; the hair of the herdsmen grows long, to protect them from the sun.*

THE WEALTH
OF THE LAND

Although there were lean years occasionally when the Nile failed to rise high enough to inundate the farmlands thoroughly, compared with other countries Egypt was spectacularly fertile. As the grain harvest began, peasants wailed a ritual farewell to Osiris, the god of vegetation, who dwelt in the corn and died again as the crop was reaped. But the inundation which came a few months later was a token of his resurrection; year after year, Osiris returned and Egypt's granaries were filled with grain for bread, beer, and seed. During the months of the inundation, from July to November, little agricultural work was possible; then the peasants were called upon to labor on the dikes or haul great stones for the temples and pyramids of the king. Once the flood had receded, however, the earth was ready for plowing, and teams of cattle, goaded on by farmboys, drew a light plow across the mud. Before the seed could be planted the ground had to be broken up once more with a hoe. Then, throughout the dry season, the fields required careful irrigation, with water laboriously drawn from the network of canals that branched off the Nile. Grain was the core of the Egyptian agricultural economy, but flax, which provided oil as well as fiber, was almost as important. Vineyards were carefully tended, and the products of the best ones were labeled, as they are today, according to their year and estate of origin. The pride of the Egyptian farmer was his cattle, however. Sometimes branded with their owner's identifying mark, they might be set free during the planting season to spend the dry months grazing in the marshes that bordered the Nile; when the inundation came again, they were penned up in their stalls for fattening, and fed by hand. Once a year, they were inspected by their owner and his scribes, and a part of the increase of the herd, like a certain percentage of all crops, was set aside for the tax gatherer.

The Eighteenth Dynasty painting above shows the harvest in a vineyard, with farm workers trampling upon the grapes. In the register below them, peasants net water birds in the marshes, and clean their catch for the table. At left, herdsmen, carrying one calf, drive their cattle across a canal. The donkeys shown in the relief at right are treading out grain on a threshing floor; one can be seen reaching down for a nibble.

ARTISANS

During the years of the Old Kingdom, Egypt maintained a simple economy based on barter; the great noble estates, with their villages and fields stretching along the banks of the Nile, remained almost completely self-sufficient. The country's finest artisans were attracted to the royal court; less skilled workmen remained in the provinces to build boats and make tools, weave linen and manufacture pottery. Like their neighbors, the peasants who tilled the soil, the craftsmen were probably bound to the estates on which they lived. Many, serving on estates dedicated to the upkeep of ancient temples, worked solely for the gods; others devoted a large part of their labor to preparing tomb equipment for their mortal masters. This was a task which consumed much wealth and manpower throughout Egyptian history. The nation's social structure changed in many respects in the New Kingdom. Egypt became richer, its cities increased in size, and a middle class arose which

Above, while their companion saws a board in half, two carpenters work on a wooden beam with mallet and chisel. The two sculptors shown in the relief below model a funerary statue.

could afford to purchase craftsmen's products. This brought little corresponding change in the social status of artisans, although certain trades did come to enjoy higher prestige than others; among the ranks of craftsmen the goldsmiths who made temple images were especially esteemed. Artists were generally considered common workmen and the word for artist and artisan was the same; illiterate sculptors and painters were scorned by the scribes who traced out hieroglyphic inscriptions for them to copy. Like other workingmen, artists usually inherited their jobs from their fathers, after serving a prolonged apprenticeship. They were organized into work gangs of five or ten, under the supervision of a foreman, who assigned them their tasks and doled out rations of food, clothing, and raw materials. Nevertheless some managed to avoid anonymity, and from the earliest times painters and sculptors depicted themselves on the walls of their masters' tombs.

At left, workmen smelting metal remove crucibles from the fire; below them, others carry mud for brickmaking. The woman shown above prepares beer by pressing mash through a sieve; below, three men cut up a tree trunk.

WINE AND SONG

The harem inmates, who were an integral and valued part of every rich man's household, were often called upon to oblige with public as well as private entertainment. At the great banquets, which Egyptians enjoyed even at funerals, the host's singing girls presented a concert, serenading the guests with songs such as the one inscribed in the hieroglyphs shown at right, above the entertainers' heads: "The earth god has implanted his beauty in every body. / The creator has done this with his two hands [as balm to his heart. / The channels are filled with water anew / And the land is flooded with his love]." Attuned to this happy state of affairs, harem girls clapped their hands in time to the music and whirled about with the sensuous rhythms Egyptian dancers still delight in. The singers and musicians who accompanied them might have attended schools to study music; from there they could advance to the royal court to perform under the direction of officials broadly entitled "superintendents of all the beautiful pleasures of the king." Court and estate banquets provided other diversions besides music. Guests were anointed with perfumed oil and garlanded with wreaths. They sniffed lotus blossoms and drank freely. "Drink not beer to excess . . . ," the scribes had written. "The words that come out of thy mouth, thou canst not recall." But despite this exemplary advice, banquets were often disordered by drunkenness.

Two Eighteenth Dynasty tomb paintings show female musicians entertaining guests at a banquet. The girls on the facing page perform on the lute, harp, and double flute; above them supplies for the feast include bunches of grapes and a garlanded wine jug. Shown above in the partly destroyed upper register are the guests at a banquet, two married couples who sit arm in arm, waited upon by a scantily clad servant girl. Below them, musicians wearing cones of pomade to perfume their elaborate wigs clap hands and sing.

While a hairdresser attends to her coiffure, the lady Kawit (below) refreshes herself with a drink. In her hand she holds a mirror of polished metal. The Egyptian word for mirror, which can also mean life, demonstrates the awe that early men felt before images. The mirror on the facing page is made of bronze, with its handle cast in the shape of a nude handmaiden. Above, an ointment spoon represents a girl swimming through the marshes, behind a bird whose wings conceal a compartment for perfume. A maiden at far left brushes rouge on her lips; next to her is another whose slender body is adorned with little besides jewelry, eye paint, and a lotus. The unfinished portrait on the facing page is probably of Queen Nefretiti; it was supposed to be covered with a wig made of stone or colored faience.

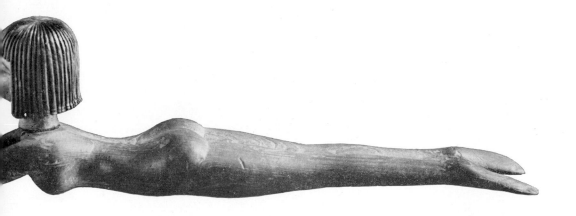

WOMAN'S WORLD

In a collection of precepts that were widely circulated during the New Kingdom, a judicious scribe advised Egyptians to treat their wives kindly: "Fill her belly; clothe her back. Ointment is the prescription for her body. Make her heart glad as long as thou livest. She is a profitable field for her lord." In Egypt women enjoyed a high status rarely equaled elsewhere in the ancient world. They had complete legal right to inherit property and dispose of it without reference to the wishes of their husbands. Monogamy was generally practiced (although the rich supported harems), and men often traced their ancestry through the maternal rather than the paternal line. Women in the next world continued to savor many of the indulgences that had gratified them on earth. The Seven Sacred Oils, a collection of perfumes, ointments, and pomades, were placed beside their mummies, and coffers were stored within their tombs, to contain the heavy wigs and braids of human hair customarily worn in Egypt, as much to guard against the sun as to lend beauty. Cosmetic jars held red paste to color the lips, and a red paint to dye fingernails and toenails, and to stain the palms and the soles of the feet. Sometimes cosmetics too had more than an aesthetic function; the eye paint used by both sexes also was a protection against the eye infections so common in Egypt.

HUNTING

Netting birds for the table or for sacrifice in the temples was a muddy job, suitable only for members of the lower classes, but nobles delighted in sailing through the papyrus marshes to hunt for waterfowl with a throwstick. The Nile Valley lies directly upon a migratory route of European game birds, and during the autumn and winter the "bird tanks of pleasure" teemed with flocks of geese, ducks, and cranes. To enjoy roast goose, which was a favorite Egyptian food, ordinary men had to net or trap the fowl, for hunting with a throwstick was a diversion in which only nobles were privileged to indulge; accompanied by a pet cat trained to retrieve game, they paddled after their quarry in small skiffs made of papyrus reeds bound together. More lethargic aristocrats spent entire days sitting in the fields, waiting to hear the "wailing cry of the beautiful bird smelling of myrrh," which flew in from Arabia and could be caught in a trap baited with worms. The most adventurous preferred to harpoon hippopotamuses in the river, but none dared hunt the dangerous crocodile; its pursuit was risky because the crocodile god of the Nile became enraged whenever his beasts were killed. The most dangerous game of all were the lions and leopards of the desert, which were usually hunted by spearmen on foot, aided only by a pack of fearless hounds.

Spearing fish (although the painter has neglected to provide him with a harpoon), a New Kingdom official named Nakht sails through the papyrus marshes with his wife and children. Above him, dead birds which he has killed with a throwing stick fall through the air. The sketch above shows one of the Ramesside pharaohs killing a lion already wounded by arrows.

GLORY
AND
DECLINE

Kingdom of the Pharaohs · III

According to Manetho, the Middle Kingdom was brought to an end by an invasion of Asiatic tribes whose leaders he called the Hyksos, a term derived from an Egyptian expression that may be translated "Rulers of the Desert Uplands," or "Rulers of the Upland-dwellers." These "upland-dwellers" were tribes from Palestine, Lebanon, and Syria, some of whom were Semitic and may have included ancestors of the Hebrews. Actually this was no sudden invasion, but rather a successful takeover bid by peoples who had already infiltrated into the Delta area and had been settled in this northern part of Egypt for generations. Such people had been in the habit of coming to Egypt, especially in times of famine or drought in their own homelands, perhaps selling some of their number into servitude in return for corn. Some, as we know from the much later Old Testament story of Joseph and his brethren, held positions of high trust.

They were a lively-minded, intelligent, energetic people; moreover they provided a link with the world of Western Asia, and brought with them innovations from that world which were to have a great influence on the conservative, valley-dwelling Egyptians. Among these were the use of bronze for implements and for new kinds of swords and daggers, and the powerful composite bow; also the horse, the wheel (almost unknown to the Egyptians before this period), and, in conjunction, the horse-drawn war chariot.

It may have been the possession of superior weapons, among other factors, which tempted them to exploit the weakness and dissension among Egypt's rulers and seize power in the Delta area and, later, to extend a loose suzerainty over the

A sculptor's preliminary study for a portrait shows the Eighteenth Dynasty king, Akhenaten who rebelled against Egypt's traditional religion and established his own monotheistic cult of the sun disk.

native Egyptian rulers who still nominally controlled Middle Egypt from Thebes. The Hyksos also entered into alliance with the rulers of Kush (Nubia), who by this time had broken away from Thebes; thus the Theban kings were hemmed in to north and south.

During this so-called Second Intermediate Period (1786–1567 B.C.) the Hyksos kings, ruling from Avaris in the eastern Delta, adopted pharaonic titles and customs; but often their outlandish names—Khyan, Anat-her, Pachnan—reveal Semitic origins. (The most intriguing of these names, found on scarabs of the period, is Yakubher which can very probably be identified with the name of the patriarch Jacob.) Something had happened in Egypt which had never happened before. In the past there had been civil wars and frontier battles, but during its already long history Egypt had never known the ignominy of foreign occupation, of alien pretenders to Pharaoh's throne.

It is easy to denigrate the ancient Egyptians for their conservatism and insularity. Yet there must have been more in what we label Egyptian culture than an elaborate governmental hierarchy, a viable economic system, and a tenacious religious tradition; it was a way of life which Egyptians valued sufficiently to fight for. During the late years of this Intermediate Period they turned on the foreign intruders with what might be called patriotic fervor. From the Asiatic settlers the Egyptians had learned much. They now proceeded to use the practical, technical innovations they had borrowed from these aliens in order to reunite the entire valley of the Nile under the sovereignty of native rulers.

The Theban prince Sekenenre is credited with being the ruler who began driving out the foreign intruders, a process followed up with increasing effect by his successors Kamose and Ahmose. Sekenenre's mummified body was among those

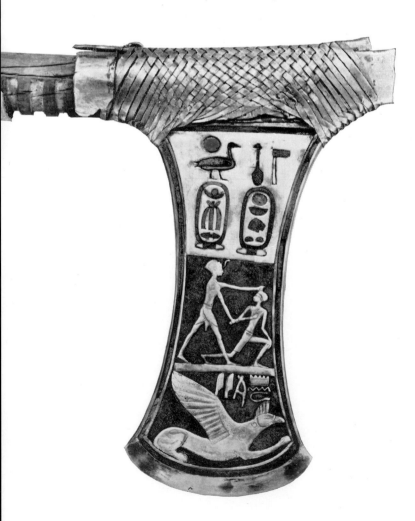

After expelling the Hyksos from Egypt, Pharaoh Ahmose carried his battle against them into Asia and re-established Egyptian sovereignty over the cities of Canaan. On the ceremonial axehead below, Ahmose is shown smiting an enemy. The horse was introduced into Egypt during the era of the Hyksos kings, whose use of the chariot revolutionized warfare in the Nile Valley. The chariot shown on the faience tile above dates from the Eighteenth Dynasty.

found in a cache at Deir el Bahri in 1881. The body was twisted as if in agony, and the skull and neck bore hideous wounds. He may well have been killed in battle, fighting the Hyksos; there is documentary proof that both he and Kamose did indeed lead a campaign against the hated Asiatics.

An inscribed stele of Kamose, discovered as recently as 1954 at Thebes, completes the story told in a document discovered earlier. The following brief extract describes the Theban ruler's northward advance. "I fared downstream in might to overthrow the Asiatics by the command of Amen, the just of counsels; my brave army in front of me like a breath of fire, troops of Medja-Nubians [mercenary soldiers] aloft upon our cabins to spy out the Setyu and to destroy their places. East and West were in possession of their fat and the army was supplied with things everywhere."

There is in this report of Kamose's campaign a militant zest which foreshadows that of the greater kings who were to follow—men such as Tuthmosis III and Ramesses II. "I spent the night in my ship, my heart happy," the account continues. "When the earth became light, I was upon him [an Egyptian collaborationist] as it were a hawk. The time of perfuming the mouth [the midday meal] came, and I overthrew him, I razed his wall, I slew his people, and I caused his wife to go down to the river bank. My soldiers were like lions with their prey, with serfs, cattle, milk, fat, and honey, dividing up their possessions . . . Your heart is undone, base Asiatic, who used to say 'I am lord, and there is none equal to me from Khmun and Pi-hathor down to Avaris.' "

The document goes on to describe how Kamose intercepts a letter passing between the Hyksos king and his ally, the ruler of Kush, whom he had corrupted and persuaded to turn against his natural lord. "I captured a messenger of his high up over the Oasis traveling southward to Kush for the sake

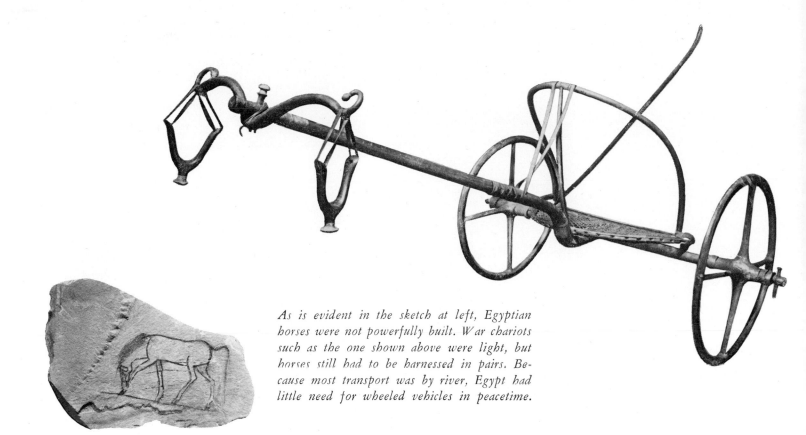

As is evident in the sketch at left, Egyptian horses were not powerfully built. War chariots such as the one shown above were light, but horses still had to be harnessed in pairs. Because most transport was by river, Egypt had little need for wheeled vehicles in peacetime.

of a written despatch, and I found upon it this message in writing from the chieftain of Avaris . . . 'Why have you arisen as chieftain without letting me know? Have you (not) beheld what Egypt has done against me, the chieftain who is in it, Kamose the Mighty, ousting me from my soil, and I have not reached him . . .'"

In about 1567 B.C. when Ahmose, Kamose's younger brother, succeeded to the throne and founded the Eighteenth Dynasty, Egyptian civilization was already more than fifteen hundred years old, three times the age of either the Greek or Roman civilizations in their prime. Our Western democratic system—which its harsher critics believe to be already in decline—has a very much briefer history. Yet with Ahmose's reign Egypt entered a period of unprecedented brilliance, known to us as the New Kingdom, which, though the traditional pattern of civilization continued, saw Egypt established as the greatest and richest power on earth.

Having pushed the "upland-dwellers" out of the Delta, the kings of the Eighteenth Dynasty proceeded to carry Egyptian conquest far into the homelands of their enemies, for they realized that it was not enough merely to close and guard the frontiers. Unless the Asiatics were pursued and subdued they would reorganize and return. So the Egyptians became conquerors and colonizers. For the first time scores of thousands of Egyptians saw the countries that lay outside their sheltered valley; lands where there were mountains more than nine thousand feet high, where there was "a Nile in the sky" (rain) and a river (the Euphrates) that "in running southwards runs northwards." Here the scribes tried to explain to their compatriots the course of a river that unlike the Nile, the father of all rivers, flowed from north to south instead of vice versa.

The Egyptians became soldiers; not conscripts recruited for brief periods, but veteran professionals one of whom (according to a popular literary composition of the New Kingdom) could write to a young and boastful colleague: "You are a *mahir* [a hero], who is skilled in deeds of valor! A *mahir,* such as you are, is qualified to march at the head of the host! Forward, O *maryen,* to shoot! Behold, there is the [ambuscade] in a ravine two thousand cubits deep, filled with boulders and shingle. You make a detour. You grasp the bow . . . you let the chieftains see what is pleasing to their eyes until your hand grows weary . . ." At this point, the old warrior even puts in a few Canaanite words, which is like a veteran of the Pacific war quoting a few words of Malay or Japanese.

"Behold, there is the narrow defile," he goes on, "made perilous by Bedouins, who are hidden beneath the bushes; some of them are of four cubits and five cubits from the nose unto the sole of the foot [a typical old soldier's exaggeration; this would have made them seven to nine feet tall], fierce of face, their heart not mild . . ." Then the author describes the plight of the *mahir,* a green young chariot officer, when he is caught in the narrow defile, with "the ravine . . . on one side of you, the mountain rises on the other. On you go and guide your chariot beside you . . . You unharness the horse, in order to repair the hand [evidently a part of the chariot] . . . ; you are not expert in the way of binding it, and you don't know how to fasten it together. The . . . [some other part of the chariot] falls from its place, and the horse is already too heavily laden to load him with it. You are sick at heart and start to go on foot . . . you fancy that the enemy is behind you. Then trembling takes hold of you. Ah, would that you had a hedge (between you and the other side)! Your horse is galled up to the time that you find quarters for the night. Now you know what pain tastes like."

And there were other hazards, not unfamiliar to the modern soldier. At a later stage the *mahir* encounters a girl, "a fair maiden who keeps watch over the vineyards. She takes you to herself as companion and shows you the color of her bosom. You are recognized [by the enemy] . . . and put on trial, and your tunic of good Upper Egyptian linen, you sell [as a bribe to facilitate escape] . . . You sleep every evening with a piece of woolen cloth about you, you slumber and are inert. They [steal] your bow, your knife, your quiver, and your reins are cut in the darkness.

"Your horse is gone . . . The road stretches out before you. The chariot is smashed . . . your weapons fall to the ground and are buried in the sand . . ." And so on; possibly an exaggeration, but the writer of that satire, who died some three thousand years ago, has said enough to make it clear that ancient Egyptian soldiers of the New Kingdom were fully familiar with the hazards of campaigning in a strange and hostile country.

A succession of pharaohs of the Eighteenth Dynasty extended Egypt's conquests far into Syria. The greatest of these was Tuthmosis III who finally rid himself of his detested stepmother, Hatshepsut, who had ruled as a pharaoh for twenty years. (We do not know what may have happened to this dominating female; she simply disappears from the records.) By his own boast Tuthmosis III was "the smiter of the rulers of foreign countries who had attacked him." It is recorded that he fought at least seventeen successful campaigns, the most extensive of which carried him beyond the Euphrates River. After each victory he returned to his capital at Thebes, bearing the spoils of war to lay before the Theban god Amen-Re. The god was well pleased with his all-conquering son and, in a famous paean inscribed on one of the temple walls, praised the pharaoh in grandiose terms.

Built by Amenhotep III, the court-yard shown at right is part of a temple dedicated to the divine triad of Amen, Mut, and Khonsu, "in a place where the prayers of gods and of men are heard." The god Amen was especially revered at Thebes and his colossal temples dominated the right bank of the Nile. On the opposite side of the river were tombs of Middle and New Kingdom pharaohs. Many of the new buildings that adorned the imperial capital were constructed by slave laborers, who had been brought back from the conquered provinces of Asia.

Come thou to me, rejoicing to see my beauty, O my son, my champion, Tuthmosis. . . .
I give unto thee valor and victory over every land;
I place thy might and the fear of thee in all lands,
And the terror of thee as far as the four supports of the sky. . . .
The chiefs of all lands are united in thy grasp—
I stretch forth mine own hands to bind them for thee;
I bind the Nubian Bedouin in ten thousands and thousands, and the northern peoples in hundred thousands.

I cast thine enemies beneath thy sandals, and thou destroyest the recalcitrant,
Even as I have committed unto thee the earth in its length and in its breadth,
While the Western peoples and the Easterners are under thy control.
Thou treadest every foreign land with joyful heart, and none ventureth himself in thy vicinity;
But as I am thy guide, so thou reachest out unto them. . . .

I cause them to see thy majesty as a fierce lion: thou makest them into corpses throughout their valleys.
I have come to cause thee to trample the tail of the world; that which the sea encircleth is enclosed in thy grasp.
I cause them to see thy majesty as a soaring falcon that taketh what it perceiveth according to its desire.

I have come to cause thee to trample those who dwell at the head of the world; thou bindest the sand-dwellers in captivity.
I cause them to see thy majesty as an Upper Egyptian jackal swift of feet, the runner that prowleth throughout the Two Lands.

I have come to cause thee to trample the Nubians; everything is in thy grasp as far as Shatiu-djeba.
I cause them to see thy majesty like thy two brothers [Horus and Seth], whose arms I have joined with thee in victory.

On the walls of the temple, also, Tuthmosis is depicted wielding a mace and grasping the hair of his Asiatic enemies, almost exactly as Narmer was shown seventeen hundred years earlier on his commemorative slate palette. The only important difference occurs in the scale. The palette is less than two feet long; the temple of Amen-Re at Karnak rises to a height of more than one hundred feet. The idea behind both scenes is the same, and nothing more clearly suggests the essential conservatism of the Egyptian outlook.

To celebrate his victorious reign Tuthmosis caused to be erected from time to time commemorative obelisks, in accordance with old tradition. The subsequent travels of four of these monuments, proclaiming the might of this great conqueror, are memorable in themselves: one now stands in the Hippodrome at Istanbul; a second was erected during the Renaissance in the piazza of St. John Lateran in Rome; another stands on the Thames Embankment in London; and the fourth, a gift of Egyptians to the United States, towers beside the Metropolitan Museum in New York's Central Park.

The foreign campaigns of Tuthmosis brought wealth pouring into Egypt in the form of gold and other precious metals; captives to serve as mercenaries and to work in bondage on the projects of the pharaoh and his nobles; horses, cattle, and other animals in great quantities; and above all regular tribute from the newly established colonies and satellites. Not all this new wealth came from conquest, however; there were increased trading contacts, and in some of the Theban tombs we see paintings of embassies from as far away as the island of Crete, bringing the products of their lands in exchange for Egyptian goods.

Egypt experienced increasing influences from foreign lands. Sons of Syrian princes were brought to Thebes as hostages, educated at the Egyptian court, and sent back to govern

their own lands as Egyptian vassals. Princesses from foreign lands married into the royal and noble families, or were added to the harems of such households. Amenhotep III, the luxury-loving pharaoh who spent his life enjoying the fruits of his predecessors' conquests, added Mitannian princesses to his international assemblage of wives and favorites. When local medical help failed him in his illness, he asked the king of Mitanni for a statue of the Ninevite goddess of love, Ishtar, hoping that her celebrated healing powers would relieve his symptoms.

His son, Amenhotep IV, the so-called heretic king, initiated a short-lived religious revolution, the philosophical content of which is still a matter of discussion. Some believe the king was mad, or at least mentally unbalanced; others, like James Henry Breasted, have called him "the first individual in history," a man who had the courage to defy the powerfully entrenched priesthood of Amen-Re, and with his beautiful wife Nefretiti to establish a new capital at el Amarna, where he devoted his life to teaching a novel religion. This was based on the worship of the Aten, the "One God," whose symbol was the sun's disk. The pharaoh changed his name to Akhenaten, meaning "he who is serviceable to Aten." In a single stroke he tried to abolish the innumerable deities whom the Egyptians had inherited from predynastic times; all were to be swept away, even Osiris, god of the dead, who by this time had almost come to equal Amen-Re in importance. This religious revolt was accompanied by an equally short-lived revolution in art; the statuary and tomb reliefs of the so-called Amarna period, of which the best known is the Berlin portrait bust of Nefretiti, are distinguished by a startling realism that contrasted sharply with the traditional canons of Egyptian art. Akhenaten encouraged his sculptors to depict him as he really was, with

Campaigning in Asia, King Amenhotep II "saw a few Asiatics coming furtively, adorned with weapons of warfare, to attack the king's army. His majesty burst after them like the flight of a divine falcon. The confidence of their hearts was slackened . . . His majesty killed them by shooting." Scribes and artists were kept busy recording royal military triumphs. The painted relief at right, from a temple of Ramesses II, shows a group of Syrian warriors overwhelmed by the Egyptians. Opposite, decorative tiles show a Nubian captive and a bearded Asiatic.

swollen belly, elongated jaw, and pronounced effeminate characteristics; also to show him, not in the conventional austere pose of the god-king, but, with informality, as a devoted spouse and parent, kissing and fondling his infant daughters (he had no sons).

The Hymn to Aten, which is attributed to the heretic pharaoh and which is inscribed on the walls of several tombs near his capital, contains passages of lyrical beauty; the sun is not merely the fierce, all-pervading heat, driving men into the shade of midday, but the gentle source of life in all created things.

Thou appearest beautifully on the horizon of heaven,
Thou living Aten, the beginning of life!
When thou art risen on the eastern horizon,
Thou hast filled every land with thy beauty.
Thou art gracious, great, glistening, and high over every land;
Thy rays encompass the lands to . . . all that thou hast made:
As thou art Re, thou reachest to the end of them;
(Thou) subduest them (for) thy beloved son.
Though thou art far away, thy rays are on earth;
Though thou art in their faces, no one knows thy going.

When thou settest in the western horizon,
The land is in darkness, in the manner of death.
They sleep in a room, with heads wrapped up,
Nor sees one eye the other.
All their goods which are under their heads might be stolen,
(But) they would not perceive (it).
Every lion is come forth from his den;
All creeping things, they sting.
Darkness is a shroud, and the earth is in stillness,
For he who made them rests in his horizon.

At daybreak, when thou arisest on the horizon,
When thou shinest as the Aten by day,

Thou drivest away the darkness and givest thy rays.
The Two Lands are in festivity every day,
Awake and standing upon (their) feet,
For thou hast raised them up.
Washing their bodies, taking (their) clothing,
Their arms are (raised) in praise at thy appearance.
All the world, they do their work.

All beasts are content with their pasturage;
Trees and plants are flourishing.
The birds which fly from their nests,
Their wings are (stretched out) in praise to thy ka.
All beasts spring upon (their) feet.
Whatever flies and alights,
They live when thou hast risen (for) them.
The ships are sailing north and south as well,
For every way is open at thy appearance.
The fish in the river dart before thy face;
Thy rays are in the midst of the great green sea.

Creator of seed in woman,
Thou who makest fluid into man,
Who maintainest the son in the womb of his mother,
Who soothest him with that which stills his weeping,
Thou nurse (even) in the womb,
Who givest breath to sustain all that he has made!
When he descends from the womb to breathe
On the day when he is born,
Thou openest his mouth completely,
Thou suppliest his necessities.
When the chick in the egg speaks within the shell,
Thou givest him breath within it to maintain him.
When thou hast made him his fulfillment within the egg, to break it,
He comes forth from the egg to speak at his completed (time);
He walks upon his legs when he comes forth from it.

How manifold it is, what thou hast made!
They are hidden from the face (of man).
O sole god, like whom there is no other!
Thou didst create the world according to thy desire,
Whilst thou wert alone:
All men, cattle, and wild beasts,
Whatever is on earth, going upon (its) feet,
And what is on high, flying with its wings.

Thy rays suckle every meadow.
When thou risest, they live, they grow for thee.
Thou makest the seasons in order to rear all that thou hast made,
The winter to cool them,
And the heat that they may taste thee.
Thou hast made the distant sky in order to rise therein,
In order to see all that thou dost make.
Whilst thou wert alone,
Rising in thy form as the living Aten,
Appearing, shining, withdrawing, or approaching,
Thou madest millions of forms of thyself alone.
Cities, towns, fields, road, and river—
Every eye beholds thee over against them,
For thou art the Aten of the day over the earth. . . .

Thou art in my heart,
And there is no other that knows thee
Save thy son Neferkheperure Waenre,
For thou hast made him well-versed in thy plans and in thy
    strength.
The world came into being by thy hand,
According as thou hast made them.
When thou hast risen they live,
When thou settest they die.
Thou art lifetime thy own self,
For one lives (only) through thee.
Eyes are (fixed) on beauty until thou settest.
All work is laid aside when thou settest in the west.

(But) when (thou) risest (again),
[Everything is] made to flourish for the king . . .
Since thou didst found the earth
And raise them up for thy son,
Who came forth from thy body:
the King of Upper and Lower Egypt . . . Akhenaten . . .
and the Chief Wife of the King . . . Nefretiti, living and
youthful forever and ever.

There is a tenderness in this poem, which is far removed from the aggressiveness in the paean of Amen-Re, delighting in blood and conquest. Both in its content and in its structure it has often been compared with the 104th Psalm. Yet as critics have said, it contains no moral instructions, no system of ethics. It is doubtful if this new religion affected more than a minority of sophisticated courtiers. Most Egyptians probably continued to worship the traditional gods, even though the pharaoh in his fanaticism caused the name Amen-Re to be erased from every monument his agents could reach. When after less than forty years the royal heretic died, Egypt returned to her old familiar polytheism. In reaction to his reign, the name of Akhenaten was in turn removed from some of his monuments, and the temple dedicated to Aten, at Karnak, was completely destroyed. The Eighteenth Dynasty, which had begun gloriously under the warrior and liberator Ahmose, finally flickered out, leaving behind a legacy of idealistic pacifism, a neglected empire, and a powerful new enemy—the Hittites of Asia Minor. These people, "the abominable Kheta" as they were termed in one wartime manifesto, were pushing into Syria and terrorizing the remaining loyal Egyptian colonies into submission.

Among the few who stood out against the invader and remained faithful to Egypt was a certain Ribbadi, governor of Byblos, in Lebanon. By a fortunate chance his desperate ap-

Accompanying singers at a banquet, the blind musician at right plays upon his harp. In showing one arm realistically placed behind the harp, the sculptor has departed from one of the classic conventions of Egyptian art. The relief on the facing page shows a stone carver preparing a coffin. With mallet and chisel, he applies the finishing touches to its surface as an official watches, and an apprentice walks by with a basket upon his shoulder. Eyes were customarily painted on sarcophagi so that the dead could see out.

peals to Akhenaten, filed in the pharaoh's foreign office at el Amarna, have survived to tell their own story. "Behold Aziru [king of Amurru, a region north of Lebanon, who was conspiring with the Hittites against the pharaoh] has fought my chiefs, and the chiefs whom I dispatched to the city Simyra he has caused to be seized in the city. Both the city Beruta [Beirut] and the city Ziouna are sending ships to the city. All who are in the land of the Amorites have gathered themselves . . . I need men to save the rebellion of this land . . . Give me soldiers!"

And later, when the traitor Aziru, with the aid of his Hittite masters, had taken Simyra, Ribbadi wrote again to Akhenaten: "Behold what has befallen the lands of the king on account of him; and he cried peace unto the land, and now behold what has befallen the city of Simyra—a station of my Lord [the pharaoh], a fortress . . . and they spoil our fortress . . . ah, the cries of the place . . . a violent man and a dog!"

One's heart goes out to the old governor when one reads his last letter to the pacifist pharaoh, who passed on these appeals to his foreign office clerks, while consoling himself with the mysteries of his esoteric faith. "March against him," implores Ribbadi, ". . . March against him and smite him . . . the land is the king's land [Egyptian territory]; and since I have talked thus and you have not moved, the city of Simyra has been lost. There is no money to buy horses; all is finished, we have been spoiled . . . give me thirty companies of horses with chariots . . . men, men . . . there is none of this for me . . . not a horse . . ." And that is the last we hear from Ribbadi.

But it was not the end of Egypt's imperial claims. A new dynasty of pharaohs, the Nineteenth, won back most of the territory lost through the indolence of Amenhotep III,

Akhenaten, and their successors. There is something astounding and superb in the way this civilization, now almost two thousand years old, rose again to the call of destiny. Conservative and tradition-bound it may have been; but it was not effete. Monarchs such as Sethi I and Ramesses II recovered much of their Asian territory, and commemorated their exploits with inscriptions on the walls of the enlarged and beautified temple of Amen-Re at Karnak. Whatever the degree of his success, or lack of it, the campaigns of Pharaoh were always shown, by timeless convention, as absolute, complete, and personal triumphs. Ramesses II met the Hittites at Kadesh, in Syria, and fought a battle which, though inconclusive, he celebrated as a crushing victory for Pharaoh. In any event, this stand off engagement resulted in a treaty which established a peace between these great empires that was never broken. Copies of the agreement signed by Ramesses II and the Hittite king, Hattusilis, have been preserved both at Thebes and at the Hittite capital of Boghazkoy in Asia Minor. Now they are no longer "the abominable Kheta." In the treaty Hattusilis is referred to as "the great king . . . the valiant," in accordance with diplomatic usage of the day. Ramesses even took to himself a Hittite princess whom he found "fair of face [like] a goddess . . . and he loved her more than anything."

Less than a century later Ramesses III, of the Twentieth Dynasty, had to meet an even more deadly threat. In his reign (1198–1166 B.C.) there was a great movement of peoples throughout Western Asia, Asia Minor, and the Aegean. It was the time when the Dorian invaders were pouring into Greece, dispersing the Mycenaeans; a time when the Hittites, so lately allied to Egypt, were being swept out of power in Asia Minor by new invaders; a time when not only armies but whole peoples—with their cattle, and baggage trains—

Throughout Egyptian history, men and women of obscure origins were able to rise to high rank. The low-born Senenmut, whose portrait appears at right, became the chief minister of Queen Hatshepsut. He also served as tutor to her daughter, and the builder in charge of her funerary temple, within which his own image frequently appears. Akhenaten's general, Horemheb, who is shown below being decked with collars of gold as a sign of royal favor, even rose to become Pharaoh. Before he became king, Horemheb enjoyed an impressive number of official titles. He was Chief Commander of the Army, Attendant of the King in his Footsteps, Sole Companion, Fanbearer on the King's Right Hand, and although apparently not of royal blood, Hereditary Prince.

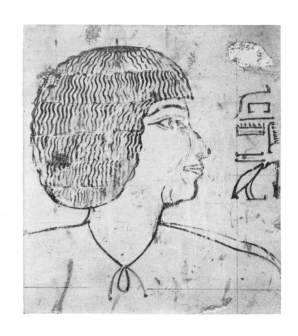

were swarming down the eastern coast of the Mediterranean, seeking new and more promising lands in which to settle.

Ramesses III met them, at sea and on land, and hurled them back from the gates of Egypt. In the commemorative scenes which he ordered carved on his temple walls at Medinet Habu we see the ships of one of these invading peoples, the biblical Philistines, rammed and sunk by the pharaoh's war galleys. One scene depicts an encounter between an Egyptian and a Philistine ship somewhere in the Nile Delta or the sea beyond it. From the crows' nest of the Egyptian battleship an archer snipes at the deck of the Asiatic vessel. The Egyptian oarsmen, protected by high bulwarks, haul on their oars, while Egyptian marines hack, slash, and fire arrows at their enemies. This is one of the earliest representations of a naval conflict in the world; and it was a decisive battle. At the end of that day the drowned bodies of thousands—Asiatics and Egyptians—floated in the Nile swell, alongside the broken, derelict hulks of their vessels. And though the surviving invaders were able to cling to the seacoasts of Lebanon and Palestine, they did not dare attempt to enter Egypt again.

In Thebes the results of the imperial conquests were reflected in many significant ways—especially in architecture, tombs, and rich furnishings. The sepulchers of the Theban rulers during the Hyksos domination were handsome, but not particularly remarkable. But once Thebes had become the supreme capital of Egypt, it rose to a magnificence surpassing even that of Memphis, from which the Old Kingdom pharaohs had ruled a thousand years earlier. The Theban god Amen, originally a minor deity, had been amalgamated with the sun god Re as king of gods under the name Amen-Re, as we have seen. His temple at Karnak, enlarged and glorified by successive generations of pharaohs—the Tuthmosides, the Amenhoteps, and the Ramesside kings—became the largest

Queen Teye (right) came from a humble background, but she was chosen by Amenhotep III as his Great Royal Wife, taking precedence over all other women in the royal harem. For her recreation, Amenhotep built a mile-long pleasure lake beside his palace. The scarab below commemorates the event; one side carries one of the king's titles; the other tells about the excavation of the lake.

religious building in the world, and no other built in subsequent times has exceeded it in size.

The Hypostyle Hall of this immense complex, the largest single chamber of any temple in the world, covers fifty-four thousand square feet, almost equal to the space occupied by one of the greatest cathedrals of medieval Europe—Canterbury in England. A number of its one hundred and thirty-four columns are twelve feet thick and sixty-nine feet high, each about the size of Trajan's column in Rome, and crowned by capitals of such size that one hundred men could stand upon them; the rest are forty-three feet high. But this many-columned hall was only the central feature of a building complex which would cover much of mid-Manhattan. Within the walls of the temple there would be room for St. Peter's in Rome, the Milan Cathedral, and Notre Dame in Paris. The outer walls would comfortably enclose ten European cathedrals.

Stretching for miles along the east bank of the Nile were the palaces of the kings and the villas of the nobles, each enclosed within its walled gardens. Here also were the wharves crowded with goods from Asia, Crete, and the Aegean Islands. On the west bank lay other palaces, including that of Amenhotep III with the great pleasure lake he had had made virtually overnight for his favorite queen, Teye; here also was the necropolis, the City of the Dead, housing the mortal remains of kings and nobles. The pharaohs still made their Houses of Eternity in the West, where Re "went to his horizon." The mud-brick mastabas of the early dynastic period, the stone pyramids of the Old and Middle Kingdoms, all had failed to protect the embalmed and consecrated body of the king. So now the architects devised a new stratagem; pyramids were abandoned, and instead the kings were buried in rock-hewn chambers deep in the cliffs, approached by long,

sloping corridors. All the pharaohs of the New Kingdom tunneled their last resting places in the living rock of the Theban mountains, in a lonely defile beyond the eastern face of the cliff, the famous Valley of the Tombs of the Kings.

Every trick used by the tomb builders of the Middle Kingdom to thwart plunderers was employed, besides some new ones: "puzzle-passages," deep pits in the floor of the corridor, blind alleys, and false burial chambers beyond which flights of stairs tunneled still deeper through the rock to the final chamber. The tomb of Sethi I has several such devices; the tomb chambers of Hatshepsut extend for more than five hundred feet, starting high up in the Theban cliffs, the entrance obscure and difficult of access. But despite all these precautions the tomb robbers got through; aided, no doubt, by corrupt officials who hoped to get their percentage of the loot.

Documents have survived that report the trials of certain malefactors who were apprehended while pillaging the sepulchers of earlier kings. "We went to rob the tombs in accordance with our regular habit," the culprit explained to his inquisitors, "and we found the pyramid of King Sekhemreshedtaui, the son of Re, Sebkemsaf, this being not at all like the pyramids and tombs of the nobles which we habitually went to rob. We took our copper tools and forced a way into the pyramid of this king through its innermost part. We found its underground chambers, and we took lighted candles in our hands and went down. Then we broke through the rubble that we found at the mouth of his recess, and found this god lying at the back of his burial place. And we found the burial place of Queen Nubkhas (his queen) situated beside him, it being protected and guarded by plaster and covered with rubble. This also we broke through, and found her resting [there] in like manner. We opened their sarcophagi and their coffins in which they were, and found the

noble mummy of this king equipped with a falchion; a large number of amulets and jewels of gold were upon his neck, and his headpiece of gold was upon him. The noble mummy of this king was completely bedecked with gold, and his coffins were adorned with gold and silver inside and out and inlaid with all kinds of precious stones. We collected the gold we found on the noble mummy of this god, together with . . . his amulets and jewels which were on his neck and . . . the coffins in which he was resting [and we] found [the] queen in exactly the same state. We collected all that we found upon her likewise, and set fire to their coffins. We took their furniture which we found with them consisting of articles of gold, silver, and bronze, and divided them amongst ourselves."

That is the contemporary report of a court investigation which was made in Egypt some three thousand years ago. There had always been such looting, but in the Twentieth Dynasty it became epidemic. This was a time of stress when hungry and desperate men were prepared to defy the beliefs of their forefathers and pillage the deep-hidden tombs of their god-kings. The transcribed report is obviously a smoothed-over version of what the robber actually said. But no doubt the fluency and accuracy of his own account owed something to the lash which was applied regularly to the soles of his feet.

Tomb robbery was a risky trade, made even more dangerous because it outraged Egyptian religious ideals. But it also served an important economic function, as the Egyptologist John Wilson has suggested. The thieves restored to circulation an immense amount of silver and gold which had been stored away for the dead and thus withdrawn from the national economy. With the ending of the Bronze Age, Egypt had become poorer. It could no longer profit by mining the

copper of the Sinai peninsula and manufacturing bronze for an eager foreign market. Now it had to import iron itself for tools and weapons; and the fall of the Hittite empire, and the resultant breakdown in communications kept iron very expensive. As a result, grain prices rose and the government was unable to provide rations for the workmen who labored on the tombs in the necropolis at Thebes. Some of them went on strike for their pay—the first recorded example of a labor dispute. Others chose a more direct and more effective method for getting the money they needed. They tunneled into the tombs and plundered them.

Unlike the austere, unadorned galleries within the pyramids, the corridors of the later tombs were covered with painted reliefs depicting the progress of the dead pharaoh in the sun god's boat as it passed through the twelve caverns of the Underworld—the subterranean Nile upon which Amen-Re journeyed during the hours of night. Above and below these scenes are columns of hieroglyphic texts which recite spells from the Book of Him Who Is in the Underworld, in which the pharaoh is interrogated by the good and evil spirits he will meet during his subterranean journey.

In the Book of the Dead, another compilation of religious formulas, the primitive charms and spells of the Pyramid Texts that had served pharaohs of the early dynasties, were modified and expanded to fit the needs of persons of lesser rank. Such popular tomb magic probably meant as little to the average Egyptian as it does to us, but with the "democratization" of the Osiris cult, it was intended to guide the departed spirit of every man through the realm of the gods. After winning an infernal game of questions and answers (he could hardly fail to win since he was provided with the correct answers), the dead man appeared before Osiris, judge of souls. The depictions of this scene, which often illuminate the

Weeping before the tomb of her husband, a widow (left) sits in a necropolis at the desert's edge. The garden behind her, with its date palms and sycamore, contains a table of offerings for the dead. Both this panel and the sphinx at right, a standard for a sacred bark, date from the Late Period, and demonstrate the persistence of religious and artistic traditions that remained almost unchanged all throughout Egyptian history.

papyrus rolls, usually include a pair of balances with the soul in one pan and the feather of *maat* in the other.

In the New Kingdom, as in former times, the Egyptian love of life still predominated. On the walls of the tombs of the nobles, cut out of the rock of the eastward-facing cliffs at Thebes, we can recognize most of the subjects with which we have become familiar in the mastabas of the Old Kingdom — hunting, fishing, and party-giving. If anything they are less inhibited, as in one tomb that pictures a servant holding a bowl before a woman who has been overcome by her potations. Yet there was the other side to this picture.

> *(One) generation passes away*
> *And others remain (in its place) . . .*
> *The gods that were aforetime*
> *Rest in their pyramids;*
> *Nobles and glorified likewise,*
> *Are buried in their pyramids.*
> *They that built houses,*
> *Their places are no more;*
> *What has been done with them?*
> *I have heard the sayings of Imhotep and Djedefhor,*
> *With whose words men still speak so much,*
> *What are their places?*
> *Their walls have crumbled,*
> *Their places are no more,*
> *As if they had never been.*
> *None cometh from thence*
> *That he might tell their circumstances,*
> *That he might tell their needs,*
> *And content our heart*
> *Until we have reached the place*
> *Whither they have gone . . .*

When the guests sat at their tables, heavy with wine, sated with music and the antics of dancing girls, an old blind man would pluck the strings of his harp and in his high voice sing an ancient song steeped in pessimism.

All the pharaohs of the New Kingdom from the beginning of the Eighteenth Dynasty to the end of the Twentieth were buried in the Valley of the Kings. Each was accompanied by such richness—in furniture, jewelry, arms, clothing, and personal adornment—as to make it certain that during those brief centuries this short and lonely valley contained a greater quantity of sheer wealth—in golden treasures and other works of art—than any place on the earth's surface. Of all these tombs only one survived almost intact, and that merely the small, cramped sepulcher of a minor king, Tutankhamen. The fact that it kept its secrets down to the twentieth century is due to several factors. Tutankhamen, a boy-king who died at about eighteen years of age, reigned briefly at the end of the Eighteenth Dynasty, very shortly after the Akhenaten interlude; he was related to, and had been brought up at the court of, Akhenaten; and although he himself returned to orthodoxy, as his name indicates, his memory may have suffered from association with the heretic. It so happened that when the tomb of one of the later pharaohs was tunneled into the hillside above Tutankhamen's tomb, the chippings from these operations hid the entrance to the young king's much more modest sepulcher.

So that, whereas even as far back as Roman times many of the tombs in the Royal Valley had become empty showplaces for curious visitors, that of Tutankhamen escaped detection by the tomb robbers. More than a hundred generations had walked past that obscure grave, yet not one man in all that long time realized that so very near in the hillside lay treasures which, when discovered in 1922, would astound the world. The king's body was enclosed in a coffin of solid gold,

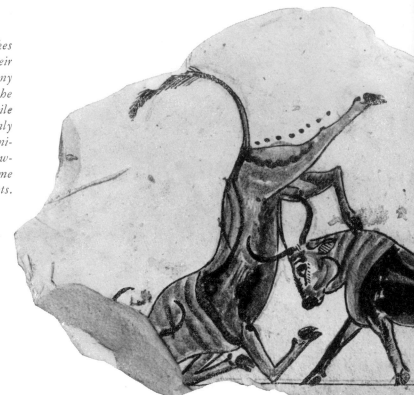

Artists used ostraca, which were potsherds or flakes of limestone, to make preliminary sketches for their major works, or to practice freehand drawing. Many of them have a humorous and satirical content. The one below shows a cat chastising a young child, while a mouse, who probably represents an official, solemnly watches the scene. Such sketches often showed animals engaged in human activity. In the papyrus drawing seen at the bottom of the page, a venturesome gazelle challenges a lion to play a game of draughts.

so heavy that it required four men to lift it. This coffin nested within two outer coffins of wood, richly ornamented with gold, carnelian, and lapis; and these in turn were surrounded by a nest of timber shrines, plated with sheet gold, all richly worked and inscribed.

The objects found in the adjoining chambers now fill several of the principal galleries in the Egyptian Museum in Cairo. They range from the king's chariots and hunting gear down to the tiniest and most exquisitely made jewelry. There are the pharaoh's couches, chairs, and beds; chests containing his clothing, ebony and ivory caskets filled with weapons, toilet articles, and toys, including a game played with movable pieces, rather like checkers. There were statues covered with gold, vases, and other palace ornaments of translucent alabaster; rings, pectorals inlaid with semiprecious stones, and, on the head of the body, a portrait mask of solid gold. All this treasure, the property of a minor pharaoh, was crammed into four small chambers cut like the others from the rock— one of the smallest royal tombs ever found. One can only speculate on the treasure that once filled the chambers of such great kings as Tuthmosis III, Sethi I, and Ramesses II and III.

By another miracle the bodies of these and other of the mightiest New Kingdom pharaohs were found in 1881, hidden in a forgotten tomb shaft on the eastern side of the Theban cliffs, where they had been stacked by the necropolis priests in a final, successful effort to protect the royal dead. The bodies had been rewrapped, in certain cases several times, but of the rich regalia with which they must have been surrounded in their original tombs hardly anything remained.

The bodies themselves lay undisturbed for three thousand years, so that today privileged visitors to the museum in Cairo can look into the faces of monarchs who once "held the world in awe." Sekenenre is there, still showing the wounds

caused by the clubs and daggers of his enemies; so is Tuth-mosis III, with the intelligent face recognizable from his statues; the powerful, heavy-jawed face of the conqueror Sethi I; and the emaciated features of Ramesses II, who reigned for more than sixty years, and raised such numerous and massive monuments that he passed into legend as the mightiest of pharaohs.

None of the kings who followed even approached the power and magnificence of these New Kingdom pharaohs, though, with interruptions, native Egyptian dynasties continued to reign down to the fourth century B.C. Even then, when one of Alexander's generals founded a new dynasty, these Greek-speaking, Greek-thinking conquerors became sufficiently Egyptianized to adopt pharaonic titles, religion, and customs. After three thousand years the valley dwellers' civilization was still tenacious, and even through this long, slow period of decline, the pharaohs occasionally attempted to reassert their ancient power.

They had strong rivals—the priests. Through the munif-icence or superstition of the pharaohs of the Eighteenth and Nineteenth Dynasties, the temple foundations gained a stranglehold on the economy of Egypt, and with it, on the government as well. The great temples had always been an important force in Egyptian life, but by the time of the Ramesside pharaohs they may have controlled as much as one-tenth of the population. Eventually, the high priest of Amen ruled the southern half of the Nile Valley, from Thebes, while a merchant dynasty controlled the Delta region in the North. Even when the pharaoh did not bear the title of high priest, questions of state were often decided by a consultation with the oracles of the gods, with the priests interpreting the answers. It was a god who decided whether an erring officeholder should be brought to trial,

Tomb paintings and monumental reliefs allowed artists little freedom to experiment. Artistic canons were strict, and in large compositions painters were expected to arrange their stylized figures in conventional poses. But on ostraca, artists experimented freely, and studies of motion, such as the scene of fighting bulls (above at left) were common. The sketches of an acrobatic dancer (above), and of a young girl (below) fanning an oven fire with her breath, disregard traditional rules for representing the human figure.

or determined the allotment of a disputed inheritance; a god chose new government officials from a list submitted to his shrine. This reliance on oracles meant that in essence the priests shared sovereignty with the king. This was not the only symbol of the changes which occurred in the religion of Egypt during the Late Period. Egyptians had always been concerned with ceremonial observances; but now ritual became of fanatical importance, with punctilious attention paid to detail. In earlier ages, certain animals had been revered as manifestation of the gods; now they were worshiped themselves. Thousands of them were piously tended during their lives and carefully mummified upon their death. Extensive cemeteries were set aside specifically for the interment of sacred cats or crocodiles. The Greeks looked on these features of Egyptian religion with curiosity and awe; the Hebrews with scorn.

Apart from a few references to the *Habiru,* a name which may denote the Hebrew tribes, Egyptian chronicles rarely mention the Jews, and no one can state definitely under which pharaoh Moses lived. The biblical account of the captivity in Egypt records that the children of Israel "built for Pharaoh treasure cities, Pithom and Raamses." Raamses was probably the city of Tanis in the Delta, renamed after Ramesses II when he established his capital there. It may have been Ramesses who was the pharaoh during the Exodus, which many scholars date to the thirteenth century B.C. In any case it is likely that the Jews left Egypt before the time of his successor, Merneptah; on a memorial stele boasting of his conquests, that ruler announces, rather prematurely, "Israel is laid waste, his seed is not."

We are on much more firm ground when about three hundred years later the Old Testament mentions "Shishak, King of Egypt," to whom Jeroboam fled "and was in Egypt unto the death of Solomon." This king was undoubtedly Sheshonq, first king of the Twenty-second Dynasty who invaded Palestine and Judea in the fifth year of his reign (945 B.C.). According to the Book of Kings, Shishak "came up against Jerusalem. And he took away the treasures of the house of the Lord, and the treasures of the king's house; he even took away all: and he took away all the shields of gold which Solomon had made. . . ."

The tomb of one of this king's successors, also named Sheshonq, was discovered as recently as 1940 by Professor Montet at the Delta city of Tanis, almost certainly the Old Testament Zoan, and the capital of Egypt at this period. He and the other pharaohs of the Twenty-first and Twenty-second Dynasties were Libyans. Although Thebes still was the focus of religious power, dominated by priest-kings who did not recognize the authority, such as it was, of the northern rulers, Tanis had become a great capital. One day, we can hope, some lucky excavator at Tanis may recover the treasures which Sheshonq took from Solomon's temple.

This was the first time in three hundred years that an Egyptian king had invaded Palestine; and it may have seemed, at the time, that the days of Egypt's imperial glory were about to return. But soon other powers—the Assyrians, Babyloni-

ans, and later the Persians—took the place that the kings of Egypt's imperial age had once occupied. Egypt relied increasingly on foreign troops, and except for one last revival never again commanded the resources and the militant patriotism of a united realm. Moreover she was outclassed in weapons and military tactics.

In the Old Testament the Assyrian envoys sneer at the Judean king for relying on the king of Egypt—"this broken reed"—as an ally. Between 715 and 300 B.C. Egypt was occupied for shorter or longer periods by various foreign conquerors: by the Kushites, the Assyrians, the Persians, and the Macedonians. The Kushites established a brief dynasty, the Persians ruled from the time of Cambyses (525 B.C.) down to that of Darius II (424–404 B.C.), son of Xerxes. Yet between the Twenty-fifth (Kushite) and the Twenty-seventh (Persian) Dynasties Egypt knew an Indian summer under the Saites—native Egyptian kings who came from Sais, and governed the land for more than a century during which Egyptians assiduously imitated the art and literature of the Old Kingdom in an attempt to revive the glories that had so long been a part of the past.

It was during this period that the Greeks began to enter Egypt, at first as mercenaries, then as traders and merchants. They found the three-thousand-year-old civilization still in being, its political power waning but its ancient culture remarkably enduring. The Greeks marveled at it, and in the writings of Herodotus we can feel the wonder and respect that these questing, intelligent, curious people felt when confronted by the Egyptian colossus. Although he has been dubbed "the father of lies," Herodotus was accurate in many of his conclusions. Like a conscientious modern journalist he listened to and reported what he was told, without necessarily believing it, and like a modern journalist he sometimes repeated hearsay with tongue-in-cheek. Much of the information that he gained from the Egyptian priests has since been proved to be true; and at least he had the enviable opportunity of seeing Egyptian civilization still in being, magnificently surviving the misfortunes of defeat and foreign occupation.

A little over a century after Herodotus' visit the Ptolemies came to Egypt and founded its last dynasty. Sophisticated Hellenes though they were, the Ptolemies too succumbed to the lure of this all but timeless civilization—the longest-lived of all ancient cultures. They became pharaohs, and are represented in sculpture very much as were their predecessors who had ruled Egypt thirty centuries earlier. And when Cleopatra, last of the Ptolemies and the last native ruler of ancient Egypt, died, she did so with a gesture which is dramatically appropriate to her nature. For the "asp" that Shakespeare tells of the slave bringing into Cleopatra's presence in a basket was the royal cobra—the symbol that Egyptian pharaohs had worn on their crowns since the beginnings of dynastic history. Cleopatra was killed by one of the most ancient deities of Egypt—the goddess Wadjet, guardian of Buto, in the Delta where Egyptian civilization budded and flowered so many long centuries before.

THE AGE
OF EMPIRE

Ruling Egypt at a time when the empire stood at the zenith of its power, Amenhotep III (above) boasted that he was the "smiter of Naharin" and the "captor of Shinar." Amenhotep probably took part in only one military expedition, for few nations dared challenge the supremacy of Egypt. His interest in foreign affairs was expressed less militantly —in delicate negotiations to arrange marriages with the daughters of the kings of Babylon, Arzawa, and Mitanni. In his cosmopolitanism, Amenhotep was typical of the pharaohs who ruled Egypt during the New Kingdom at a time when the Nile Valley was no longer isolated from the rest of the Near East. Typical too was his taste for extravagant building projects. In Nubia, Amenhotep built two temples at which he and his wife were worshiped as gods. In Egypt, he dedicated several others to the god Amen. His own funerary temple rose overlooking the Theban plain; before it stood the two giant statues of him which were later to be called the Colossi of Memnon.

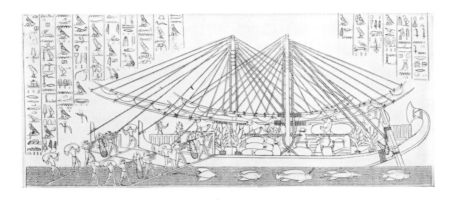

In the Land of Punt, Egyptian traders (left) load their ships with myrrh trees and incense; their cargo also includes several apes, who can be seen perched on the deck of one vessel. The trees were destined for Hatshepsut's temple, shown below, which stands under awesome cliffs on the western bank of the Nile. The portrait of Hatshepsut as a sphinx (right), now carefully restored, was smashed to pieces by her successor when she died.

HATSHEPSUT

The royal ladies of Egypt were an independent breed. Pharaoh's wives and sisters (and to ensure dynastic purity, they were often the same women) participated freely in public affairs—most notably during the years of the New Kingdom. Occasionally they were shown less than life-size, fondly clinging to the knees of a majestic spouse; but often they too were portrayed as colossal figures. The most enterprising of them all was Hatshepsut, who usurped the double crown and ruled as a pharaoh herself for seventeen years "with the form and spirit of a god." On the walls of the great temple that she built at Thebes, royal sculptors depicted her birth as a boy, as well as the moment in which her mother conceived her with the aid of the god Re, father of all Egyptian kings. This visual evidence was enough to prove her right to rule as a king, for to the Egyptians images or words had a magic power to create reality; when Hatshepsut's nephew Tuthmosis III finally inherited the royal power that she had stolen from him, he vengefully defaced as many of her portraits as he could. But Hatshepsut's immense temple remained to testify to the interest in commercial expansion that marked her reign. Loyal to tradition, her scribes compared her to a raging crocodile, but reliefs on her temple walls recorded a peaceful trade expedition, instead of the military exploits in which other Egyptian rulers took pride. Because ancient legend located the home of the gods among the myrrh terraces of Punt on the Somali coast, Hatshepsut imported myrrh trees from that distant land to decorate the terraces of her new temple. In the past, bold traders had often sailed there for incense and ivory, panther skins and gold. These expeditions were a royal monopoly, but they were neglected during periods of political instability. This re-establishment of trade was an early token of the New Kingdom's increasing strength.

Preparing to smite his enemies, Tuthmosis III (right) treads on rows of bound Asiatics, each representing a conquered city. The king holds his kneeling prisoners captive by twining their long hair about his staff. Below, Syrian supplicants, dressed in white robes, offer tribute to their conqueror. Tuthmosis gratefully shared credit for his military success with the god Amen, whose gold image appears on the opposite page, and after a battle rewarded him with presents for his temple. Above, the king pours out a libation before the throne of his divine patron. During the New Kingdom, the temples of Amen grew so rich that they controlled more than one-tenth of Egypt's cultivable land. The high priest of Amen became head of the nation's priesthood, and rivaled the king in power.

TUTHMOSIS III

Tuthmosis I had planted a victory monument on the distant banks of the Euphrates, and returned from battle with the broken body of an enemy prince hanging head downward at the bow of the royal barge. But it was the warrior king Tuthmosis III who finally established Egypt as a great imperial power. Marching north into Palestine, he conquered city after city, and besieged the important stronghold of Megiddo until its princes knelt before him to "beg breath for their nostrils." His predecessors had been content with occasional shipments of tribute, but Tuthmosis organized a permanent administration to drain the revenue from his Asiatic territories. He built a fortress commanding the highway to Lebanon, imposed an oath of fealty upon the Canaanite princes, and carried their sons back to Egypt with him, where they were indoctrinated to remain loyal to their Egyptian overlords after they had inherited their fathers' titles. The conquered provinces gave more than their princes to Egypt however; they provided ideas as well. When Egyptian soldiers came upon the Euphrates River and saw, to their astonishment, its "inverted water" flowing from north to south—contrary to the direction of the Nile—their accustomed view of the universe had to be modified. But Asia's chief contribution was its wealth; the new provinces were so rich that large ships had to be built to carry their tribute from Syrian ports. These treasures enriched a new class of officials who had arisen to administer the vast empire; but the chief beneficiaries were the god Amen and his earthly representatives at the temple at Karnak. For as his priests were quick to proclaim, it was Amen who cast Pharaoh's enemies beneath his sandals, and gave him the earth "in its length and breadth."

PHARAOH'S
WARRIORS

When Pharaoh marched into battle wearing the blue crown
of war, with his standard bearer carrying an ostrich feather as
a token of victory, Egypt's enemies were obliged to flee. For
as Egyptian dogma proclaimed, in fighting against the king
they were foolishly attempting to upset the unalterable order
of the universe. Still, foreigners sometimes won their battles,
and to defeat them Egypt had to rely on mundane as well as
cosmic forces. The well-trained armies of the New Kingdom,
dominant for centuries on the battlefields of Asia, were led
by an elite chariot corps which attacked the foe with spears
and arrows; for defense, its soldiers carried shields and wore
coats of leather or wadded cloth. Their highly maneuverable
chariots could range over the battlefield, harrying the farthest
ranks of the enemy. Fighting alongside them was the in-

fantry, divided into squadrons named after the major gods, and equipped with lances and swords or daggers. Earlier warriors had been drafted to labor on roads and canals as well as to fight; the New Kingdom army was a professional one, largely made up of foreign mercenaries, or prisoners of war who earned freedom by fighting against their compatriots. Although ranking officers were required to achieve a high standard of education, the army remained one route through which obscure men could still rise to a high social position in the increasingly stratified world of the New Kingdom. Ordinary soldiers could advance to become standard bearers or company commanders; officers became overseers, palace tutors, and viziers, and at least one, with more exalted ambitions, even managed to usurp the royal power itself.

Egyptian lancers and Nubian bowmen march together in a group of wooden models which represent an Eleventh Dynasty squadron. The Egyptian warriors are shown at right; for protection they carry hide-covered shields on their arms. OVERLEAF: *Because Egyptian convention required that Pharaoh be shown as an invincible conqueror, the peaceable young King Tutankhamen was depicted as a warrior, his plumed horses mercilessly trampling the bodies of Nubian enemies.*

THE
AMARNA
HERESY

To build a new capital where the worship of the sun disk might flourish, King Akhenaten chose a site today called Amarna, midway between Egypt's northern and southern borders, on virgin land never before dedicated to any god. After offering a solemn sacrifice, he mounted his golden chariot and rode across the plain, until the sun's rays shining on him told him to stop; there he fixed the boundaries of his city and vowed never to leave it until he was dead. The new city stretched from horizon to horizon; within it, the heretic king worshiped one god only—the Aten or sacred sun disk. Amarna doctrine proclaimed that the new god "lived on truth," and truth became the watchword of the revolution. Artists strove to copy nature and architects built temples open to the sky, unlike the dark sanctuaries of other gods who were often called "the hidden ones." There were great occasions when the king and Queen Nefretiti scattered gold to their favorites from a palace window, but the royal family often defied tradition to act like ordinary mortals in public, and Pharaoh was even portrayed kissing his children. But orthodox forces determined to crush the heresy, and Akhenaten eventually appointed a co-regent to rule Egypt while he attended to the sun. In the power struggle, Nefretiti was pushed aside and exiled to another palace. Still she remained faithful to the sun disk, praying that its cult might last ". . . until the swan grows black and the raven becomes white, until the mountains rise up to walk and the waters flow uphill"; but as soon as Akhenaten died, his heresy was suppressed and the old gods regained their power.

Akhenaten and Nefretiti are shown in the relief at upper right playing with their daughters under the life-giving rays of the sun disk. Like the life of the royal court, the art of Amarna was informal. At right, figures of an alert servant girl and the languid King Amenhotep III display a naturalistic spirit that was to reach its most memorable expression in the famous portrait of Queen Nefretiti shown on the facing page.

ROYAL TREASURES

When his young relative Tutankhaten succeeded to the throne which Akhenaten had held for almost twenty years, the triumph of the priests of Amen was made complete. The young king had been brought up to worship the sun disk, but now he dutifully incorporated Amen's name into his own and became Tutankhamen. He restored the shrines which had been neglected by his predecessor, and as one inscription records, "doubled, tripled, and quadrupled" the temple treasures. A grateful scribe acclaimed the results. "The hearts of the gods and goddesses who are in this land are in joy," he wrote. "The possessors of shrines are rejoicing; the regions are in jubilee and exultation . . . The good [times] have come!" But unlike his priests and his gods Tutankhamen had little chance to benefit from the good times. For the young king's reign lasted barely nine years, and he died when he was eighteen, the last male heir of the Eighteenth Dynasty pharaohs who had brought the Egyptian empire to its greatest heights. Although Tutankhamen's tomb was modest compared with those of other rulers, its four small rooms contained a dazzling array of treasures—the richest uncovered in modern times. The king's fingers and toes were sheathed with gold. The inmost of the three royal coffins was made of solid gold as well, and the outer two were encased in gold leaf. Beside the shrine and the funeral coffins within it, were alabaster vases and gorgeously decorated thrones, funeral boats, gilded idols, and precious inlaid chests. These treasures provide more evidence of the passing of the cult of the sun disk. The royal throne, too valuable to destroy, still retains a heretical scene showing the king under the protection of the sun disk, although in some of the inscriptions upon it, the old royal name had been rubbed out and written in again as Tutankhamen.

His solid gold inner coffin (above) shows Tutankhamen holding the symbols of royal authority—a crook and a flail. The vulture pectoral shown at right was found resting upon his chest. Among the furnishings of the tomb were a pair of golden horse blinders (below) and an ivory headrest (above left) which represents the god Shu supporting the sky so that the king's head might rest in heaven. The gilded lion shown opposite was one of a pair which decorated a funerary couch.

THE DECLINE OF EGYPT

As the New Kingdom declined in power, monumental temples continued to rise along the Nile, but they were often more remarkable for their imposing size than they were for architectural style. Their walls displayed vainglorious lists of conquered towns, but Ramesses III merely copied his list from that of the great Ramesses II, who in turn had already appropriated the list of another pharaoh. Ramesses III also named his children and his horses after those of Ramesses II, for Egypt was determined to remain unchanging. Although foreign conquerors seized the double crown, the concept of divine kingship survived until kingship passed from Egypt; then its memory lived on until even the most learned scribe could no longer decipher the mysterious hieroglyphs that had been carved in ancient times to keep the royal name alive for eternity. Egypt fell prey to imperial powers which themselves would perish in turn; its monuments were neglected; but the temples and pyramids that awed Greek and Roman, Arab and Turk, have outlasted empire after empire, to proclaim the glory of the pharaohs.

His crown shattered, Ramesses II (opposite) surveys his funerary temple, the Ramesseum, now fallen into ruins, like the towering colossi of Amenhotep III shown above. No less eloquent in recalling the vanished power of Egypt is the tiny plaque at right, an artist's sketch showing the king slaying an enemy captive.

SUMER
DAWN OF CIVILIZATION

Land Between the Rivers · I

Several of the world's earliest civilizations developed in the crescent-shaped area of southwestern Asia that stretches from Palestine on the Mediterranean, curving around northern Arabia, to the Persian Gulf in the east. From time immemorial mountaineers from the northern uplands and nomads from the deserts to the south struggled for possession of these lands. Most of the eastern half of the crescent, the land that slopes down in grassy steppes from the mountains of Armenia and follows the Tigris and Euphrates Rivers to their outlet in the Gulf, falls within the territory of modern Iraq.

The visitor to Iraq will look in vain for anything comparable to the natural and man-made wonders to be found in Egypt. Few awesome ruins remain to recall the mighty civilizations which flourished there. The stony uplands of the north give way to brown plains of almost unbearable flatness which extend from horizon to horizon. From the air, this desolate landscape looks like sand, but on landing, say, at Baghdad, the visitor will find that it is in fact dried alluvial mud brought down by the two great rivers, the Tigris and Euphrates, the sole sources of Iraq's fertility. As they flow across the broad flatlands on their way to the Persian Gulf, these twin arteries meander erratically, often changing their course. They are uncontrolled by natural barriers. No cliffs hem them in, and the only constraints put upon them are those erected by men—the great embankments or levees that throw long shadows at sunrise and sunset. In the southern valley one can trace a network of straight lines that is hardly visible at ground level but can be seen from the air, marking the pattern of long-vanished irrigation canals.

This finely carved figure of gypsum stood at a temple altar in Nippur about 2700 B.C. as a woman's constant suppliant before her goddess. Its gold mask was once attached to a wooden head.

Apart from Islamic cities such as Baghdad, and clusters of black Bedouin tents, one sees few signs of human habitation. Here and there a modern pipeline, a dam, and a glinting reservoir; the rest appears to be wasteland. South of Baghdad, near Basra, the rivers filter through a broad marshland and join to form a single large stream that shortly empties into the Gulf. From the air, one can see a waste of muddy water, patterned with symmetrical "stars" which one later discovers are the tops of half-submerged palm trees. The gleaming wet backs of brown leviathans occasionally rear out of the water, mudbanks on which may be discerned the moving figures of men and their cattle, and the green patches which are their crops.

This drab valley that stretches from the Gulf to the Armenian mountains in the north is the Land Between the Rivers —Mesopotamia, as the ancient Greeks called it. In and about this valley, long before the classic age of Greece, centered the great empires of Assyria and Babylonia. And here, more than two millenniums still earlier, the Sumerians developed a remarkable civilization which, antedating even that of Egypt, was the earliest known on earth.

Some four thousand years ago, the Sumerians set down in writing their conception of how their river-bound world was created, recording a myth that was ancient even at that time. The story is echoed in the first chapter of Genesis, for the Hebrew writers almost certainly derived their idea of creation, like the Garden of Eden, the tale of the Deluge, and other traditional stories in the Old Testament, from the Land Between the Rivers.

"And God said, let there be a firmament in the midst of the waters, and let it divide the waters from the waters. And God made the firmament, and divided the waters which were under the firmament from the waters which were above

the firmament: and it was so. . . . And God said, let the waters under the heaven be gathered together unto one place, and let dry land appear: and it was so."

If one thinks of the earth as a spinning globe, this biblical interpretation of creation is not easy to reconcile with known facts, except in a poetic sense. But if for *firmament* one thinks simply of the lower valley of the Tigris-Euphrates, a land of widespreading flood, marshes, mudbanks, and clouds, it does make sense. Gods and goddesses are the chief participants in the story, because these early peoples saw what we call natural phenomena as the acts of their deities or the manifestations of the gods themselves.

To the people of that valley, the fresh-water flood was Apsu, and the salt-water sea in the distance with which Apsu mingled in the primordial chaos, was Tiamat. The mingling of the two resulted in a deposit of silt brought down by the rivers, which gave birth to Enki, the god of earth, and Anu, god of heaven. Then Enlil, god of the air and the most important deity in the Sumerian pantheon, separated the heaven and earth which had been born of the waters, the way the God of the Hebrews divided the waters to make dry land appear. It was Enlil too who taught the Sumerians agriculture and gave them tools with which to build. Archaeology cannot corroborate the myth of Enlil's teaching, but it can follow the record of how the people of Mesopotamia learned to farm and build, and how the river valley slowly developed a complex urban civilization.

By 7000 B.C. the agricultural revolution had begun on the fringes of these regions; man had already begun to gather cereal crops, thus partly freeing himself from the necessity of hunting game for his food. In widely separated sites, among the mountains of Iran and in the upper Tigris Valley of Iraq and southeastern Turkey, archaeologists have discovered the settlements of these early farmers. There is one at Qalat Jarmo, in the grassy uplands of northern Iraq, close to the modern city of Kirkuk.

From the air, the site looks something like a circular mudpie from which a substantial segment has been eaten away by a stream. On the very edge of this eroded portion, one sees a series of mathematically spaced test pits in which archaeologists have dug down through twenty-three feet of occupational debris to establish their evidence. From about 7000 B.C., Jarmo was occupied by a succession of primitive agricultural communities, whose farmers used flint-bladed sickles to reap their grain; they domesticated goats, and perhaps dogs as well. They built straight-sided dwellings of bricks made of pressed mud. On the lower, that is earlier, levels of the site, the excavators found stone vessels. On higher and therefore later levels of occupation, coarse pottery appeared, and figurines of animals made of baked clay.

Jarmo is one of the most ancient settlements in Mesopotamia. Comparable sites that have been discovered by archaeologists have been assigned various dates ranging from 5500 to 4000 B.C., although precise dating is impossible. All were the settlements of primitive hunter-farmers who gradually moved down into the Tigris-Euphrates Valley seeking more desirable land. There is no historical record of these movements, except obliquely in legend, but a scientific examination of the stratigraphy of these sites, which has been undertaken in the course of many seasons, reveals a fascinating story.

At Hassuna in northern Iraq, it is possible to trace the development of the town from the time when man first camped there to the days when he had begun to make substantial buildings. Here in the bottom layer next to the virgin soil, the excavators found a camp site strewn with tools of stone and bone, crude pottery containers, and clay pellets for use

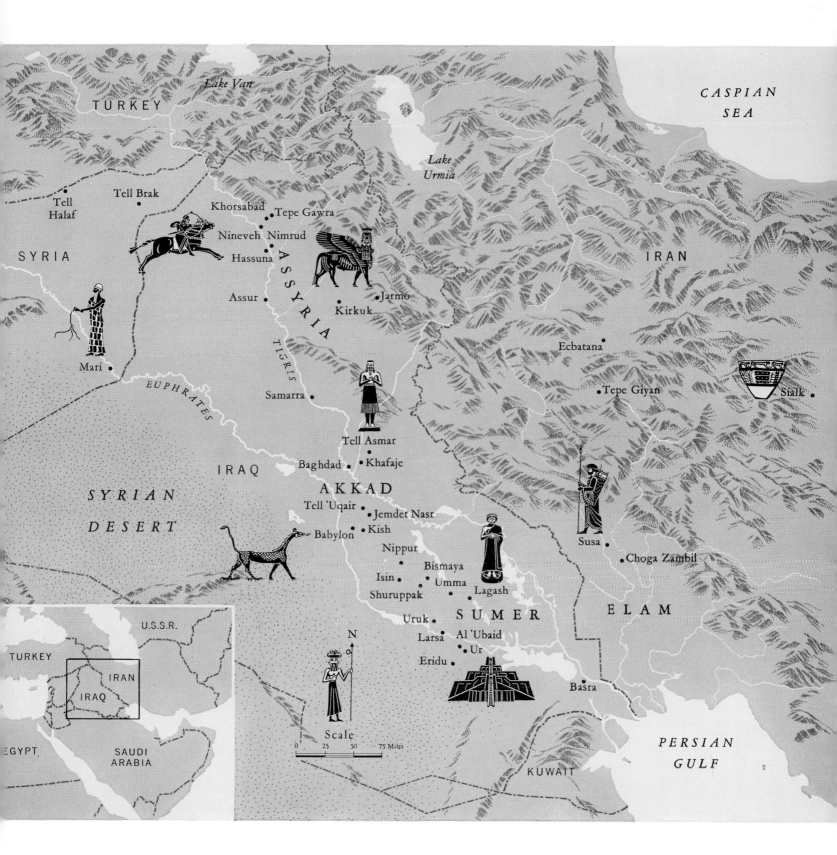

The ruins of its great ziggurat still testify to the glory of Ur, the most famous of the
Sumerian city-states in the lower reaches of the Tigris-Euphrates Valley. Sumerian culture
provided a foundation for all Mesopotamian civilizations. The Semitic kings of Mari
adopted Sumerian rituals; the long-necked dragon of Babylon derived from Sumerian
myth. Assyria's warrior-kings collected a large library of Sumerian writings. Conquest
and trade carried Sumerian influence to numerous neighboring countries. Many elements
of its original culture survived in the Land Between the Rivers until after the time of Christ.

in slings; but there was no trace of any dwelling. Here, perhaps, a group of nomads had moved down from the mountains, probably in spring, and camped on the fertile grasslands at the junction of two streams. They were attracted, no doubt, by the abundance of game and fish, and the possibility of reaping a crop of wild barley before the winter storms forced them to move on. Later, when they returned, they found that the trees were again bearing fruit, and there was more wild barley. In time the idea would occur to someone that they might settle here, and build some form of protection against winter conditions.

And this is evidently what happened. In the next stage, the nomads had learned to sow the crops which they had seen growing there; later still, mud huts appear and better pottery, until at last, near the top of the mound, were the remains of a complete agricultural community, hardly differing from that of the neighboring village of Hassuna in the twentieth century. There is no evidence to show when cattle, sheep, and pigs were domesticated, but bones of a pig were found in an early level at the site. At about 4000 B.C., prehistoric Hassuna seems to have been abandoned.

To the imaginative mind, such a story, based purely on layers of pottery fragments, mud-brick foundations, and primitive tools, is as stirring as the tale of the Tower of Babel, for here, to borrow Gordon Childe's phrase, is "man in the making." Let there be no doubt that the descendants of such people built the great Sumerian cities with their towering ziggurats, invented writing, and developed mathematics and astronomy, and created a culture that survived down to the time of the classical Greeks. There were many Hassunas; again and again in the mountains north and east of Mesopotamia archaeologists have found the remains of similar communities, and through their characteristic artifacts,

especially pottery, have been able to trace the progress of their culture into the valley of the twin rivers.

It is not easy for the layman to appreciate just how important pottery is to the archaeologist, and why he rates bits of earthenware so highly. Some half century ago, an Oxford scholar appraised its value to the researcher.

> *For 'tis not verse and 'tis not prose*
> *But earthenware alone*
> *It is that ultimately shows*
> *What men have thought and done.*

It is fairly true to say that the history of the human species as revealed by archaeology alone, without benefit of written records, is little more than a history of technology and artifacts; when he finds no written records, all the archaeologist can hope to do at a given site is to study the building foundations and objects found at various levels. Pottery is the most common of these artifacts, and part of its value lies in the fact that it provides a trade mark or "brand name" by which we can follow the development of a particular culture and observe how it spreads.

If a characteristic form of storage jar originally found at Site A turns up at Sites B, C, and D in a later context, it is reasonable to assume that the people or the culture represented by type A had spread to these other regions, either through physical conquest or the peaceful superimposition of one culture upon another. Similarly, minor variations among pottery styles are significant, for in Mesopotamia as elsewhere the beginnings and development of a civilization often can be traced only by observing the changes in its pottery, and in its tools and weapons—objects that are often small, unromantic, and of little beauty. Yet rightly interpreted, they are

no less significant than the great pyramids, the Theban tombs, and the other enormous and impressive monuments of Egypt.

Neolithic settlements like Hassuna were succeeded by those of a people called the Tell Halaf folk, who established themselves for many centuries in the hill country and plains of northern Mesopotamia. Later, to their south, a new wave of migrants entered the river valley from the highlands of Iran. These, the al 'Ubaid people, were farmers and stock-breeders, skilled in many crafts. They used implements of stone and flint, and produced greenish pots of varying shapes, with designs in black paint.

"Gallant heroes lived before Agamemnon, not a few; but on all alike, unwept and unknown, eternal night lies heavy because they lack a sacred poet," Horace said, and there must have been more than one of such forgotten geniuses who led mankind on its upward path, and whose bones lie scattered among the fragmented pottery of these Stone and Bronze Age villages. The Sargons, the Gudeas, and the Hammurabis, the great leaders of later times, were fortunate in being born after the invention of writing, and at a time when technological advances had enabled them to leave permanent memorials. The leaders who first induced their followers to settle in one place instead of wandering, and who later led them to move to more advantageous situations, against the force of tradition, have left no record. But they must have existed, if only for the reason that in historical times we know that important advances are normally initiated by such gifted and forceful individuals, and do not ordinarily arise by accident or by the drift of circumstances alone.

Who was it, for instance, who inspired the events recorded in the eleventh chapter of the Book of Genesis? "And it came to pass, as they journeyed from the east, that they found a plain in the land of Shinar; and they dwelt there. And they

Life in a Sumerian city-state was mainly rural, resembling that on a medieval manor. Most residents worked in the surrounding fields, which included a "common" whose produce went to the temple for use by priests and for later distribution at festivals or in case of famine. The lord of the manor was literally a god—the patron deity of the city, who owned the land and managed it through a human steward, the high priest. In this frieze, which shows one aspect of farming, priests are seen at work on the sacred dairy farm of Ninhursaga, the Sumerian mother goddess. At the right they milk the cows (from behind) while muzzled calves look on. To the left, past a cow barn made of reeds, one priest pours the milk through a funnel or strainer held by a seated companion; two others on either side hold large jars, in which they may be preparing butter. The figures were carved from shell and white limestone and inlaid in shale between raised borders of copper. Found at al 'Ubaid, near Ur, the frieze dates from early in the third millennium B.C.

said to one another, 'Go to, let us make brick and burn them thoroughly.' And they had brick for stone, and slime had they for mortar. And they said, 'Go to, let us build a city, and a tower, whose top may reach unto heaven; and let us make a name, lest we be scattered abroad upon the face of the whole earth.' "

Archaeology has revealed that this is indeed what happened, though not suddenly as in the biblical story that tells of the Tower of Babel, but over a long period of time. Some of the early immigrants to southern Mesopotamia (Sumer, the land of Shinar) probably did come from the east. They found a fertile land, but one without stone, so they learned to make bricks from the river mud, and eventually to burn them thoroughly in kilns. And they evolved the ziggurat, or temple tower, perhaps to remind them and their gods of the mountainous lands from which they had come.

At the site of the ancient city of Eridu excavators have found at a number of early levels remains of large temples which undoubtedly date from the al 'Ubaid period, that is, from about 4000 to 3500 B.C. But it was the succeeding Uruk period (3800–3200 B.C.) that witnessed an extensive development of monumental architecture and the evolution of the first real cities. For instance, at Uruk itself there was a large temple with its shrine built on a raised platform, a forerunner of the ziggurats or giant, many-tiered towers central to most later Mesopotamian cities. The sacred buildings in Uruk were colorfully decorated with mosaic patterns made up of clay cones dipped in pigment and decoratively arranged. At 'Uqair, another site of this period, there were wall paintings representing processions of human and animal figures. This richness and exuberance of decoration, no less than the scale of the buildings mentioned, provide impressive testimony to the level of accomplishment reached in the land of Sumer as early as the fourth millennium B.C.

But the Uruk people may be given credit for an even more important innovation, the development of writing. It is at this time that we find the first primitive pictographs from which the later cuneiform writing system evolved in a manner that can be accurately traced.

Just how writing originated we cannot be sure, but it was certainly for utilitarian reasons, through a need for keeping records. Among the early nomadic peoples trade and commerce were no more highly organized than they are in primitive African or South American tribes today. Permanent records were not needed; human memory was sufficient. But once human beings began to be organized in large and complex social groups, with varying interdependent relationships, and were faced with the problems of accumulating, storing, and distributing surplus wealth, the need for a more permanent and accurate system of recording became urgent.

The earliest intelligible examples of writing are inventories. They are lists of objects: so many head of cattle, so many jars of oil, so many captives. From early times—long before he had evolved an architecture or a written language, as we can see from examples of paleolithic art in the caves of southwestern Europe and of Africa—man has enjoyed exercising his skill in drawing the world about him. Hence it is natural that most of the earliest writing symbols were pictures: a rudimentary cow's head, a man or a woman, a wine jar, a sword or a shield, the disk of the sun or moon.

Originally these would be used as a reminder, for example, that A had agreed to exchange with B so many cows for so many jars of oil, the barter to be completed within so many months. A series of crude pictures of cows, oil jars, and moons (each representing a month) would suffice to record the bargain. Later this system would be elaborated more and

more until a time came when the pictographs gave way to a series of conventional signs, which were easier to write and which were no longer representations of objects, but of the sounds of human speech. Obviously numeration was also evolved, a series of dots or strokes representing numbers. Thus writing was born, with all its vast potential for recording not merely commercial transactions but the achievements of rulers, hymns and invocations to the gods, the practical knowledge that grew along with man's gradual mastery of his environment, the wisdom of thinkers and philosophers, and the imaginative flights of storytellers and poets.

This new means of communication appears to have evolved first in Mesopotamia. As we have seen, the idea may well have inspired the predynastic Egyptians to develop their own writing system. There is, however, a basic difference between Sumerian and Egyptian writing, which is almost certainly due to the type of writing materials that were available in the two lands. In Egypt, where stone was abundant, the pictorial form of writing survived for monumental inscriptions down to the time of Roman rule, although when writing on papyrus the scribes used a flowing, cursive form called the hieratic. In Sumer, though the system undoubtedly began as a series of pictographs, these were rapidly modified until writing became merely a series of little wedge-shaped marks (hence *cuneiform*—"wedge-shaped"). The Sumerians wrote on the same abundantly available material they used for their buildings—mud. It is difficult to write pictographs on wet clay, but wedges are easy to make. Nearly all Mesopotamian writings are on clay tablets, usually about the size of a postal card, convenient to work, to handle, and to store. Although fragile and easily crushed, thousands of them have survived and more turn up continually on the sites of ancient Mesopotamian cities. And it is from these precious writings, far

more than from the once-mighty ziggurats, temples, and palaces, that we are able to trace the history of each of the successive Mesopotamian civilizations.

For it is important to remember that in Mesopotamia we are dealing not with one but with several "lost worlds." Egypt's natural barriers protected the Nile world against unwelcome outside influence and intrusion. Unprotected by such barriers, the fertile plains and valleys of Mesopotamia attracted migrants and invaders, settlers and conquerors, who invested the land in successive waves over the course of a long time. In spite of the frequent changes that resulted, the basic pattern of civilization established by the early Sumerians remained fairly constant. The racial and linguistic affinities of the Sumerians—"the black-headed people," as they called themselves—are unknown. Their language was neither Indo-European nor Semitic. But the cuneiform script they evolved was taken over by the Akkadians, the Babylonians, the Assyrians, and other peoples who later ruled in Mesopotamia, and with it were perpetuated many of the myths and legends, the proverbs and poems, the medical and mathematical lore that made up the abundant literature of the Sumerians, and with this their basic culture.

Before 2500 B.C. the land of Sumer was occupied by a number of independent city-states. There was no single, centralized political authority as there was in Egypt. The earliest city-states were primitive democracies, ruled by assemblies of all adult men (except slaves). Only in time of crisis did the assembly elect a king and hand over absolute power to him for the duration of the emergency. But as relations among the cities became more complex and threatening, kingship became permanent rather than temporary. The kings of these early centers did not claim divine status for themselves, as Egyptians and later Mesopotamian rulers did;

in fact, the Sumerian word for king can also be translated simply as "great man." Each of these urban communities owed allegiance primarily to a local deity and each of them was surrounded by, and largely dependent upon, an extensive agricultural hinterland.

These city-states represented a new stage in social organization. They arose because circumstances in southern Mesopotamia encouraged the organized, co-operative efforts of the community. Here the land was made abundantly fertile by the river-borne mud. But before this fertility could be effectively exploited, the rivers had to be controlled, and the large-scale system of irrigation that was developed to meet this need involved a complex social organization. With an elaborate system of canals that throughout the dry summer months conserved the water brought down by the winter floods, a land which earlier sustained no more than a handful of villages could now support a prolific population. And with the surplus of produce that resulted, some part of the population was freed from devoting all of its time and energies to the unremitting task of providing food. Some men were able to function as specialists—priests, carpenters, metalworkers, sculptors, and so forth. Foremost among these were the priests and rulers, men who governed and protected the land, who understood and could interpret the mysterious, terrifying phenomena of sun, rain, flood, tempest, which ultimately controlled men's lives—the forces which would bring abundance or famine, wealth or poverty, which produced fertility or sterility in men, cattle, or crops. These were the wise men who understood how the earth began, and how the powers kept it in equilibrium.

Below this higher intellectual class, but allied with it, were the administrators and civil servants, the scribes who had learned the secret of writing and who kept records of crop

The early Sumerians traded along the rivers, using boats like the one above. It carries two oarsmen, a bull bearing an altar, and a priest. At right an offering bearer carries stalks of wheat, symbols of Sumer's flourishing agriculture. By 3000 B.C. the Sumerians had invented the first writing system. Some pre-cuneiform pictographs appear on the clay tablet at left, where the small circles represent numbers.

yields, flood levels, years of plenty or of dearth, annual returns from taxation, the movement of the stars, and the achievements of their great men. Below them were other classes: the architects and builders who planned and erected palaces and temples; the artisans who understood the craft of working clay, stone, and in time, metal; the carpenters, boatmen, jewelers; the spinners and weavers, who were usually slaves. There was also a very important class of traders and merchants who, among other things, brought in sorely needed commodities from the world outside the valley.

There were many Sumerian cities bordering the Tigris and Euphrates: Eridu, Khafaje, Lagash, Shuruppak, Uruk (which the Bible calls Erech), the great ceremonial center of Nippur, and Ur, the city where, according to tradition, Abraham the patriarch was born. Though they were scattered over a wide area, were varied in size, and owed allegiance to separate gods, their basic character was similar. They rose from a level plain, on or near a river. Their structures were almost entirely of mud bricks, but with this modest building material they achieved monumental effects. Surrounding each city there was probably a defensive wall, as for example at Uruk. At Khafaje there was a series of interior walls, graduated in height, surrounding the temple at the center of the city; within these were rows of workmen's houses and shops, stores and warehouses. If the city was on a river, wharves were provided for vessels.

Dominating the city and the fertile fields, vineyards, orchards, and pastures that surrounded it rose the temple of the chief deity, usually placed upon a high artificial mound. As early as the fourth millennium B.C. one temple complex at Uruk covered an area of almost a half million square feet, its shrine rising from a platform that was forty feet high. Later these sacred temple towers, or *ziggurats* (the Mesopota-

mian word means "to be high" or "pointed") occasionally achieved phenomenal height and bulk. Their construction must have consumed millions of man-hours of labor. They have been compared with the pyramids of Egypt, but they were of course not tombs. They served quite a different purpose. Each of these structures was in effect an artificial mountain raised by gigantic efforts of the community to bridge the gap between man and god. A temple was placed at the top of the tower to serve as a chamber of welcome for the god descending from heaven. At the ground level another shrine was usually provided for the accommodation of the deity during his stay on earth. Processional stairways linked the two, inevitably bringing to mind Jacob's vision of the "ladder" that reached to heaven, on which he saw "the angels of God ascending and descending."

We might be tempted to compare this temple complex with a cathedral, or perhaps a great monastery; but these would be false analogies. In fact there is no modern equivalent. For the god or goddess of the city was the core of its existence; the activity of the community was primarily devoted to the interests of the temple. Religion was not something which could be separated from daily life. Even the use of the word *religion* to describe Sumerian belief conveys the wrong impression, because today we stress religion's association with a system of ethics and morality. In ancient Sumer, as in other early societies, the concept of religion included more immediate and practical meanings as well.

Gods and demons controlled every aspect of life; the natural forces of wind, rain, flood, and sun, and the gods and goddesses which personified them, either permitted men to live or destroyed them. These deities required constant propitiation, and it would have been calamitous to neglect or vary the elaborate rituals which appeased them. According to leg-

129

end, the Sumerians had been created to live as serfs on the estates of the gods, to "be burdened with the toil of the gods that they may freely breathe." And the Sumerians found their divine masters as capricious as human ones.

Although they were occasionally compassionate, the gods could be angry, vengeful, and selfish. Like human beings, they appreciated good food and wine, fine clothing, and other delights of mortal civilization. Like human beings, they married and had children, and sometimes quarreled among themselves. They were also conscious of status; it would not have done, for instance, for the deity of Uruk to possess a temple inferior to that of the god who controlled Eridu.

To the Sumerians of all social classes, these deities were as real as the king and his hierarchy of priests, who administered the estates of the gods. The farmer at work in the barley fields, straightening to ease his back, would see rising above the waving grain the temple complex, dedicated to the god whose needs he supplied and whose priests in turn supplied him with seed, tools, and cattle for plowing, and food and clothing for himself and his family. The same was true higher up the social scale: the scribes who kept accounts of crop yields and stores; the privileged priests who brought the god his offerings of food, and washed his sacred image and changed its clothing; the soldiers who fought the god's wars against neighboring city-states; the merchants who exchanged wheat and barley for precious metals; the craftsmen who made beautiful objects of wood, stone, and ivory for the temples and palaces—all felt themselves to be the servants of the god.

Every Sumerian was equal before the gods. In the earliest period, all men had been assigned tasks to perform as divine service, and all were given rations from the temple storerooms, as well as allotments of land which they could farm for themselves. Eventually this system developed divisions of labor and class distinctions. The economy of the Sumerian temple community, that is, of the city-state, has been termed a system of theocratic socialism. Yet from an early date personal ownership of wealth was recognized and there remained ample opportunities for private enterprise. Imported luxuries, and luxuries of imported materials, that have been found in private tombs give but one indication that these opportunities for individual trade ventures were not neglected.

Perhaps the most extraordinary and moving example of the Sumerian spirit of collective devotion was found in the death pits of Ur, discovered by Leonard Woolley in 1923. Near the city walls Woolley came upon a cemetery that had been considerably plundered. Among its nearly two thousand graves were sixteen that clearly belonged to distinguished personages. They may have been kings and queens as Woolley thought, but we cannot be certain. The sepulchral chambers were of stone, which must have been brought from thirty miles away. Within each chamber lay a body, male or female, in full regalia of gold, silver, and semiprecious stones. Some had golden drinking cups beside them. These stone-built rooms lay at the bottom of deep pits which were approached by sloping ramps. Within the pits, and sometimes on the approach ramps, lay the bodies of scores of men, women, and animals. There were sixty-eight women in one pit, all of whom had been buried in red woolen robes, with headdresses of gold or silver. Some of the women had musical instruments, such as lyres and harps made of wood and ornamented with gold, silver, shell, lapis lazuli, and red stone. They were probably court musicians. The wood of these instruments had decayed, but its impression remained in the soil, so that the archaeologists, by taking wax casts, were able to reconstruct the harps, replacing the rich gold and silver mountings so that they may now be seen in all their

Woman's inclination toward elaborate and costly headdress appears even in this earliest of civilizations. The creation at right, probably worn over a large wig, is crowned by a tall silver "comb" decorated with inlaid flowers; beneath it are three beaded wreaths with gold pendants in the form of long willow leaves, beech leaves, and disks with lapis centers. Another beech-leaf wreath (below) shows the delicacy of the enchased pendants and the beads of lapis and carnelian. These headdresses belonged to women found in a death pit of the Royal Cemetery.

original beauty. These mounted decorations were most commonly fashioned in the form of an animal's head, that of a cow or a magnificently bearded bull. In at least one case the complete figure of a stag is represented.

In another, Woolley found the remains of two wagons, with the bones of oxen and the bodies of their riders or drivers beside them. In a third pit lay soldiers in copper helmets, their spears at their sides.

The bodies were lying in orderly rows, giving the impression that these people had met a peaceful death or that the corpses had been tidied up afterwards. The little cups that lay beside them may have contained poison or a drug. It is possible that these servitors were alive when they entered the pits and, like the "great ones" in the burial chambers, they were self-immolated. It seems not altogether unlikely that they went to their deaths calmly, without fuss. As they marched down into the pits they may even have been singing and the musicians playing.

After they became unconscious someone must indeed have entered the pits to tidy up the bodies before the earth was flung down on them; two of the harps lay *on top* of the corpses. Another poignant and significant detail is that half of the court ladies had worn gold circlets in their hair; from the presence of certain oxides in the soil Woolley suspected that the rest had worn silver circlets, but he could not prove this. Then one day he found, near one of the bodies, a little metal disk, which on examination proved to be just such a silver circlet, tightly wound up in a coil. From this Woolley deduced that each girl had been so provided, but that whereas the majority had had time to put on their circlets, one girl—late for her own funeral—had left it coiled up in a pocket in her clothing which protected it from the corrosion that had destroyed the rest of the silver fillets.

What can one make of this? It is too facile to suggest that these victims had gone to their deaths joyously because they anticipated, like Christians or Moslems, a better world to come. A *better* world? Listen to a Sumerian description of the afterlife, where

> . . . the Dead shuffle
> Under their black plumage . . . Where the food is clay
> And the drink ashes . . . whence there is no reprieve . . .

Or this passage from another, later poem:

> When Inanna ascends from the nether world,
> Verily the dead hasten ahead of her.
> Inanna ascends from the nether world,
> The small demons like spear shafts,
> The large demons like the spear shafts . . .
> Walked at her side. . . .
> They who accompanied Inanna,
> Were beings who know not food, who know not water,
> Who eat not sprinkled flour,
> Who drink not libated water,
> Who take away the wife from the loins of man,
> Who take away the child from the . . . of the nursemaid.

Obviously the Sumerians did not view death and the hereafter with the confident hopes of the early Egyptians. Yet these well-fed, well-dressed Sumerian ladies and gentlemen of 4500 years ago, whose remains Woolley found in the death pits, apparently went to their graves calmly. If they had been driven into the pits and forced to kill themselves, would not there have been some signs of violence and terror?

There can be no certain answer to all this. It seems a likely possibility that the victims, without hope of future beatitude, allowed themselves to be sacrificed because they believed it to be a religious duty necessary for the safety of the city-state,

Rivalry and frequent warfare darkened relations among the city-states of Early Dynastic Sumer. Lagash won an important victory over its neighbor Umma, and commemorated it on a stele showing (right) a phalanx of spearmen from Lagash advancing, behind a wall of shields, over the prostrate enemy. Not the city's leader, Eannatum, but its warlike god, Ningirsu, received credit for the victory; he appears (far right) holding the men of Umma in a net and bludgeoning one of them with a mace. The extensive empire of Sargon of Akkad, who brought all the cities of Sumer under his rule, was described centuries later on a tablet (left) bearing an early map of the world, with Babylon on the Euphrates at the center.

whose well-being could be renewed only by the sacrifice of a king, or a mock king, and his retainers. The epic poem about Gilgamesh describes such a custom of sending retainers to accompany the dead king to his tomb. And it has parallels in numerous ancient societies. As late as the First Dynasty in Egypt the servants of a princess were slain upon her death and their bodies interred beside hers.

What the Ur tombs do clearly reveal is the wealth and beauty and fine craftsmanship which the "great ones" of the period could command. The gold, silver, bronze, and semi-precious stones may have been imported, probably from Iran in exchange for Sumerian textiles, foodstuffs, tools, and weapons. The quality of the workmanship is highly sophisticated and reflects a long tradition of development. The fantastic headdress of one of the sacrificed women, as absurdly delightful as a modern Paris hat; the upreared figure of a he-goat in gold and lapis, which has often been compared to the biblical "ram caught in a thicket"; the splendid electrum helmet of another victim which reproduces a Sumerian style of male hairdo with chignon at the back; the beautifully wrought golden drinking vessels—all these are comparable to the best Egyptian work of the same period.

The scenes depicted in lapis and inlaid shell on the sound boxes of the musical instruments and on other surfaces present fascinating and tantalizing images of this distant and often inscrutable world. On the famous "Ur Standard" we see Sumerian infantry marching in step, spears ready, driving before them captured enemy prisoners. We see the king's chariot, drawn by wild asses (onagers), charging the enemy. These solid-wheeled chariots look clumsy compared with the graceful, spoked-wheeled vehicles of later times, but they were sturdy and no doubt powerful instruments of war at that time. On the reverse side of the "Standard" are scenes of peace, perhaps a victory banquet, showing the king and his nobles feasting, wine goblets in their hands, while a musician plays to them on his harp.

As they are represented here and in certain other inlays, reliefs, and sculptures, with their stocky figures, hook-nosed faces, bunchy skirts, and their general lack of animation, the early Sumerians would appear to have been singularly unattractive as a people. However, artistic conventions quite alien to those we are familiar with may to some degree have dictated these appearances—as they did in Egypt where, to accentuate the most recognizable aspects of a human being, the artist showed the head in profile, the torso front-on, and the legs again in profile.

On the other hand, unlike the relatively uniform and static character of Egyptian art, that of early Mesopotamia varied enormously between the extremes of realism and abstraction. The head of a bull from a harp also found at Ur, for example, is a superbly modeled sculpture that conveys to perfection the animal vitality of its subject. Still again, the famous Warka Head of a woman, fashioned in Uruk (Warka is the modern name for ancient Uruk) centuries earlier than the "Ur Standard," in its subtle modeling and serene grace might almost be from classical Greece.

And contrasted with this life-size head, there are innumerable little carved cylinders of stone or metal used for sealing documents, whose designs, ranging from highly representational scenes to almost purely decorative arrangements, are engraved with such delicacy that we can hardly believe they were executed on such a small scale without the aid of a magnifying glass. Aside from sealing inscribed tablets these attractive and practical devices were also used to identify and protect property. They were rolled over pats of moist clay that covered the fastenings of jar and basket tops. After the impres-

sion dried and hardened the container could not be opened without damaging the sealing. From the thousands of examples that have been recovered, surely a tiny fraction of those that were made, we can judge that they represented a form of popular art that persisted over a long period of time. They are indeed the only objects that have survived in sufficient quantity to provide a comprehensive view of Mesopotamian art over the ages. They were customarily attached to a necklace or wristband and were worn to the grave by their owners. Consequently every generation produced its own seals in a succession of styles that broadly display the inventiveness of the Mesopotamian designer.

Scenes such as those depicted on the cylinder seals are invariably religious in nature, and occur again and again on pottery, stone vases, and stelae. In some we can recognize a familiar figure often thought to be the epic hero Gilgamesh, grappling monsters, slaying two lions with his bare hands, and, with his companion Enkidu, performing other feats described in the famous Sumerian epic. But other figures are inexplicable, and serve to demonstrate the gulf which separates us from these highly civilized people of five thousand years ago. One shows a man kneeling at the foot of a tree while a coiled snake gnaws at his genitals. "And who," as the French archaeologist André Parrot inquires, "will ever know why?"

Mesopotamia's political vicissitudes are reflected in its art. In the Early Dynastic period (3000–2370 B.C.) monumental palaces, rivaling the temples in size, appear as prominent features of the Sumerian cities. The land was subject to repeated foreign invasions and the city-states struggled among themselves for authority over neighboring areas. The newly important political and military leadership reflected in the appearance of these palaces is also indicated by the scenes

depicted on the "Ur Standard." The fortunes of such independent city-states as Ur, Uruk, Lagash, and Eridu rose or declined in a fitful pattern of dynastic dispute, with the land subject to repeated foreign invasion, and the city-states struggling among themselves for authority over neighboring areas. A fragment of a stele found at Lagash, the so-called Stele of the Vultures (because vultures are shown, with lions, devouring naked human corpses), records a victory of that city under its ruler Eannatum over the neighboring city of Umma. With the help of the god Ningirsu, Umma was conquered and its armies captured. But although such conflicts were frequent they were rarely decisive. The various city-states continued to exist as separate, contending entities, recognizing no single ruler or central authority.

Meanwhile, other areas outside the lower Mesopotamian valley and other peoples who infiltrated the valley were exposed to the influence of Sumerian civilization. To the east, in the foothills of what is now southern Iran, the Elamites, both in war and in peace, were in constant contact with the urban Mesopotamian centers, and they absorbed the main elements of Sumerian culture. For century after century, Semitic tribesmen moved in from the deserts and the mountains to the west and north, intermingling with the Sumerians. These immigrants assimilated Sumerian culture so thoroughly that in time little but their language differentiated them from the original inhabitants of the valley.

The first ruler to bring the land of Sumer under one authority was Lugalzaggisi, king of Uruk. According to his inscribed records, which may be exaggerated, he extended the sway of the Sumerians from the Persian Gulf to the shores of the Mediterranean. His despotic reign was challenged and overthrown by the first great Semitic ruler of Mesopotamia, Sargon, a king whose exploits are abundantly docu-

133

Under the Akkadian dynasty, power was centered increasingly in the ruler. Sargon's grandson Naram-sin took a title that had belonged to certain gods—King of the Four Quarters of the World—and was himself deified. A magnificent expression of his divinity is the pink sandstone stele below, on which, wearing the horned helmet of the gods, he stands over two foes as a third falls headlong and others plead for mercy. His men, shown smaller in stature, follow him up the wooded mountain slope; but the king stands alone at the summit, close to the great gods whose stars appear overhead. The rulers of Ur's Third Dynasty also assumed the attributes of divinity; in the seal impression at right, a king sits enthroned as a goddess ushers a worshiper into his presence. Bronze figures, like the one at far right, depicting a kneeling deity driving a peg into the ground, were sometimes used as foundation deposits for new structures.

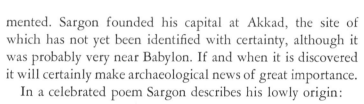

mented. Sargon founded his capital at Akkad, the site of which has not yet been identified with certainty, although it was probably very near Babylon. If and when it is discovered it will certainly make archaeological news of great importance.

In a celebrated poem Sargon describes his lowly origin:

Sargon the mighty king, king of Akkad, am I.
My mother was a changeling, my father I knew not.
The brothers of my father loved the hills.
My city is Azupiranu, which is situated on
    the banks of the Euphrates.
My changeling mother conceived me, in secret
    she bore me.
She set me in a basket of rushes, with bitumen
    she sealed my lid.
She cast me into the river which rose not
    over me.
The river bore me up and carried me to Akki,
    the drawer of water.
Akki lifted me out as he dipped his ewer.
Akki . . . appointed me as his gardener.
While I was his gardener, Ishtar granted me her love,
And for four and . . . years I exercised kingship.

To judge from a handsome bronze head found at Nineveh and often identified as a portrait of Sargon, this great king could easily pass for a Bedouin sheik of today, with his full, sensuous lips, strong aquiline profile, luxuriantly curled hair, and noble beard. He was evidently a born general capable of far-ranging strategic maneuver. He must also have had considerable armies at his command to achieve the total subjugation not only of Mesopotamia but of its neighbors. His strategic sense is evident from the manner in which he achieved his conquest. Before he attacked the Sumerian city-states to the south, he was careful to protect and consolidate his posi-

tion by taking the northern towns of Mari, Assur (one of the capitals of Assyria), and Arbil. Then, in a short time, his armies overran the Sumerian cities and established him as "King of Sumer and Akkad," the greatest to bear that name.

Sargon was more than a soldier with a knack for winning battles; he was a man of statesmanlike ability. By his conquests he incorporated the Sumerian city-states into an empire which extended westward possibly to the Mediterranean coast, eastward to Iran, and northward into Syria—an Akkadian empire which lasted about a century and a half. His energetic grandson Naram-sin pushed the frontiers into the mountains of Asia Minor, proudly boasting that he was "King of the Four Quarters of the World."

The Semites of Akkad had long traded with the Sumerians, they had adopted the Sumerian gods, and they had borrowed Sumerian script for writing their own language. But with the new-found political unity imposed by Sargon a fresh spirit finds expression in Mesopotamian culture. This is clearly evident in the plastic arts. One has only to compare the lithe, fluid line of the sculptured soldiers on the Stele of Naram-sin with the rigid, hieratic figures on Eannatum's Stele of the Vultures to notice the change. Both commemorate military victories, but that is practically all they have in common. Eannatum's stele has great historical value, but Naram-sin's is a wonderful work of sculpture. With only fifteen figures, two formalized trees, a few upward-surging lines culminating in a conventional peak, the sculptor has depicted the successful attack by Naram-sin's armies on an enemy's mountain stronghold. The whole scene is alive with movement: the steady upward march of the Akkadian monarch's troops, an enemy falling back dying, another plunging from a rocky ledge, a third clasping his hands in entreaty, while towering over all stands the heroic figure of the king.

Semitic influence shows itself in other ways, for example, in more realistic portrait sculpture and the vigorous treatment of animals, especially lions and bulls. Equally remarkable is the art of the engraver. The cylinder seals of this period writhe with life: Gilgamesh grappling with a buffalo, and on another seal locking his powerful arms around a struggling lion, snapping its neck. There is an almost explosive quality in these tiny designs which foreshadows the terrifying violence of Assyrian art in later times.

A second and more permanent effect of the Akkadian conquest was the spread of the cuneiform writing system throughout the entire Near East. Akkadian became the official language of diplomacy and was used in business transactions in lands beyond Mesopotamia for many centuries. The Sumerian language was still written, but in time it became a "learned" language, like the Latin of the Middle Ages in Europe that survived in schools and in religious rituals.

There were further dynastic changes in Mesopotamia, of which only the broadest outline concerns us here. An invasion by eastern barbarians, the Guti from the Zagros Mountains, a people "who knew not kingship," destroyed what was left of Sargon's Akkadian empire late in the third millennium. Once again there was disorganization in the land of Sumer.

The city of Lagash managed, probably by paying tribute, to escape the general chaos caused by the Guti. Its governor, Gudea, beautified Lagash with temples and palaces and with sculptures of such quality that they have become famous in our own day. Few people interested in the ancient world can not have seen these serene statues with piously folded hands, Sumerian in their static dignity and repose, but carved out of hard diorite with the skilled precision of the best Akkadian workmanship. Most of these represent Gudea himself, and like virtually all Mesopotamian portraits they were intended to show the worshiper in ceaseless vigil confronting his god in the temple. A remarkable man, he ruled Lagash at least fifteen years, but for some reason never took the title of king. In time Sumer revived under a new line of kings ruling from some of the older Sumerian cities, notably Ur and Uruk. This Neo-Sumerian Period, which covered most of the twenty-second to the twenty-first centuries B.C., marked a new golden age, in which such kings as Ur-Nammu and Dungi created enormous buildings during what is called the Third Dynasty of Ur. Of these the greatest was undoubtedly the great Ziggurat of the Moon God at Ur, the remains of which can still be seen on the lower plains of Mesopotamia. Even in decay it is impressive, but in its original glory it reared into the sky to a height of eighty feet and, with its steep flights of stairs rising to the topmost tower, it must have been comparable in splendor to the Egyptian pyramids. This achievement is even more remarkable when one considers that the largest building unit was but a small brick fifteen inches long.

Ur-Nammu was responsible for this and other buildings which lent luster and importance to his own capital. In fact he rebuilt a substantial part of the city. His dynasty endured for more than a century, and during this Sumerian renaissance, literature flourished. It was in this period that scribes compiled many of the memorable examples of Mesopotamian literature that survive today. Weights and measures were standardized. Trade, overseas and overland, seems to have been extended even as far as the Indus Valley, indirect though this latter contact may have been.

Toward the end of the third millennium B.C. the power of the last Sumerian dynasties cracked under another invasion, this time by the Elamites from Iran and by the Amorites from the northwest, who established themselves at several places in the valley and whose cities flourished. For about a hundred years there was internecine warfare as the various city-states of Mesopotamia—Isin, Larsa, and Eshnunna in the south, Assur in the north, and Mari on the middle Euphrates—struggled for supremacy, until Babylon became the dominant power under Hammurabi in the eighteenth century B.C.

Of all these contending cities Mari is particularly interesting, for here in fairly recent years French excavators under Parrot have revealed a Mesopotamian city of the early second millennium, in a unique state of preservation. Temples, palaces, dwelling houses, cemeteries, superb works of sculpture, painted frescoes, and no less than twenty-five thousand cuneiform tablets have been brought to light, revealing, in Parrot's words, "hitherto undreamt-of aspects of the Mesopotamian genius." The plan of the great palace that has been uncovered is staggering in its complexity. It contains over two hundred and fifty rooms, ranging from the residential quarters of the king, through the scribal school (where the tablets were found), to the stewards' offices and storerooms. With its large central courts, its wall paintings, throne room, and maze of storage magazines, the palace at Mari is reminiscent of that at Knossos in Crete. The flounced dresses of the women shown in the brightly colored frescoes, the spiral bands, and certain naturalistic details in the decoration are also a little like the paintings found in Minoan Crete. It

would be unwise to overstress these resemblances, but they do suggest a cultural contact between the two lands.

Of all the ruined cities of Mesopotamia, Mari brings one closest to the spirit of those long-dead people. Here are the temples in which they performed those strange, complicated rites in honor of their gods; here are the sculptured figures in stone and bronze of deities, worshipers, and hieratic beasts, which once adorned their courts; here, opening out of a labyrinth of corridors, are the very rooms in which scribes made and filed their records, copied those poems and proverbs, the medical and mathematical lore, and other writings of varied interest, depositing, like bees in a honeycomb, the hoarded richness of two thousand years of civilization.

On a wall of one of the courts could be seen the painting, reproduced on pages 162 and 163, which appears to show the investiture of the king of Mari. A goddess in a narrow, flounced skirt and tall headdress presents the king, who receives from Ishtar the royal insignia. Winged, human-headed beasts, faintly recalling both the Egyptian sphinx and the Minoan griffin, flank the picture; two other goddesses pour out ritual libations, and a powerful human-headed bull stands with foot upraised. As Parrot has suggested, these strange creatures who stand guard before stylized trees may be the precursors of those cherubim of the Old Testament who forbid access to Eden and the tree of life. Thus, too, in an adjoining panel, the four streams that gush forth from vases held by two goddesses may prefigure the four rivers of Paradise. In this and other Mari frescoes the main strands of Syrian and Mesopotamian civilization meet and mingle: the rigid, hieratic formalism of Sumer, and the freer, more fluid art of Syria—in this case represented by a delightfully naturalistic picture of two men climbing a date palm, apparently oblivious to the ceremony taking place below them. But it is one thing to see these paintings in a museum or reproduced in the pages of a book; it is quite another to walk immediately across the very floor upon which this and similar rites were performed. One can do that at Mari, but not, alas, in Babylon, which rose during the early years of the second millennium B.C. to become the great capital city of the land, subduing Mari in the process.

With the decline of the great Third Dynasty of Ur the last Sumerian revival had ended, and for the following fifteen centuries Semitic races dominated the civilization of Mesopotamia. Hammurabi was the sixth king of the Semitic dynasty that was founded at Babylon in the nineteenth century B.C. It was about 1792 B.C. that this great leader came to the throne, and during the forty-three years of his reign he built an empire whose glory lingers to the present day.

Although the Sumerians ceased to constitute a significant political or military force, the culture they had developed was fused with that of the newcomers. The names of the gods were subject to change, but their functions remained the same. Babylonian temples were elaborations of Sumerian prototypes, and the deities were worshiped much as before. Babylon's city god, Marduk, became the chief god of the Mesopotamian pantheon, and his temple called Esagila became the chief sanctuary of Hammurabi's empire.

CITIES OF
THE GODS

The world's earliest civilization arose some six thousand years ago in the marshlands of Sumer in southern Mesopotamia. There isolated farming settlements developed into the first cities, and in them evolved the earliest known system of writing. The city-states of Sumer remained separate and independent for more than a millennium, growing in size and wealth, and contending for supremacy. Sargon of Akkad, for whom the bearded, turbaned Akkadian above may have fought, succeeded in bringing them under a single rule, but his dynasty fell before barbarian tribes. Some cities prospered anew, only to be engulfed by fresh waves of invaders. For this pattern of recurrent conquest, which persists through Mesopotamian history, the terrain is partly responsible: as an aerial panorama of Ur suggests (overleaf), the flat valley land provides no natural defenses. Yet here, amid the scars of violent storms and floods, in cities ruled by the whims of the gods, was born a splendid culture whose spirit pervaded the ancient East.

The awe and utter dependence felt by the
Sumerian toward his gods are manifest in
these stone figurines from the Square
Temple at Tell Asmar. They were found
together near the altar of Shrine II (see
plan below). Most represent worshipers,
but the two tallest, with their enormous
eyes, may be a god and goddess, and the
clean-shaven man in front of them is a priest.

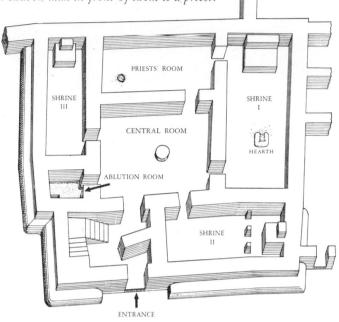

RELIGION

Religion in Sumer encompassed all of life: the will of the
gods might be discerned in the least phenomenon. The
most important deities in the Sumerian pantheon corre-
sponded to powerful elements in the cosmos—Anu the
heavens, Enlil the storm, Ninhursaga the earth, Enki the
waters of the earth. Man was merely the gods' servant;
they paid him little heed, but he sought constantly to win
their presence in his city and to earn their favor, for
everything depended on them. To this end the early city-
states were organized. Each was considered the property
of a god or goddess; the main shrine, atop the ziggurat,
was the deity's dwelling place, and the ensi or governor
of the city was his high priest. The ensi and his staff
parceled out land for private cultivation, supervised work
by citizens on the "common" and on the dikes and irrigation canals, kept records, regulated trade, administered
justice, and commanded the army. Fundamental to all these
duties was his role as interpreter of the divine will, revealed through signs or dreams. The ensi provided hospi-
tality for the god, whose image was fed and cared for with
all possible elegance. Though all men were considered
equal before the god, only the highest priests and officials could enter the temple shrine where his image rested.
The ordinary man required the intercession of a minor, personal god in order to appeal to one of the great deities.

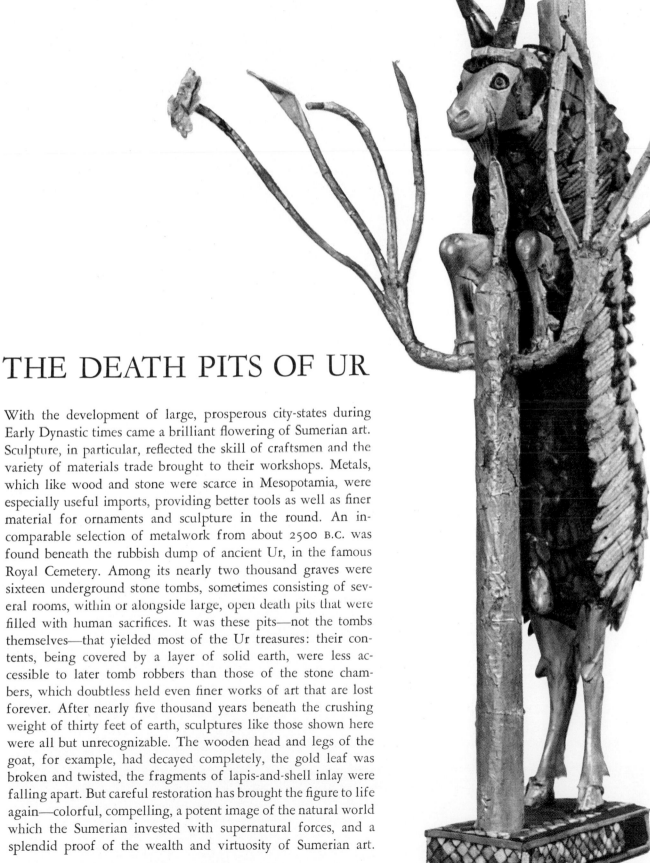

Animal and vegetal forms, symbolizing dual aspects of nature's fertility, were often combined in Sumerian art, but rarely with such elegance as in this figure of a goat and tree. Twenty inches high and made of gold foil, shell, and lapis over a wood core, it was found in the Royal Cemetery. So was the magnificent bull's head at left, which is attached to the sound box of a harp; the inlaid plaques show mythological figures, and animals as servants and musicians.

THE DEATH PITS OF UR

With the development of large, prosperous city-states during Early Dynastic times came a brilliant flowering of Sumerian art. Sculpture, in particular, reflected the skill of craftsmen and the variety of materials trade brought to their workshops. Metals, which like wood and stone were scarce in Mesopotamia, were especially useful imports, providing better tools as well as finer material for ornaments and sculpture in the round. An incomparable selection of metalwork from about 2500 B.C. was found beneath the rubbish dump of ancient Ur, in the famous Royal Cemetery. Among its nearly two thousand graves were sixteen underground stone tombs, sometimes consisting of several rooms, within or alongside large, open death pits that were filled with human sacrifices. It was these pits—not the tombs themselves—that yielded most of the Ur treasures: their contents, being covered by a layer of solid earth, were less accessible to later tomb robbers than those of the stone chambers, which doubtless held even finer works of art that are lost forever. After nearly five thousand years beneath the crushing weight of thirty feet of earth, sculptures like those shown here were all but unrecognizable. The wooden head and legs of the goat, for example, had decayed completely, the gold leaf was broken and twisted, the fragments of lapis-and-shell inlay were falling apart. But careful restoration has brought the figure to life again—colorful, compelling, a potent image of the natural world which the Sumerian invested with supernatural forces, and a splendid proof of the wealth and virtuosity of Sumerian art.

143

THE WARS
OF SARGON

A new chapter in the history of Sumer opened about 2300 B.C. when Sargon of Akkad brought all the city-states under his rule. In the past one city or another had won brief preeminence over its neighbors, and late in the twenty-fourth century B.C. Lugalzaggisi of Umma had gained military supremacy over all the cities. But, devoted as they were to local sovereignty and local gods, the Sumerians had never had a king who ruled over the whole land. Sargon was not a Sumerian but an Akkadian, a Semite from the north, and he probably shared the wider loyalties, based on kinship, that are common among Semitic peoples. For that reason he considered himself more than a local king, and after conquering all of Akkad he marched south, defeated Lugalzaggisi— whom he enclosed in a cage at Nippur, religious capital of Sumer, to signify his victory and his favor with the gods— and asserted authority over all of Sumer and Akkad. These two lands, despite different racial and linguistic roots, had been linked for centuries by a common culture, essentially Sumerian, so that Sargon was not considered a foreigner in the south. But with his accession stronger Akkadian elements began to appear in Mesopotamian art and statecraft. Sargon appointed his followers as governors of the Sumerian cities, and wooed the support of the people by setting himself up as their legal protector. Despite these measures the cities attempted periodically to regain their independence and were held in line only by force. To subdue them, safeguard his empire, and secure new trade routes to it Sargon waged no less than thirty-four wars. He established his borders to the east in Elam (now southern Iran), and to the north, in what was later Assyria; then he turned west toward Mari and the rich lands near the Mediterranean. According to one epic he led his army deep into Anatolia to protect the interests of Mesopotamian merchants who traded there. Sargon also had overseas contacts with Arabia and perhaps with the Indus Valley. He reigned for fifty-six years, and his dynasty remained in power, by dint of constant warfare, for two centuries.

This imposing Akkadian head of bronze, here slightly larger than actual size, reflects the majesty of Sargon, whom it is thought to portray. The eyes, inlaid with gems, were gouged out by thieves.

Infantrymen like these, marching with their spears upon their shoulders, fought in the frequent local wars that took place among the Sumerian city-states. Territorial disputes were a common cause of warfare. One, between the towns of Lagash and Umma, is recorded by the stele on which these soldiers are represented. The war was begun by the king of Umma, who removed a boundary stone and despoiled fields belonging to the patron god of Lagash. Lagash defeated him in battle, and marked a definitive boundary between the two cities by digging a ditch along the border and erecting shrines to the gods nearby to guard it.

Victory was celebrated by a feast such as that shown on the "Standard" from the Royal Cemetery at Ur. In the upper register the king sits facing his officers while, at the right, a female singer or dancer and a musician with a bull's-head harp provide entertainment. The middle register shows bulls, rams, and fish being taken to the banquet table. At the bottom are teams of captured onagers, and porters carrying other booty; two use packs with straps that cross the forehead. The mosaic, twenty-two inches long, adorned one side of a box.

Intertwined snakes, representing vital powers associated with Gudea's personal god, decorate this fragment of a steatite lamp or dish from his reign. The continuous, interlocking motif, common in Sumerian art, appears again on the plaque below, named for Dudu, a high priest of early Lagash, who stands at upper right. Behind him are the emblem of the city god Ningirsu—a lion-headed eagle grasping two lions—and a recumbent calf. Such plaques may have supported maces that were used in oath-taking ceremonies.

GUDEA,
RULER OF LAGASH

In the twenty-second century B.C. the city of Lagash stood like a sunny, tranquil island in a dark and threatening sea. Most of Sumer was then occupied by the Guti, a mountain people from the northeast who had overthrown the Sargonid Dynasty. Lagash probably maintained its freedom through a combination of military strength and payment of tribute to the invaders. Led by its outstanding governor, Gudea, the city enjoyed a period of exceptional prosperity and cultural attainment. Great new temples were built, old ones were reconstructed, and quantities of precious materials were imported to embellish these shrines. "They brought from Susa, from Elam, and the western lands copper for Gudea," one text reports; logs of cedar and ebony from distant forests, stone for statuary, gold and silver and alabaster—all these and more were shipped down the rivers to Lagash. The impulse was, as always in Sumer, service of the gods: the grandeur was for them, not for man. The more splendid their temples, the more likely they were to visit the city and allow it to flourish. A contemporary account tells how Gudea undertook the rebuilding of Ningirsu's temple. After the Tigris, which the god controlled, had failed to rise and flood the fields, Gudea retired in alarm to the sanctuary. There he dreamed of a winged figure, "boundless like heaven," with lions on his left and right—clearly Ningirsu himself. Gudea sought the advice of a goddess skilled at interpreting dreams, who told him first to offer the god gifts, and then to rebuild the temple. Gudea did so, saying: "Ningirsu, thy house I shall build for thee; but I have not my specific orders." The god replied with a promise to revive the floods: "I will call up in heaven a humid wind. It shall bring thee abundance from on high. And the country shall spread its hands upon riches in thy time." He also gave instructions for building the new temple. Gudea set to work, seeking the guidance of the god at every juncture, for a wrong step could provoke divine anger. The first brick, for example, was molded by the governor himself in an elaborate ceremony, and the finished product was reverentially displayed: "Like a pure crown lifted toward the sky . . . he brought it to his people." This spirit of piety which marked Gudea's reign was no doubt intensified by the circumstances threatening Lagash's prosperity. The gods granted the city deliverance from the Guti, but soon Lagash and the rest of Sumer came under the hand of a new master—Ur.

This statuette of Gudea, showing him wearing a simple robe and a woolen cap, is one of a series of more than thirty similar figures that document his governorship of Lagash. Carved from diorite, a very hard stone here polished to unusual brilliance, and seventeen inches in height, the statue emphasizes Gudea's strength and serene piety. It was placed in the temple to mediate between him and the god of the city and was thought to have a power of its own: Gudea addressed one such figure, "Statue, say to my king . . ."

The cuneiform texts on the prism at left comprise the Sumerian King List, which chronicles the passage of "the kingship" from one city of Sumer to another, from the time it was "lowered from heaven" till about 2000 B.C. The account was written in the incorrect belief that individual kings had always reigned over the whole land. In fact the first Sumerian king to rule over a united realm was Urnammu, founder of Ur's Third Dynasty. On a stele that may commemorate his building of the city's ziggurat, he appears (opposite above) pouring a libation before a seated god, who holds a measuring ring, line, and staff, the symbols of justice; and (below) carrying construction tools.

KINGS OF UR

Under the rule of the Third Dynasty of Ur, Sumer enjoyed its final century of greatness. Urnammu, first king of the dynasty, gained control of Sumer and Akkad in 2125 B.C. He transformed his city by erecting a series of magnificent buildings, of which the Ziggurat of the Moon God is the most famous. His son Dungi consolidated a Mesopotamian empire that enjoyed uncommon unity and peace. The Third Dynasty rulers departed from the tradition of local sovereignty; like the Akkadian kings they claimed national authority and divine status. But in spirit they remained Sumerian: they ruled as servants of the great gods, aware that kingship might be taken away at any time. In 2025 B.C. it was lost to Sumer forever; and two thousand years of Sumerian supremacy in Mesopotamia came to an end.

THE AGE OF
HAMMURABI

Land Between the Rivers · II

It used to be said of Hammurabi that he drew up the world's first legal code. At Susa, in Iran, explorers unearthed a diorite stele bearing his name and cuneiform inscriptions that set forth a comprehensive system of laws. This monolith, which had been carried to Susa by Elamite conquerors after one of their periodic raids on the Euphrates Valley and which may now be seen at the Louvre in Paris, is a document of enormous interest. However, we now know that though Hammurabi may have been one of the world's greatest law-givers and administrators, he had much earlier legal documents in the Sumerian language to draw upon. For instance, there exists the code of Lipit-Ishtar, the fifth ruler of the Dynasty of Isin, who ruled a century and a half before Hammurabi. Like Hammurabi's, this code consists of three parts —a prologue, the legal text, and an epilogue. In the prologue the king states: "I, Lipit-Ishtar, the humble shepherd of Nippur, the stalwart farmer of Ur . . . established justice in Sumer and Akkad in accordance with the word of Enlil . . . I made the father support his children and . . . the children support their father; I made the father stand by his children and . . . the children stand by their father . . ."

There are thirty-eight known laws in this code, some of which seem entirely equitable by our modern standards. For instance: "If a man turned his face away from his first wife . . . [but] she has not gone out of the house, his wife which he married as his favorite is a second wife; he shall continue to support his first wife . . . If a man's wife has not borne him children but a harlot from the public square has borne him children, he shall provide grain, oil, and clothing

Mesopotamian art became freer and more realistic under Akkadian influence. This finely modeled head of a divinity wearing a triple crown comes from a Sumerian city, but is Semitic in style.

for that harlot; the children which the harlot has borne him shall be his heirs, and as long as his wife lives the harlot shall not live in the house with his wife."

Another law code, written in Akkadian and found at Tell Obu Harmal near Baghdad, contains such practical regulations as the following: "If the boatman is negligent and causes the sinking of the boat, he shall pay in full for everything the sinking of which he caused. . . . The wages of a hired man are one shekel of silver; his provender is one pan of barley. He shall work for one month. . . . If an ox gores another ox and causes its death, both ox owners shall divide between themselves the price of the live ox and also the equivalent of the dead ox."

Another law, that was designed to protect the interests of a returned prisoner of war, strikes a familiar note to us today: "If a man has been made prisoner during a raid or an invasion or if he has been carried off forcibly and stayed in a foreign country for a long time, and if another man has taken his wife and she has borne him a son—when he returns, he shall get his wife back."

Still earlier codes, dating at least as far back as the celebrated Sumerian king Urnammu, have survived. But Hammurabi's much larger and more comprehensive code is one of the most important documents in human history. For here, nearly two thousand years before the codification of Roman law, is an organized and comprehensive legal system governing most human activities. There are laws concerning marriage, divorce (including a husband's responsibility for his wife's debts), property rights, liability for military service, sale of wine, deposits and debts, murder and assault, theft, and the responsibility of professional men to their clients. The death sentence was imposed for theft, adultery, bearing false witness in cases involving the defendant's life, and for

false accusations. There were also laws concerning agriculture, commerce, inheritance, adoption, wages, and slaves.

Although Babylonian women did not enjoy the same social status as men, their civil rights were safeguarded under Hammurabi's code. For instance, a wife whose husband neglected her could obtain a divorce, provided she could prove she had lived a blameless life. A concubine who had borne children to a man who sent her away was entitled to take with her whatever dowry she had brought to him, and he was obliged to give her an income from "field, garden, and movables" to support her and his offspring. It is an interesting fact that the higher the social rank of the injured party, the harsher were the penalties for crime. Some of the penalties imposed on negligent professional men seem excessive, but have a certain rough justice. If a doctor, through carelessness or inefficiency, caused his patient to lose the sight of an eye, he lost one of his own eyes. If a house fell on its owner, the builder of that house might be subject to death or at least to a heavy fine. However, contemporary records of lawsuits show that these more savage penalties were imposed only on rare occasions.

These rules of law as they were applied to all social classes in everyday affairs, and the numerous records of lawsuits that have survived, help to create a more intimate impression of this vanished world than can be gleaned from the physical remains of cities and temples and the lengthy chronicles of kings. But the picture would be still far from complete without permitting the ordinary men and women of Mesopotamia to speak for themselves. For this we must turn to the little cuneiform tablets on which the folk wisdom of the people was summed up in their proverbs. So many of these axioms and adages, recast in a modern idiom, would seem immediately familiar to us of the twentieth century.

A restless woman in the house
Adds ache to pain.

Who has not supported a wife or child,
His nose has not borne a leash.

We are doomed to die; let us spend;
We shall live long, let us save.

Who possesses much silver may be happy,
Who possesses much barley may be happy,
But who has nothing at all can sleep.

The poor man is better dead than alive;
If he has bread, he has no salt,
If he has salt, he has no bread,
If he has meat, he has no lamb,
If he has a lamb, he has no meat.

You can have a lord, you can have a king;
But the man to fear is the [tax collector].

Blunt, shrewd, and cynical, these are the typical complaints and observations of civilized human beings in any epoch. Here, at this very early stage of recorded history, the inevitable drawbacks of civilized life already begin to appear —the burden of taxation, the onerousness of military service, the responsibilities of wealth, the penalties of poverty, and the trials of married life.

But other Mesopotamian writings express the highest aspirations of mankind. There is the *Epic of Gilgamesh,* the story of the first great tragic hero known to history. This superb dramatic poem, most of it originally Sumerian, antedates the Homeric epics by at least fifteen hundred years. It was transmitted through the later Babylonians and Assyrians with some modifications, surviving for thousands of years amid the rubble of vanished ancient cities until its rediscovery

by archaeologists within the last century. Its hero, the mighty Gilgamesh, was a legendary king of Uruk, which claimed to be the oldest of Sumerian cities. "The theme of that story is twofold," the modern British scholar D. G. Bridson has written, "man's conquest of his environment and his yearning for immortality. . . . Out of a folk hero [the Sumerian poet and his successors] have created a symbol for mankind —transmuting a cycle of mythical adventures into a moving allegory of human courage and aspiration."

In the heroic figure of Gilgamesh are embodied the effort and striving, the terror and trials of the anonymous masses who contributed to what we label the Tell Halaf, al 'Ubaid, Uruk, and Jemdet Nasr cultures. With his close friend and companion, the formidable Enkidu, he invades the mountain forests to fell a cedar, probably an allegorical summary of the innumerable forays made by Sumerian plainsmen into the hostile uplands in quest of the wood they lacked and needed. They enter the dark ranks of cedars and confront the god Humbaba, the frightful guardian of the forest and, according to modern interpretations of the epic, a symbol of evil.

And it was only the last barrier of the mountain forests,
Lined up elbow to elbow like infantry,
That was an irritation to them . . .
For the clustering cedars
Made the way difficult and the going slow.
And as a first indication of their true intentions
In those parts, both Gilgamesh and Enkidu
Set their hands to the axes and attacked the trees . . .
Then the forest god Humbaba, struck back
And leaping up fully armed at the first onslaught
They fought back valiantly at the malignant anger
Unleashed upon them . . . And there was no pausing
For axes then, but swung swords began the sickling

Of all between them and that scourge . . . and the whirlwind
Scoured after them through agony of the cedar trees
Like a searching of bullwhips . . . and the thunderbolts
Bounced off the body-armor of those two heroes—
A pattern of spent sparks off an anvil . . . And lightning crackled
About them balefully while they struck new knotted
Virulences of light out of the flame-forks
And cut them down . . . And there was just no harness
To put upon fighting bulls like those, as they drove on—
Battering down, trampling, and crushing the indiscriminate
Heart out of that anger—forcing a final
Stranglehold of subjection upon their danger . . ."

That is Bridson's paraphrase of passages from the epic. Below, in a more literal translation of a later cycle, is the story of how Gilgamesh, fearing death and longing for immortality, approached the sun god Utu:

"O Utu, a word I would speak to you, to my word your ear,
I would have it reach you, give ear to it.
In the city Man dies, oppressed is the heart,
Man perishes, heavy is the heart.
I peered over the wall,
Saw the dead bodies . . . floating in the river;
As for me, I too will be served thus; verily it is so.
Man, the tallest, cannot reach heaven,
Man, the widest, cannot cover the earth.
Not yet have brick and stamp brought forth the fated end.
I would enter the 'land,' I would set up my name,
In its places where the names have been raised up . . ."

"I would set up my name . . ." It is man's eternal attempt to arrest the current of time, to set a lasting stamp upon life, before he moves on to the unknown realm of the dead.

Many of the tablets from which we learn so much of Babylonian civilization, and its inheritance from ancient Sumer,

date from the first half of the second millennium B.C. and are written in Sumerian cuneiform. The rest, translations and modifications of earlier versions, were found among the remains of the library formed at Nineveh by Assurbanipal, "written down according to the original and collated in the palace" of this last great king to rule the Assyrian empire before it collapsed in the seventh century B.C.

Among those archives was found a version of the story of the Deluge, incorporated with the Gilgamesh epic but derived from independent poems which in the earliest known forms date about fifteen hundred years before the biblical story of Noah was set down, not earlier than 800 B.C., by a Hebrew scribe. This is not to suggest that the Hebrews were not familiar with the story at a much earlier date. There is every indication that the two versions stem from a common tradition. (There is no archaeological evidence of one great deluge in Mesopotamia, although the valley was subject to periodic local inundations, as Woolley discovered in his diggings at Ur, and these floods may have been disastrous within their limits.) As it was transcribed from the Assyrian archives the story reveals a close resemblance to the account in Genesis, as may be judged from the following excerpts.

Man of Shuruppak, son of Ubar-Tutu
Tear down this house, build a ship!
Give up possessions, seek thou life.
Forswear worldly goods and keep the soul alive!
Aboard the ship take thou the seed of all living things.
The ship that thou shalt build,
Her dimensions shall be to measure.
Equal shall be her width and her length.
Like the Apsu shalt thou ceil her. . . .
Ten dozen cubits each edge of the square deck.
I laid out the contours and joined her together. . . .

Then comes the dramatic description of the Deluge itself:

Consternation over Adad reaches to the heavens,
Who turned to blackness all that has been light.
The wide land was shattered like a pot!
For one day the south-storm blew,
Gathering speed as it blew, [submerging the mountains],
Overtaking the [people] like a battle.
No one can see his fellow,
Nor can one be recognized from heaven.

But the hero in his ship escapes disaster, riding the flood until at last the vessel comes to rest on "Mount Nisir."

Mount Nisir held the ship fast,
  Allowing no motion. . . .
When the seventh day arrived,
I sent forth and set free a dove.
The dove went forth, but came back;
Since no resting place for it was visible, she turned round.
Then I sent forth and set free a swallow.
The swallow went forth, but came back;
Since no resting place for it was visible, she turned round.

And so on until at last the flood finally recedes; a "raven went forth and, seeing that the waters had diminished, he eats, circles, caws, and turns not round."

Babylonian boys of good families who were sent to school to learn writing would probably have been obliged to copy such portions of the Gilgamesh epic, as well as other tales, hymns, lamentations, and wisdom literature, to familiarize themselves with the Sumerian language and the cuneiform writing system. The schoolboy also learned the timeless myths surrounding Enki, Enlil, Inanna, and other deities, much as our youngsters memorize passages of our own great classics.

Although the women of Mesopotamia were permitted some independence, they were not as free as their contemporaries in Egypt. Their lives, like those of their modern descendants, revolved about the home. Like the amiable Sumerian lady shown at right holding hands with her spouse, women were generally treated tenderly by their husbands. If they were not, they could have recourse to laws that offered protection to ill-used wives. The terra-cotta plaque reproduced on the facing page depicts a woman nursing her child. Next to her, a high-born Elamite lady is shown spinning while an attendant fans her.

And probably at that age they bored him as much. But writing was the first essential step to any kind of responsible office within the hierarchy. The following, although written by a Sumerian schoolmaster for amusement, probably sums up fairly accurately the behavior and attitude of a typical pupil, of that era as well as of ours:

"[Arriving at school in the morning] I recited my tablet, ate my lunch, prepared my new tablet, wrote it, finished it; then they assigned me my oral work . . . When school was dismissed, I went home, entered the house, and found my father sitting there. I told my father of my written work, then recited my tablet to him, and my father was delighted. . . . When I awoke early in the morning, I faced my mother and said to her: 'Give me my lunch [one hopes he said "please"], I want to go to school.' My mother gave me two 'rolls' and I set out . . . In school the monitor in charge said to me, 'Why are you late?' Afraid and with pounding heart, I entered before my teacher and made a respectful curtsy."

The schoolboy learned how to write first by making individual signs and then by combining them in complete words. To help him, long word lists were written out on clay tablets—lists of insects, birds, stones, minerals, countries, cities, and so on, which were intended to be copied by primary students. A considerable number of these "text books" have been unearthed, dating from the latter half of the second millennium. Numeration was also taught as a preparation for the study of arithmetic. Addition and subtraction, multiplication and division sufficed for ordinary account keeping. Students intended for higher posts would go on to more complex mathematics, which included algebra and geometry and which were taught, as they are today, by the setting and solving of problems.

The following is one from the time of Hammurabi:

" 'An area A, consisting of the sum of two squares is 1000. The side of one square is 2/3 of the side of the other square, diminished by 10. What are the sides of the square?'

"This leads to the equations:
$$x^2 + y^2 = 1000$$
$$y = 2/3x - 10$$

of which the solution can be found by solving the quadratic equation

$$\frac{13}{9} x^2 - \frac{40}{3} x - 900 = 0$$

which has one possible solution: $x = 30$."

In the actual cuneiform text, however, the problem is solved by simple enumeration of the numerical steps that must be taken. In a thorough treatment of the subject, the mathematician Dirk J. Struik notes that while the Egyptians of the same period could solve simple linear equations, the Babylonians also knew how to work with quadratic equations in two variables, as well as with cubic and biquadratic equations. The Babylonians had multiplication tables based on a well developed sexagesimal system, and they were the first people to indicate the value of a number by its position in a line of numbers; thus 1 followed by another 1 was equal to 61 (using the figure 60 as a unit as we would use the unit 10 in our decimal system).

It was obviously much more efficient to use this system in writing numbers than it was to employ the system developed so much later by the Romans. It was of particular advantage when dealing with hundreds and thousands. Our division of the hour into 60 minutes, or 3600 seconds, and of the circle into 360 degrees is an inheritance from the sexagesimal system of early Mesopotamian times.

Mathematical skills would be needed by a student if he wished to become, say, a builder, surveyor, land appraiser,

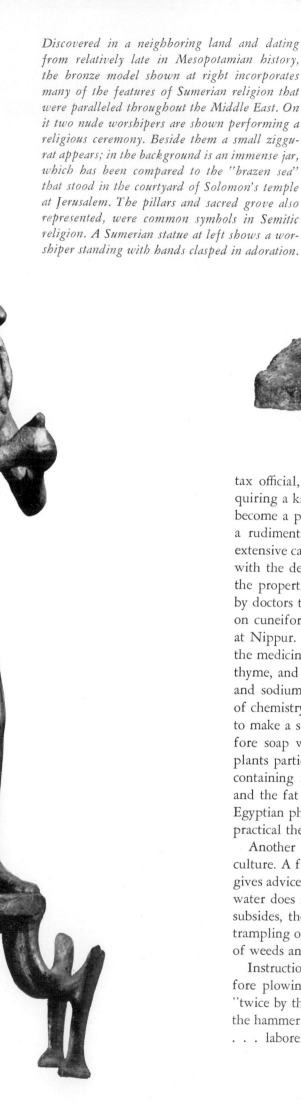

Discovered in a neighboring land and dating from relatively late in Mesopotamian history, the bronze model shown at right incorporates many of the features of Sumerian religion that were paralleled throughout the Middle East. On it two nude worshipers are shown performing a religious ceremony. Beside them a small ziggurat appears; in the background is an immense jar, which has been compared to the "brazen sea" that stood in the courtyard of Solomon's temple at Jerusalem. The pillars and sacred grove also represented, were common symbols in Semitic religion. A Sumerian statue at left shows a worshiper standing with hands clasped in adoration.

tax official, or temple astronomer—to perform any job requiring a knowledge of measurement. But he might wish to become a physician instead, in which case he would acquire a rudimentary knowledge of anatomy and surgery and an extensive catalogue of incantations and exorcisms for dealing with the demons who caused sickness. He would also learn the properties of many drugs, some of which are still used by doctors today. Over five hundred such drugs are recorded on cuneiform tablets discovered by American archaeologists at Nippur. Sumerian and Babylonian physicians understood the medicinal properties of such plants as myrtle, asafoetida, thyme, and cassia, and of such minerals as potassium nitrate and sodium chloride. They commanded enough knowledge of chemistry to be able to make filtrates, and discovered how to make a substance resembling soap, thousands of years before soap was "invented" in Europe. The ashes of certain plants particularly rich in soda were mixed with a substance containing natural fats; the interaction between this alkali and the fat produced a soap-like ointment. Like the ancient Egyptian physicians, Sumerian doctors were able to prescribe practical therapy for cases of ophthalmia and earache.

Another subject that might have been taught was agriculture. A free interpretation of one tablet, in which a farmer gives advice to his son, directs: "Care must be taken that their water does not rise too high over the field; when the water subsides, the wet ground must be carefully guarded against trampling oxen and other prowlers; the field must be cleared of weeds and stubble and fenced about."

Instructions are given for the breaking of the ground before plowing, which, the young farmer learned, should be "twice by the mattock and once by the hoe. Where necessary the hammer must be used to pulverize clods. . . . Stand over . . . laborers and see to it they [do] not shirk their work."

"Keep an eye on the man who puts in the barley seed," the instructions continue, "that he make the seed fall two fingers uniformly." Then follows some careful advice about stages of growth at which the crops must be watered, on the treatment of a certain plant disease called *samana,* and about manners of harvesting, threshing, and winnowing the grain.

But these great scribal schools were more than mere vocational training centers. It has been suggested by the noted scholar Samuel Noah Kramer that they resembled modern universities; the teachers did more than teach. They were also engaged in scientific study, or in copying and editing ancient literature. But like the medieval universities of Europe, the schools were closely linked with religion. The texts copied were often the sacred myths. The stars were studied in order to determine the exact timing of the annual religious festivals. Mathematical learning was applied to measure land, much of which probably belonged to the god of the city. And many "graduates" of the scribal schools became priests.

The mathematical problems, the schoolboy's essays, the medical pharmacopoeia provide us with an immediate, understandable link with the past. And there are hundreds of similar links. But if the student rose to high rank in the priestly hierarchy, he would have to give equal attention to learning spells and rituals which to us seem little more than black magic, although they were just as serious and meaningful to him as the mathematical problems were. The ritual to be followed when covering the temple kettledrum, for instance, runs on for about one hundred and fifty lines of closely written cuneiform instructions. An unblemished black bull had to be led into a certain chamber whose floor had been purified with water; it was placed on a reed mat, and its legs were tied "with a bond made of goat's hair." Seven loaves of barley bread, seven loaves of emmer bread, honey

Nude, with two enormous jars balanced on their heads, the two men shown wrestling above may be participating in a religious ritual whose significance is still not understood by scholars. The pair probably served as the base of an offering stand. Throughout Mesopotamian history, votive statues such as the ones shown on these pages were deposited in sanctuaries. These wrestlers, found in the temple at Tell Agrab, date from the first half of the third millennium.

and cream, dates, flour, wine, beer, and milk were to be offered to the god. This however was only the beginning. Before the bull was sacrificed, the practitioners were instructed, "You shall draw the curtains shut. On the bull you shall perform the rite of Washing the Mouth. . . . You shall whisper through a reed tube into the bull's left ear the incantation entitled *Alpu ilittu Zi attama* . . . You shall draw a ring of *zisurra*-flour around the bull. Standing at its head you shall sing [the composition called] *Nitugki niginna* to the accompaniment of a bronze *halhallatu*. . . . Then you shall cut open that bull and start a fire with cedar. You shall burn the bull's heart with cedar . . . and *mashatu*-flour before the kettledrum. You shall remove the tendon of its left shoulder and shall bury the body of that bull (wrapped) in a single red . . . cloth. You shall throw some *gunnu*-oil on it (and) arrange it so that its face points to the west. . . ." And so on through line after line.

It is worth noting the precision with which the rite is described. We may be sure that if one small detail were omitted the spell would be considered ineffective, as in modern science the least deviation from correct and controlled procedure can be disastrous. The world of the Babylonians, like the worlds of the ancient Egyptians, the Hittites, the Maya, and others, was controlled by supernatural forces, and magic was employed as a practical, systematic technique to control those forces. Its aims, at least, approximated those of science, but its practices were undifferentiated from the religious observances which, in all these ancient societies, gave form to human fears and aspirations.

In one case, however, science did emerge from superstition. The Babylonians believed that the movements of the heavenly bodies controlled the life of man. The precise observations they made in following the progress of the planets and the stars gave rise to the science of astronomy. They identified the major constellations. They named the planets we call Mercury, Venus, Mars, Jupiter, and Saturn after the gods of their own pantheon, Nabu, Ishtar, Nergal, Marduk, and Ninurta, and watched their position in the sky to determine the will of these deities. They studied eclipses of the sun and moon and tried to predict them. If one occurred at a certain time, it might mean that agricultural prices would rise, or that the king would die and his dynasty come to an end. They developed the zodiac, as a map of the sky, the route along which the heavenly bodies traveled. With its aid, astronomers were able to cast horoscopes, and determine which days were propitious and which malign. Most of the surviving cuneiform literature treating with astronomy dates from late in Babylonian history, but the omens to which the observations are linked are very ancient, and it is evident that the Babylonians had long been attentive to the heavens.

They studied the sky with awe and foreboding, for baleful forces were always to be feared. The earth too was full of dangers, and it was to guard against them that the god Marduk, who represented order, was forced to battle anew each year against the powers of chaos, represented by the goddess Tiamat, as he had before the creation of the world.

(Echoes of this ancient story occur in the Bible, when the prophets and the psalmist rejoice at God's conquest of Leviathan.) In celebration of the battle between Marduk and Tiamat, there was an annual festival in Mesopotamia, usually held in the spring before the vegetation had sprouted and while the land was still in bondage to the forces of death. At Babylon, the statues of the gods were assembled in one room in the temple of Esagila; there they conferred all of their divine powers on Marduk, so that his triumph would be assured. As the priests in the temple recited the great mythological account of Marduk's struggle, the populace fought mock battles in the streets of the town, hoping to promote the victory of their god through sympathetic magic. Marduk represented the spirit of vegetation, as well as order, and his victory would promise fertility for the forthcoming year. To help secure fertility, the king engaged in ritual intercourse within the precincts of the temple with one of the temple prostitutes, as another act of sympathetic magic. But these rituals were not enough; the gods still had to be assembled once more to ratify the favorable destiny of the city, before survival during the forthcoming year could be assured.

It was during religious festivals such as this, when strangers flocked into the towns, that the temple prostitutes were most assiduously employed. These women were divided into two classes. The "brides of the god" were votaries who supposedly served the pleasures of the god each night. The others, ordinary temple prostitutes, accommodated the citizens of the town, and travelers. Babylonians felt no compunction about the public display of love. Indeed, the public squares and streets of the town were considered appropriate places for love-making. Harlots who made their headquarters in the taverns provided competition for the temple prostitutes. The tavern strumpets were so liberally rewarded that many amassed ample dowries, and made respectable marriages upon termination of their careers.

The "Town of the Sacred Courtesans" was Uruk, a place sacred to Ishtar, the goddess of love, beauty, and fertility; she is only the Sumerian goddess Inanna given a Semitic name. Ishtar was the courtesan of the gods. One of her hymns proclaims that she is "clothed with pleasure and love."

Some of the elements of ancient civilization coincide with our own, and can be isolated. Such are the more practical forms of medicine, advances in astronomy, architecture, engineering, and mathematics, and those expressions of human emotions which we still can share. Other elements, however, can quickly shatter the comforting illusion that these remote ancestors of ours are "just like us." In many ways, they are also similar to members of primitive African or South American tribes, which still live today under the influence of witch doctors and rain makers. Certainly the culture of Babylon and Mesopotamia was sophisticated, highly organized, and basically a culture of civilized men. But it was still rooted in the practices of those primitive ancestors of the Sumerians who moved down from their hills to settle in the marshy country along the banks of the Tigris and Euphrates Rivers, six, seven, and eight thousand years ago.

THE GREAT KING
OF BABYLON

Before embarking on his conquest of neighboring lands, Hammurabi ruled as king of Babylon for thirty years. He devoted much of that time to strengthening his army; several clauses of his law code are designed to ensure that conscripts do not evade military service. When the king finally did begin his wars, his progress was swift. He conquered the Sumerian cities to the south and seized control of the powerful kingdom of Elam. In the north he subjugated Assyria and mounted two campaigns against the city of Mari, which finally succumbed to his power. The stone portrait above may represent the king; on it the sculptor has sensitively recorded the marks of age and care. A fresco from the palace of Mari, which Hammurabi destroyed, is shown on the following two pages. It depicts a religious ceremony watched over by the gods. In one corner a delightful genre scene shows two men climbing a date palm, on which a large bird is perched, a peaceful contrast to the fierce animals common in Mesopotamian art.

THE CITY OF MARI

Commanding the caravan route between Mesopotamia and the Mediterranean ports, the ancient city of Mari reached the zenith of its power at the beginning of the second millennium. It was so famous as a center of wealth and sophistication that one foreign prince felt his education incomplete until he visited its palace. The archives that have been discovered at Mari date from this period. They include letters that chronicle military expeditions, as well as reports from petty functionaries. "The king gave me a chariot," one official complains, "but during my circuits across the country and the mountains this chariot was broken . . . And now when I must go here and there I no longer have a chariot to drive." Although chariots have been outmoded, the official's problem can still evoke a sympathetic response today. Several dispatches from Mari's ambassadors at Hammurabi's court also sound curiously modern; they are deceptively reassuring about the peaceful intentions of the king whose armies eventually conquered the city.

Helmeted warriors like the one at left fought in Mari's final battles.

Best preserved of all the royal residences discovered in Mesopotamia so far, the palace at Mari (opposite) covered more than eight acres. The statue of a goddess (shown above) was found at the site. In her hands, the figure holds a vase through which libations could be poured. The sculptor has shown the vase overflowing with water, which streams down along her skirt. Flowing water, which symbolized fertility, was an important motif in the art and religion of Mesopotamia. The worshiper carrying a sacrificial lamb to the altar (right) was another ancient religious motif; it survived in Christian art in representations of the Good Shepherd.

THE LAW CODE
OF HAMMURABI

On the capital of the stele on which his law code is written, Hammurabi is shown standing on a mountaintop before the sun god Shamash (above). The god, his shoulders aflame, orders Hammurabi to write down the law for his people. The praying figure opposite has its hands and face, the noblest parts of the body, covered with gold leaf; dedicated as a votive offering for the king's well-being by one of his subjects, the statue represents either Hammurabi himself or the donor, Awil-nannar.

In the epilogue to his law code Hammurabi recorded the benefits that his rule had conferred on the people of Sumer and Akkad. "I, Hammurabi, the perfect king, was not . . . neglectful of the black-headed people [the Sumerians] . . . I sought out peaceful regions for them; I overcame grievous difficulties; I caused light to rise on them. . . . I made an end of war; I promoted the welfare of the land; I made the people rest in friendly habitations . . . In my bosom I carried the peoples of the land of Sumer and Akkad; they prospered under my protection . . . I sheltered them in my wisdom in order that the strong might not oppress the weak, that justice might be dealt the orphan and the widow." The inscription goes on to commemorate the placement of Hammurabi's law code in a temple where anyone could consult it. "In Babylon . . . in Esagila, the temple whose foundations stand firm like heaven and earth, I wrote my precious words on my stele, and in the presence of the statue of me, the king of justice, I set it up in order to administer the law of the land, to prescribe the ordinances of the land, to give justice to the oppressed. . . . Let any oppressed man who has a cause come into the presence of the statue of me, the king of justice, and then read carefully my inscribed stele . . . may he understand his cause; may he set his mind at ease!"

Hammurabi is best known today for his law code, but he also established the foundations of a Babylonian kingdom that managed to survive for almost two hundred years, a period that marked the zenith of Old Babylonian civilization. The king improved irrigation to increase the cultivable land within his realm, and established halting and watering places. He strengthened his army by imposing harsh penalties on those who failed to respond to conscription, which was compulsory for all; only indispensable men, such as a town's one baker, were exempted. His religious reforms were as important as his legal ones. Mesopotamian religion was centralized about the Esagila temple at Babylon, with Marduk as the supreme god of the pantheon. The king restored many provincial temples, but the age in which each Sumerian city was devoted solely to its local god had long since passed. Each city still worshiped its own deity, but now it also owed allegiance to the cult of Marduk, god of Babylon, who assumed the role of protagonist in the ancient Sumerian myth that described the triumph of order over the forces of chaos.

BABYLONIAN LIFE

During the age of Hammurabi, Babylonian society was divided into three classes. Landowners, government officials, and the rich merchants who made the city of Babylon a thriving commercial center comprised the upper class. As a mark of status, they never shaved their hair, in the reverse of the Egyptian custom. The lower class was called the *muskenu* and consisted of men without land of their own, either peasants who labored on the farms of the rich, or artisans in the towns. They served in the army, but not as soldiers; if they thirsted for military glory, they had to be content with following the troops as cooks or porters. Even though they had little power in society, they were still free men. Hammurabi's law code differentiates between these two classes in punishing crime. The upper class invariably had to pay a harsher penalty for wrongdoing; often the *lex talionis* was applied to a member of the upper class, when one of the *muskenu* could get away with merely paying a fine.

Hammurabi's empire also contained a large population of slaves, many of them obtained through purchase from abroad. Others were prisoners of war, descendants of slaves, or debtors who had been reduced to bondage. Slaves were branded on the forehead with the mark of their owner, which it was a crime to hide or remove. In many respects, however, they were humanely treated. If they were debtors, their service was limited by law to a few years, and if they were enterprising enough, they could run their own businesses and purchase freedom. They were even permitted to marry free men or women. Most Babylonian slaves belonged to the temples or to the royal court; it was rare that a family owned more than two or three of them.

Hammurabi's law code was completely secular in nature. There are a few sections that treat of temple property and votaries, but as a whole the clauses are concerned with the most mundane problems of commerce and family life, military service, adoption, slavery, and agriculture. As varied as the situations described in the law code are the many terra-cotta votive plaques that have been discovered, dating from the same period and showing the ordinary people of Mesopotamia in scenes of daily life. In the next column, excerpts from Hammurabi's law code appear next to descriptions of some of the plaques.

1) A nude female figure, perhaps a fertility talisman: "If a seignior wishes to divorce his wife who did not bear him children, he shall give her money to the full amount of her marriage price and he shall also make good to her the dowry which she brought from her father's house and then he may divorce her."

2) This street entertainer, with his performing monkeys, would be welcome at a tavern; more boisterous guests were frowned upon: "If outlaws have congregated in the establishment of a woman wine seller, and she has not arrested those outlaws and did not take them to the palace, that wine seller shall be put to death."

3) A married couple: "If a woman so hated her husband that she has declared, 'You may not have me,' her record shall be investigated at her city council, and if she . . . was not at fault, even though her husband has been going out and disparaging her greatly, that woman, without incurring any blame at all, may take her dowry and go off to her father's house. If she was not careful, but was a gadabout, thus neglecting her house and humiliating her husband, they shall throw that woman into the water."

4) A carpenter at work: "If a builder constructed a house for a seignior, but did not make his work strong, with the result that the house which he built collapsed and so has caused the death of the owner of the house, that builder shall be put to death."

5) Farmers in an orchard: "When a seignior borrowed money from a merchant and his merchant foreclosed on him and he has nothing to pay it back, if he gave his orchard after pollination to the merchant and said to him, 'Take for your money as many dates as there are produced in the orchard,' that merchant shall not be allowed; the owner of the orchard shall himself take the dates that were produced in the orchard and repay the merchant for the money . . . in accordance with the wording of his tablet . . .'"

6) A peasant riding upon an ox: "If a seignior hired an ox and has caused its death through carelessness or through beating, he shall make good ox for ox to the owner of the ox."

7) Two soldiers armed with throwsticks: "If either a private soldier or a commissary, whose dispatch on a campaign of the king was ordered, did not go or he hired a substitute and has sent him in his place, that soldier or commissary shall be put to death, while the one who was hired by him shall take over his estate."

The fierce bronze lion below was one of a pair guarding the entrance to a temple at Mari. Atop a cosmetic box (above) another lion is shown devouring a bull.

ANIMALS IN ART

Many of the clay tablets that school children copied in order to learn how to write contain long lists of animals. Some record the names of domestic beasts only; others list wild animals or different kinds of serpents. A third group catalogues imaginary beasts, such as the "great lion demon" and the "monstrous pig." These lists find a counterpart in Mesopotamian art, which is rich in representations of animals. Many are fantastic creatures—bulls with human faces, or lion-headed eagles. Sometimes wild animals are shown engaged in human activities, playing musical instruments, or serving at a banquet. In the earliest period of Sumerian history, animals were never shown solely for aesthetic reasons; their images always had a religious purpose as well and were designed to guard their owner or to ensure fertility in the herds. Occasionally that purpose is self-evident, as in the case of the small figures of dogs, which were buried under thresholds to protect houses. Eventually animal sculpture lost much of its magic significance and was used simply for decoration. In all periods, however, artists were exceptionally skilled in the representation of animals, which were often portrayed more realistically than humans.

The onager, or wild ass, seen at right standing atop a rein ring, was found in one of the royal tombs at Ur.

GILGAMESH

The hero Gilgamesh was as "strong as a savage bull." When he attacked, no one could withstand him. He conquered monsters and descended into the underworld, and dismayed even the gods with his strength. They created another powerful hero, Enkidu, to rival him, but Gilgamesh thwarted them by defeating and befriending the only man who might have been his equal. Gilgamesh was as proud as he was strong; he proclaims himself "most splendid among heroes . . . most glorious among men." In his pride and strength, as well as in his exploits, Gilgamesh is a prototype of later epic heroes. His descent into the underworld parallels that of Odysseus. His friendship and mourning for Enkidu foreshadows the story of Achilles and Patroclus. Again like Achilles, he is the son of a goddess who grieves at her child's sufferings. "Why, having given me Gilgamesh for a son," she complains to the sun god, "with a restless heart didst thou endow him?" The Gilgamesh story is also similar to the Greek epics in echoing history. When Gilgamesh consults the elders of his city before he battles an attacking enemy, his deference to them recalls the primitive democracy that once existed in Sumer.

The theme of a hero's struggle against two fierce beasts is a common one in Mesopotamian art. It is often supposed that representations of the contest illustrate the battle that Gilgamesh and Enkidu waged against the "bull of heaven," for many such scenes depict bulls as the conquered animals; but lions and mythological beasts also appear in confrontation with the hero. The small group of gold figures above shows the hero grappling with two bulls.

A detail (above) from the soundbox of a harp discovered in one of the royal tombs at Ur and illustrated in full on page 142 depicts the hero's conquest of two human-headed bulls. The primitive stone plaque at left, the support for a ceremonial macehead, is earlier in date. On it appears a man who is taming a pair of lions. Opposite is another, later representation of the hero's struggle, a detail of a fine Assyrian relief that shows him holding a lion cub.

The headless, life-size statue of an
Elamite queen, Napir-asu, that is shown
at left dates from the thirteenth century B.C., when Elamite power was at
its height. It was Napir-asu's husband
who built the five stage ziggurat at
Choga Zambil, near his capital of
Susa. The bronze statue of the
queen weighs almost two tons; cast in
one piece, it is a majestic example of
the skill of Elamite metalworkers. The
ceremonial axehead illustrated at upper
right was also discovered at Choga
Zambil. Its blade is of bronze; behind
it is the head of a boar, made of electrum and naturalistically rendered. The
bronze head shown below the axe may
portray an Elamite monarch or a priest.

THE ELAMITES

Waves of Semitic invaders sweeping in from the desert were not the only foreigners to assimilate the culture that the Sumerians had originated. In the north the Hurrians adopted some of the Mesopotamian gods. The Canaanites and Hebrews repeated Sumerian myths, and Mesopotamian artistic motifs reached as far as Greece. But of all the peoples outside Mesopotamia, it was the Elamites in the mountains and plains of southwestern Iran who were influenced most strongly. There were frequent trading contacts between the two lands, of which the most notable example was Gudea's expedition into Elam to bring back copper. There was warfare as well. Naram-sin, Sargon's grandson, seems to have made Elam an appendage to his empire. Years later an Elamite king marched against Ur and joined the coalition of forces that overthrew Sumerian hegemony for the final time. Susa, Elam's capital, eventually became one of the centers from which the Persian empire in later times dominated all of Mesopotamia for centuries.

It is in Elamite art that the contacts between the two cultures are most evident to us today. The earliest Sumerians derived many pottery styles from the area of Susa. In succeeding centuries the current was reversed, and many forms of Sumerian art were at home in Elam too. One of the finest remaining ziggurats is located at Choga Zambil in Elam; it was over one hundred sixty feet high. Like the Sumerians, the Elamites depicted fantastic animals, offering bearers, and presentation scenes that showed a worshiper before his god. They imitated decorative devices that had first been used in the Tigris-Euphrates Valley. Elamite art is often less sophisticated than that of the Sumerians, but at its finest it equaled and sometimes surpassed the Mesopotamian models on which it was based.

KINGS

OF THE

WORLD

Land Between the Rivers · III

After the death of Hammurabi, the Babylonian empire began to disintegrate. The incursion of the Kassites, an Indo-European tribe from the east, threw Mesopotamia into a turmoil. Kassite rulers conquered Babylon and all of southern Mesopotamia and controlled it for centuries, but their rule there was contested by other dynasties and other tribes. In this age of internecine warfare and foreign domination, the valley world declined culturally and politically.

With Babylon no longer an important force in the northern hills of Mesopotamia, a new Semitic people rose to power on the banks of the upper Tigris—the Assyrians, a ferocious, violent people whose profession was war. Until the time that archaeologists began to uncover the remains of their cities and palaces, knowledge of the Assyrians had been based mainly on the accounts of them in the Old Testament, mostly bitter tirades against the kings who "laid waste all the nations." Then in the mid-nineteenth century pioneer archaeologists, such as the Frenchman Paul Emile Botta and the Englishman Austen Henry Layard, unearthed the ruins of Assyrian cities, and the Western world read their reports with awe and wonder. A generation familiar with the Old Testament accounts of Assyrian conquests and the stories of their persecutions was now confronted with the visible remains of their cities, palaces, and temples and could look on images of the very people for whom the Hebrew prophets had reserved some of their harshest denunciations.

When Botta and Layard began digging and unearthed spectacular remains of great palaces, both knew that they had discovered the ruins of the greatest Assyrian cities—Nineveh and Calah—but they were not sure which was which.

Winged bulls with human heads stood guard at the gates of Assyrian palaces. Sculptors endowed them with five legs so that they would look realistic when viewed from either the front or the side.

Nor did they know the names of the kings to whom these palaces had belonged. The decipherment of the Assyrian inscriptions, however, undertaken while these excavations were still in progress, solved the problem of identification. Botta had found Nineveh, the modern Kuyunjik, and Layard the ancient town of Calah, now called Nimrud. The cuneiform inscriptions also revealed much of the political, religious, and military aspects of Assyrian life. Together with magnificent carved reliefs, they amplified the traditional image as it is set forth in the Old Testament.

Still, the reliefs showed one scene after another of warfare. Tall, bearded kings with cruel lips are shown standing in their war chariots watching the sack of an enemy city. Prisoners are being impaled on pointed spikes; an enemy ruler, staked out on the ground, is being slowly flayed alive by men with knives. Women and children are driven away captive; headless bodies float down the river. The fiercest denunciations of the Hebrew prophets do not damn the Assyrians more effectively than some of their own pictures and inscriptions. In one of these an Assyrian king boasts: "My officers . . . put to the sword the inhabitants, young and old, of the town . . . they did not spare anybody among them. They hung their corpses from stakes, flayed their skins and covered with them the wall of the town."

These savage scenes are executed with such ferocious strength, such feline suppleness of line, such violent yet disciplined force of imagination that they take the breath away. One cannot approach them without experiencing the same awe, almost terror, that they inspired at the time of their discovery over a century ago. Moreover, they may have a message for us that escaped their Victorian admirers; for here we see stated for the first time a relatively new force in civilization, a force still potent today—the power of advanced technology, ruthless discipline, and naked terror narrowly ap-

plied to one end—domination. To the Assyrians life was war; and their genius was concentrated on it. Their nobles belonged to a military caste; their armies were highly organized, and used iron weapons and such formidable engines as battering-rams and siege towers, which, when pushed up to the walls of an enemy city, enabled them to pour down fire on their enemies while they themselves were protected by armor. They added to the normal accompaniments of conquest, sack, and pillage, the calculated use of violence and terror.

Who were these people who could sever the skin from the bodies of their enemies with seeming nonchalance and yet execute such beautiful works of art?

Sometime in the third millennium B.C. a stocky, dark-haired Semitic people came from the west and settled on the upper Tigris in a region that is now northern Iraq. Assur (the modern Sharqat), from which the name of these people was taken, became their chief city. It served as a northern outpost of the Sumerian civilization that dominated the valley of the two rivers, but with the fall of the Third Dynasty of Ur, around 2000 B.C., the Assyrians were able to break away from Sumerian control. In a land filled with ambitious rivals and racked by frequent foreign invasions, independence was precarious; in the eighteenth century B.C. Assyria became part of Hammurabi's empire and was ruled from Babylon, and though eventually the country regained its freedom, for centuries thereafter it was held in check by the presence of powerful kingdoms on its northern and western borders—the Mitanni and the Hittites.

About 1200 B.C., when the collapse of the Hittite empire removed the threat of opposition in the north, Assyria began to expand. During the next hundred years a succession of powerful kings held the throne. Tiglath-pileser I, one of the most memorable of these early rulers, not only rebuilt the temples and palaces of the land and restored its public works.

but struck out in all directions at contesting tribes and principalities. In retaliation for earlier attacks from Babylonia he swept down into the valley and took the city of Babylon. By 1100 B.C. the Assyrians had pushed their conquests west to the Mediterranean and north to Lake Van. But soon the nation lapsed into a period of decline lasting almost two hundred years. The reasons for this decline are unknown; there are no written records and few sculptured remains. Perhaps the country lacked forceful rulers or was crowded out by its neighbors. At any rate, Babylon and the western territories were lost. It was a dark age for Assyria.

Then, in the ninth century B.C., Assurnasirpal II came to the throne, and Assyria began its march to power. This aggressive military genius reorganized the Assyrian army and led it as far as the Phoenician coast, collecting tribute from the weaker cities and prudently bypassing towns that might offer strong resistance. But the strongholds closest to the Assyrian borders could not be ignored; these were battered into submission and annexed to the king's domain. Assurnasirpal chose Nimrud, on the Tigris, as the capital of his empire and magnificently restored this ancient city.

Assurnasirpal's son, Shalmaneser III, continued his father's campaigns and waged furious war against his neighbors, especially those in the west. Twelve kings of Palestine and Syria, including Ahab the Israelite, joined in an alliance against him, but in 854 B.C. Shalmaneser defeated the coalition; he boasted that he had "scattered their corpses far and wide and covered the face of the desolate plain with their widespreading armies. With my weapons I made their blood to flow down the valleys of the land. . . . With their bodies I spanned the Orontes as with a bridge." Later Shalmaneser exacted tribute from Ahab's successor, Jehu, the king of Israel, in the form of "silver, gold, a golden bowl, a golden beaker, golden goblets, pitchers of gold . . ." The booty was listed on the side of an obelisk of black alabaster, over six feet tall, which illustrated Shalmaneser's victories and showed row after row of conquered enemies bringing tribute to him.

The Assyrian yoke was heavy, and the subject peoples were always eager to shake it off. At the end of Shalmaneser's reign twenty-seven districts revolted; under his successors other rebellions greatly weakened the Assyrian government. But rebellion against the power of Assyria rarely met with success, and the unhappy subject nations that were rash enough to revolt found their exactions doubled and their rights limited more severely than ever. These were the lucky rebels; those less fortunate were slaughtered or, in line with a traditional policy, carried into exile. Many of the captives were enslaved and brought back to Assyria, where they labored to build the magnificent palaces, the lofty ziggurats, and the gigantic walls that made the Assyrian cities the wonders of their time. When Israel and Damascus allied themselves once more against Assyria, in the middle of the eighth century B.C., King Tiglath-pileser III overran Israel, carrying off "40,500 of its people, together with their possessions, their spoil, their property and goods, [the king's] wife, his sons, his daughters, and his gods . . ."

Even allowing for excessive enthusiasm on the part of the ancient chroniclers, the number of captives that must have been carried off is astonishing. Tiglath-pileser's successor, Sargon II, claimed he led away as prisoners almost twenty-eight thousand inhabitants of Samaria (the capital of Israel). He banished "the rebellious inhabitants of Carchemish . . . and brought them to Assyria," and formed "from among them a contingent of fifty chariots, two hundred men on horseback, and three thousand foot soldiers" to add to his army. The annals of Tiglath-pileser list town after town conquered in the district of Damascus; one provided eight hundred prisoners, another seven hundred fifty, and a third five hundred fifty.

Fleeing from their Assyrian enemies, who pursue them with a rain of arrows, a group of refugees swims across a river to seek shelter in a fortified town. To help themselves keep afloat they cling to animal skins that have been filled with air. The walls of the Assyrian royal palaces displayed many such representations of warfare; within the palace gates both the king and his visitors were constantly surrounded with visible proof of the royal supremacy. The earlier sculptures were conventionalized, with the figure of the king dominating the scene of battle. Later, as in the relief shown here, greater attention was paid to the rendering of naturalistic detail.

Year after year the Assyrians pursued this policy throughout their domain, depopulating entire districts, eradicating entire nations, and carrying images of gods from their native lands.

Sargon chose Khorsabad as his capital and "built a city with the labor of the peoples of the lands which my hands had conquered . . . and I called its name Dur-Sharrukin [the citadel of Sargon]." The city was carefully planned as a huge fortified square with seven gates. In the northwest section were the palace and the ziggurat, which was probably dedicated to the god Assur. Sargon lined the walls of the palace with reliefs of enemy towns that had succumbed to his armies: "I had them set up around their interior walls; I made them objects of astonishment. Reliefs of the towns of the enemy lands, which I had captured . . . I used as adornments in those palaces, thanks to the sculptor's art."

Sargon's son Sennacherib abandoned Khorsabad and made Nineveh his capital. The palace he built there was adorned with gold, silver, copper, alabaster, ivory, and precious woods. The ceilings were white, and there were rich curtains draped back across silver bosses. In the extensive parks and gardens, mountain streams specially diverted through canals provided water for exotic trees and flowers imported from other lands. All that power could furnish and art embellish was used to beautify the new Assyrian capital.

When it rebelled against his rule, Sennacherib destroyed Babylon: "The city and its houses, from its foundation to its top, I destroyed, I devastated, I burned with fire. The wall and outer wall, temples and gods, temple towers of brick and earth, as many as there were, I razed and dumped them into the Arahtu canal. Through the midst of that city I dug canals, I flooded its site with water, and the very foundations thereof I destroyed."

Into the palace of the king, the royal records continue, "I entered joyfully and I opened his treasure house . . . I

brought out, I counted as spoil, I seized." It is no wonder then that the Hebrews were terrified when Sennacherib's armies marched against Judah and besieged Jerusalem, where, the Assyrian annals tell, he shut up King Hezekiah "like a caged bird" in his royal city. "The terrifying splendor of my majesty overcame him, and the Urbi [Arabs] and his mercenary troops which he had brought in to strengthen Jerusalem, his royal city, deserted him." The grim story is continued in the Bible. To avoid the fate of Babylon, Hezekiah handed over to the Assyrians "all the silver that was found in the house of the Lord, and in the treasures of the king's house. At that time did Hezekiah cut off the gold from the doors of the temple of the Lord, and from the pillars . . . and gave it to the king of Assyria."

Egypt was next. Sennacherib's son, Esarhaddon, marched into the Nile Delta and conquered Memphis, the ancient capital of the pharaohs. "I am powerful, I am all powerful," he exulted, "I am a hero, I am gigantic, I am colossal, I am honored, I am magnificent, I am without an equal among all kings . . ." Esarhaddon was indeed without an equal among all kings. No one could withstand the mighty Assyrian armies. Nineveh was a thousand miles away from the Nile Valley, and the Egyptians tried to expel their Assyrian masters, but within a few years they had to pay the price. This time, the Assyrians traveled up the Nile to Thebes, the center of Egyptian resistance, and sacked the city so thoroughly that it never recovered its ancient eminence.

There must have been some special quality in the character of the Assyrians that gave them their formidable prowess in war and their efficiency as rulers; perhaps it was a love of order and discipline akin to that of the later Romans. There was nothing in the nature of their homeland that could have given them special advantages; indeed, geographically, it suffered from several military disadvantages, and it may have

been this very fact that forced the Assyrians to construct such cunningly devised fortifications.

In a number of other ways the Assyrians resembled the Romans of the Imperial Age. They were extremely capable engineers, devisers of ingenious military machines, and experts in siege warfare and the techniques of undermining the walls of a fortress. Their armies were well drilled and well disciplined and were organized in regular formations arranged according to arms—chariotry, cavalry, heavy infantry, light infantry, and sappers. Such tight organization was not common in armies before that time; even the mighty Persian armies of the fifth century B.C. were organized according to tribes and not the type of arms they carried.

In Assyria, as in pharaonic Egypt, the prolific royal family formed the nucleus of the ruling class; generals, governors, high court officials, and the higher echelons of the priesthood were often drawn from its ranks. Like most Oriental despots, the Assyrian king had numerous children, not only by the queen but by the women of the royal harem. Such concubines were recruited partly from among the daughters of defeated or vassal kings and princes. Conspiracies among them were frequent, since not unnaturally each wanted to advance the career or even secure the succession of her own favorite son; the queen herself does not appear to have possessed much political influence, but the queen mother often did. Such intrigues over the succession to the throne constituted one of the few weaknesses of the Assyrian system.

As the chief priest and the central figure of the cult of Assur, the king was mediator between god and man. He presented the people's cause to the god and told the will of Assur to the people. The king was totally sacred; he belonged to the god. Removed from the public, he lived an isolated existence in his palace, aloof from all except his entourage of court officials, soldiers, and slaves, and, of course, the women

of the harem. Visiting dignitaries often received no more than a glimpse of his figure, far off in the throne room. When they were allowed into his presence, they could address him only after kissing the ground at his feet.

Nevertheless, this aloof king was never very far from the sights and sounds of the battlefield. Even on those ceremonial occasions when he feasted among his nobility, sculptured scenes of battle, conquest, and the hunt were visible in the flickering light of massive torches. These were the subjects most beloved by the Assyrian aristocracy. Looking at such reliefs, in which battering-rams pound the walls of enemy cities, or the king in his war chariot leads his spearmen to victory, Assurbanipal and his predecessors must have recalled with pride that, as the inscriptions state, an Assyrian king shared fully in the hardships and dangers of a campaign. One such inscription has been translated: "I had pitched my camp at the foot of the Nipur mountain and with my select bodyguard and my indomitable warriors I advanced like a strong wild ox. Gorges, mountain streams, and cataracts, dangerous chasms I traversed in my palanquin. If it were too precipitous for my palanquin I proceeded on foot. Like a young gazelle I ascended the high mountain peaks in pursuit of [the enemy]. Whenever my knees gave way under me I sat down on a rock and drank cold water from a waterskin to quench my thirst."

The contrasting pictures of the king presiding in godlike state over his groveling courtiers and the king leading his warriors through wild and rugged country is arresting. In Egypt such expressions of military ardor were sometimes—though not invariably—conventional, but one feels that if an Assyrian monarch were unable to demonstrate his soldierly qualities he probably would not have remained king for long.

The native subjects of the king may be divided into three classes corresponding roughly to the aristocracy, the freemen,

As his court musicians entertain him and birds in the treetops chirp in accompaniment, King Assurbanipal reclines on a couch within his garden, enjoying a peaceful dinner. His wife sits beside him on a high, throne-like chair. The scene is not completely idyllic; at the far left of the relief the severed head of an Elamite king can be seen hanging from a tree, a gruesome trophy of Assurbanipal's ferocious wars against the Elamites. At left, four musicians are shown playing upon lyres, cymbals, and a small drum; they may be one of the small military bands that went off to war with campaigning soldiers, who customarily clapped their hands and sang as they marched along.

and the slaves. From the aristocracy the king chose all of his dignitaries—governors, priests, court officials, and so on. Occasionally women filled some of these high positions. There are records that tell of women who governed provinces, and one Assyrian queen, Sammuramat, prototype of the legendary Semiramis, ruled as coregent for a time and was immortalized by Herodotus as a great conqueror who led the Assyrian armies to victory after victory.

The cuneiform tablets discovered in the ruins of the Assyrian cities tell us much about the middle classes. These classes included not only what we would call professional men, such as bankers and scribes, but also many kinds of craftsmen. Though each profession had a different status, all appear to have been organized into guilds. Every freeman had to pay taxes, generally in the form of produce or labor. All fit males of this class were liable for military service; besides their standing army of regular troops, the Assyrian rulers recruited mass levies in time of war. A man of means, however, could avoid service by providing a slave to replace himself.

There were merchants who must have profited greatly from the caravan trade in order to afford the twenty-five per cent interest that was charged for loans. These merchants traded in slaves, horses, camels, and manufactured goods, especially fabrics. Gold, silver, and copper were the metals used for exchange, and by the eighth century B.C. coinage had come into use. A very ancient Assyrian trading station dating from early in the second millennium was discovered at Kultepe in Anatolia, with its cuneiform business documents and letters still preserved in their files. From these it is clear that at an early date Assyrian trade was highly organized and extended over a large area; Kultepe was obviously an entrepôt at which Assyrian manufactured goods were traded for copper and other valuable metals of Anatolia.

In late Assyrian times there was a large class of agricul-

tural slaves attached to the land; if the farm they lived on were sold, they went along to its purchaser. Most slaves, however, lived in the cities and were engaged in domestic work. Despite their status, slaves could still own personal property, and there were some who possessed land of their own. Their lot on the whole was comfortable; indeed, the condition of the slave in Assyria seems to have been better than in any other ancient society.

Life at the court of the king is easier to visualize than the existence of the common people. Because of the lengthy personal accounts recorded by the king, all his habits and surroundings can be recreated. This is particularly true of Assurbanipal, the last of the great Assyrian kings. During his reign, from about 669 to 626 B.C., the splendor of the empire reached its greatest height. Assurbanipal continued the embellishment of the royal capital at Nineveh. Its mighty palaces were enriched with precious metals and fine woods, and its parks and gardens were adorned with exotic flowers and trees. It must have been a rich jewel in that somber landscape. Visitors to the mud-brick mounds that are Nineveh today find difficulty in imagining it as it was, when its streets and courts were thronged with richly dressed, bejeweled women and swarthy men with square-cut, curling beards, when the smartly turned-out Assyrian troops, armed with spears and bows, clattered past echoing palace walls as they escorted some great official in his chariot through the town.

At the court and in the homes of the powerful there was wealth and luxury. Singers and musicians entertained guests at royal and noble banquets, as we can see from the depictions on stone reliefs. But the king was probably more stately and austere than in Sumer or even in Egypt. Underlying all this richness and sophistication one senses uneasily the overwhelming power of those kings; that power informs the hundreds of sculptured scenes, carved on massive blocks of stone, that are

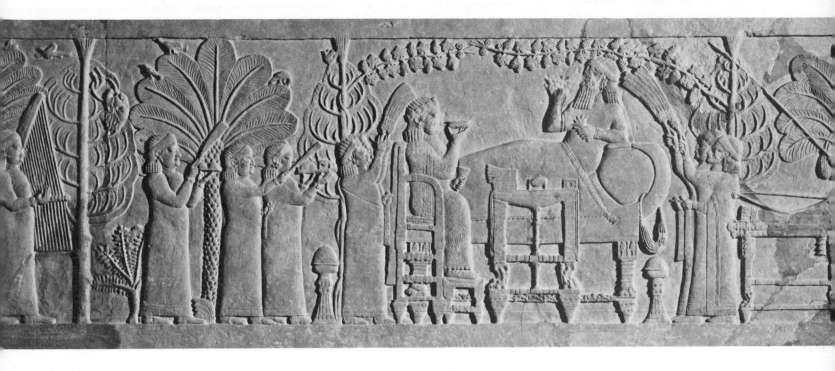

the most impressive and most durable legacy of the Assyrians.

The best of these reliefs date from the time of Assurbanipal, when the tribute of hundreds of foreign towns poured into the royal coffers to pay for the adornment of Nineveh. On them, the king, larger than his courtiers, grasps a lion by its mane and plunges his sword into its chest, or appears as the awesome conqueror, with abject foreigners under his sword. Assurbanipal's ferocious war against the Elamites is depicted at length, the enemy fleeing in panic from Assyrian warriors, whose spears and arrows are everywhere. In all this, there is that astonishing muscularity and vigor so characteristic of Assyrian art.

Certain motifs appear over and over again—chariots and horses, bowmen in the midst of battle, cities besieged, captives being led into exile. The subject matter, with its continual obsession with warfare, its armies endlessly ravaging nation after nation, is ruthless, often to the point of monotony. But there are more genial aspects to the art of Assyria. The colossal winged bulls that guarded the entrances to the palace courtyards were overpowering; they stood some sixteen feet high. Still, they represented protective geniuses, and their benevolence is manifest. Among the delicate ivories found at Nimrud, mostly Phoenician in style, are some done by Assyrian craftsmen, revealing that they were equally capable of working with more peaceful themes.

It is hard to believe that merely fourteen years after the reign of Assurbanipal, "the great king, the legitimate king, the king of the world," the Assyrian empire collapsed. One possible explanation for the downfall might be that Babylonia, as well as many other captive territories, had never wholly bent under the yoke of Assyria, but had continued to resist its domination. Undoubtedly Assyria's financial resources had been drained by the necessity of suppressing rebellion. Another reason could be that the frequent foreign wars had

taken a great toll of Assyria's fighting men. After a while the incessant demand for more native soldiers to fill the army's ranks could not be met, and the kings were forced to rely on their subject nations for soldiers. Inevitably, this led to a deterioration in the quality and the loyalty of Assyria's forces.

"Woe to the bloody city!" the Hebrew prophet Nahum had proclaimed against Nineveh. "It is all full of lies and robbery; the prey departeth not; the noise of a whip, and the noise of the rattling of the wheels, and of the prancing horses, and of the jumping chariots. The horseman lifteth up both the bright sword and the glittering spear: and there is a multitude of slain, and a great number of carcasses . . ." After a three-month siege by the combined forces of Babylonians and Medes, the Assyrian capital finally fell in 612 B.C., suffering the same fate that the Assyrians themselves had so often meted out to other proud capitals. Assyria was divided between its two conquerors. The Medes took the region east and north of the Tigris River, the Babylonians, under the leadership of Nebuchadnezzar, the region to the west and south, and with it the control of a vast empire.

About twenty-four hundred years ago the Greek traveler Herodotus, having made the difficult journey from the Mediterranean coast across the mountains and deserts of Syria and then down the Euphrates, stood entranced looking down at the streets of Babylon. He was not a naive, inexperienced visitor, but a widely traveled and cultivated man. He had, in his time, visited most of the eastern Mediterranean countries, including, of course, Greece and the Greek islands (he was born in Asia Minor). He had coasted along the shores of Palestine, toured North Africa, examined the pyramids of Egypt, and had long discussions with the priests of Memphis. He had passed through the Dardanelles, cruised along the western shores of the Black Sea as far as the mouth of the Dnieper in modern Russia, and studied the customs of the

Scythians of the steppes. If ever there was a "man of the world" in the literal sense, it was Herodotus. He was not a man who was very easily impressed.

This is part of what he wrote in the fifth century B.C. concerning Babylon. "Babylon lies in a wide plain, a vast city in the form of a square with sides nearly fourteen miles long and a circuit of some fifty-six miles, and in addition to its enormous size it surpasses in splendor any city of the known world. It is surrounded by a broad, deep moat full of water, and within the moat there is a wall fifty royal cubits wide and two hundred high. . . . On the top of the wall they constructed, along each edge, a row of one-roomed buildings . . . with enough space between for a four-horse chariot to turn. There are a hundred gates in the circuit of the wall, all of bronze with bronze uprights and lintels. . . . There is a fortress in the middle of each half of the city: in one the royal palace surrounded by a wall of great strength, in the other the temple of Bel [or Marduk], the Babylonian Zeus."

Admittedly there are serious discrepancies between Herodotus' description and the excavated remains—so many, in fact, that it has been doubted whether the Greek historian had ever been to Babylon. But this is an extreme view and not generally accepted. His description of the city seems reliable in most respects, although the measurements he gives are exaggerated. The excavations of Babylon at the beginning of this century, by a German expedition under the direction of Robert Koldewey, established the circumference of the walls surrounding the ctiy as about eleven miles; but Herodotus' estimation of fifty-six may have included the walls of the nearby town of Borsippa, which stands directly to the south on the Euphrates. The thickest of these walls was found to be only thirteen feet wide, a considerable difference from the figure of eighty feet reported by Herodotus. Since most of the walls have disappeared or have been greatly reduced in height,

we have no means of checking whether they were originally three hundred forty feet high, as Herodotus claimed; but it has been pointed out that walls that high would require a base far wider than thirteen feet to support them.

There are other difficulties in reconciling Herodotus' account with the visible remains. The city appears to have been rectangular, not square in plan, and to have contained three main districts, not two, as Herodotus claimed. Within the section called Babil stood one of the large palaces of the renowned king Nebuchadnezzar. The district of Amran, to the south, contained Esagila, the temple of Marduk, adjoining the lofty ziggurat Etemenanki, the "tower of Babel." Between these two districts was the center of the city, the Kasr, where stood the main palace of Nebuchadnezzar and its Hanging Gardens, the great Gate of Ishtar, and the celebrated Processional Way. This road was flanked on each side by cliff-like walls of gleaming glazed tiles, on which enormous reliefs of lions glowered down on the visitor as he approached the great temple of Marduk. Various of these, discovered by Koldewey, stand in museums around the world, and in the Berlin Museum is a reconstruction of the Ishtar Gate that incorporates several of the reliefs of bulls and dragons that decorated the original structure.

Built on a mound high above the city, Nebuchadnezzar's palace with its many courtyards must have been an overwhelming sight. In the throne room was a splendid wall relief of glazed bricks, representing a procession of yellow lions. Above them were garlands of colorful flowers and tall graceful columns shown against a background of rich blue tile. "I laid the foundation of the new palace firmly," the king wrote, "and built it up mountain-high with bitumen and baked bricks. Huge cedars I caused to be laid for its roof, door leaves of cedar mounted with copper, thresholds and hinges made of bronze I fitted to its gates. Silver, gold, pre-

Herodotus records that the people of Babylon always wore a seal stone on a cord tied around their wrists. The cylinder seal shown at right, made of carnelian, is incised with a characteristic motif—the hero in conflict with two wild beasts. An attacking lion, with its right paw raised, can be seen on the seal itself; on the impression reproduced on the facing page the winged hero is shown with one hand holding a scimitar and the other grasping a bull. The Babylonians used such seals for more than signing their names. Sometimes they closed their doors with wet clay and marked it with a seal, in order to discover if anyone had broken into a house that was left unguarded.

cious stones, all that is costly and glorious, wealth and goods, ornaments of my exaltedness I stored within it, an immense abundance of royal treasures I accumulated in it."

In the northeast corner of the palace, overlooking the Ishtar Gate and as if suspended between the earth and the sky, were the so-called Hanging Gardens, which the Greeks named one of the Seven Wonders of the World. In the course of his excavations Koldewey came upon a large vaulted structure, the roof of which was protected by an unusually thick layer of earth. In one of the chambers underneath the roof he found a curious well consisting of three shafts side by side, the largest being in the center. "I can see no other explanation," wrote Koldewey, "than that a mechanical hydraulic machine stood here, which worked on the same principle as our chain pump, where buckets attached to a chain work on a wheel placed over the well."

Though still not proved, it could well be that this substructure supported the gardens, that the trees and lawns may have been planted on the thick layer of earth and kept moist by water pumped up from below. But there is another equally fascinating feature of this building; perhaps the Babylonians had learned to defeat the torrid heat of their summers by cooling the air. Koldewey concluded: "The air that entered the chambers [surrounding the gardens] . . . through the leaves of the trees must have been delightfully cooled by the continuous watering of the vegetation. Possibly the palace officials did a great part of their business in these cool chambers during the heat of summer."

The word *hanging* is in any case a misnomer, the result of faulty translation. The term used by the Roman historian Quintus Curtius Rufus is *pensiles,* which could mean either "hanging" or "in the form of a balcony." What made the Babylonian balconies one of the Seven Wonders of the World was the fact that they had extensive gardens laid out upon

them. Not that the Romans ever saw them. Long before they appeared in Mesopotamia Babylon had been deserted and its buildings were crumbling to dust.

The city that Herodotus and other Greek travelers saw was mainly the work of Nebuchadnezzar and his successors of the seventh and sixth centuries B.C. In those years it must fully have deserved the description accorded it by St. John the Divine in the Book of Revelation: "That great city Babylon, that mighty city! . . . The merchandise of gold, and silver, and precious stones, and of pearls, and fine linen, and purple, and silk, and scarlet . . . all manner vessels of ivory, and all manner vessels of most precious wood, and of brass, and iron, and marble . . . ointments, and frankincense, and wine, and oil . . . and horses, and chariots, and slaves, and souls of men."

What stands out very clearly is that the Babylonians, from the time of Hammurabi onward, derived much of their wealth from trade and commerce. They were a nation of merchants. The units of currency that occur so often in the Old Testament, the talent and the shekel, are Babylonian. A great many of the cuneiform tablets found at Babylon, Nineveh, Ur, Nippur, and other Mesopotamian sites are bills, receipts, business contracts, accounts, and invoices. Babylon's caravans moved along much-traveled routes to and from Iran, Syria, Palestine, and Asia Minor. Its ships sailed down the Euphrates and through the Persian Gulf to Telmun, to bring back the produce of Arabia and India. Its rafts, or *keleks,* made of reeds and inflated skins, floated down to Babylon bringing minerals from Armenia. Among its own exports were barley, dates, and wools, and woven stuffs and other manufactured products. But despite their wealth the Babylonians were not able to control their empire for very long.

Nabonidus, the last king of Babylon, who reigned from 555 to 538 B.C., was of Aramaean origin and chose to worship his native god, Sin, rather than the Babylonian Marduk. When the priests of Marduk, and eventually the people, turned against him, he withdrew to the town of Harran and left his son Belshazzar in charge of the capital. It was while Belshazzar was ruling in Babylon that Cyrus the Persian succeeded in the apparently impossible task of taking the city. Despite the protection of its enormous walls, despite the fact that the citizens had provisions and water to withstand a long siege, Babylon fell. The Euphrates ran through the city, but it was of such a depth as to be unfordable. So the Persian king, Herodotus reports, employed "all his noncombatant troops" in digging a canal that drained off the river into a marsh. "The Persian army which had been left at Babylon for the purpose entered the river . . . and making their way along it, got into the town. If the Babylonians had learned what Cyrus was doing or had seen it for themselves in time, they could have let the Persians enter and then . . . caught them in a trap and wiped them out. But as it was they were taken by surprise. . . . owing to the great size of the city the outskirts were captured without the people in the center knowing anything about it; there was a festival going on, and even while the city was falling they continued to dance and enjoy themselves, until hard facts brought them to their senses. That, then, is the story of the . . . capture of Babylon."

Herodotus certainly could not have read the Hebrew chronicles of that disaster. Yet the latter part of his calm historical narrative confirms the impassioned poetic description of the prophet Daniel, an unwilling guest of Belshazzar at that festival: "Belshazzar the king made a great feast to a thousand of his lords, and drank wine before the thousand. Belshazzar, while he tasted the wine, commanded to bring the gold and silver vessels which his father Nebuchadnezzar had taken out of the temple which was in Jerusalem; that the king and his princes, his wives and his concubines, might drink therein. They drank wine, and praised the gods of gold, and of silver, of brass, of iron, of wood, and of stone." (As noted, Nabonidus, not Nebuchadnezzar, was the father of Belshazzar.)

The greatest of the "false gods" was Marduk, who had assimilated the characteristics of the Sumerian god Enlil. All the deities worshiped in Babylon, though they bore Babylonian names, were in fact directly linked with the gods and goddesses who had been honored in Mesopotamia for more than two thousand years. At the time, the ancient religion could not have seemed more impregnable; it was as firmly established as the temple that Nabopolassar had rebuilt for Marduk, which, in the words of that king, had "its foundations firm to the bosom of the Underworld."

Yet the world was changing; the foundations of the old faiths were crumbling, and the Hebrew poet, with prophetic insight, knew that one of the heaviest blows at those foundations was being delivered that night. While Belshazzar "drank wine before the thousand," Cyrus' men waded through the shallow river and burst in upon the unsuspecting city. "In the same hour came forth fingers of a man's hand, and wrote . . . upon the plaster of the wall of the king's palace:

and the king saw the part of the hand that wrote. . . . And this is the writing that was written, *Mene, mene, tekel, upharsin* . . . Thou art weighed in the balances, and art found wanting. Thy kingdom is divided, and given to the Medes and Persians."

So Babylon fell to the Persians, who did not destroy it, as Sennacherib had done, but preserved the city as part of their Achaemenian Empire. Later it rebelled and was retaken by the Persians under Darius. Even then, though its defenses were thrown down, the Persians spared Babylon, so that Herodotus, when he went there in the next century, could still see much to admire. A century still later, when Alexander the Great passed that way, he planned to rebuild and revive Nebuchadnezzar's capital, making it one of the principal towns of his eastern empire. But after his death, when the Seleucid Dynasty inherited this part of Alexander's dismembered dominions, Babylon was abandoned and deserted. But its ancient civilization, its gods, its literature, and its cuneiform writing survived down to the beginning of the Christian era; and by then elements of its culture had passed almost imperceptibly into that of Greece, which has transmitted them to us.

The picture that remains is that of Herodotus, one of the earliest representatives of our Western civilization, looking down at this moribund relic of the ancient East. He had never heard of Sumer and Akkad, let alone Tell Halaf, al 'Ubaid, or Uruk. But his description of Babylon in the fifth century B.C. might well have been applied, in broad outline, to a Sumerian city built two thousand years earlier. Both had the same basic structure—rings of defensive walls, the palace of the king, and the temple and towering ziggurat of the great deity. Beyond the walls he could see fields irrigated and cultivated by the same methods the Sumerians had developed.

Today Babylon and the other once-great cities of Mesopotamia are little more than desolate, dun-colored mounds of dried mud, surrounded for the most part by desert or scrubby little fields. Around them, abandoned irrigation works—silted canals, mounds, and ditches—are all that remain where thousands once labored in fields of waving wheat and barley for the glory of their gods. Yet the world these people created lives on and not only in their written records and in the buildings and artifacts restored by the patient labors of archaeologists. It survives within our minds, even among those who have never heard of Sumer or Akkad. Every time we look at a watch or a compass, or use a protractor, we are thinking like the Babylonians, in multiples of sixty. When we study star maps or, at a less scientific level, read a column on astrology in a popular newspaper, we share something with the Sumerian and Akkadian priests who watched the cloudless heavens from their temple roofs. For all who read the Bible, the world of ancient Mesopotamia is reflected in the voices of the Old Testament prophets and psalmists. The more we learn of the world of the Sumerians and their cultural descendants in Babylon and Assyria, the more we understand our debt, spiritual and material, to the civilization that first flourished in the Land Between the Rivers.

ASSYRIAN EMPIRE

"I, Assurnasirpal . . . the mighty king, king of the universe, the king without a rival . . . the mighty hero who treads on the neck of his foe . . ." When he commissioned his scribes to write this inscription, Assurnasirpal II, who is portrayed above, hardly exaggerated the truth. His armies had marched triumphantly from the eastern hills of Mesopotamia to the shores of the Mediterranean. The chronicles of his reign list one campaign after another, recording the conquest and destruction of town after town and the receipt of plentiful tribute. Assyria's kings built as well as they destroyed, however. Assurnasirpal restored the ancient capital at Nimrud, and at Balawat built a palace and a temple dedicated to the god of dreams. He and his son adorned the temple gates with scenes of warfare and the hunt, a detail of which appears on pages 190 and 191. Many magnificent palace reliefs, often inscribed with annals, celebrate the nation's victories and make Assyria one of the best documented of all ancient civilizations.

THE
WAGES
OF
WAR

When an enemy fortress held out against the formidable armies of Assyria, the besiegers tried persuasion before they showed their strength. An Assyrian envoy called a truce and stood before the walls, pleading with the defenders in their native tongue to succumb to his power. Generally it was a wise move to follow his advice; as one inscription boasts, Assyria's enemies usually "fled like young pigeons." If his efforts were unsuccessful, the army went to work. Battering-rams pounded against the walls, and sappers began digging beneath the fortifications. Timber would be placed under the walls and burned to make them collapse, unless the defenders themselves succeeded in deflecting the sappers by tunneling under their work. Once the city was captured the Assyrian king set up his throne beside the city gate. The captives were marched before him with their ruler at their head. They might be killed and their heads piled one on top of another to make a memorial pillar outside the town; if not, they would surely be exiled or enslaved. Their leader was tortured, perhaps confined in a cage, and then finally executed. The captured town was thoroughly despoiled, for during times of war the Assyrian armies relied on booty for their pay; indeed, warfare played an important role in the economy of the nation, and neighboring provinces were regarded as storehouses from which tribute could be taken regularly. Part of the spoil was destined for the temples, for the god Assur was given credit for every victory; some of the prisoners slaughtered after each battle were regarded as a sacrifice to him.

While their comrades march off laden with plunder, a contingent of Assyrian soldiers (left) demolishes the fortifications of the burning town of Hamanu. The bricks and timber dislodged by their pickaxes can be seen tumbling from the walls. Above, an Assyrian shoots an Arab warrior whose camel has been wounded. OVERLEAF: *The bronze gates of Balawat show the inhabitants of the island of Tyre rowing ashore with tribute for the king of Assyria. In the lower register, chariots and infantrymen leave a circular campsite (left) to attack an enemy town.*

Carrying their possessions on their shoulders, a group of captives marches into exile (opposite) guarded by bowmen of the Assyrian army. Two of the men pull a cart piled high with goods, upon which two women are seated. In the bottom register a small child is led along by his father. A fragment of a wall relief (below) shows an emissary from the king of the Medes bringing two finely caparisoned horses as tribute to the Assyrians. It was the Medes who joined with the king of Babylon and finally overthrew Assyrian power.

CAPTIVE PEOPLES

Assyria was the first of the despotic empires that were to dominate the history of Western Asia. With her rule the age of the small, independent kingdom, or city-state, came to an end. A series of shifting alliances joined the kingdoms of Anatolia and the Levant with the Babylonians and Elamites to the east in the struggle against her; but for centuries the power of Assyria prevailed. A revolution in Sidon and Tyre in 700 B.C. was suppressed so fiercely that these Phoenician cities never regained control of Mediterranean trade, which later passed to Carthage and Greece. The Elamites were punished so vindictively that their ancient civilization vanished; the bones of the Elamite kings were exhumed and carried off to Assyria so that their souls would never be at rest. The rebellious kingdom of Israel was wiped out and its inhabitants, the "ten lost tribes," resettled in the far corners of the empire; into its capital, Samaria, were brought the ancestors of the Samaritans—Persians, Babylonians, Elamites, and exiles from the ancient Sumerian town of Uruk. Besides the prophets of the Bible, scribes in other lands cried out their hatred against the oppressors. The Assyrian king, one Babylonian proclaimed, "had evil intentions, he thought out crimes . . . he had no mercy for the inhabitants . . ."

THE LION HUNT

"Since I took my seat upon the throne," King Assurbanipal wrote, ". . . the reeds of the marshes have shot up so high there is no getting through them. The young of the lions grew up therein in countless numbers . . . they became fierce and terrible through their devouring of herds, flocks, and people . . . They keep bringing down the cattle of the plain, they keep shedding the blood of men." Hunting lions to protect the population was a royal duty as well as a sport. In preparation for the hunt, beaters went through the fields, driving lions before them; the beasts were trapped within cages, from which they would be let loose one by one after the king had entered the enclosure in which the sport took place. Once they were released the lions ran forward to be met with a rain of arrows; if one failed to run within shooting range, beaters would drive him ahead, or the king would ride by in his chariot and twist the beast's tail. Only an enraged lion was a worthy adversary for the royal hunter. Sometimes the king dismounted and fought on foot, armed only with a sword, his hand covered with goat's wool to guard against mauling.

Above, a wounded lion attacks King Assurna-sirpal as he rides across the hunting field. Beside the royal chariot another beast lies dying. One of the finest of all Assyrian sculptures (left) shows a dying lioness; although partially paralyzed, the beast still has enough strength to rise on its forelegs. OVERLEAF: A wooden bow, an embroidered robe, the horse's trappings, and the king's tightly curled hair form an intricate and subtle pattern in one of a series of magnificent reliefs that illustrate Assurbanipal's lion hunt. Another of the reliefs, reproduced on the following two pages, shows the king pouring a libation over the slaughtered animals, perhaps to appease their angry spirits.

THE ARTS
OF PEACE

Under Assurbanipal, who ruled in the middle of the seventh century B.C., Assyrian civilization reached its greatest heights. The power of the empire was evident in the splendor of its capital, Nineveh, and in the palace that the king erected there with the aid of foreign slaves. An early ruler, Sennacherib, had already built a palace in the city and surrounded it with gardens and orchards and fields of cotton plants, or "trees bearing wool." But it was during Assurbanipal's reign that learning flourished most and that royal sculptors created the most memorable examples of that characteristic Assyrian art, the carved stone relief.

Assurbanipal was also responsible for collecting the greatest cuneiform library ever assembled; all the important texts that the king could find were copied down by his scribes and deposited in his library. "When thou receivest this letter," Assurbanipal wrote to one provincial official, "take with thee . . . the learned men of the city of Borsippa and seek out all the tablets, all those that are in their houses and all those that are deposited in the temple . . . Hunt for the valuable tablets which are in your archives and which do not exist in Assyria and send them to me." In another inscription the king boasts of this work: "Row upon row of all existing characters I wrote on tablets, imprinted and perused them, whereafter I placed them in my palace so that I can peruse them and read them aloud." Assurbanipal was proud of his exploits in war and his skill at hunting, like most Assyrian rulers, but he was also vain of his learning. He smugly proclaims that the gods have endowed him with "great ears," that is, an excellent memory, which in that age was the prime requirement for scholarly achievement.

Under a canopy that protects him from the sun, King Assurbanipal (left) rides in his ceremonial chariot. The pages behind him carry fly whisks to chase insects away from the royal presence. Even when he strolled through his palace, the king always had servants walking before and behind him. At right, cedar logs are transported through waters filled with marine animals; they are probably destined for use as beams in a palace.

A HOST OF DEMONS

The Babylonians kept a special set of ragged clothes to wear on those days when evil forces were abroad. On the seventh day of the month, the king did not dare ride out in his chariot or issue commands. On certain dates in the autumn, garlic was taboo; if one ate it then, one risked a scorpion bite or the death of a kinsman. Sometimes a man had to take care in going up to the roof; if he did venture to ascend, then "the handmaiden of the wind demon will espouse him." Both the Assyrians and the Babylonians lived in a universe filled with evil spirits. Men and nations suffered sudden and terrifying reverses of fortune and constantly had to be on guard against the demons who caused them, demons who were always lying in wait ready to work more mischief. Special precincts were set aside within every temple, where malevolent spirits could be exorcised, and priests assembled hundreds of spells that might frustrate their efforts. There were thousands of demons everywhere, many of them restless souls of the dead who had been improperly interred. The fiercest of all was the she-devil Lamashtu, whose name alone, when uttered aloud, was enough to terrify people. She dwelt in the mountains, the marshes, and the waste places and took special delight in causing miscarriage in women and in beasts. One incantation, used as an exorcism against her, describes her vividly: "Angry, fierce, terrible, frightful, enraged, furious, terrible, rapacious is she. . . . Her fist is a scourge. . . . She turns upside down the inside of the pregnant woman. . . . Her head is the head of a lion. . . . She howls like a bitch."

A mask of the frightful monster Humbaba appears below. Because his ominous features, foreshadowing evil, were sometimes seen in the innards of a sacrificed beast, his face was envisaged as a mass of entrails.

The evil forces in nature were powerful, but the gods could help guard mankind against them. The Assyrian relief at left shows a protective genius, commonly depicted on palace walls, touching a sacred tree; he may be sprinkling it with holy water. On the plaque below, an unidentified god kills an evil monster with his sword. The Babylonian idol shown above represents a god who faces in all four directions at once.

All the Assyrian ivories that have been discovered date from sometime after the ninth century B.C., when King Assurnasirpal conquered the rich trading cities along the Phoenician coast. The carving above, which represents a cow and calf in a lotus thicket, and the one below, of a woman at a window, are both in the Phoenician style. It has been suggested that the woman represents Ishtar, the goddess of love, or one of her sacred harlots; a similar figure appears on many ivory plaques. The carving at left, the handle of a fly whisk, was probably made by Assyrian craftsmen; it shows two figures kneeling by a sacred tree.

IVORY IN ART

The Assyrian policy of transplanting subject peoples from one part of the empire to another was designed to suppress revolution. Rebels were sent into exile; in an alien land they would find few trustworthy allies to join them in battle against the Assyrians, even if the local population did share their discontent. But the transfer of peoples also served to diffuse ideas throughout the lands of the Near East, and the era of Assyrian supremacy fostered a rich cultural exchange. The city that Sargon built at Khorsabad was filled, according to one of the king's inscriptions, with people from "the four quarters of the world," who spoke "differently and in a foreign tongue." Nineveh, one of the capitals of the empire, may even have had a majority of foreigners in its population.

When the Assyrian armies stormed enemy cities, craftsmen stood a better chance of surviving than other captives did; they could be useful to their conquerors. Among the exiles transported to Assyria were Syrian and Phoenician artisans, who had brought to perfection in their own country the craft of working in ivory. Ivory carving had long been practiced in the Levant. Until the eighth century B.C. the elephant could still be found there. Both technique and style were derived from Egypt, which had always been a major influence on Levantine art. Many of the ivories found in the ruins of Assyrian palaces are carved in the Phoenician manner; some bear a close resemblance to a group of ivory furniture ornaments found at Samaria, in the ruins of the palace of a king of Israel, who evidently had also imported Phoenician craftsmen or the products of their workshops. Some of the Assyrian ivories are done in a native style, however, and must have been carved by local artisans who had learned their trade from foreigners.

Foreign craftsmen were not the only prizes that the Assyrians brought back from their military expeditions. The royal records of tribute show that when the kings marched out against an enemy, they returned home with silver and gold and spices, and "linen garments with multicolored trimmings," with elephant hides and chariots, musicians, concubines, and camels, and at least in one instance, with a collection of stuffed animals, including "wild birds whose spread-out wings were dyed blue."

Part of a horse's trappings, the ivory cheekpiece above is Egyptian in style and shows a sphinx with a sacred sun disk upon its head. The ivory retains traces of a dye; in Anatolia during the same period, according to Homer, women also stained "ivory with purple to make a cheekpiece for horses." A remarkably similar piece, in bronze, has been found in Cyprus. The fine plaque below, decorated with gold leaf and inlaid with glass paste and semiprecious stones, shows a lion mauling a Nubian.

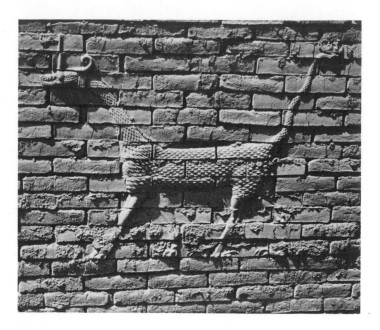

The ruins of the West Gate (right) can still be seen at Babylon. Another entrance to the city, the Ishtar Gate, was decorated with tile reliefs of bulls and the dragon of Marduk (above).

FALL OF BABYLON

"I established Babylon, the sublime city . . ." King Nebuchadnezzar wrote. "On the threshold of her gates I set huge bulls and footed serpents, such as no other king before me had wrought." During Nebuchadnezzar's long reign Babylon grew to be even more splendid than Nineveh was before it had been destroyed. The city's population may have reached a million; its wealth, drawn from caravan routes that extended from India to Egypt, made it the world's richest city. In the long history of the Land Between the Rivers this age was unrivaled in glory. But its glory was destined to be brief. After less than a century of imperial power Babylon was overthrown, and the civilization that had been born in Sumer millenniums before began to perish. Mesopotamia became a province ruled by Persians, Greeks, and Romans. Even when kings did reassert the independence of the land for a time, Babylon was no longer their capital. In one period of forty years the city changed rulers nine times. Little by little its population was exiled, its buildings crumbled. By the time of Christ the city was deserted and its great ziggurat a heap of rubble, a desolate site like so many of the ancient and famous cities now fallen into ruins on the Mesopotamian plain.

THE
VALLEY
OF THE
INDUS

The story of the primitive founders of the Indus Valley civilization, who ventured down from their mountain homelands and tamed the dangerous, inhospitable, but fertile valley of the great Indus River, has all the elements of a heroic saga. Yet compared with the civilizations of Egypt and Mesopotamia, the Indus Valley culture, which arose about 2500 B.C., lacks apparent glamour. As far as we know, the Indus people created no poetic myths and chronicles, as did the Sumerians. We have no Indus equivalent of the great epic of Gilgamesh and Enkidu; the names of their gods and kings (if indeed they had kings), their sages and heroes are unknown. Only scatters of pottery and tools—"culture spreads"—patiently traced by archaeologists from the valley to the mountains provide evidence of unremitting work and struggle.

From this civilization, which lasted for about a thousand years, there are substantial remains of two great cities—Harappa and Mohenjo-daro—and numerous smaller sites covering an immense area, from the Simla hills (the foothills of the Himalayas) in the Punjab to Sutkagen-dor near the coast of the Arabian Sea, a total distance of some one thousand miles. Southeast of the river's mouth, other evidence of the Indus culture has been found near the coast as far as the Gulf of Cambay, the broad inlet just above the modern city of Bombay; and in 1958 typical Indus artifacts were found within thirty miles of New Delhi, far beyond the frontiers of jungle and desert, which archaeologists thought would have prevented the culture's eastward expansion.

It is an absorbing story, with the added appeal of relative newness. The Indus Valley civilization—frequently called

There are few clues to help identify the image at left, one of the rare stone sculptures from the Indus Valley. Its stern visage suggests authority, and it may represent a deity or priest-king.

the Harappa civilization—is one of the most recently discovered cultures of the ancient world. Only in 1921, when an Indian archaeologist began to unearth the buried remains of Harappa, did it become evident that the Indus could take its place beside the Nile and the Tigris-Euphrates as the begetter of a great riverine culture of the ancient world—a culture that might be traced back almost forty-five hundred years into the past. Part of its fascination lies in the grim fact that it appears to have foreshadowed some of the economic features of the totalitarian state. Admittedly there is insufficient evidence on which to form definite conclusions, but the barrack-like buildings, the huge granaries, and the raised platforms on which rows of workmen pounded grain all suggest a life of controlled communal activity. This is one interpretation, and it is not universally shared by archaeologists, but only further study and excavation can prove it true or false.

Much still remains to be learned. No royal tombs have been discovered. The Indus Valley people had a writing system, but we cannot read the writings that have been uncovered. Our knowledge of their social customs is as uncertain as what we know of their origins. Even the reason for the collapse of their long-established culture is not known with certainty, though there may be clues in the *Rig-Veda,* a collection of Hindu religious hymns that, like Homer's *Iliad* and *Odyssey,* may prove to have a historical basis.

The *Rig-Veda* is the saga of the Aryans, Indo-European invaders who swept down from the northwestern hills to the Punjab about 1500 B.C. and eventually settled throughout India. Their greatest god was Indra, from whom the subcontinent takes its name. It used to be assumed that the land these warriors seized was, before their coming, a barbarous country to which they brought the light of civilization. But scholars note that one of Indra's names was *puramdara,* "fort

destroyer." In one passage he is described as destroying ninety forts; in another he "rends forts as age consumes a garment." The word *pur,* meaning "rampart" or "stronghold," occurs frequently in the *Rig-Veda;* some are built of stone (*asmamayi*), others of mud brick.

What were these forts? Until this century there was not one known building in all India that could be dated earlier than 500 B.C. Historians generally dismissed the "forts" as mere stockades, such as primitive people might raise for protection. But with the first excavation of Harappa, archaeologists began to read the *Rig-Veda* in a new light. The Indus Valley, it now appeared, had been the seat of a major civilization for a thousand years before the Aryan invasion. The forts that Indra's people stormed may well have been Harappa, Mohenjo-daro, and the other Indus cities. Perhaps Indra himself was the human leader of the conquering race, later deified by his grateful followers. If so, we know what brought the Indus civilization to its violent end, after it had been in existence for roughly a thousand years.

"What is most important in history?" asks a distinguished archaeologist. "Is it ideas or faith, technology or great men, property systems or geography?" The archaeologist, faced with a society whose few surviving written records are still undeciphered and whose oral tradition has been lost, has to make what he can of what does remain, and in the case of the Indus Valley people the remains are scanty. We know nothing about their ideas or faith, or about their great men, and can only guess at their economic system. One is left with technology and geography. The lay reader may be surprised at what has been learned despite these handicaps. In fact, the revelation of the Indus Valley civilization is a classic example of what archaeology can achieve by the interpretation of material remains—non-written evidence—alone.

Archaeologists had long been intrigued by the huge mounds of mud brick at Harappa, a site near the former course of the Ravi River, one of the chief tributaries of the Indus. The first excavations were carried out by Rai Bahadur Daya Ram Sahni, a young Indian on the staff of Sir John Marshall, at that time Director-General of Archaeology in India. In his preliminary excavations Sahni found a number of tiny seal stones bearing animal designs of great beauty, together with what was evidently some form of picture writing that bore no resemblance to any known script.

Precise dating was impossible, but from tools and other objects discovered deep in the mound it was clear that the builders of this buried city, whoever they were, had lived before the coming of the Aryans. They had reached only a chalcolithic stage of development, which was an intermediate stage between the ages of stone and bronze, when implements fashioned from both materials were in use. (In Mesopotamia and Asia Minor the Chalcolithic Period lasted for about two thousand years before the beginning of the Bronze Age in about 3500 B.C.) The lowest level of the Indus culture at Harappa—that is, the earliest level—has since been given a provisional dating of about 2500 B.C.

The Harappa mound was difficult to excavate, being partly overlaid by the modern village; moreover, in the nineteenth century it had been heavily plundered for ballast by the builders of the Lahore-Multan railway. Despite these handicaps the excavators were able to establish some of the principal features of what had been a city of some three miles in circumference. Certain of these features were unique and have no parallel outside India. Most remarkable was a great citadel roughly 460 yards long and 215 yards wide, rising high above the lower city and surrounded by a mighty baked-brick wall, 45 feet wide. There were projecting bastions,

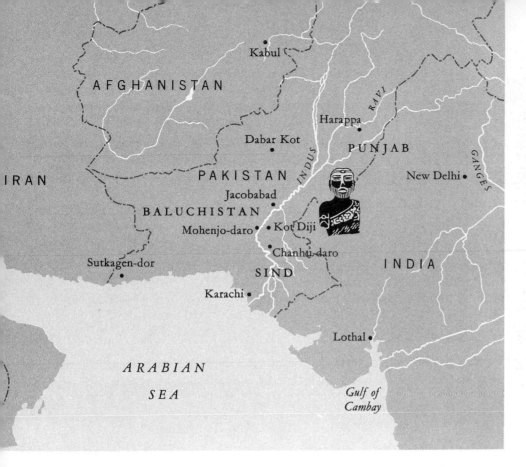

ramps, and gates protected by guardrooms. This grim military structure frowned down on the city and the plain beyond.

To the north of the citadel the archaeologists came upon a complex of buildings that they eventually identified as a double row of barrack-like dwellings, and a further double range of huge granaries. Nearby were remains of eighteen circular brick work platforms, each with a central hole in which had stood a heavy wooden mortar. Fragments of straw and barley found in these holes indicate that the platforms had been used for pounding grain. There is nothing unfamiliar in the presence of threshing floors; a similar system of pounding grain with pestles is used in Kashmir today. What may be significant is that the work was evidently done under the supervision of watchers in the citadel. This and the uniform rows of barracks strongly suggest government planning and control of at least this aspect of the economy.

The granaries, a little to the north of the work platforms, had been of remarkable size. They were arranged in symmetrical rows, and the floor of each was supported on low walls with projecting air-vents, to allow the air to circulate and thus keep the grain dry. The total floor space of the complete system of granaries, each of which measured fifty by twenty feet, amounted to twelve thousand square feet. In view of the vast size and the apparent systematic planning of the whole complex, the uniformity of the buildings, and the dominating presence of the citadel, it is difficult to escape the conclusion that these were state granaries. In addition, the excavators found evidence that the granaries were entered to the north from the banks of the river, which suggests that the grain was drawn from distant as well as nearby areas.

More substantial evidence came to light when another member of Marshall's staff, R. D. Banerji, excavated the city mound at Mohenjo-daro, nearly four hundred miles to the southwest, in the province of Sind. Here there were few overlying buildings, and the excavating team, employing hundreds of workers, was able to strip the great mound of the accretions of some thirty-five hundred years and reveal a sight that astonished archaeologists, who flocked to see it.

For there was no doubt this time. Here, bared to the fierce Indian sun after lying in darkness for probably thirty-five centuries, lay the skeleton of a vast city that had once swarmed with ant-like activity. The comparison with ants, though banal, can hardly be avoided. Even the architect's plan of Mohenjo-daro reminds one of the type of many-chambered structures these insects construct. Apart from the citadel, a great bath, and a granary, there is little evidence of monumental architecture. Temple and palace there may have been, though they have not been definitely identified. Instead we see hundreds of small buildings, many of uniform size and construction, laid out on a gridiron plan. The main thoroughfares were roughly thirty feet wide, but the houses, with their windowless outer walls, fronted on narrow lanes that appear to have been deliberately dog-legged in order to break the force of the prevailing winds.

Some of the houses were of reasonable size and planned with a feeling for spaciousness and dignity. A typical example has a porter's lodge at the entrance, and a passage leading to a pleasant courtyard that opens onto several rooms. Most of these buildings were of baked brick faced with plaster, and may have had an upper story approached by stairways that still survive. They contained bathrooms and latrines, often on two floors. Everywhere is clear evidence of controlled urban planning; earthenware drains encased in brick—one of the distinguishing marks of the Indus Valley civilization—carried sewage away from the houses, and numerous inspection holes show that they were regularly cleared.

There were many shops, including one that contained sockets in the floor, possibly for wine jars, and that may have been a restaurant; numerous wells, both public and private; and small "sentry boxes" that may have been for police or watchmen. As Sir Mortimer Wheeler, the great student of the Indus Valley civilization, has remarked, the whole plan of the city is evidence of "middle-class prosperity with zealous municipal supervision."

And, as at Harappa, Mohenjo-daro (the name may mean "the hill of the dead") had its towering citadel and state granary, though in this case they were better preserved. The citadel was built on an artificial mound about forty feet high, protected by a massive wall of mud brick with towers reinforced by timber. Within was a huge bath or tank, made watertight with mortar, bitumen, and four layers of brick. Nearby buildings, it has been suggested, may have belonged to a college of priests, but this is as yet unproved. The conspicuous emphasis on bathing, probably for purposes of purification, brings to mind current Hindu religious ritual; this and other evidence suggest that certain features of the Indus Valley civilization did indeed survive the Aryan invasion. (Religious practices in particular may have been adopted by the conquerors and handed down to present-day Indian culture.)

The citadel and the state granary at Mohenjo-daro were as elaborate as those at Harappa, and so similar in construction as to make it appear that these were the twin capitals of a common civilization, even though they were four hundred miles apart. No Indus cities of comparable size have since been found, but the numerous villages and small settlements stretching from the hills in Simla to the coast, and for a considerable distance along that coast, all bear the unmistakable marks of the Indus culture—the characteristic seals, often with pictographic writing, the triangular terra-cotta "cakes"

(the purpose of which is not known), the painted pottery, the tools, weapons, and architecture. The total area is more than twice that of Egypt or Mesopotamia.

It was a truly indigenous culture, owing nothing to Egypt, and except perhaps for the germinal concept of organized communal life, owing little directly to Mesopotamia; however, seals with Sumerian motifs, as well as beads, ornaments, and occasionally tools, prove that there were at least trading contacts with the Land Between the Rivers. In an age when no place on earth is more than two days' journey away, it is difficult to comprehend a world in which three great civilizations—Egypt, Sumer, and the Indus Valley—could grow up independently, each with its own characteristic art, technology, and religious and social system. The area in which these three self-contained worlds developed could be spanned by a jet plane in about seven hours.

Where did the founders of the Indus Valley civilization come from? This question has been partially answered, though much remains to be discovered. They were not colonists from the already developed civilization of Sumer; the evident differences between the two cultures are too great to admit that possibility. But neither could they have come from the east or south; the earliest cultures of central India and the Ganges area are later than that of the Indus. Thus the search is narrowed down to the border regions of Baluchistan and eastern Iran. We have already noted how some of the peoples who founded the civilization of Sumer came from the western mountain valleys of Iran; it now seems likely that on the eastern slopes of the Iranian massif lived other agricultural communities, and it was among these that some of the earliest Indus Valley settlers originated.

To reach the fertile Indus, such Iranian immigrants would have had to traverse Baluchistan or Afghanistan. Intelligently

directed, systematic digging in those areas might well yield interesting evidence. Here, surely, lies a promising field for archaeologists, as suggested by Sir Mortimer Wheeler, who apparently awaits the development of such a program with some impatience. "The high mound of Dabar Kot in the Zhob Valley of northern Baluchistan," he notes, "exhibits in its sides the Indus culture bracketed above and below by other cultures, and would amply reward a single season's excavation carried out with skill and purpose."

Lacking conclusive evidence from a number of sites, we can assume from what has already been found at Dabar Kot, at various sites in Sind, and at Kot Diji, twenty-five miles east of Mohenjo-daro, that beginning about 3000 B.C. the farmer-hunters of the hill communities in Baluchistan began to move down into the Indus Valley. At Kot Diji, where there are sixteen successive levels of occupation, the third from the bottom has been given a carbon-14 dating of 2700 B.C. The three topmost layers were identified by characteristic Indus pottery and other artifacts. The fourth layer revealed both Indus and pre-Indus material; the layer below that, which has been dated to about 2400 B.C., showed evidence of a conflagration and contained objects so different from those found in the topmost layers as to make it certain that they belonged to an antecedent culture, which has now been labeled Kot Dijian. All the layers below this belonged to the same pre-Indus culture. Because of the resemblances between Kot Dijian artifacts and those found in the Baluchistan region, it now seems likely that these early valley dwellers were directly related to the tribal immigrants who had begun moving down from the northern hills in the early third millennium. But these early settlers lacked the distinguishing characteristics—and techniques—of the civilization builders who followed them several centuries later.

The implication is fairly clear; newcomers arrived in the middle of the third millennium B.C. Probably they took and then burned the settlement, and afterwards rebuilt it, living there and establishing their own culture. They were more advanced than the people they superseded. For example, copper and bronze occurred in the Indus layers, together with walls of baked brick. The lower levels contained only stone tools and stone and mud-brick foundations. Similarly, at Harappa, excavations in 1946 revealed in the occupation layers below the citadel defenses a non-Indus culture related to those of north Baluchistan; and a similar situation was found to exist at Amri, south of Mohenjo-daro in Sind. Other sites await the spade, and no doubt a time will come when we shall be able to trace the newcomers back to their homelands, just as in Mesopotamia we can trace back the highly civilized Sumerians to the al 'Ubaid and Tell Halaf peoples.

The most important thing these mountain people who were to build the Indus culture brought with them to the valley was not, perhaps, their bronze tools or weapons, but the concept of a civilized society. Such a society, whose people had the knowledge of writing and led a complex, organized life centered in cities, had earlier developed in Mesopotamia. It may well have been that the hill people of Baluchistan were aware of these developments beyond the Iranian plateau in Mesopotamia and profited from this knowledge.

For centuries they had lived a closed, precarious, and difficult existence in their mountain homes, managing only to grow enough food and raise sufficient stock to eke out what they gained by hunting. But not far away lay the broad, fertile plains of the Indus and its tributaries, a dangerous land of deep jungle and wild animals. Like the valleys of the Tigris and Euphrates it could, if tamed and civilized, yield a richer and more abundant life. The land, perpetually fertilized by

river-borne mud, was rich. There was an abundance of game and fish. And the river itself provided a natural highway linking and uniting a vast area. At some time, perhaps cautiously at first, the people from the hills began to move down onto the plain. The diseases that only recently began to yield to modern science surely took a heavy toll. There were wild animals against which the only weapons were the bow and the spear, and the later settlers had to contend with hostile peoples as well. The mighty river when in flood was like a god in anger, fierce and uncontrollable, sweeping away farms, fields, men, and beasts. Yet the immigrants stayed on and fought. Thousands died, but others arrived to take their places and gradually learned to control their environment sufficiently to make urban life possible.

Within not more than a thousand years these people had created their own civilization with a heavy dependence on irrigation, flood control, and communal farming on a large scale. They built at least two big planned cities; they traded extensively with many other cultures, perhaps both by overland caravans and by small, sea-going vessels. They created a massive, if somewhat dull architecture and developed a system of pictographs, which were engraved on seals presumably used for labeling and identifying the ownership of property. And yet before the end of those ten centuries their civilization had begun to decline, and in 1500 B.C. it was overwhelmed—at least in its Indus Valley homeland—and eventually disappeared almost without trace.

Compare this relatively rapid growth and decay with the long-lived civilizations of ancient Egypt and Mesopotamia, each of which lasted three thousand years, and it will be seen that the Indus Valley culture was not the product of slow, inevitable growth. It could hardly have happened save by a conscious effort of will on the part of people who had a de-

fined objective. This, at least, is Wheeler's theory. He writes: "The benefits offered on so formidable a scale by an environment at the same time so vast, so exuberant, and so menacing are dependent, and dependent from the outset, upon the power of man to master and constrain. The situation was one which can have brooked no pusillanimity, no piecemeal compromise. A society strong in heart, disciplined, numerous, and imaginatively led grasped the problem and, we may be sure, simultaneously solved it; else it had perished."

In sum, we have a picture of people driven to tame and civilize a hostile but potentially rich region, perhaps inspired by the example of another group of human beings who had done the same. As an analogy, modern European civilization has roots that penetrate thousands of years into the past. The peoples of Africa, for example, will not need thousands of years to reach a similar level of civilization. So it may have been with the Indus Valley people.

Yet we have only the vaguest clues to the type of society that they created. We know practically nothing of their religion, though the presence of numerous female figurines—possibly of a fertility goddess—suggests that in the Indus Valley, as in Sumer and Crete, the earliest deities were female. And since in Egypt, Sumer, Hatti, and other centers of civilization the intellectual leaders were the priests, who claimed to understand and control the forces of nature, it is reasonable to assume that a similar situation would have applied in the Indus Valley. Yet to date, no temples have been positively identified, though on seals and among the statues of stone, terra cotta, and bronze unearthed at Harappa and Mohenjo-daro are figures that may represent gods. One seal depicts a three-faced figure sitting on a low stool flanked by a buffalo and a rhinoceros; below the stool are two antelopes or goats. Sir John Marshall has suggested

that this figure may have been the prototype of the later Hindu god Siva, in his aspect as lord of beasts.

There are also small clay statuettes representing female figures, nude except for intricate necklaces and large, wide-spreading headdresses. Some of the figures have a cup on each side of the headdress, and from the smoke stains occasionally found in them it has been assumed that they were used for burning incense. Occasionally one finds seals with figures reminiscent of certain Sumerian mythological scenes; for example, a horned tiger being attacked by a bull-man or minotaur recalls numerous Sumerian representations of battles between minotaurs and various composite animals.

Besides the seals with Sumerian motifs, there is evidence of another Mesopotamian parallel with the Indus Valley culture; this is the basic concept of controlling a flooding river by diverting its waters, in order to irrigate and fertilize large tracts of arid land. Yet in most respects the Harappan civilization was quite individual. The plans of the Indus cities, with their citadels and granaries, the construction of the buildings, the pottery, tools, and weapons, the statuary and ornaments bear little resemblance to their counterparts in Sumer and other cultures. Those Sumerian objects that have been found were clearly imported in the normal process of trade. The entrepôt of this trade, Telmun, can probably be identified with the island Bahrein in the Persian Gulf, reached by sailing down the Indus and then westward along the coast of the Arabian Sea. Sumerian cuneiform tablets describe Telmun as a trading center and refer occasionally to a land called Meluhha, which may have been the Indus Valley.

The inhabitants of the Indus were a great trading people. They imported not only Sumerian products but gold from southern India, silver, copper, and lapis lazuli from Afghanistan, and turquoise from Iran; in return their merchants may have shipped abroad copper, stone, ivory, wood, and certain animals. Among their agricultural products were wheat, barley, melons, peas, sesame, and possibly dates, and they domesticated humped cattle, buffaloes, and possibly horses, asses, cats, pigs, and camels. They also grew cotton and exported it to Sumer; they are the earliest people known to have cultivated this plant.

The Harappans had an effective system of weights and measures, a necessity for both the domestic and the foreign commerce of their thriving cities. At the Indus sites weights have been found ranging from very large to tiny units. The former are in some cases so large that ropes and metal rings were required to hoist them; the smallest weights were probably used by jewelers. The higher weights, along with measures of length, followed the decimal system, although the binary system was used for lower denominations.

But the principal source of wealth in the Indus Valley was the land, which, though richly fertile, had to be protected. Bitter experience must have taught the people how violent and unpredictable were the Indus floods. They learned to build dikes and dams and to raise their cities on mounds out of reach of the floodwaters. It must have been a constant, bitter struggle involving the communal effort of many thousands. Admittedly the Indus settlers had one notable advantage over the Egyptians and the Sumerians, who had to learn the technique through trial and error over a vast period of time. As Wheeler says, the Indus people at least had the assurance that it had been done before and could therefore be done again. Even so, the Indus presented its own special problems, which the settlers solved, or partially solved, in their own individual way. The state granaries, huge and severely functional, drew their supplies from a wide area, as has already been pointed out. At Mohenjo-daro archaeologists

were able to identify an unloading area into which grain wagons were evidently driven. Above this area was a platform onto which the sheaves of barley could be hauled by ropes, after which they would be stacked in the huge, castle-like structure, whose steep, forbidding walls were clearly designed to resist attack. For grain was life, and the dusty, sweating drivers with their oxcarts, bringing in the harvest from fields far out across the plain, knew that by so doing they were protecting themselves against the results of flood, famine, and foreign invasion.

However, it is only fair to mention that this theory is not universally shared by archaeologists. Some students of the Indus Valley civilization have put forward a different interpretation, according to which the great cities of Harappa and Mohenjo-daro were merely cult centers dedicated to the worship of a god or several gods; the tributes of grain were intended for the deity; and the real centers of the Indus Valley civilization were the smaller towns and villages. It is a theory that has few adherents, for the ancient civilizations of which we have better records—Egypt, Sumer, and Crete—were oriented on palaces or cities in which lived not only the temporal or spiritual rulers of the state, but the administrators, record keepers, and tax collectors who controlled its economy. Nevertheless, it is true that to date nothing resembling the files of accounts, receipts, and tax returns—such as one might expect to find at an archaeological city-site—has turned up at either Harappa or Mohenjo-daro.

What sort of life was lived by the inhabitants of Harappa and Mohenjo-daro during the millennium that their civilization endured? Again we have to rely entirely on remains of buildings, tools, weapons, pottery, and a few examples of statuary, seals, and ornaments. Yet much may be learned even from this sparse evidence. The cities were planned with an eye to convenience, efficiency, cleanliness, and protection from the baking sun. The sanitary system and the numerous baths would have helped to keep down the plagues and epidemics that threaten large communities of people, especially in hot countries. Some of the buildings were commodious and exhibit a certain bourgeois comfort, if not grace, and even the smallest dwellings, though cramped and of dreary uniformity, were probably no worse than the homes of millions of Indian and Pakistani artisans today. In the important respects of sanitation and water supply, they were superior.

Rich burials, like those that tell us so much about the peoples of Egypt and Sumer, have not yet been encountered; such graves as have been discovered are evidently those of average citizens. Several pots and trinkets accompany a corpse, and that is all. Nor is there anything strikingly beautiful in the pottery, though it is interesting that some pottery fragments have been found inscribed with those intriguing pictographs that have so far defied interpretations. (Michael Ventris, decipherer of the Cretan Linear B script, was about to begin work on the Indus pictographs when he died.) Such jewelry as has been found, especially the necklaces of gold, faience, carnelian, and steatite, is pleasing but unremarkable. Perhaps the most beautiful, as well as the most characteristic, Indus artifacts are the tiny seals, about an inch in width. Unlike the cylindrical Sumerian seals, these are usually square, though some are disc-shaped and a few cylindrical examples have been found. Each was carved in stone with a minute but delicately executed design, usually featuring an animal, and from these we know the types of wild beasts with which the Indus Valley folk were familiar. They include the crocodile, rhinoceros, elephant, tiger, and antelope; also a strange ox-like creature that appears to have only one horn. (Sir Mortimer Wheeler has noted that according to both Aristotle

None of the ancient ruins of Mohenjo-daro has yet been identified as a formal place of worship, but it has been pointed out that if the city had a temple, it might logically have stood at the highest point of the citadel. That area is today covered by a Buddhist shrine, or stupa (background, left), erected over two thousand years after the people of the Indus Valley built their city. No such hindrance kept archaeologists from uncovering the circular brick threshing floors (right) at Harappa. Bits of barley, wheat, and straw have been recovered from the central holes in the platforms; these indentations may have served as the mortars in which Indus workers ground grain with wooden pestles.

and Ctesias, a Greek historian, the unicorn came from India.)

The seals were usually perforated for hanging around the neck or wrist and usually had short pictographic inscriptions. These may have been names, though not necessarily always of individuals; some may indicate a title or a trade. The seals were probably used for stamping the clay sealings that identified the ownership of certain goods—jars of oil or wine, for instance, bales of cloth, or other properties. A similar method was used in both Mesopotamia and Egypt. Apart from their interest as minute works of art, these seals may perhaps eventually provide clues that will lead archaeologists to the original homelands of the Indus Valley people; they are so characteristic of this culture that they provide a readily recognizable clue to an Indus site, wherever it may be found. In contrast to the currently favored theory that the origins of the Indus people may ultimately be discovered in both Iran and Baluchistan, Stuart Piggott, an authority on Indus Valley archaeology, has pointed out that virtually no seals have been found in the Baluchistan settlements; he maintains that the people who carried what was to become Harappan culture down from the uplands must therefore have come directly from Iran, and not from Baluchistan.

Few examples of Indus statuary, either in stone or bronze, have been found; those that exist indicate that Harappan artisans were not particularly interested in portraying the human form. An exception is the slim, nubile figure of a dancing girl, her hand provocatively resting on her hip, and naked save for her numerous armlets. This little bronze figurine has such a contemporary Indian quality as to make it probable that artistic elements of the Indus Valley culture, as well as the religious customs already mentioned, were absorbed by the Aryan invaders and transmitted to later Indian cultures. Of the small stone sculptures, perhaps the

The columnar tower above was once a sunken well. Excavators left it standing when they dug through earlier city-layers to find the first level at Mohenjo-daro.

most striking is the steatite figure of a bearded man, found at Mohenjo-daro. It has a powerful but sinister face, with narrow eyes, prognathous jaw, and receding forehead, impressive in a somewhat repellent way—the kind of face one can well imagine frowning down from the citadel on the ranks of laborers pounding grain on the work platforms.

There is a large number of little terra-cotta models of animals, executed with keen observation of the character of the beast depicted, and with masterly technique. There are also terra-cotta toy carts with movable wheels, much like the peasant carts seen in India today; small, clay, box-like shapes, thought to have been mousetraps, and terra-cotta rattles and dice have also been found. The dice remarkably resemble those used in games today, but the dotted markings on opposite sides do not add up to seven; one dot appears opposite two, instead of opposite six.

Finally we must ask why the Indus Valley civilization, after only one thousand years of existence, failed and disappeared. The most widely accepted answer, previously discussed in connection with the *Rig-Veda,* is that it was overthrown about 1500 B.C. by the Aryan invaders under their war god Indra, the fort-destroyer. The Aryans seem to have come from the southern slopes of the Himalayas and may have been related to other warrior peoples who were moving into Asia Minor and Greece both at the beginning and at the end of the second millennium B.C. One may speculate that *Hari-Yupuya,* described in the *Rig-Veda* as the site of an Aryan victory, may have been Harappa. And at Mohenjo-daro the excavators came upon piles of skeletons of men, women, and children who had been cut down, stabbed, or clubbed to death and left to rot where they fell. It was a grim sight; in one house thirteen skeletons, still wearing rings and bracelets, lay sprawled in the agony of death. Sword cuts in the skulls of two skeletons showed how they had perished. Not far away was a public well, and here two other skeletons, one of them female, lay stretched across the stones, apparently struck down as they had tried to escape. In another place lay nine more contorted skeletons, five of which were those of children. All this pitiful human debris lay in the highest level of the city, the last one inhabited by Indus-culture people.

This is the catastrophic end of the story uncovered by archaeologists. As they sank their shafts through the layers of the city they revealed a record of progressive deterioration and decay. At the lower levels were fine, well-made buildings of impressive size and construction. But higher up in the mound the buildings became shoddier and smaller. As generation succeeded generation, each generation building on the partly demolished structures of its forebears, the living quarters became more cramped, the construction progressively poorer. It seemed as if "squatters" had moved in, breeding prolifically, no doubt, and no longer enjoying the wealth that the city had been able to command in the days of its greatness. It was as if once-dignified town mansions had deteriorated until they had become slum dwellings.

Finally, it may be surmised, the state decayed to the point where its defenses were neglected, and the Aryans moved down into the valley just as the ancestors of the Indus people had moved down in the distant past. Indra had come, and the thousand-year experiment in civilization was at an end.

What caused this decline? Groping in semidarkness, without the light of written records or the testimony of neighboring or successor peoples, we can find no certain answer, but must fall back on theory. There could have been a breakup of the strong controlling power, and a succession of impotent rulers; there could have been a switching of trade routes, or a deterioration of the soil, which if neglected soon becomes saline, as one can see in the Sind desert today. (The white crust on the surface has been described by one writer as "a satanic mockery of snow.") Or there could have been a breakdown in the vast system of controls needed to hold in check the floods of the great river.

One ingenious theory is based on the simple fact that in building and rebuilding their cities, towns, and villages the Indus Valley people used enormous amounts of baked bricks. Baking naturally needs fire, and the principal fuel in the Indus would have been timber. Five thousand years ago large forests grew on the hills bordering the valley. The remorseless stripping of this forest cover over a period of ten centuries could well have increased the flooding of the Indus, just as deforestation has altered the climate of other lands; the heavy rainfall, no longer partially absorbed by vegetation, could have stripped off the surface soil and swelled the already affluent river to unmanageable proportions. Against such power the highest dikes would fail unless continually rebuilt and maintained. The results of such neglect may well be imagined. (It must be remembered too that only within the last century have we begun to understand the relationship between deforestation, soil erosion, and flooding.)

Compared with the much richer and better known civilizations of Egypt and Sumer, the Indus Valley civilization surely seems a far less dramatic and splendid achievement. We cannot tell how much of its contribution has been permanently lost, or what remains to be learned—especially not until the inscriptions are deciphered; even the incomplete picture we now have of the Harappans in their bustling cities may prove to be inaccurate. Yet we can respond to the drama that lies in the total effort of a people who after untold centuries of hard-won existence in the mountains of southeastern Iran and Baluchistan suddenly exploded into the fertile but perilous valley of the Indus. They cleared the jungle, fought the wild beasts, tamed the flooding river, planned and built their cities, and created within a relatively short time a thriving civilization. We do not know who they were or, with any certainty, where they came from. Gods, kings, heroes, thinkers, poets, all alike are forgotten. When we first encounter them they are already in possession of a mature, highly developed culture; we know nothing of the early failures that must have occurred before they secured a foothold in that untamed land. But we do know that they succeeded, and that it was through their toil that a true civilization was born.

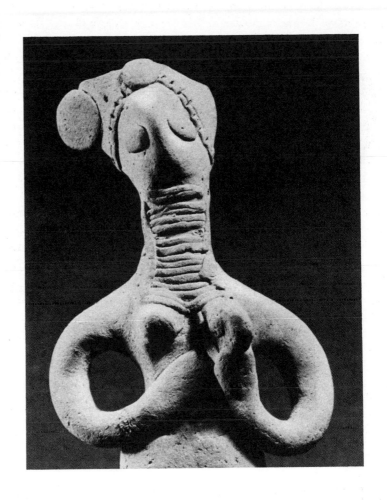

INDUS IMAGES

With faces pinched from clay, crude figures like the terra-cotta image above may have represented the fertility goddess of the ancient Indus Valley civilization. Such figurines, found in the ruins of many cities, sometimes appear with bellies swollen in pregnancy; others lie upon little clay beds or feed infants at their breasts; still other female representations give birth to rivers and to plant life, denoting the broad powers of creation that usually belong to the mother goddess. There is good reason to find fertility symbols in these images, but there is no general agreement about their function. If Mohenjo-daro and Harappa were secular, urban communities, as is broadly supposed, the figures could have been fertility idols from household shrines, as well as models of petitioners, and even dolls; some have been found in drainage systems, suggesting that they were dropped by children at play. If, as others believe, the same cities were elaborate ceremonial centers, the effigies may have served solely as sacred fertility-cult objects.

Modeled animals similar to the terra-cotta bull above make up almost three-fourths of the clay images found thus far at Indus Valley sites. The monkey below is finished with a faience glaze. Unlike the animals portrayed on seals, such as the tiger on the facing page, these figurines show no markings that would suggest a sacred use, but they may have been votive idols nonetheless.

THE
WORLD
OF
BEASTS

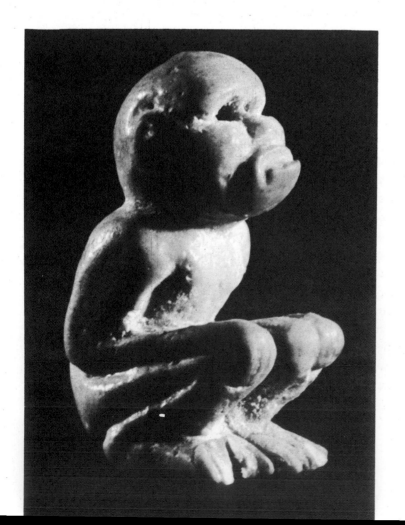

The artists of the Indus Valley lavished their talents upon portraits of the animals that lived in the ancient river valley; thousands of careful representations of bulls and buffaloes, tigers, elephants, and many other creatures have survived, mainly on the minute seals that are characteristic of the culture. Like other early peoples, the valley dwellers must have cherished the beasts of burden upon which their economy so heavily depended; at the same time they no doubt viewed the powerful predatory beasts of the forest with respect and terror. In time, regard for these animals may have grown into formalized reverence, for on seals the humped and the short-horned draft bull and the ferocious tiger were frequently portrayed with a strange emblem believed to have had ritual significance. One human figure is shown on the seals in a seated, yoga-like posture, surrounded by animals, and may represent a Harappan deity in the role of ruler of animals. The worship of bulls in India today may also descend from the religious traditions of the Indus Valley culture, long thought to have perished with the great Harappan cities when the Aryans, under their war god, invaded the land.

The bronze figure on this page is 4½ inches in actual height. The pot at left, found in Baluchistan, is Iranian in shape. The humped bulls it features, however, are typically Indian animals; their presence may indicate a flow of influence from the Indus Valley westward into Baluchistan.

SOURCES OF CULTURE

Mohenjo-daro was probably not the birthplace of the girl who served as the model for the famous bronze dancing figure (right and above); although found at that site, the statuette is said to resemble a young Baluchi woman, identifiable by her bracelets and the heavy plait of hair gathered to one side of her neck. Those who see such a likeness speculate that the model may have come to Mohenjo-daro with Harappan traders, who on trips to Baluchistan could have brought back dancing girls to amuse "the tired businessmen" in the thriving valley cities. The origin of the people who built a civilization in the Indus Valley is even more difficult to determine. Settlers moving down from the Baluchistan hills, carrying with them influences from the Iranian plateau and perhaps Mesopotamia beyond, are said to have played the major role. One theory bars Baluchistan as a point of origin, however, and traces the source of Harappan civilization directly to Iran. It is also possible that an indigenous population helped to define the culture that developed in the valley. The discovery of the Indus Valley civilization is so recent and investigations are still so incomplete that the problems surrounding its origin cannot yet be solved.

ROMANCE OF REDISCOVERY

There has never been a time in the known history of man when he has not indulged in speculation about the past and tried to learn more about his antecedents by collecting and studying the relics of earlier times. The Greeks had a word for the discussion of antiquities, from which we have derived our own word *archaeology*. But the Greeks emerged relatively late in the history of civilization. Antiquarianism was already a respectable pursuit before their time. The ancient Egyptians were the first Egyptologists. The pharaohs of the Nile Valley often showed a reverent regard for the achievements of their predecessors, and from time to time revived and copied the arts of the more distant past.

In the sixth century B.C. the princess Belshalti-Nanner, sister of Belshazzar, set aside a room to house her collection of local antiquities; among its ruins was found an inscribed clay drum which could be called the earliest known museum label. The princess must have been inspired by her father, Nabonidus, who was the last king of Babylon and who apparently devoted a large part of his time to antiquarian research. During his excavations at the age-old ziggurat at Ur, Nabonidus uncovered an early foundation stone which, he reported with an understandable mixture of awe and satisfaction, "for thirty-two hundred years no previous king had seen." Then, with the handwriting on the wall, the kingdom of Nabonidus collapsed, and in the years to come his resplendent capital crumbled into dust.

Today we know much more about the ancient past of Mesopotamia than Nabonidus knew. In the world of archaeology, the last century and a half has been an age of exploration as rich in adventure and discovery as the age of Columbus and Magellan that first found its way about the seven seas of the globe. Expeditions have pushed the charted limits of history back to the unexpectedly remote beginnings of civilization on this planet. Their reports have disclosed large regions of human experience which had been lost to the memory of man in some cases for millenniums and whose wealth of interest was unimaginable. The revelation that such a great part of man's accomplishment and thought, his dreams along with his deeds, lay buried beneath the ground came with a shock of surprise that has been felt over and over again during the last four or five generations with every fresh report from these long-lost worlds.

The first major penetration into the mysteries of the preclassical past was a by-product of Napoleon's ill-fated Egyptian campaign of 1798. Along with his formidable army the young general transported a whole corps of savants—scientists, antiquarians, and artists—whose mission it was, among other things, to compile a faithful and complete record of the valley of the Nile and its timeless monuments, and to gather what evidence it could for shipment back to France.

The publication of the records kept by the expedition was a great early landmark in the history of archaeology. Scores of volumes were issued during the early years of the nineteenth century. Their abundant illustrations from on-the-spot drawings provided a detailed, accurate visual record of the face of Egypt that came as a complete novelty to all but the most privileged travelers. The impact of these strange and wonderful sights fired public curiosity. What seemed an excess of popular excitement over these matters was lampooned in a number of contemporary prints and drawings. But such burlesques hardly exaggerated the interest that mounted from then on with every new archaeological venture into the faraway corners of time. As Napoleon's acquisitive tactics foretold, antiquities became counters in a game of international prestige that has not yet been played out.

The men in the field played their part in the game with an enthusiasm that at times resembled downright abandon. In their impatience to break through the barriers of time they occasionally resorted to battering-rams and gunpowder, methods that served the immediate purpose without regard for the evidence destroyed in the process. Giovanni Battista Belzoni, literally a giant in the early history of Egyptology (he stood six feet seven inches tall and had been a professional strong man), wrote of his visit to the necropolis near Thebes that with every step he "crushed a mummy in some part or other . . . [and] could not avoid being covered with bones, legs, arms, and heads rolling from above." It was Belzoni too who battered his way into the secret recesses of sealed tombs. But the treasures he unearthed and shipped off to England—the colossal torso of Ramesses II among them— became the proud possessions of London museums; and the narrative of his often perilous and always spirited adventures in the land of the pharaohs carried an infectious enchantment that spread wherever his book was read.

The great monuments of Egypt had stood firm before the passage of centuries to remind the world of their hidden secrets. But the cities and temples of ancient Mesopotamia had crumbled into dusty mounds, their very location in most cases confused or forgotten, as had long before been observed. "As for Nineveh . . . it is already gone," wrote Lucian seventeen hundred years ago, "and there is not a trace of it left; you couldn't even say where it was. . . . But there is Babylon, the well-towered city with its enormous walls, before long it will be as hard to find as Nineveh."

The first man to probe with good purpose into the heaps of rubble that, according to tenacious traditions, had once been mighty Babylon and Nineveh was another of those prodigious figures whose intrepid spirit and rare talents dramatized the development of archaeology. Claudius James Rich was a self-taught linguist who while still a youth had mastered Arabic, Persian, Turkish, Hebrew, Syriac, and other Eastern languages, including some Chinese—not to mention French and Italian. As "political resident of the honorable East India Company at Baghdad," he had opportunities to indulge his tireless curiosity about the ancient Near East, at times dressed in native garb and passing successfully as a native of more than one Eastern country. On one occasion he impersonated a Georgian Turk and traveled with a horde of pilgrims to Mecca, "completely unsuspected by the most vigilant and fiercest Mussulman bigotry."

Rich died in 1821 at the age of thirty-four while he was nursing the victims of a cholera epidemic in Shiraz. His collections of oriental manuscripts and cuneiform tablets were sold to the British Museum. But before his death, his reports of discoveries at the site of Babylon and elsewhere awakened an interest in the archaeology of Mesopotamia that was remarkable enough for Lord Byron to memorialize in a section of his poetic work, *Don Juan.*

Less than a generation later, Rich's compatriot Austen Henry Layard, another brilliant linguist with a "passionate desire for exploring the East," excavated the mounds at Nimrud and there uncovered the remains of the great royal palace of Assurnasirpal II, then at Nineveh the palace of Sennacherib, and that of Assurbanipal with its great library of cuneiform tablets. The fabulous treasures he found at these sites, which he shipped home to the British Museum, surpassed anything that had yet come out of the ancient Near East. Here, among other things, were examples of those monstrous human-headed winged beasts that had guarded the entrance to Assurnasirpal's royal capital. When the first of these was unearthed, Layard wrote, its great head "rising from the bowels of the earth might well have belonged to one of those fearful beings which are pictured in the traditions of the country, as appearing to mortals, slowly ascending from the regions below."

Layard was an able writer and a fine draftsman and his reports made major news stories when they were published in England. The growing popular press kept pace with archaeological developments and fed public curiosity with every intelligence that came from the field. When George Smith, an assistant in the British Museum, found among Layard's tablets a portion of the Gilgamesh epic that seemed to tell in cuneiform the story of the Deluge, the London *Daily Telegraph* immediately looked for a scoop.

One crucial passage of the story was missing, and the newspaper dispatched Smith to Nineveh to find the tablets that would complete this part of the epic, paying his way in exchange for an exclusive right to publish the findings. Smith's search took on the character of a great public detective story. (Gilbert and Sullivan noted the popular excitement in these decipherments in *The Pirates of Penzance,* in which the Major General boasts that he could "write a washing bill in cuneiform.") By fantastic good fortune Smith found precisely what he had gone looking for, what he needed to convince the world of the astonishing and, to some, shocking, parallel between the Hebrew and the earlier Babylonian accounts of the flood. Subsequently Smith deciphered other tablets which contained, he reported, a "continuous series of Babylonian legends, giving the history of the world from the Creation down to some period after the Fall of Man."

Two centuries before these revelations, the archbishop James Ussher, by the most laborious calculations based on the Hebrew date of the flood, 2348 B.C., and the data in Genesis 1, had set the time of creation on a certain Sunday evening in the year 4004 B.C. It was a remarkable display of erudition and commanded enough authority to be noted in the margins of reference editions of the Authorized Version of the Bible. The disclosures of archaeology were only beginning, but it became increasingly difficult to cling to that precise date with any real assurance. The course of history seemed to trace not a straight line or a steady curve, but a cycle that Aristotle had seen as a continuous "coming to be and falling away"—reaching indefinitely in either direction, in time.

The growing realization that there had been unheard-of civilizations that had once flourished mightily and had then vanished from the face of the earth had melancholy implications that satisfied the romantic mood of the nineteenth century. In 1791 Constantin Volney had issued his book *The Ruins*. Volney had roamed the world from the ruin-dotted lands of the East to the virgin forests of America, and in these brooding pages he meditated on the causes of the downfall of empires—a theme paraphrased by Shelley twenty years later in *Queen Mab*. The thought that there might be sinister forces which in the end would defeat the efforts of man, as they had done repeatedly in the past, haunted the imagination of the century and gave artists in every medium an excuse to indulge both their somber speculations and their most exotic fancies.

Long before Layard and others had made their spectacular disclosures, Byron invoked the image of the semifabulous Assyrian tyrant Sardanapalus in order to weave a gaudy tragedy on the theme of death and destruction. In a climactic episode, the great king foresaw the collapse of his empire, gathered his harem, his slaves, his dogs, and his horses and had them slaughtered in his presence before they were all put to the torch on his own funeral pyre. Just who Sardanapalus may have been has never been determined, although he has been confused with Assurbanipal, the remains of whose beautiful and famous palace at Nineveh Layard had yet to study. But Byron was responding to the temper of the day, which looked to the faraway in space and time for dramatic materials that anticipated the sensational truths that the archaeologists would in fact so soon provide. A few years later, the French painter Eugène Delacroix emphasized the point by borrowing Byron's slaughter scene for the subject of one of his most impressive and colorful canvases.

However, neither the poets nor the painters could in their most imaginative moments envision the tales of wonder that continued to unfold as men searched the globe looking for what might have been lost and forgotten of their human heritage. Deep in the rain jungles and amid the highlands of Middle America, it was reported by men of serious mind who had been there, were visible remains of white temple-cities which could have been those of the lost Tribes of Israel or, if not that, of even more venerable representatives of the human race—perhaps of the inhabitants of Plato's lost Atlantis. Disbelievers and those who were unaware of the evidence remained satisfied that before the coming of the white man America had been peopled only by savages.

One of the most enchanting chapters in the entire history of archaeology was written by the American John Lloyd Stephens who in 1839, with the English-born artist Frederick Catherwood, hacked his way through the trackless wilderness of Central America to learn the truth about the mysterious monuments that had been reported there. Both men were experienced travelers; Catherwood was an accomplished artist and Stephens was a writer of surpassing charm. The hazards and the difficulties of their expedition were more formidable than anything that they had foreseen or hitherto known. But when they penetrated to the site of Copan in what is now western Honduras and beheld the evidence that lay scattered about, half-buried in the earth or enveloped in a tangled mesh of tropical growth, they peered into an entire new world of discovery. Here, and subsequently at other sites, this gifted pair found evidence that confounded almost everything that had been said about America's ancient past. These steaming jungles had for centuries veiled the temple-cities of the Maya, a purely native civilization that had flowered into complex growth in Central America long before Europe had heard of a New World in the west.

"America, say historians, was peopled by savages; but savages never reared these structures, savages never carved these stones . . . ," Stephens wrote later of Copan. "Architecture, sculpture, and painting, all the arts which embellish life, had flourished in this overgrown forest; orators, warriors, and statesmen, beauty, ambition, and glory had lived and passed away, and none knew that such things had been, or could tell of their past existence . . . The beauty of the sculpture, the solemn stillness of the woods disturbed only by the scrambling of monkeys and the chattering of parrots, the desolation of the city, and the mystery that hung over it, all created an interest higher, if possible, than I had ever felt among the ruins of the Old World."

Not many explorers into the past were such talented storytellers as Stephens. But even the most prosaic reports gave promise of distant worlds still to be revealed; and they came from all over—from the windy heights of Anatolia where a strange people, the Hittites, once held sway with great authority; from the remote tropical interior of Cambodia, where at Angkor, it was reported, some unsung Oriental Michelangelo had raised temples of dazzling and exotic beauty; from the shores of the Aegean, where the fabulous legends of our own classical past suddenly became true.

To a public whose schooling was rooted in the literature of ancient Greece and Rome, the reports of Schliemann's discoveries at Troy and Mycenae brought the romance of archaeology back close to home. The facts of Schliemann's life and work are hardly more plausible than most fairy tales. As a poor child in Germany he had put his faith in the historical reality of Homer's epics; as a grown man, he never renounced his youthful dream that he might one day actually find Troy and King Priam's treasure. When he was a rich man, by the stubborn persistence of his faith, he awakened the world to a vision of the past in which "the topless towers of Ilium" rose like a beacon of truth rediscovered.

As Carlyle observed a century or so ago, there is poetic meaning in the very word *past,* a meaning that grows clearer the farther we recede in time from the events that are considered. In the pursuits of archaeology, imagination, seeking the facts, finds in them the true poetry of human history.

The results of the observations and studies made by the learned specialists who accompanied Napoleon's expedition were published in a series of gigantic volumes entitled Description de l'Egypte. No country had ever before been so thoroughly delineated. The frontispiece of the first volume (above) presents a telescopic panorama of the principal monuments of the Nile Valley, from the Delta to the cataracts. An illustration from another volume (left) shows a member of Napoleon's intellectual task force directing the exploration of a passageway within the Great Pyramid.

C. Richard Lepsius, leader of a Prussian archaeological expedition to Egypt, made many superb drawings of the land and its monuments

hey appeared in the 1840's. These were reproduced in twelve huge volumes of plates. This view shows the temple of Sethi I at the right.

The nineteenth century burgeoned with venturesome travelers who sought out long-untrodden paths to the past. In the 1830's, the Frenchman Charles Texier journeyed into the forbidding uplands of Turkey and discovered, high above the ruins of an ancient city he could not identify, a great gallery of curious figures carved along the walls of the rugged cliffs. The illustration (upper left) from the report of his travels is labeled as the site of Pteria, scene of the famous conflict between Croesus and Cyrus. Texier had in fact found the Hittite sanctuary known as Yazilikaya. Only a few years later, Stephens and Catherwood rediscovered the ruins of Tulum, the walled Maya city that the conquistadores had claimed rivaled Seville in size and splendor. Catherwood pictured its principal building, the Castillo (below), as native workmen hacked at the entangling jungle. Earlier in the century, discoveries in various parts of Italy had excited fresh interest in the Etruscan past. In a scene from an early nineteenth-century account (lower left), a well-dressed artist records the gloomy interior of a plundered Etruscan tomb by the light of a torch held by one of his two companions.

Giovanni Belzoni, shown at left in Oriental garb, was known to England before his Egyptian expeditions as a performer in Sadler's Wells and other music halls. In 1821, after returning to London, he staged a display of his Egyptian discoveries (below), which The Times hailed as an "extraordinary exhibition" that contained a "multitude of collateral curiosities." The showing was held, appropriately, at Egyptian Hall in Piccadilly, and attracted a crowd of almost two thousand paying visitors on opening day. At the Universal Exhibition held at Paris in 1878 Europe had its first view of the world of the ancient Khmers (right), strangely beautiful images that had been retrieved from the forest that had engulfed them for five hundred years past.

The exposure of the head of one of the huge stone figures at Layard's Nimrud excavation (above) caused great excitement among the native workmen who believed they had uncovered an effigy of Nimrud himself. The colossal figure was hauled to the river, for transshipment to England, by three hundred shouting men, preceded by relays of musicians, followed by shrieking women, and attended by wildly dashing horsemen (above left).

The architect who made this rendering of Assurnasirpal's palace at Nimrud had little to go on except the ground plans revealed by Layard.

His imagination was obviously influenced by the contemporary exposition at the Crystal Palace, for which he had designed the Nineveh Court.

Egyptian Hall, where Belzoni held his celebrated exhibition, was an extravagant interpretation of the Egyptian "style" set in the Georgian calm of a London street. It had been built in 1812 shortly after the appearance of the first volumes of Description de l'Egypte. In 1822, one year after Belzoni's show, the hall was hired by the English artist John Martin for an exhibition of his paintings. Like other artists of the romantic period, he dealt with sublimity and horror on a colossal scale and inevitably turned to themes from the distant past to add grandeur to his presentations. In his Seventh Plague of Egypt (left), as told in Exodus, Moses stretches forth his rod toward heaven, and thunder, hail, and fire are loosed on the land of Pharaoh. The structures in Martin's painting are an assortment of Egyptian halls grown larger and ever more indifferent to archaeological fact. Throughout the last century, artists played to a large audience with allegorical and historical subjects drawn from areas of the past where archaeologists were making their finds. The respectability of such themes often provided a gloss for otherwise highly sensual pictures. The success of this formula is suggested by the fact that Edwin Long's Babylonian Marriage Market (above left) was sold for seven thousand guineas in 1875.

OVERLEAF: In The Death of Sardanapalus Eugène Delacroix depicted the last moments of the Assyrian empire as Byron had retold it, with highly romantic flourishes, from the accounts of early Greek writers. Besieged in Nineveh, the great king foresees the fulfillment of ancient prophecy and impassively orders the slaughter of his favorite women. When shown to the public in 1827 the painting created a sensation because of the unrestrained opulence of its bold colors and what seemed at the time its confused composition.

CRETE

THE ISLAND OF MINOS

Europa was the daughter of Agenor, the king of Tyre. She was so beautiful that Zeus himself, the king of gods, fell in love with her. Europa and her companions were used to stroll near the seashore at Tyre, where Agenor's herds of cattle grazed. Zeus assumed the shape of a snow-white bull and mingled with them. Seeing the beautiful beast, Europa caressed it, whereupon Zeus contrived to get her on his back and swam with her across the sea to the far-off island of Crete. There he assumed the shape of an eagle and lay with the girl; the resultant offspring were Sarpedon, Rhadamanthus, and Minos, who became king of Crete.

Aegeus was king of Athens. He had a son, Theseus, by the daughter of Pittheus, king of Troezen, in whose palace the boy was brought up. When he grew to manhood Theseus went to Athens in search of his father. Medea, wife of Aegeus, tried to poison the young man before his father could recognize him, but she failed. Later Theseus, already renowned for many feats of heroism, volunteered to sail to Crete as one of the seven youths who, with seven maidens, were sent every ninth year by Athens as tribute to King Minos.

In the labyrinth of his palace, Minos kept a monster, part bull and part man, the progeny of his wife, Pasiphaë, whom the sea god Poseidon had caused to be enamored of a bull. Until Theseus arrived the fourteen youths and maidens were invariably devoured by the monster. Ariadne, the daughter of Minos, fell in love with the handsome Athenian, and gave him a ball of thread which he played out behind him as he penetrated the labyrinth. When he met the Minotaur in the dim depths, Theseus slew him "by smiting him

To mark the spot as sacred, horns of consecration such as those shown on the facing page were set atop the palace of Minos at Knossos; they probably represented the horns of sacrificed bulls.

with his fists," and then, by following the thread, found his way out and into the arms of Ariadne. The two lovers fled to the island of Naxos, where Theseus deserted Ariadne. On his return to Athens he forgot to hoist the white sails that were the prearranged signal of his success in Crete. The stricken King Aegeus saw the ship's black sails—the signal that Theseus had lost in his encounter with the unnatural beast—threw himself into the sea, and drowned. Ever since it has been called the Aegean. So Theseus, in his turn, became the king of the Athenians.

The Greeks of the classical age believed these two familiar Greek myths. The Romans probably had doubts, and every succeeding age down to this one has regarded them as legends and nothing more. But nowadays we hardly know where we are. Historians, linguists, and practical-minded archaeologists comb the myths, the works of Homer, Hesiod, and other Greek poets in search of clues to archaeological sites. No one raises an eyebrow if a philologist like Leonard Palmer or an archaeologist such as Carl Blegen mingles his linguistic researches or excavation reports with references to what Homer said about King Nestor of Pylos or King Priam of Troy. This was not always so. In 1846 the monumental history of Greece by George Grote contained these words: "I begin the real history of Greece with the first recorded Olympiad, or 776 B.C. . . . For the truth is, that historical records, properly so called, do not begin until long after this date: nor will any man who candidly considers the extreme paucity of attested facts for two centuries after 776 B.C. be astonished to learn that the state of Greece in 900, 1000, 1100, 1200, 1300, 1400 B.C.—or any earlier century which it may please chronologists to include in their computed genealogies—cannot be described to him upon anything like decent evidence." These earlier times, Grote observed in his

Throughout the Near East the bull was a symbol of male potency, and frequent representations of it in Minoan art suggest that it served as the masculine counterpart to the fertile mother goddess whom the Cretans worshiped. Whether they actually considered the bull a god as well is not known. The bull's-head rhyton shown at right was discovered in a cult center of the palace complex at Knossos. It was probably used for libations, which were poured into it through a hole at the top of the neck, and trickled out through an opening in the mouth.

writings, belong to the region of "epic poetry and legend. To confound together these disparate matters is, in my judgment, essentially unphilosophical."

What has happened to alter this view so radically? The answer is simply the development of scientific archaeology. We have seen how a number of Old Testament records relating to ancient Egypt and Mesopotamia have been confirmed. But there was more gratification than surprise when the religious chronicles of the Hebrews were corroborated by archaeological discoveries. It *was* surprising, however, to find not only Homer's story of the Trojan War, but even the most fantastic myths and legends partially confirmed by the evidence of the spade. But the matter is much more complex than whether or not such and such a legend described actual beings, circumstances, and events. The modern archaeologist does not believe in the literal reality of Poseidon or the Minotaur or Europa any more than Grote did. But at the same time it is no longer possible to take refuge in the idea that these myths express mere poetic or symbolic truths. The reality lies somewhere in between, for now the myths have been proved to contain elements of historical truth.

To make matters more difficult, the story is still unfolding, the pattern changing, even as these words are being written. No sooner does one think one has found a way out of the labyrinth than some scholar shouts, "No! Not that way—it's a blind alley." And so we go on groping—but with what zest!

The area with which we are here concerned comprises Crete, the Aegean Islands, the mainland of Greece, and western Asia Minor. As we have seen, by about 2800 B.C. two major civilizations had developed, one in Africa and the other in the Near East. (A few centuries later a third civilization emerged in the Indus Valley, much farther to the east, but that does not enter into this picture.) Egypt was already in

trading contact with the coast of Lebanon and Palestine in predynastic times. During the Old Kingdom she established colonies there, and was trading also with the Aegean Islands. A glance at the map will show that there is a chain of islands linking Greece with the Turkish mainland; the southernmost of these is the long, narrow, mountainous island of Crete. South of Crete there is nothing but sea until one reaches the African coast; not a wide stretch by modern standards, but in days when ships rarely sailed out of sight of a coast, sufficient to make Crete fairly remote from Egypt, which at that time was the nearest civilized power.

During the nineteenth century, archaeologists had devoted most of their attention not to the islands of the Aegean, but to the mainland. Between 1870 and 1884 the brilliant, eccentric German amateur archaeologist, Heinrich Schliemann, had excavated at Troy, near the Hellespont, and at Mycenae, Tiryns, and Orchomenos in Greece. He believed that the Trojan War was not legendary, but a historical event, and he confounded the skeptics by discovering remains of buildings, and arms, ornaments, and other works of bronze, gold, and ivory, some of which closely resembled objects described in the *Iliad* and the *Odyssey*. These finds—which included daggers of gold-inlaid bronze; gold diadems, dress ornaments, and rings; gold drinking vessels, offering vases (rhytons), and cult objects—were of a type not previously found in Europe. The art was exquisite—sensitive, vigorous, yet disciplined, the goldwork being especially fine. About ninety years ago, when these treasures were first discovered, precise archaeological dating did not exist. No one knew exactly how old Schliemann's finds were, but in his enthusiasm he confidently attributed them to the period of the Trojan War, traditionally dated about 1190 B.C., although it is now placed somewhat earlier by a good many important scholars.

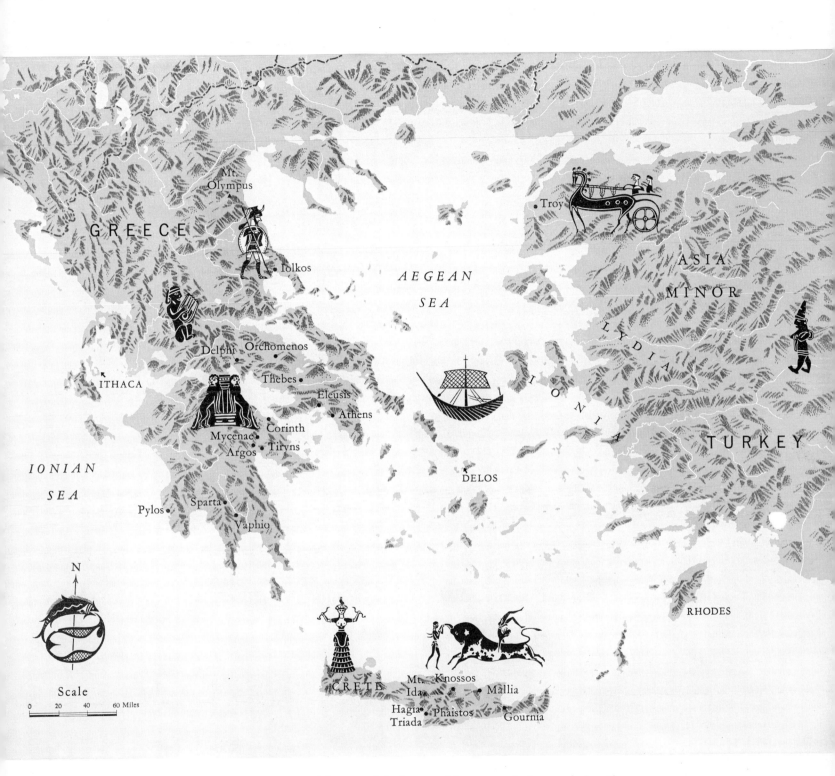

"Their weapons were of bronze, their houses of bronze, and they worked with bronze," the Greek poet Hesiod wrote about the men who had lived in Aegean lands long before his own age. Two civilizations flourished in Greece during the Bronze Age. On the island of Crete the Minoans built splendid palaces, not of bronze, but of stone, with cult centers dedicated to the mother goddess and walls displaying pictures of the bull games in which the Cretans delighted. The warlike Mycenaeans of the mainland made more use of bronze weapons; they conquered the palaces of Crete and sailed off to war with Troy. Eventually their massive strongholds were stormed and captured by the Dorian Greeks, but the tales of their heroes have survived, transmitted by the bards of later times.

Arriving at the palace of Minos at Knossos from its port four miles away, visitors could see a fresco of a charging bull within the portico above the entrance; the tapered columns of the portico (left), narrower at the bottom than at the top, were characteristic of Minoan architecture. They probably derived from the tree trunks which had once been used to support buildings, and which were placed upside down so that they would not take root and sprout again. The paved ramp that ascended into the palace courtyard may have been a roadway for carts.

But there were other scholars who were not so easily satisfied, and controversy waxed bitter during the twenty years following the initial discoveries at Troy. One critic attributed the goldwork of Mycenae to the Byzantine period. Others, including the English scholar Arthur Evans, believed that it was older than the period of the Trojan War. Meanwhile all such artifacts, wherever found, were labeled Mycenaean, from the name of the type-site. Evans (who was later knighted) met Schliemann in 1883 in Athens and spent much time examining the Mycenaean treasures. The Englishman had a sensitive, almost intuitive understanding of the changes and developments of artistic style; Mycenaean art fascinated and intrigued him. Handling the gold cups and the diadems, jewels, and intaglios in Schliemann's great villa, Evans wondered who could possibly have produced such art. It had been found in Greece, yet there was little in it of the classical Greek spirit. But it was not Oriental either. Evans was excited and puzzled by what he considered possible Near Eastern influences. He politely listened when the old German pointed out enthusiastically the resemblances between the twin-handled cup with its feeding doves that he had discovered at Mycenae and the Cup of Nestor described by Homer. But he was more interested in the problem of Mycenaean origins than he was in tracing connections with Homer. Objects of such beauty and craftsmanship must be the products of a long period of civilization. The evidence uncovered by Schliemann obviously indicated a pre-Greek culture along and about the Aegean coast. Might it not have been literate, as Egypt's was? Evans had almost microscopic eyesight when viewing things at close range. The conviction grew on him that the tiny marks on some of the smaller objects might be pictographs, elements of a hitherto unknown language.

Evans' eye for very small, significant detail had been help-

The alabaster throne still standing in the Knossos Throne Room is evidently modeled after a wooden prototype; it may have been carved out of stone instead of wood to conform with ritual requirements. The room itself was part of a complex beside the Central Court of the palace devoted to ceremonial functions. Painted griffins are stationed on either side of the throne to symbolize the divine protection given to its occupant; the fresco which shows them crouching among lilies in a stylized landscape is a modern replica of the original found by Evans.

ful to him in his study of numismatics, though this was only one of his many interests. He was an extremely complex character, well-read in many fields—especially ancient history and prehistory—sensitive to art and beauty, yet no mere aesthete or academician, but a vigorous man of action. Before meeting Schliemann in 1883 he had traveled widely in Sweden, Finland, and the Balkan countries which he most loved. When Bosnia and Herzegovina revolted against their Turkish oppressors, Evans championed them enthusiastically, became a war correspondent for the Manchester *Guardian,* and eventually was arrested as a spy and expelled. And yet throughout all these political and journalistic activities he found time to follow his archaeological bent—copying inscriptions or collecting coins and other antiquities—when he was not swimming a swollen river naked (except for a hat into which his notebook was tucked), or entering a Moslem stronghold wearing his red-lined cloak inside out and trying to look as Oriental as possible. The year after his meeting with Schliemann, Evans, at the age of thirty-three, was appointed Keeper of the Ashmolean Museum at Oxford, in which academic post he succeeded in consolidating the scattered archaeological material at Oxford into a central museum of art and archaeology. This accomplished, he found considerable time for foreign travel once again.

These personal details are extremely relevant to the story of Evans' discoveries. His forceful, positive character imprinted itself on whatever he did. The storm of debate that still rumbles around the conclusions he drew from his archaeological discoveries and studies is proof of this. Twenty-one years after his death he remains a figure of controversy.

During the fifteen years following his success at Oxford he made several trips to Greece and Sicily, at intervals in his museum work. The question whether prehistoric Greece had a writing system that had long been lost was never far from his mind. In 1893 he was in Athens with John Myres (later Sir John)—that "black-bearded Ulysses"—with whom he spent time "grubbing . . . below the 'Pelasgian' wall of the Acropolis and picking out fragments of pre-Mycenaean vases which nobody here seems to have heeded before," to quote from one of his letters. And he studied Mycenaean rings. One day Evans was searching among the trays of the antiquity dealers in Shoe Lane in Athens when he came upon several tiny bead seals, some four-sided, some three-sided, drilled with a hole for thread. Scrutinizing them with his remarkable eyesight, Evans thought again that he could detect "squiggles" that might be writing symbols.

He asked the dealer where they came from and was told that they were from Crete. The seals were called *galopetres* —"milk stones"—because the peasant women there wore them around their necks as charms when they suckled their children. Subsequently, in Crete, he could not persuade a nursing mother to sell her "milk stone"; to have parted from it, she believed, would have imperiled her child's health.

The year 1893 was a critical one in Evans' life. In that year his much-loved wife, Margaret, died after a long illness. Partly to distract his mind from this tragedy, but largely because he felt he had found an important clue to his mystery, he decided to go to Crete. Almost from the moment he set foot on Cretan soil Evans fell in love with the island, as so many travelers have done since. He loved the mountainous landscape, with snow-crowned Mount Ida, where Zeus himself had been born, and Mount Juktas, where lay the legendary tomb of the god. With a guide he explored the island on foot and on muleback. Not only did he find many more "milk stones," but potsherds, gems, and, among other things, remains of prehistoric settlements. Evans had come to Europa's

island. Here, as Homer had written, was "a rich and lovely land, washed by the waves on every side . . . and boasting ninety cities. . . . One of the ninety towns is a great city called Knossos, and there . . . King Minos ruled and enjoyed the friendship of almighty Zeus."

Knossos—a mere village now—still existed, a few miles from the port of Herakleion. Schliemann, of course, had also been well aware of Homeric allusions to this and other places on the island, and had planned to dig at Knossos, but a hitch in negotiations over the land had been followed not long after by his death. Evans' interest in things Homeric was at that time only peripheral. His main concern was to find further evidence of a writing system. At Knossos there was a large, flat-topped mound where a Cretan investigator (appropriately named Minos) had already dug and found remains of massive walls and many huge pithoi, or storage jars. Another Mycenaean palace, perhaps? It was enough to make up Evans' mind. If there was a palace there might be archives, like those discovered at Assurbanipal's palace at Nineveh.

After Crete was freed from Turkish rule in 1899, it became possible for Evans, with the help of the Commissioner of Crete, Prince George of Greece, to secure a share of the site for archaeological exploration. In March, 1900, he returned to the island and was joined by two companions, D. G. Hogarth and Duncan Mackenzie, both experienced archaeologists. He arrived in the midst of a great storm; thunder pealed from the crags of the mountain where the god of lightning had been born. After this singularly dramatic introduction Evans began digging, and almost at once he uncovered a great labyrinth of buildings.

He soon found the palace storerooms—the great stone-built magazines with their rows of smoke-blackened pithoi, more than man-high, that had once contained olive oil, wine,

honey, figs, and other products of the island. And not far away Evans came upon what he had been looking for: the first hoard of clay tablets, inscribed with symbols—not Egyptian hieroglyphs, not Sumerian cuneiform, but a script he remembered having seen on another such tablet that had come from Knossos.

Even before he began digging Evans had written: "The great days of Crete were those of which we still find a reflection in the Homeric poems—the period of Mycenaean culture, to which here at least we would fain attach the name 'Minoan' [after King Minos of the Greek legend]. . . . Nothing more continually strikes the archaeological explorer of its ancient remains than the comparative paucity and unimportance of the relics of the historical period. . . . The golden age of Crete lies far beyond the limits of [that] period . . ." But only a month after the start of his excavations he could write in his diary: "The extraordinary phenomenon: nothing Greek—nothing Roman . . . Even geometrical [Greek pottery of the preclassical period] fails us —though as tholoi found near [the] central road show, a flourishing Knossos existed lower down. . . . Nay, its great period goes at least well back to the pre-Mycenaean period."

At the age of forty-eight Evans had found his destiny, which was to devote the rest of his life to excavating and interpreting Knossos. The gods of Crete had claimed him, and, like Theseus, his task was to penetrate the Minoan labyrinth.

Evans was right in his intuition; the civilization that had flourished in Crete was extremely ancient. When the development of sequence dating by pottery styles and by stratification enabled archaeologists to affix reasonably accurate dates to objects, it became evident that the oldest shaft graves that Schliemann had found at Mycenae did not date earlier than 1600 B.C. At Knossos, however, Evans was able to trace a

Daylight streaming through a light-well illuminates the Grand Staircase of the Knossos palace, seen at right. Five flights of steps still remain, ascending through the domestic quarters of the palace. Adjoining them were the queen's apartments, the remains of which are shown opposite. The Cretans made no attempt to achieve symmetry in their architecture; palaces were a maze of rectangular rooms and long corridors, added to with no regular plan. The Knossos palace is essentially a series of apartments surrounding a central court, with the domestic quarters and artisans' workrooms bordering its eastern side, and reception and ceremonial chambers located opposite them.

sequence of almost continuous development from about 3000 B.C. down to about 1150 B.C. Yet from the beginnings of this Minoan civilization (Evans' name for it has stuck) the style of pottery, fresco painting, arms, and ornaments resembled the type that had been previously called Mycenaean. So-called Mycenaean objects appeared to be only a late development of this style, and one plausible inference was that mainland sites such as Mycenae were Minoan colonies. This is what Evans believed, but as we shall see, the facts are considerably more complex.

Evans devoted thirty years and, even though he was helped for a while by the Cretan Exploration Fund, a considerable part of his personal fortune to the excavation and restoration of the Knossian palace. Although he early recognized that the clay tablets were lists or inventories of some sort, he never succeeded in deciphering them; but his interest in the Minoan writing system remained undiminished.

Lacking intelligible written documents, apart from legends and traditions recorded by later poets and historians, Evans and other early workers in Cretan archaeology had to rely on material evidence for their interpretation of Minoan civilization. Evans' monumental work of scholarship, *The Palace of Minos,* is, with the restored palace, a permanent memorial at once to his genius and to his firmly held beliefs. But numerous other gifted scholars have helped to unravel the mystery, and not all have agreed entirely with Evans' conclusions. Federigo Halbherr, the distinguished Italian archaeologist, worked for many years in the south with an expedition at the great palace of Phaistos and at Hagia Triada, having in fact preceded Evans in other parts of Crete. Harriet Boyd Hawes worked at Gournia and Richard Seager at other sites in the east. R. C. Bosanquet and R. M. Dawkins and colleagues dug at Praisos and Palaikastro. French scholars unearthed another

Minoan palace at Mallia. Spyridon Marinatos and other Greek archaeologists have made distinguished contributions, both in excavation and interpretation. Again, on the Greek mainland the work of Alan Wace and John Papadimitriou at Mycenae and Carl Blegen at Pylos have cast fresh light on the later period of Aegean civilization. These and a number of other significant contributions have indeed caused a drastic revision of earlier opinions.

The efforts of these men and women have enabled us to draw an impressive, though still incomplete, picture of Europe's earliest civilization. But for the full impact of the initial discoveries as they were revealed year after year, we have to turn to Evans. During the first few years of his excavations at Knossos he made discoveries that astonished the archaeological world. He revealed that the palace, built around a large central courtyard on top of a mound called Kephala, was truly labyrinthine in its complexity. About the Central Court, which one approached via one or another of several long corridors, was a veritable maze of halls, private chambers, storerooms, staircases, ramps, and other areas to serve special purposes. And on one of the plastered interior walls Evans came upon the first representation of a Minoan man to have been discovered. It was a painted fresco, in a fragmentary condition, but sufficient to recall to Evans a painting that had been found in the tomb of the Egyptian vizier Rekhmire at Thebes.

Rekhmire, chief minister under Pharaoh Tuthmosis III (1504–1450 B.C.), had had depicted on the walls of his tomb the reception of certain visiting foreigners, referred to as the *Keftiu.* They were completely non-Egyptian both in physique and in dress: very thin-waisted, elegant, with their dark, curled hair worn in a side-lock, or sometimes two locks, falling over one shoulder, and attired in short kilts. Similar

247

"La Parisienne" (right) was one of a group of youths and maidens portrayed in a ceremonial scene. The knot at the back of her neck may be merely a fashionable detail of dress, or it may be a sign that she was a priestess, for sacral knots were a common religious symbol. One is shown beneath a band of roses on the cup below, which combines the religious and floral designs most commonly used for vase decoration. In their skill at utilizing a variety of forms and adapting surface designs to them, Minoan potters were unsurpassed in the ancient world. Some of their work was so delicate that cups and vases were covered with painted designs to strengthen fragile walls as well as to decorate them.

figures appear in other Egyptian wall paintings. In some instances the "gifts" they carried to present to the Egyptians resembled in style objects discovered by Schliemann at Mycenae. One of the figures, indeed, carried a rhyton in the form of a bull's head, almost exactly like the rhyton found in one of the shaft graves.

The fresco that Evans' workmen uncovered included a figure of just this kind, slightly larger than life-size, and with details that were missing from the Egyptian artists' paintings. To Evans the head was not classically Greek, but recalled an indigenous Cretan type. The body, though firm and muscular, nevertheless was slim and suggested a delicate refinement. The skin was a kind of russet-brown, the kilt was orange with a blue band near the base, the hands carried a tall rhyton, painted blue to indicate, by convention, that it represented silver—all similar to those shown in the Egyptian paintings. The figure had been one in a procession of similar figures painted on the walls of the corridor. Here then was one of the mysterious *Keftiu* who had traded with Egypt in the fifteenth century B.C.

From the west side of the Central Court opened a number of rooms, the most dramatic of which was the Throne Room. It was a comparatively small, rectangular chamber, divided on one side from a second room of about the same size by a balustrade surmounted by columns. The floor of this second room was at a lower level, forming a kind of pit. Evans thought at first it might be a bath, but later concluded that it was a lustral basin, probably used for ceremonial purposes. Against the wall facing the basin stood a thirty-four-hundred-year-old alabaster throne, the oldest in Europe. Flanked by stone benches that ran along the wall, it was rather like the bishop's throne in the chapter house of a medieval cathedral. Fragmented wall frescoes showed that on each side of

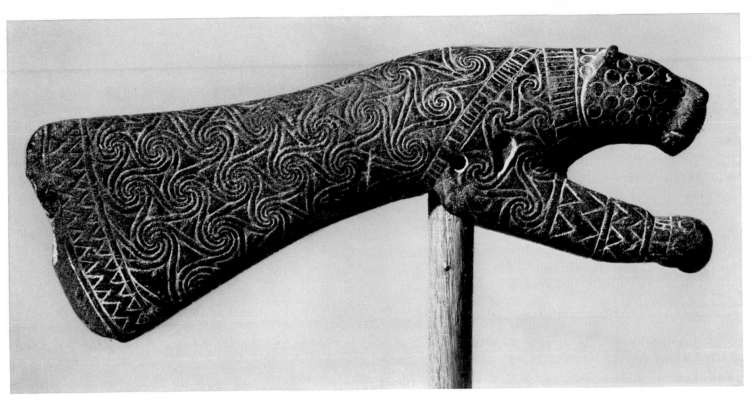

Made in the shape of a running leopard, this ceremonial axe or macehead is decorated with the spiral pattern so common in Minoan art.

the throne had been painted pictures of griffins and conventionalized foliage. Nearby on the floor lay vessels, evidently used in some kind of religious ceremony, but they had been overturned and were in disorder.

West of this room, and separated from it by a corridor, lay the long, rectangular magazines that contained the huge pithoi: these, clearly, were the palace storerooms, the repositories of Minos' wealth—olive oil, wine, cereals, fruits; in the floors were sunk cists or "safe deposits" which may have contained gold and other treasure similar to that which Schliemann had found in the graves at Mycenae. (As in ancient Egypt, wealth was in kind, not in currency.) At the end of one corridor was found a complex of smaller rooms, the offices of the scribes and clerks, who had kept records of this wealth on clay tablets in a script that Evans could not read. And there were not only offices, but other rooms which had clearly been the workshops of craftsmen and artisans—metalworkers, potters, stone carvers, and so forth. In one such chamber the excavators found a block of stone half sawed through, as if abandoned suddenly by the craftsman.

In many places were the marks of fire, particularly in the magazines, where some of the pithoi were blackened by the smoke of the oil that they had once contained and that had burned. By noting the direction of these smoke stains, it was even possible to establish that the wind was blowing from the south on the day that fire destroyed Knossos. The palace must have burned fiercely, because there was much wood in its construction. The walls had been reinforced with timber supports; the pillars, which tapered from capital to base, were also hewn out of timber, and Evans found the charred remains of the columns in their original stone bases.

Still farther north, on the side of the palace facing the sea, the excavators came upon a monumental gateway, the North-

ern Entrance or Sea Gate. This too had been magnificent in its time, with an ascending stone-paved road passing between porticoes with downward-tapering columns and leading to the Central Court. But what was most remarkable was that on the pavement beneath one of the portico walls overlooking the passage were found fragments of a vivid painted plaster relief of a charging bull. By this time Evans and his collaborators, though more methodical and scientific than Schliemann had been, began partly to share the German amateur's respect for the ancient myths. The story of Theseus, Ariadne, and the Minotaur had begun to loom large in their minds; the image of a bull had recurred in fact and fable. There was the bull's-head rhyton found at Mycenae, and the story of Europa who had been carried to Crete by Zeus in the shape of a bull. One encountered the creature again and again.

Evans was a romantic, though a scholar, but it is doubtful whether he or any of the various archaeologists, architects, and other specialists who from time to time worked with him were given to fantasy. They were looking for facts, not trying to justify an earlier formed hypothesis, as Schliemann had tried to do. But the facts were there before their eyes. Not only did they discover the famous relief of the charging bull, but other frescoes that brought them much nearer to the legend of Theseus and Ariadne. One of these depicts another charging bull, but this time it is not alone. There are three human figures, two female and one male. The girls (identifiable by their lighter skins, by a convention similar to that applied in Egypt) stand at each end of the painting. One appears to be grasping one of the bull's horns; the second, standing behind the animal, is poised on the balls of her feet, her arms outthrust. And in the center of the picture a male athlete (wearing, like the girls, only a loincloth) is in the act of somersaulting over the bull's back.

The seven youths and seven maidens sent from Athens to be sacrificed to the bull-monster—the labyrinth—Theseus and Ariadne—Pasiphaë, wife of Minos, who fell in love with a bull—were these, after all, mere poetic fantasies? They had appeared to be, and yet here was a picture of a young man and two young women performing a feat that recalled the ancient myth, a feat so difficult that it seemed impossible. If this were a true record of fact, then perhaps it might be proved that the legends themselves were not completely implausible. One may imagine the discussions and arguments that went on between Evans and his colleagues in the Villa Ariadne, the house that he had built near the palace. In an attempt to reconstruct how the bull-leaping trick might have been done, Evans suggested that each athlete in turn grasped the animal's horns, vaulted in a somersault over its head, landed upright on its back, and then leaped off over its tail, probably in another somersault, into the arms of a waiting companion. A cowpuncher from Arizona who was consulted thought this was quite inconceivable, however, since a charging bull lowers its horns and twists its head sideways. Anyone rash enough to attempt to grasp the horns, he claimed, would undoubtedly be gored and tossed aside.

The excavators of Knossos discovered another related fresco, which depicts a large number of men and women seated or standing in a kind of grandstand and evidently watching some public performance. The women are apparently court ladies in full coiffure of curled hair beset with jewels. Their puffed sleeves, their flounced, bell-shaped skirts, and their general air of sophistication made a French visitor to the site in the early nineteen-hundreds exclaim, "Why, they are *Parisiennes!*"

But their breasts are bared and even the *Parisiennes* of the early twentieth century would hardly have dared to appear at

the Opéra in such full décolletage. In any event these Minoan ladies, gossiping and chatting as they wait for the ceremony to begin, do not seem to be self-conscious. To all intents they might be chic women at a party who are waiting for something exciting to happen. In the same fresco are depicted hundreds of male spectators, mere caricatures indicated by only a few strokes of the draftsman's hand, crowded into the grandstand almost as if to fill up space. It is hardly an exaggeration to say that this scene could have been sketched by a talented newspaper illustrator to adorn a gossip column. What are these rows of *soignée* women and girls and the men behind them waiting for or looking at?

It is possible that they were anticipating, or watching, the performance shown in the other fresco, and that this was part of a religious ceremony or ritual. In the center of the audience scene there is what appears to be a shrine, with downward-tapering pillars and conventionalized representations of the horns of a bull—the "horns of consecration," to use Evans' phrase—a motif that appears frequently in the decoration of Minoan palaces and on seals and pottery. There can be no doubt that the bull-leaping sport was in some way associated with the observance of religious practices.

For what presiding deity was this shrine intended? Although the Cretans of later times boasted that their island was both the birthplace and burial place of Zeus, king of the gods, there is little evidence in Minoan art of a prominent male deity. Admittedly men appear in religious or cult scenes, but always in subordinate positions. The principal deity is always a goddess. As in other, eastern religions the male god associated with her may have been her son or her lover; and as in such other religions he may have been ritually sacrificed each year. But the goddess reigned eternally. One sees her in delicately modeled, slim-waisted figurines, with belled or

With the harvest season ended, a procession of farm workers (left) marches in from the fields singing. Over their shoulders they carry farm implements probably used for threshing grain or picking olives. They wear the characteristic Minoan turban and their waists are tightly bound. The religious ritual that celebrated the harvest may have been led by a singer such as the one shown on the seal impression at far left, whose beard probably marks him as a member of a priestly caste. A votive offering, the figure shown at right represents a worshiper, his hand reverently raised to his brow.

flounced ankle-length skirts. Sometimes her back and upper arms are covered. She also appears frequently on Minoan and Mycenaean seals, rings, and gems, usually alone, but sometimes accompanied by male or female figures, and very often near a sacred tree or grove. Occasionally an altar is shown, before which women, dressed like the goddess in flounced skirts, are dancing. One of the most fascinating of the seals depicts two rampant lions supporting a central pillar—recalling the Lion Gate at Mycenae, but here the pillar is crowned by a goddess. In some frescoes the women appear to be wearing puffed sleeves onto which their dark hair falls in ringlets; but always the breasts are bare, and on some of the intaglios the goddess is naked to the waist.

In the Central Sanctuary of the palace at Knossos the excavators discovered what had evidently been the shrine of a goddess, and here they found an exquisite little statuette in faience. It represents a woman whose whole body is clothed save for her face, forearms, and bosom. In each outstretched hand she grasps a writhing snake, and on her head is a circular headdress adorned with the miniature figure of a leopard. Her bodice is so tight that it forces the breasts into unnatural prominence, and below the wasp-like waist an elegant skirt falls in pleated flounces to her feet. Among primitive peoples, even today, the snake is frequently associated with the earth and with earth worship, and for that reason it is equally apt to call this obviously hieratic figure either the snake goddess or the earth goddess.

In ancient religions in which sexual and fertility symbols are prominent, the archetypal figure of the mother goddess, or the earth mother, is almost universal. One finds her in paleolithic times, usually represented as a crude figure with enormous breasts, big buttocks, and a swollen belly. In the Near East she survived long into historical times as Diana

of Ephesus, or in more shapely aspects as Ishtar. In Minoan Crete she became sophisticated, even elegant. When the smart ladies of the court of Knossos exposed their bosoms in public, as shown in the palace frescoes, it would seem they followed a custom amply sanctioned by old religious traditions.

In various aspects, the mother goddess survived in the religion of classical Greece. Demeter represented her as the earth mother who nourished mankind and increased the fertility of the fields. Aphrodite continued her role as the goddess of love. Athena was the goddess as warrior, and Artemis, the chaste huntress, inherited her power over the wild beasts. (Minoan representations frequently show the mother goddess taming lions and bulls, or fabulous animals such as griffins and sphinxes.) The Central Sanctuary, where the goddess' image was discovered, was not the only area of the Knossos palace dedicated to her. The whole palace was sacred in character, a fact that has given support to the theory that the sacral role of the Cretan princes was as important to the country as their secular functions were.

The living quarters and the state rooms of the palace, approached by the Grand Staircase, lay in the southeast wing of the structure and were built at various levels above and below that of the Central Court, into the steep hillside that falls away toward the river Kairatos. This wing, by far the most impressive remaining part of the great building, owes its present dignity and splendor as much to Evans' painstaking restoration and reconstruction as to the efforts of the original architects. As the palace fell into ruin this section suffered less than the others. By the time the wooden columns supporting the Grand Staircase and the state rooms collapsed or decayed, the debris from the roof and the upper walls had formed a compact filling, resting on the lower parts of the building and serving as a continued support for

Carrying fine pottery vases, musical instruments, and rhytons made of precious metals, a painted procession of offering bearers marched along a palace corridor at Knossos. One of them, the rhyton bearer shown on the right in the restored fresco opposite, was the first Minoan portrait seen by Evans. The elegance of the people who built the Cretan palaces is evident in their jewelry as well as in the portraits that have survived. The golden pendant at left, which represents two hornets with wings raised, could have been designed to adorn either a man or a woman.

much of the remains of the staircase and the upper structure.

Through this deposit of fifteen hundred years Greek miners engaged by Evans tunneled their way, shoring up walls and roofs. Meanwhile the resident architect, Christian Doll, carefully examined and made plans of the remains. Here were the bases on which the wooden pillars had once rested; there, on parts of the walls that were still standing, were fragments of plaster with painted scenes still adhering to them. Bit by bit, with infinite care and patience, Evans and his colleagues restored the staircase and the rooms to which it led.

The result is awe-inspiring. Admittedly, to visit unrestored Phaistos with its ruined walls and staircases open to the sky and with snow-capped Mount Ida in the distance is a moving experience. In a different way, so is it to see Mallia, Gournia, and other open sites. But the very openness of their ruins, bathed in sunlight, gives a false impression of what a Minoan palace was like. Whereas when one descends that shadowed Knossian staircase, with its colonnades opening onto a light-well, or when one stands in the dimly lit, frescoed rooms of state, one feels nearest to those remote people whose character has been aptly described as "a curious mixture of religious formalism and a real *joie de vivre* of a somewhat heartless and childlike nature."

Evans himself felt this strongly. In a memorable passage from *The Palace of Minos* he wrote: "During an attack of fever, having found, for the sake of better air, a temporary lodging in the room below the inspection tower that has been erected on the neighboring edge of the Central Court, and tempted in the warm moonlight to look down the staircase-well, the whole place seemed to awake awhile to life and movement. Such was the force of the illusion that the Priest-King with his plumed lily crown, great ladies, tightly girdled, flounced, and corseted, long-stoled priests, and after

them a retinue of elegant but sinewy youths—as if the Cup-Bearer and his fellows had stepped down from the walls—passed and repassed on the flights below."

At Knossos and other Minoan sites archaeologists have come upon pillars, often set in or beside small stone-lined basins let into the floor of a room and inscribed with the sign of the *labrys,* or double axe. Many actual examples of such axes in bronze and other metals have come to light, some of them, no doubt, strictly functional objects. But the form, sometimes set on a base or between the horns of consecration, also appears in materials and sizes unsuitable for any practical purpose. It was clearly a sacred symbol. Evans and other scholars have suggested that it might have been associated with some rite intended to propitiate the infernal powers, a theory supported by the fact that Crete is subject to earthquakes, some of which have been catastrophic.

Because he found such symbols on its walls, Evans called one of the state rooms of the Knossos palace the Hall of the Double Axes. By means of double doors that swung on rectangular pillars, the inner area of this hall could be closed off—on the one side from an area with two porticoes facing spacious light-wells, and on the other from what Evans referred to as an audience chamber, since here he found evidence of a canopied throne. Painted on a spiraliform frieze on the walls of another nearby room—the Hall of the Colonnades—Evans had found representations of the huge leather figure-of-eight shields so often encountered in Minoan—and Mycenaean—art. On the upper walls of the Hall of the Double Axes he found traces of the same frieze, but no shields. Evans conjectured that real shields once hung there, and had replicas made. For this and other touches of disciplined, if bold, imagination he has been criticized by men with a more cautious approach to archaeology.

Not far from this hall, but approachable only via a dark, winding corridor, is another suite of rooms, the largest room of which Evans called the Queen's Megaron. There is no certain proof that these were indeed the queen's chambers, but their privacy and a certain femininity in the decoration strongly suggest it. Also they were linked by a private stairway with the quarters directly above. On one side, opposite the main door, a colonnade opens onto a light-well which softly illuminates the interior. Fragments of painted frescoes enabled Evans' artist, Edouard Gilliéron, to restore the main scheme of the delightful mural decoration. Dark blue dolphins sport on a light ground, against which one also sees smaller fish, sea plants, and other marine life of diverse colors. The walls and the ceiling are ornamented with the characteristic Minoan spirals and rosettes, and a dancing girl appears on one of the pillars.

One of the smaller adjoining rooms had an earthenware bath, like a Victorian hip-bath, still *in situ*. Even more remarkable was the clear evidence, found in another small chamber, of a latrine. Evans wrote: "The aperture leading to the main drain, partly masked by a curious projection, deviates from the center of the seat, thus leaving room on the right for some vessel used for flushing the basin. As an anticipation of scientific methods of sanitation, the system of which we have here the record has been attained by few nations even at the present day."

At Knossos, Gournia, and Hagia Triada there is evidence of brilliant hydraulic engineering. Knossos in particular has been called a "plumber's paradise." Each area of the palace was served by a drainage system that fed into the main channel which, in turn, emptied into the river east of the hill. From the roof, rainwater was led through channels in the walls to underground drains ventilated by air shafts.

Manholes gave admittance to these sewers, some of which were so large that Evans' excavators could spend whole days working in them without inconvenience. Two other features show the knowledge possessed by the Minoan engineers of more than thirty-five hundred years ago. In some cases water was taken through terra-cotta pipes with fitted sections that were tapered to produce a greater head of water and prevent accumulation of sediment. In another instance an open channel was cut beside a steep flight of steps that leads from a bastion of the Central Court down to the river. Each flight of steps was at a right angle to the next; if the base of the channel had been smooth the water would have rushed down like a cataract and spilled over the sides. But the Minoan builders constructed the channel in a series of parabolic curves, of such a shape and size as to slow down the flow of water and enable it to take the right-angle turns without overspilling.

Though they varied in size and planning, other Minoan palaces and private villas were built in a manner generally similar to the great Knossian palace. All had stone walls reinforced by timber, tapering wooden columns, light-wells, large halls, and usually bathrooms and toilets. The palaces had open courtyards from which opened a maze of rooms, corridors, and staircases; in a number of instances important rooms were covered with delicately painted frescoes in the general style of those we have already considered. On the ground floor there were frequently lustral basins and pillar rooms with one or more sacred pillars, often inscribed with representations of the double axe.

Again, in the other principal palaces at Phaistos and Mallia there were, as at Knossos, storage magazines, offices for clerks and administrators, and workshops for numerous craftsmen. Knossos was by far the largest palace, covering some three acres and capable of housing several hundred

people. These buildings were, in fact, not only royal or princely residences, but also cult centers, manufactories, arsenals, and administrative headquarters, all combined in one huge, multistoried, multiroomed structure.

But of course only the ruling families and their retinues lived in palaces. Around each palace are the remains of sizable towns; the ruins at Knossos, which mark the site of one of the most ancient towns in Europe, are extensive enough to keep archaeologists busy for generations. There were also towns without such great palaces, and numerous luxurious private villas—some almost as large as the palaces—which stood alone on superb natural sites, as at Vathypetro, south of Knossos, and at Hagia Triada. There were ports and harbors and well-paved roads linking the various centers of population. Indeed, Crete was, Homer claimed, "densely populated . . . boasting ninety cities." Along the streets many of the houses were two or three stories high, constructed of brick or stone, with windows on each story. Each house probably had a roof terrace, which could also serve as a summer bedroom. A unique group of faience plaques, discovered at Knossos and representing a street scene, gives us a trustworthy idea of the appearance of Minoan cities.

In Cretan palaces and towns archaeologists have found extensive remains of workshops. The town at Gournia, for instance, seems to have been occupied almost entirely by craftsmen. Harriet Hawes, digging there some sixty years ago, came upon many small dwellings that had been both the homes and workshops of these artisans. In one house she found a whole carpenter's kit concealed in a cranny and, nearby, the rotted remains of a wooden shelf that had supported fourteen loom weights arranged in order. One house contained a vat for refining olive oil still resting on its stone bench, with a place in front of it for an amphora into which the sediment

could be poured. The products of such concentrated industry were certainly intended not only for home consumption but also for foreign trade.

Among the finest products of the Cretan workshops were the jars and vases in which the Minoans stored olive oil and wine. The introduction of the potter's wheel to the island early in the second millennium had fostered a remarkable development in the art of pottery. Craftsmen learned to make the famous "eggshell ware," beautifully decorated vessels of exceptional delicacy, with walls that were literally almost as thin as eggshells. The painting of vases became a fine art, and a variety of forms was evolved, many of them highly sophisticated. In the later periods, vases became more ornate; they were adorned with fanciful blossoms made of clay and baked onto the outer surface. The Minoan pottery that survives today remains one of the finest manifestations of the island's culture. Indeed, it deserves to rank among the most beautiful that has ever been made.

The Minoans would not have been able to develop such a rich and powerful civilization but for their extensive maritime trade. Their neolithic ancestors had arrived by sea, and they themselves became a great seafaring people. "The first person known to us by tradition as having established a navy is Minos," wrote that most reliable historian, Thucydides. "He made himself master of what is now called the Hellenic sea, and ruled over the Cyclades [islands between Greece and Asia Minor], into most of which he sent the first colonies . . . appointing his own sons as governors; and thus did his best to put down piracy in those waters, a necessary step to secure the revenues for his own use."

There is abundant evidence of Minoan ports and other coastal settlements, for example at Amnisos, which appears to have been a port for Knossos, and at Nirou Khani, another

port four miles farther to the east. There is also another harbor at the mouth of the river Kairatos, two miles west of Amnisos. Three harbors within a short distance of the northern capital suggest a large fleet and much sea-borne trade. Even in early Minoan times representations of ships appear frequently on bead seals; the remains of wharves at Nirou Khani are in fact the most ancient harbor works ever discovered along the shores of the Mediterranean.

The excavations at Crete have revealed no signs of fortifications, which suggests that Minoan maritime power freed the island from the fear of foreign invasion. That the Minoans colonized the Cyclades, as Thucydides believed, seems unlikely, although they may have exercised some control over local settlements there. One must be careful in claiming that the Minoans controlled the seas by means of a formidable navy. The Minos of whom Thucydides wrote could have been an Achaean from the mainland, for at a somewhat later period a confederacy controlled from the mainland did in fact dominate the eastern Mediterranean. Nevertheless there is ample evidence that long before the mainland Achaeans occupied Crete, the Minoans traded extensively in the eastern Mediterranean, with the Aegean Islands, the Greek mainland, Malta, Cyprus, Syria, and Palestine, as well as with Egypt. There is evidence of Minoan activity to the west as far as Sicily. To what extent the early Cretans established colonies is uncertain, but many of their trading posts in various distant places did become permanent settlements. Thucydides was apparently not far wrong, though he wrote more than a thousand years after the events he described.

The material remains of Minoan civilization are like a palimpsest, in which one picture has been painted over another, and another one above that. The picture provided by the remains of palaces at Knossos, Phaistos, and Mallia is

the uppermost one, representing the ultimate phase of that civilization just before it was destroyed about 1400 B.C. (though minority opinion favors a later date). After revealing these heights of accomplishment Evans and other archaeologists set about the more difficult task of uncovering the beginnings of this earliest civilization in Europe, and of tracing it through successive stages from neolithic times down to the Late Bronze Age. In this Evans was the most fortunate, since the lowest levels of the mound on which Knossos stands go back to before 3000 B.C. The examination of these levels was aided by the fact that some of them contained Egyptian objects which could be dated with relative precision. Evans eventually worked out a chronological system for Minoan history which he divided into early, middle, and late periods, extending roughly from the beginning of the Old Kingdom in Egypt through the Middle and New Kingdoms (about 2700–1100 B.C.). Each of these broad divisions was subdivided into three sections, based mainly on changes in pottery styles. This system, first presented in 1904, is still generally accepted, although in recent years disputes have arisen over the dating of various periods and particularly over the dating of the last years that witnessed the decline of Minoan civilization.

There are hundreds of islands in the east Mediterranean, three of them—Rhodes, Crete, and Cyprus—of considerable size. A large number of these islands has been occupied by human beings at least since the Early Bronze Age. Crete was the only one to achieve an indigenous civilization as highly developed as the other great contemporary civilizations we have been considering—those of Egypt, Mesopotamia, and the Indus Valley. These three grew up along fertile river valleys. But Crete is a mountainous island with no large rivers and few plains of any size. What, then, were the conditions

that favored the development of such a highly distinctive culture and that allowed it to flourish for so long a time?

There is no certain answer, but we can distinguish a number of factors that probably contributed. The most important of these is Crete's geographic position. Both Rhodes and Cyprus are near Anatolia, and Cyprus is not far from Syria; both were subject to invasion and strong foreign influence from early times, whereas Crete—"out in the wine-dark sea," as Homer says—was sufficiently remote from the nearest civilized power, Egypt, to develop an independent culture. Yet it was near enough to Africa and Asia to receive influences from both continents via trade and the peaceful immigration of people, some of whom brought with them new techniques, notably bronze working.

Another interesting fact, pointed out by Spyridon Marinatos, is that even in remote antiquity Crete had few dangerous or noxious animals. The ancient Greeks said that Heracles had cleansed Crete of "wild animals like bears, wolves, snakes, and the like." This is not true of snakes; there are some, including a poisonous variety, and scorpions are common. But whereas the Greek mainland and some of the Aegean Islands had wolves, foxes, bears, lions, and boars, Crete's wild animals most likely consisted only of the harmless mountain goat and the porcupine. To primitive settlers this relative absence of dangerous and destructive animals would have been an advantage. Again, Crete has sufficient cultivable land to support a considerable population. The soil of the plains is fertile, and in many places the lower slopes of the hills can be terraced and cultivated.

In ancient times, forests of oak, fir, cypress, and cedar, which have long since disappeared, provided an abundance of timber for fuel and for building. They also helped to conserve the winter rainfall which nowadays rushes down

the mountain slopes, scouring off the topsoil and exposing the arid, ochre-colored rocks so characteristic of the present Cretan landscape. The abundant springs that once nourished the soil have largely dried up. Crete is still a "rich and lovely land," as Homer describes it, but in 3000 B.C. it must have been much more fertile than it is today.

We do not know precisely when Crete was first settled. It is conceivable, however, that between 5000 and 4000 B.C. people who possessed stone tools and who practiced agriculture and stock-raising had begun to move into Greece and some of the Aegean Islands. It does seem almost certain that most of the early immigrants came from the east, where these skills and techniques were understood. Some would have come from Asia Minor; others may have sailed from Syria and Palestine, or even from Egypt and Libya. Judging from their pottery styles they did not all come from the same place or at the same time; one must imagine a slow infiltration by relatively small groups. By 3000 B.C. some of these wandering peoples had settled in Crete. Their remains have been found in caves, which were their homes and which also sometimes served as burial places. In some respects their pottery is not unlike pottery of the same period found in Palestine. They fashioned crude clay figurines, possibly of a mother goddess. But not much more is known of these neolithic inhabitants of the island.

During the five centuries following 3000 B.C. the Cretan settlers prospered, multiplied, and gradually spread over most of the island, though they remained largely concentrated on the Messara plain and in eastern Crete. Even at this early stage they were in touch with Egypt (indeed, as earlier suggested, some settlers may have come from there) and Egyptian stone vases of the Predynastic and Early Dynastic Periods have been found on the island. The Cretans

learned to make excellent stone vessels for themselves, judging from some handsome examples that have been discovered in veined limestone, in polychrome steatite, and in other stones. They made palettes for grinding eye paint, an idea which may also have come from predynastic Egypt. They grew the papyrus plant, and sugar cane, which a tradition claims was brought to Crete by the ancient Egyptians.

These people learned to build settlements with houses of complex plan and with many rooms. They raised herds of oxen, sheep, and swine, kept fowl, grew corn and vines, and cultivated the olive tree. They seem never to have suffered foreign invasion, although they were beset by earthquakes and had to learn to strengthen their buildings by a half-timber construction. A bountiful supply of wood made this method the easiest for the Cretans to use.

The earliest copper implements found in the Minoan graves were imported. But by about 2500 B.C. there appear molds for making tools and weapons of this metal, proving that the craft of metalworking had reached the island, as indeed it had the Greek mainland. It was the dawn of the Aegean Bronze Age.

Some archaeologists have suggested that the change from stone to metal tools may have been precipitated by political disturbances in Egypt. At the end of the Sixth Dynasty, about 2200 B.C., the Old Kingdom was destroyed, and as we have seen, there was both civil strife and an invasion of foreigners in the Delta. Sinclair Hood suggests that at this time there was a mass migration of peoples from Anatolia down the coast of Syria and Palestine toward Egypt, and that in the resultant disturbances refugees may have crossed over to Crete and other Aegean islands. Although Crete had been trading with Egypt from a very early date, contacts became closer and more frequent, and reciprocal influences become

increasingly evident in the arts and crafts of both countries.

Some Cretan ships with high prows seem to have closely resembled Egyptian vessels. By the beginning of the Egyptian Twelfth Dynasty, about 2000 B.C., the Cretans were imitating Egyptian scarabs and other objects, and slightly later Minoan pottery, with Minoan fashions in decoration, was being exported to Egypt. But there were other influences affecting Crete, represented, for instance, by a characteristically Anatolian jug with a spout, which appeared first in Greece and then in Crete. It is reasonable to assume that Minoan civilization throughout its development gathered ideas and techniques from both African and Asian sources, but adapted them to its own use.

But one fact must be made clear. Though we speak of the "Greek" mainland, up until about 1900 B.C. (the date must remain very approximate) both Greece and the Aegean Islands were occupied by people who spoke non-Greek languages. Names ending in *-ssos,* such as Knossos and Tylissos, or those ending in *-inth,* such as Corinth and labyrinth, belong to a group of non-Greek languages. Similar word endings appear in Anatolia, especially in the names of mountains and rivers. This strongly suggests that the pre-Greek inhabitants of the Aegean Islands and the mainland spoke the same language (or group of languages) as the peoples of Anatolia, whence some of their ancestors may have come.

Was there a written form for the Cretan language, as there was for the Egyptian and Sumerian languages of the period? A primitive form of writing, in the shape of simple pictographs, has been detected on seal stones and clay tablets of the Early Bronze Age in Crete, though there is as yet little evidence that it existed on the mainland. But there is no doubt that it was this script that later developed into what Evans called Linear A, one of the two linear systems that

he recognized on the Knossian tablets. It was a syllabary, in which each sign represented the syllable of a word. Linear A has been found only in Crete; the various attempts at translation that have thus far been made, as well as conjectures regarding its ultimate origins, remain a matter of debate.

The introduction of bronze working into Crete had revolutionary effects; the advantage of metal weapons and implements is obvious. Crete developed its own characteristic variety of spears and daggers, and metal tools gave new powers to the stonemason and the carpenter. Instead of rough stone, builders were able to use finely cut ashlar masonry, which they did mainly for the outer walls of palaces and great houses; copper and bronze saws made it easier to fell trees and cut up the timber into suitable lengths for the framework of buildings. However, the metal was expensive; metal vessels were imitated in pottery and stone tools continued to be used for a long period.

By 2000 B.C. the island civilization was well established, and most of its characteristic features had appeared. It was at this stage that the foundations of the first palaces at Knossos, Phaistos, and Mallia were laid. Hitherto there had been extensive settlements at each of these places, but nothing resembling the residence of a king. Then, apparently quite suddenly, the Cretans began building enormous residential and administrative units for their rulers. Several hundred years later the palaces were destroyed and new structures were raised on the same sites, but enough of the earlier buildings was incorporated into the later ones to provide the excavators with some indication of their character. The early palaces at Knossos, Phaistos, and Mallia had three courts, a large rectangular one around which were grouped the main buildings, a second to the west, and a third, smaller court to the north. The main court was oriented on a north-

Although little is known about the cult of the dead in Crete, a painting on a sarcophagus discovered at Hagia Triada has been interpreted as representing the veneration of a dead man, whose effigy or body appears at far right. As a musician plays upon his lyre, two women offer libations. Beside them three men bring other offerings to the deceased man—two calves and, following contemporary Egyptian practice, a funeral boat as well. At far left can be seen two high pillars supporting double axes; the birds that are shown perched on them could be representations of the mother goddess, but are more probably spirits of the dead.

south axis, and the general layout of the buildings was similar to that of the palaces that were later built on the site.

No one has yet satisfactorily explained the sudden innovation of those first palaces. There is no evidence of an invasion by newcomers who could have brought with them a tradition of monumental architecture; it might be that by this time, at the opening of the second millennium, power had become sufficiently centralized to make it possible for three potent chiefs each to set up an administrative unit, controlling an area from which it drew its wealth. Who these rulers were we do not know, though one is reminded of the Greek legend that stated that Zeus had three sons by Europa—Minos, Sarpedon, and Rhadamanthus.

No doubt these palaces, like those of later periods that replaced them, had shrines that served for formal worship of the established royal cult. Elsewhere on the island—on mountaintops, in sacred groves with walled enclosures, in caves, and most frequently in rock shelters—archaeologists have discovered sanctuaries that were evidently cult centers of the popular religion.

From the innumerable votive offerings left in such sanctuaries by worshipers almost four thousand years ago, we can speculate on the nature of Minoan religion. There are little clay figures representing the familiar Minoan man tightly belted and wearing a loincloth, and with a typical Cretan dagger at his waist (the men of Crete still wear daggers). There are delightful figurines of women wearing long, full skirts, like the representations of goddesses we have considered earlier—and, also like the goddesses, naked from the waist up. The hairdos of these ladies, it might be noted, are varied and enchanting.

Some votive offerings clearly reveal the occupation of the donor. One clay bowl represents a shepherd with his flock; another with a flying bird may be the offering of a wildfowler asking the goddess to grant him success in his hunting. There are many painted cattle, and most significant of all, statuettes of bulls with little human figures clinging to their horns. One has a young man, apparently naked, hanging onto one of the bull's horns as he strives to maintain a grip on its neck with his legs. On a later seal stone a bull is shown kneeling (perhaps it is tethered) while an acrobat grasps the horns and leaps over its back. Could this have been an athlete in training? The more one studies these fascinating little figures the more one wonders whether the palace performances, as depicted in the Knossos fresco, which must have involved elaborate training and a formal ritual, originated as a sport among the young herdsmen of the plains.

The deity to whom these offerings are made is a goddess, probably the same goddess under different aspects—as queen of the animals, the sea, the mountains, or the infernal powers. Sometimes she is shown with a bird, at other times with a flower, the horns of consecration, or a snake—as in the faience figure from the Knossos shrine. To caves high up in the mountains, so high that in winter they are snowbound, the Cretans made their toilsome way with their offerings. In those gloomy caverns, where the glistening stalactites and stalagmites reflected the flickering lamps of the worshipers and bats fluttered in the shadows, they must have felt very close to their deity. Even today these caves are hardly less mysterious, since few visitors have the stamina needed to reach them, and one treads about on piles of fragmented pottery left there over three thousand years ago. Some caves have enclosing walls and the remains of altars, and from time to time new caves are discovered, which sometimes yield hoards of bronze objects and pottery. No doubt still more await discovery. Everywhere in Crete, in palaces and in remote caves,

one encounters evidence of religious worship or observances; but the evidence is never monumental. Unlike their contemporaries in Egypt and Mesopotamia, the Cretans built no great temples and they raised no large statues of their deities. Unlike the Egyptians and the Mesopotamians, we might conclude, the Minoans were not unduly awed by the supernatural.

Minoan civilization appears to have enjoyed its greatest flowering between about 1700 and 1400 B.C. Early in this period the great palaces were rebuilt and the first large mansions were raised. It was the remains of these later palaces that first claimed the attention of Evans, Halbherr, and other excavators. Why there was need for rebuilding has not been satisfactorily explained. However, Crete has been subject to earthquakes at fairly regular intervals during the past seven hundred years at least, and presumably this was so in ancient times as well. Such temblors may well have damaged the earlier structures. Evans, who found evidences of frequent rebuilding at Knossos, became absorbed by this problem, particularly when he came upon a part of the Knossian palace that bore clear evidence of earthquake damage and that had been rebuilt after due sacrifice to the infernal powers. He carefully examined the records of earthquakes that had occurred during the past seven centuries. "That space of time," he wrote, "almost exactly corresponds with the duration of the great Minoan palace in its successive phases, and we are almost bound to infer that the same natural forces must largely account for the signs of ruin that here mark the successive stages of the building."

One day in April, 1922, when Evans' workmen had just cleared the remains of the so-called House of the Sacrifice in which bulls had evidently been sacrificed to the earth goddess, there came suddenly "a short, sharp shock, sufficient to throw one of my men backwards, [which was] ac-companied by a deep, rumbling sound . . . experienced on the site and throughout the entire region."

In Minoan Crete the trident, emblem of the god Poseidon, the "earth-shaker," often appears. Evans recalled that Homer had written in the twentieth book of the *Iliad,* "in bulls does the earth-shaker delight." In 1900, just as Evans had arrived to begin digging at Knossos, he had been welcomed by Zeus with one of the fiercest thunderstorms within living memory. Twenty-six years later, in 1926, Poseidon the "earth-shaker" was also to manifest his menacing power. On a warm summer night in June Sir Arthur was resting in one of the basement rooms of his house, the Villa Ariadne. He wrote, "My own mind was thus full of past earthquakes and the foreboding of a new convulsion when on June 26 last, at 9:45 in the evening of a calm, warm day, the shocks began. They caught me reading on my bed in a basement room . . . and, trusting to the exceptional strength of the fabric, I chose to see the earthquake through from within. . . . The movement, which recalled a ship in a storm, though only of a minute and a quarter's duration, already began to produce the same physical effect on me as a rough sea. A dull sound rose from the ground like the muffled roar of an angry bull; our single bell rang, while through the open window came the more distant jangling of the chimes of Candia Cathedral . . .

"It is something to have heard with one's own ears the bellowing of the bull beneath the earth who, according to a primitive belief, tosses it with its horns. It was doubtless the constant need of protection against these petulant bursts of the infernal powers that explains the Minoan tendency to concentrate their worship on the chthonic aspect of their great goddess, wreathed with serpents as Lady of the Underworld." Evans, despite his great gifts and dedicated labors over thirty years, may have been wrong in some of his conclusions concerning Minoan Crete. But his burning imagination and insight break through in those words.

The last, most catastrophic destruction of the Minoan structures is generally believed to have taken place about 1450 B.C. when virtually every center was ruined, except Knossos which survived another half century. Then it too was destroyed. At Knossos and a number of other sites on the island there are the unmistakable marks of fire. Evans believed that after this disaster Minoan civilization went into a rapid decline, although some sort of life continued at Knossos during what he called the Reoccupation Period, from 1400 to 1100 B.C., when "squatters" occupied the great palace. But Phaistos, Mallia, and other centers did not revive.

The main question, of course, is what caused this final destruction? Was it, as Evans suggested, an earthquake, such as Crete had suffered before? Or was it, as others have believed, the result of armed attack? There are various reasons for believing that the island suffered a sacking by hostile invaders. Minoan civilization had, after all, recovered from earlier disasters caused by earthquakes, but this time it did not survive the calamity. Also, in modern cities, with their gas and electricity supplies, earthquakes often cause catastrophic fires, but this was not necessarily true in the ancient world. Yet many Minoan settlements apparently went up in flames at about the same time; charred timber and smoke-blackened oil jars show this only too clearly, suggesting that the palaces may have been deliberately set on fire after sacking. At this time, it is certain, the Mycenaeans of the mainland were powerful and warlike. After the destruction of Knossos they became dominant in the Aegean, and Minoan influence practically disappeared.

The late J. D. S. Pendlebury, who for years was Evans' assistant at Knossos, favored the "sack" theory, and thought he saw evidence of it in the condition of the Throne Room, where ritual vases had been overturned, as if, in his own words, "[they] were in the act of being used when the disaster came. It looks as if the king had been hurried there to undergo too late some last ceremony in the hope of saving the people. Theseus and the Minotaur! Dare we believe that he wore the mask of a bull?"

That the Theseus of legend represents the leader of an armed invasion by Mycenaeans, and that he overcame King Minos, wearing the mask of a bull as he performed some hasty last rite, is a romantic conjecture. As Pendlebury conceded, "Such imaginings may not be suitable to archaeology." But, he added, "with this possibility in mind, I defy anyone to enter the Throne Room without a strange thrill."

As discussed at greater length in the following chapter, the question is made more complicated by the fact that many tablets found amid the ruins of Knossos were inscribed in the Linear B script. According to the recent decipherment of the script, Linear B records an early form of the Greek language used by the Mycenaeans. This at least indicates the possibility of strong Mycenaean influence at Knossos sometime before the destruction of the palace. Other theories suggest that there was a civil uprising within Crete, perhaps assisted by foreign invaders, or simply another earthquake that struck Crete at a time when her civilization was already in decline, and from which the Cretans were unable to recover. Marinatos combines two of these theories by suggesting that the Mycenaeans exploited the confusion caused by the earthquake to occupy the island, and then set up an Achaean prince to rule at Knossos.

When Homer composed the *Odyssey* in the eighth century B.C., Crete was a relatively unimportant island in the Mediterranean world, but legends of its past had persisted over the centuries. In the cosmopolitan and densely populated world of Crete, "out in the wine-dark sea," as Homer describes it, "Each of the several races of the isle has its own language. First there are the Achaeans; then the genuine Cretans, proud of their native stock; next the Cydonians; the Dorians, with their three clans; and finally the noble Pelasgians."

Homer purported to describe the Crete of the years after the Trojan War, when, we assume, the Achaeans still ruled the Aegean. But to round out his story he obviously drew on materials that had survived from various stages of the island's history, as well as on the reports of his contemporaries, who may have seen the island. Among his sources may have been fragments of stories that reached far back to the time when Minoan culture was at the height of its glory. It is tempting to surmise that his description of the island of Phaeacia, on which Odysseus is shipwrecked and where he meets the fair Nausicaä, may hold memories of the fascinating Minoan world that Evans rediscovered at Knossos just two short generations ago.

The king of the island explains to his stranded guest that his people "can run fast and . . . are first-rate seamen. But the things in which we take a perennial delight are the feast, the lyre, the dance, clean linen in plenty, a hot bath, and our beds." In another passage Nausicaä, the king's daughter, says, "there is no man on earth, nor ever will be, who would dare to set hostile feet on Phaeacian soil. The gods are too fond of us for that. Remote in this sea-beaten home of ours, we are the outposts of mankind . . ." Phaeacia may have been an imaginary island, but the emphasis on remoteness—"the outposts of mankind"—maritime skill—"first-rate seamen" —and the uninhibited delight in the luxuries of civilization— "the feast, the lyre, the dance, clean linen in plenty, a hot bath, and our beds"—are all suggestive enough of the evidence revealed by Evans from his excavations in Crete.

The Minoans, like the Etruscans, suffer from having their history written by others. Unlike the later Greeks, or the Egyptians, the Sumerians, the Babylonians, or the Assyrians, they cannot speak to us directly—at least not until their Linear A script is thoroughly translated, and possibly not even then. We are left only with buildings, frescoes, bead seals, pottery, and the superb Cretan landscape, which is still wide enough, high enough, and remote enough to excite our imagination.

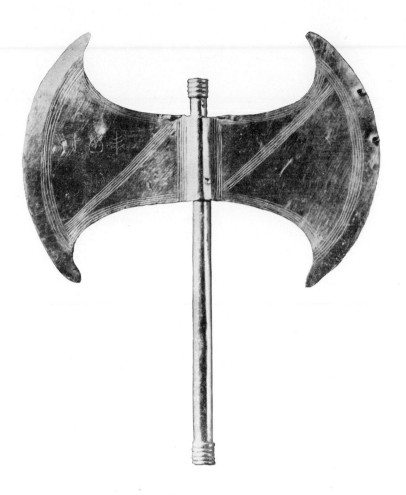

THE LAND OF
THE DOUBLE AXE

Unlike other peoples, the Cretans built no temples. Instead they performed rituals in sacred areas within the palace precincts, or before domestic altars; they built shrines in the open air beside pillars or trees, or in sacred groves. Worshipers carried votive offerings up the mountainsides to sacred caves dedicated to the mother goddess. Mount Ida, shown overleaf, beyond the ruins of the palace of Hagia Triada, held several such sanctuaries. Sacred places were often marked by the horns of consecration, and by the double axe (above), the most common Minoan cult object, as omnipresent a symbol in Cretan religion as the cross is in Christianity. It was revered either as a fetish in itself, or as a symbol of divinity. Its connection with the worship of the mother goddess is certain, if still imperfectly understood. Bulls sacrificed to the goddess were probably slain with a double axe; representations of the goddess often show her holding a double axe in her hand, or appearing before her worshipers perched upon one in the guise of a bird.

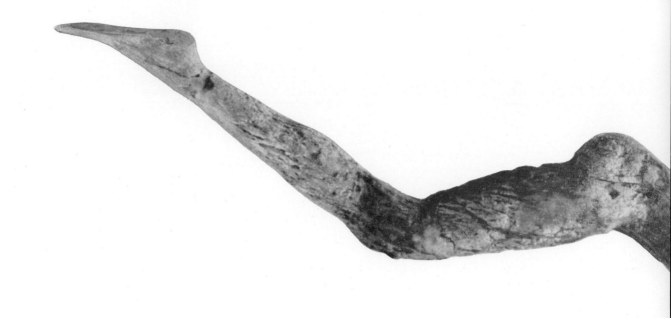

THE MINOAN SPORT OF BULL LEAPING

Performances of the Minoan bull games took place in the great palaces of the island on festival days. The populace of the surrounding city streamed into the palace courtyard, where the games were probably played, to watch from behind waist-high barriers, while the court overlooked them from colonnaded passageways above. Before the bull-leaping games began, there were other sports to watch, ritual dances perhaps, and foot races and boxing bouts, in which the contestants vigorously battled each other with both their hands and their feet. Boxers were well equipped for these combats; they often wore helmets to protect their heads, sometimes with cheekpieces attached. Leather thongs were bound about their hands—"thongs carefully cut from the hide of a ranging ox," Homer calls them in a description of a later boxing bout. One Cretan vase shows boxers very similar to those depicted in the *Iliad*. Indeed, the Greeks may well have inherited their fondness for athletics from the Minoans. Every Greek shrine at which games were held shows traces of Minoan influence.

It is still uncertain whether the bull games originated in a religious ritual, or whether they were secular to begin with and, like the American rodeo, developed out of the acrobatic stunts of the herdsmen of the plains. The ritual role of bulls is of great antiquity in Crete. Sacrificial bulls have been discovered buried under a house foundation at Knossos, and skulls of bulls that had been offered to the gods were probably nailed to the side of altars. But by the time that Minoan civilization reached its height, the performance was primarily secular, although there is some evidence that the bull was sacrificed to the mother goddess after it had been "conquered" for her by the acrobats who leaped over its back. Leaping over the bull was a very dangerous feat. Acrobats may have conditioned themselves for it by practice-leaping upon the backs of animals that had been tamed especially for their training. To ease their landing, the stone pavement of the courtyard arena could have been covered with a layer of sand.

Traces of the barriers that protected the audience still remain at Mallia; there too a ramp still leads up to the Central Court from within the palace, probably to provide the bulls with access to the arena. From relics discovered at Knossos, it seems likely that the palace there held a miniature model that showed the bull games in progress, including a representation of the shrine of the mother goddess that overlooked the court. Its miniature bulls were made of faience, with spotted markings on their coats; the acrobats, one of which appears above, were of ivory and were probably stained red. Bronze wires attached to their heads simulated long locks of hair, which streamed out behind them as they performed their daring leaps.

One of a group of models representing the bull games, the ivory acrobat at left was shown leaping over a bull. Equal skill but less boldness was required for ordinary acrobatic feats, such as the handstand performed by two tumblers shown on the seal impression at right. The sealing beneath it was long thought to represent the capture of a bull as it drank at a water tank. Now it is supposed that the square in its corner is a platform from which the bull leapers began their daring jumps. The bull leaper's most difficult feat, shown in the bronze below, required him to grasp the bull's horns and somersault over its back. OVERLEAF: A fresco from the palace at Knossos shows acrobats performing this feat. At left, a girl puts her arm around the horn of the bull so that he will lift his head in anger and attempt to toss her. With the aid of this momentum, she will somersault over his back, as another acrobat can be seen doing. The girl standing behind the bull is poised ready to catch the leapers and steady them as they reach the ground.

THE SACRED DANCE

According to Homer's description, Achilles' shield was decorated with a scene of youths and maidens dancing on "a dancing floor, like the one that Daedalus designed in the spacious town of Knossos for Ariadne of the lovely locks. . . . Here they ran lightly round . . . and there they ran in lines to meet each other. A large crowd stood round . . . with a minstrel among them singing divinely to the lyre, while a couple of acrobats [kept] time with his music . . . in and out among the people." Theatre areas similar to such a dancing floor have been excavated beside the palaces of Knossos and Phaistos—oblong paved areas, bordered by shallow stone steps on which an audience could sit or stand. With Minos and his court in attendance, these theatres were probably used for a religious performance of some kind, most likely a sacred dance to summon the mother goddess. The Cretans customarily danced for this purpose in front of a sacred grove, pillar, or tree, as well

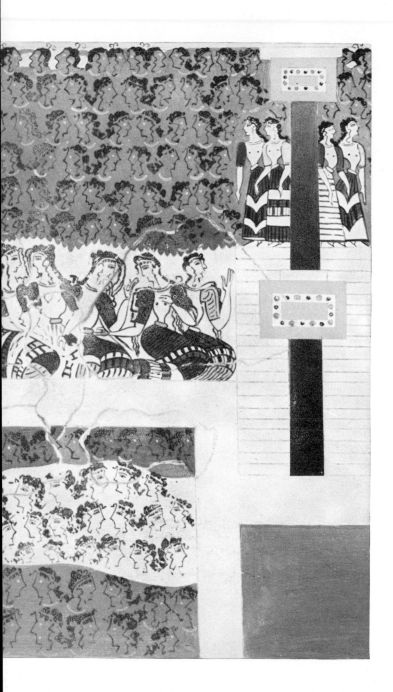

Watching a ceremonial dance or a bull-leaping performance, an audience of courtiers and ladies gathers beside the shrine of the mother goddess, in a copy of a fresco from the palace at Knossos. The shrine at the center is marked by horns of consecration. The artist has depicted most of the audience with a few impressionistic strokes and devoted careful attention to drawing the colorfully dressed court ladies. Above, a seal impression showing a chariot drawn by two goats may represent a scene from a pageant. The figure below, the so-called Priest-King, has been considered the portrait of a Minoan ruler. He wears a necklace of fleurs-de-lis about his neck and a high crown of peacock feathers upon his head.

as in theatre areas, and dances such as these may have been a source from which later Greek dramatic performances developed. It was a female deity who was honored by these dances, and women played an important role in the ceremonies, as they did in the bull games. Then they wore simply a loincloth; but for ritual dancing they often attired themselves in full court costume, with flounced skirt and tight bodice, their hair elaborately curled and their bosoms bare. Men adorned themselves as fancifully as women did at the court of Minos. Both sexes wore bracelets and necklaces. Women twined gold filigree through their hair; men secured their long curls with strings of beads. They wore anklets about their legs and, invariably, a seal stone attached to a cord around their wrists. As early as the age of ten, boys and girls began to bind themselves with tight belts, probably made of metal and designed to keep their waists extremely slim.

Crete's dependence on the sea is echoed in its art. The fresco of dolphins shown above is from the palace of Knossos; the amphora below displays the picture of a writhing octopus.

SEA TRADERS

In high-prowed ships equipped with both oars and sails, the Cretans dominated the commerce of the Mediterranean. They carried cedarwood from Lebanon to Egypt, and Egyptian luxuries to the ports of the Greek mainland. They carried copper from the mines of Cyprus; to make bronze, it was mixed with the tin that they may have fetched from as far away as the coast of Spain. The cargoes from Crete itself were mainly fine wine and olive oil, sent abroad in the beautiful jars for which the Minoans are justly famous. The Mycenaeans and the classical Athenians were also to grow wealthy exporting oil and wine; in Minoan times this trade enriched the princes who built the three major palaces on the island. Their great storerooms, capable of holding immense quantities of wine and oil, may have served as warehouses for the export trade. The palace of Phaistos, near Crete's southern coast, probably commanded most of the commerce with Egypt. Knossos, facing north, traded with the Greek mainland. Aside from those connected with the major palaces, there were other ports along the coast; some still retain traces of ancient wharves cut into the rocky shore, the oldest man-made anchorages found in the Mediterranean.

Upon the mountainous northern shore of Crete a terra-cotta provision jar still stands among the ruins of the palace of Mallia (opposite), once a great Minoan trading center.

MYCENAE

THE WORLD OF HEROES

According to Greek mythology Thessaly, in the northern part of modern Greece, was the birthplace of gods; it was the legendary scene of the creation and of the flood, and the home of the wise Centaurs. It was also the home of the great immortals who dwelt on Mount Olympus, the highest of the mountains that hem in the broad, fertile Thessalian plains. We do not know when the first mortals settled in Greece but, significantly, the earliest remains of human activity in that land, which date from paleolithic times, have been found in Thessaly and in nearby Boeotia.

In Thessaly there were also numerous neolithic settlements. One such, at Dimini near modern Volos, consisted of a number of relatively simple dwellings grouped around the house of the local ruler. The inhabitants grew barley, wheat, some fruits and vegetables, and raised cattle, pigs, sheep, and goats. Even at this early date they apparently found it necessary to fortify their settlement with concentric walls, evidence of the insecurity so long felt by the mainland people but virtually unknown among the early Minoans of sea-girt Crete.

The chief's house at Dimini was of a type that occurs in more developed form again and again on the Greek mainland. An open court led to a porch, beyond which lay the main two-room building. This would appear to be the ancestor of characteristic structures found by excavators at later palace sites, incorporating the kind of kingly hall that was uncovered at Mycenae, Pylos, and Tiryns. This type of building occurs somewhat later at Troy, and elsewhere in Anatolia. From this it is assumed that the early settlers in Greece had

The massive stone wall surrounding the citadel at Mycenae is pierced by the Lion Gate; above it two lionesses still guard the entrance to the ancient city where Homer's heroes flourished.

strong ties with that land; some of them may have come from there. (Troy stood at a strategic point commanding the passage of the Dardanelles, which lay athwart the important land route from the western Anatolian coast to Greece.)

There are no written records, but it is confidently assumed that these settlers of some five thousand years ago were not Greeks, that is they did not speak the Greek language. Schliemann's excavations at Mycenae and subsequent investigations there and at different sites on the mainland, on the other hand, revealed a vigorous and in many ways distinctive Late Bronze Age culture of Greek-speaking peoples. Judging from the findings in the shaft graves this so-called Mycenaean civilization burgeoned suddenly and dramatically about the turn of the sixteenth century B.C. and flourished for four centuries or more. Particularly in its early stages it showed strong influences from Minoan Crete. Later, from about 1400 to 1200 B.C., it became itself a dominant influence in the Aegean area and beyond. Then, shortly after the Trojan War, it rapidly declined, leaving only legends of its glory and the ruins of its impressive monuments.

The main questions to be answered are: when did the first Greek-speaking people enter Greece; where did they come from; what was their level of culture; what were their relations with the Minoans of Crete; and what accounts for the sudden deterioration of their civilization? These questions can be only partly answered. At the beginning of the second millennium B.C. high civilization was just beginning, both in Crete and on the mainland. Bronze was coming into use, of course. Outside Athens, at the site of an early fortified town that dates as far back as the third millennium, molds for casting bronze implements, weapons, and other objects and the remains of smelting furnaces have been found. Other of the sites later called Mycenaean, such as Mycenae

itself, the stronghold of Agamemnon, had been occupied longer. But little has been learned of the pre-Greek inhabitants of this city; because it was built on rock and was frequently enlarged, its stratification is archaeologically frustrating and earlier levels are difficult to establish. Nevertheless, according to the late archaeologist Alan Wace, who dug for many years at Mycenae, the plentiful pottery finds there prove that the site was occupied by 3000 B.C. Tiryns and Pylos were also old, established communities. There are remains of an immense circular building at Tiryns that date back five thousand years, but they underlie a later Mycenaean palace and have not been explored. Many of these sites are in the Peloponnesus, in southern Greece, where prehistoric settlements were often built on rocky eminences.

Between 2000 and 1700 B.C., when the first palaces were being built in Crete, the mainland was subject to waves of invasion or immigration. Most specialists in Aegean archaeology believe that the newcomers were the first Greek-speaking people to enter Greece. These people could have come there from somewhere in the north. From Schliemann's time, the legend of blonde Aryans from northern Europe who invaded Greece and founded a warrior aristocracy such as that described by Homer has had many adherents. It flatters Anglo-Saxon vanity that Homer refers to "the fair-haired Achaeans," and that "the fair Helen" might have been a Nordic blonde.

But there is little evidence to support the theory that these first Greeks were of such origins. It seems more probable that, like the earlier settlers, they came from Anatolia. In passing, it is worth mention that the invaders of Greece brought with them a pottery-making technique, represented by a drab but highly distinctive product known as Gray Minyan Ware, that they shared with but one other people—the people who invaded Troy and settled there at this same time, roughly about 1950 B.C. This ware was also known to the neighboring areas of western Anatolia that fell within the range of Trojan influence.

Wherever they came from, whatever dialect they spoke, the immigrants early in the second millennium came within the cultural sphere of the Minoans of Crete. Until the evidence has been studied further and the results made known, it is difficult to judge the exact relationship of the two cultures over the next several hundred years. However, during the sixteenth and fifteenth centuries B.C., when Minoan culture was at the height of its development, its artistic influence on the mainland became widespread.

Sir Arthur Evans believed and maintained to the end of his life that the Cretans colonized not only the islands of the Aegean, but also parts of the Greek mainland, and that such centers as Mycenae and Tiryns were originally Minoan dependencies. It seems a sound enough theory; many of the objects found in the Mycenaean shaft graves, which can be dated between 1600 and 1500 B.C., are surely from Crete, or at least were made by Cretan craftsmen. Others imitate the styles of Crete. There are gold signet rings with typically Minoan scenes of goddesses; the warriors or huntsmen represented on gold-inlaid daggers are tightly belted in the Minoan manner and carry Minoan figure-of-eight shields; and there is a bull's-head rhyton that is highly reminiscent of such a vessel unearthed at Knossos. All this glory suddenly begins to appear in these burials of the sixteenth century B.C.; the earlier graves discovered at Mycenae are pitifully small, furnished at most with a few funeral offerings.

Yet there was opposition to Evans' point of view, led chiefly by Wace, who worked for many years at Mycenae. He and others pointed out that there were substantial differ-

ences between Mycenaean and Cretan palaces, bespeaking distinctive cultural heritages. At Mycenae, Tiryns, and the later-discovered Pylos, the principal architectural feature was not the central court of the Cretan palaces, but the megaron —a squarish hall that contained the king's throne and a large, fixed circular hearth in the center. This hearth was surrounded by four pillars which supported the roof; sometimes there was a second, smaller megaron, possibly for the queen, and a staircase leading to an upper story.

The best-preserved example of such a megaron is at Pylos in the Palace of Nestor, most venerable of the Homeric leaders in the *Iliad*. It is very like the building described by Nausicaä when she directs Odysseus to her father's palace. "Directly you have passed through the courtyard and into the buildings, walk quickly through the great hall [megaron] until you reach my mother, who generally sits in the firelight by the hearth, weaving yarn stained with sea-purple, and forming a delightful picture, with her chair against a pillar and her maids sitting behind. My father's throne is close to hers, and there he sits drinking his wine like a god."

As in the early building at Dimini and its Anatolian analogues, the principal megaron was usually approached via an open courtyard and a pillared porch. In another passage Homer tells of Telemachus who, searching for news of his father, visits Menelaus in Sparta and spends the night there "in the portico" of the palace—on the porch, we may assume —while Menelaus sleeps in his room "beside the lovely Helen." Homer also describes the hearth at which Menelaus sits and where he is joined by Helen, no longer the *femme fatale*, but a model of domestic propriety—though it may be noted in passing that she still needs three handmaidens to carry the sewing, and that her workbasket runs "on casters and [is] made of silver finished with a rim of gold."

At this time, buildings of the Mycenaean plan did not exist in Crete. There the palaces consisted of many rooms opening off a central courtyard. There was no permanent central hearth and no principal porch like those of mainland structures. The influences that shaped Mycenaean civilization came from various sources besides the neighboring island of Crete. The two famous grave circles with their royal shaft graves, discovered by Schliemann and John Papadimitriou at Mycenae, have predecessors seven hundred years older at Alaja Huyuk in central Anatolia. Further, as Sinclair Hood comments, "the shaft graves show a striking mixture of the barbaric and the civilized." Aside from the artifacts that reflect the sophisticated taste of contemporary Crete, there are, for instance, amber beads that may have come from the Baltic. Some of the metalwork seems to stem from the Caucasus or the northern steppes rather than from the Aegean. The horse-drawn chariots that appear on the Mycenaean grave stelae were certainly not representations of anything Cretan; they came from Western Asia.

However, the influence of Minoan art was pervasive and enduring. What accounts for this? Cretan gold- and bronze-work could have been acquired either by peaceful trading contacts or by looting Minoan settlements, by inducing Cretan craftsmen to work on the mainland or by carrying them off as slaves and obliging them to do so. Examples are not lacking from later times of hardy, less developed people acquiring a taste for more civilized living, and so it may have been in prehistoric Greece. As one scholar has pointed out, the influence of Minoan art on the Mycenaeans, so dramatically demonstrated by the finds in the shaft graves, may represent nothing more than a newly adopted fashion. It does not necessarily mean that Crete dominated and controlled the mainland. In eighteenth-century Europe there was a great

craze for chinoiserie, but this does not indicate a Chinese conquest of Europe. It should be noted, however, that Minoan art continued to be in fashion on the mainland over the course of many centuries.

Then there is the knotty question of Homeric parallels, first raised by Schliemann. The traditional date of the Trojan War is the beginning of the twelfth century B.C., although recent studies place it a half century or more earlier. The *Odyssey* and the *Iliad* were probably composed about four hundred years later. Both poems are a strange mixture, portraying partly the society that Homer himself knew, and partly an archaic way of life that resembles the one revealed by the excavations at Mycenae and similar sites. We read of bronze swords, of chariots, and of Hector's great oxhide shield, which tapped his neck and his ankles as he walked. On the inlaid daggers found in the shaft graves at Mycenae are depicted large body shields just like those described in the *Iliad*. The buildings and ivory-mounted furniture that have been unearthed are remarkably like those lovingly described by Homer. His description of a golden cup decorated with feeding doves is, again, very like an actual example found in a shaft grave; and his account of a formidable helmet strengthened by slivers of boars' tusks closely corresponds to those represented on several Mycenaean ivories.

Yet in Homer's own time warriors no longer fought from chariots, they used iron rather than bronze weapons, and they carried much smaller shields. And certainly during the so-called Dark Age when these two epics took final shape, kings and rulers did not possess either palaces or furnishings of the richness attributed by Homer to the kings of Mycenae, Pylos, Sparta, and Troy at the time of the Trojan War.

Homer drew on legends that had been transmitted orally from generation to generation for centuries past. Among these were stories of gods and heroes, and of people who may actually have lived—men who fought in the Trojan War, and kings and princes who had dwelt in the palaces of Mycenaean cities that in Homer's own day were for the most part little more than ruins. He composed these tales into two great epics, the *Iliad* and the *Odyssey*. The first tells of the "wrath of Achilles" and describes the Trojan War; the second deals with the wanderings of Odysseus and his return to his home in Ithaca. But it is very apparent that Homer was only using part of the material available to him. Other, later poets, such as Hesiod, and Greek dramatists of the classical periods, such as Aeschylus, Sophocles, and Euripides, had access to the same material and tell us stories that Homer does not mention. All must be based to some extent on the Mycenaean civilization that has been revealed by archaeologists. When Homer described the hall in which Odysseus slew the suitors of Penelope, he was no doubt using the description of an earlier poet who had seen and perhaps actually sung in such halls.

But he drew also from the life he saw about him, from his observed experience. So in one part of the *Iliad* he has Agamemnon carrying spears characteristic of Homer's own day. The four-horse chariot described in the story of Nestor's war in Elis seems to have been an innovation of the eighth century B.C. Throughout, the Homeric stories are laid over with such "modern" embroidery, details that were present knowledge only to those who lived four or five centuries after the heyday of Mycenaean heroes.

The Homeric epics and some of the later writings on the same theme deal not only with the Trojan War but with the events that preceded and followed it. For instance, Aeschylus, in his trilogy the *Oresteia,* tells how Agamemnon, king of Mycenae and leader of the Greek host, who had sacrificed

Although much Mycenaean pottery imitated Cretan styles, the use of scenes from daily life for the decoration of vases was a Mycenaean innovation; the fragment opposite shows two warriors driving a chariot. Craftsmen also derived many artistic traditions from the Near East. The ivory plaque at left depicts a theme common in Mesopotamian art—a lion attacking a bull. The golden octopus at right was used as a dress ornament. Octopuses were a frequent decorative device in Aegean art; this one is novel, however, in having only seven tentacles.

his daughter Iphigenia to obtain fair winds for his expedition to Troy, was slain upon his return by his wife, Clytemnestra, and her lover, Aegisthus. Later we learn how Orestes, Agamemnon's son, avenges his father by killing Clytemnestra and Aegisthus and is in turn pursued by the Erinyes—the Furies—because he has committed matricide. But this cycle of bloodshed, violence, murder, and revenge goes back much further, to the time when Atreus, the father of Agamemnon and Menelaus, revenged himself on his brother Thyestes by killing his children and serving them up to their unsuspecting father at a banquet.

Thus the Atridae, the two sons of Atreus, bore the bloodguilt of their father, and there began the ghastly cycle of murder breeding murder, revenge breeding further revenge, through generation after generation, with the gods looking on implacably. Another cycle concerns the rulers of Thebes, in Boeotia, in which the same relentless powers that govern men's destinies impel Oedipus first to kill his father Laius, king of Thebes, and then unwittingly to marry his own mother, Jocasta. It forms the theme for Sophocles' greatest tragedy, *Oedipus Rex.*

From a strictly archaeological viewpoint, these legends have a peculiar interest. They abound in place names such as Mycenae, Thebes, Orchomenos, Tiryns, Pylos, Iolkos—all apparently the residences of Mycenaean, or as Homer terms them, Achaean royal families. And when archaeologists began to investigate these and other places with the spade, they found the actual remains of Mycenaean settlements. However, in classical Greek times (the sixth century B.C. and later) most Mycenaean cities had ceased to be of importance, the centers of power having shifted elsewhere, except in a few places such as Athens, Sparta, and Thebes.

In one sense this "lost world" was never lost. The classical Greeks believed the stories and knew many of the cities that were their setting. They remembered these places as the homes of their ancestors, though the Mycenaeans had flourished at least seven hundred years earlier. Some had remained inhabited; others were mere ruins, the remains of buildings and of walls built of massive stone blocks, which the later Greeks called Cyclopean, believing that only the Cyclopes, who were giants, could have built them. Homer wrote of "Tiryns of the great walls" and "Mycenae, rich in gold." The great walls of Tiryns are still there to be seen, and Schliemann found that Homer's description of Mycenae was confirmed by the excavations.

But long before the German archaeologist appeared on the scene, Greek and Roman visitors had seen and described Mycenae. In the second century A.D. a Greek traveler, Pausanias, visited the site and made a careful study of its topography. "Parts of the wall are still preserved," he wrote, "as well as the gate over which lions stand. These also they say are the work of the Cyclopes . . . There is a tomb of Atreus, and there are also tombs of all those whom Aegisthus murdered on their return from Troy after entertaining them at a banquet. . . . Clytemnestra and Aegisthus were buried a little outside the wall, for they were not deemed worthy of burial within it, where Agamemnon lies and those who were murdered with him."

The "gate over which lions stand," once the main entrance to the fortified citadel, is still there. The two great sculptured beasts that are posed in confrontation, filling the pediment above the opening, once gazed down on the approaches to the gate. Their heads, which were probably of material different from the limestone figures and which were doweled onto the necks, have long since disappeared, but the rest of the composition remains as the oldest surviving ex-

ample of monumental sculpture in Greece. And it is one of the most famous. Beneath these figures and through this portal Agamemnon led his followers at the start of their expedition to lay siege to Troy.

The Cyclopean walls that girdled the fortress may also still be seen, almost in their entire length of more than half a mile. Built of huge stone blocks, each "so large that a pair of mules could not even stir the smallest of them" (as Pausanias said of the walls of Tiryns), these great enclosing walls are in some places more than thirty feet thick. At one point, near the Lion Gate, they are built around the shaft graves where Agamemnon and those others "deemed worthy" were said to have been interred. Schliemann, following literally Pausanias' description, ignored the tombs outside the walls and started his excavations within the citadel. He was rewarded by finding the royal shaft graves with their fabulous treasures of gold, silver, and bronze. He believed these were in fact the burial places of Agamemnon and his companions, but we now know they were dug about four hundred years before that great king was treacherously murdered.

What of the tombs built "a little outside the wall"? We can still see them today, and they still bear the titles given them by Pausanias, such as the Treasury of Atreus and the Tomb of Clytemnestra. These renowned tholoi or beehive tombs mark a new departure in burial practices, first appearing in the fifteenth century B.C. Although they are later than the shaft graves, most of them date from a time before the Trojan War. Each of these magnificent funerary monuments is in the shape of a gigantic stone beehive, usually built into the hillside and approached by a long, stone-walled corridor called a dromos. The so-called Tomb of Aegisthus, near the Lion Gate and the Tomb of Clytemnestra, is built of unhewn stone, with a simple entrance, and dates from about 1450

B.C. The most majestic example is a later tholos, the Treasury of Atreus, which lies to the left of the road as one approaches Mycenae from the south. This is also sometimes called the Tomb of Agamemnon, although it was probably built before the Trojan War and may indeed have been the tomb of Atreus, father of Agamemnon.

About fifty feet in diameter at the base and almost as high from floor to apex, it is built of carefully hewn and fitted stones which rise in a perfect conical corbeled vault, the layers of masonry being graded, with the widest at the bottom and the narrowest at the top. One gets the impression that the tomb is almost twice as high as it is wide, whereas the width is actually slightly greater than the height. The massive inner lintel above the seventeen-foot-high doorway, accurately curved on the inside to fit the circular tomb, weighs more than one hundred tons, a more massive building unit than any used even in the great Egyptian pyramids. The interior walls were originally studded or faced with bronze ornaments. On the exterior façade, engaged carved columns of green stone flanked the entrance. Above this opening was a decorative panel of variously colored, carved stone, fragments of which are scattered about in half a dozen European museums. This three-thousand-year-old sepulcher is one of the architectural marvels of the ancient world.

Similar but less monumental tombs have been found at other Mycenaean sites on the mainland, and some mausoleums of this character have also been found in Crete. Most of them have long since been robbed of their contents. One or two have been found almost intact, however, with the skeletons of the royal dead lying amid the treasures that accompanied them to their graves. Such a tomb at Dendra, near Mycenae, yielded exquisitely embossed and inlaid cups of gold and silver, jewelry, weapons, and other parapher-

nalia, which had all belonged to members of a royal family.

Agamemnon, Achilles, Nestor, Odysseus, and other Homeric heroes belonged to a warrior race, unlike the peaceful Minoan islanders. They are legendary figures, but they represent historic personages; and it was men like them who built and lived within the frowning walls of Mycenae and Tiryns, who raided far and wide by sea and land, occupying territory and ruling their subject peoples. "I have captured twelve towns from the sea, besides eleven that I took by land," Achilles boasts in the *Iliad*. There need not necessarily have been many warriors; they could have been few in number, but formidable in strength and military skill—a warrior aristocracy, like the Normans of much later times.

The mainland of Greece, with its fortified citadels often within a very short distance of each other, as in the case of Mycenae and Tiryns, was not a unified realm, but rather an assemblage of kingdoms. The Achaean heroes were for the most part kings in their own right. Although they all seem to have owed feudal allegiance to Agamemnon, they fought against as well as alongside each other.

The kingdom of Achilles and the dominions of his father, Peleus, who was still living at the time of the Trojan War, were in Thessaly. The wide Thessalian plains are nearer to Troy and to Asia Minor than is the Peloponnesus, where Agamemnon ruled, and remote enough from the latter's stronghold to encourage the heroic spirit of independence so emphatically demonstrated by Achilles in the *Iliad*. In the last year of the siege of Troy this "swift-footed" hero turns his wrath on his overlord, when the Mycenaean king claims the slave girl Briseis "of the lovely cheeks," whom Achilles had won as a battle prize: "You shameless schemer . . . always aiming at a profitable deal! How can you expect any of the men to give you loyal service when you send them on

Although lions never existed in Crete, they did live on the Greek mainland; representations of them were common in Aegean art, and stories about them occur in Greek mythology. The Mycenaeans were profoundly impressed by the power of the beast; its image may have been placed over the main gateway at Mycenae as a symbol of divine protection. The bronze dagger above shows a group of huntsmen attacking a formidable lion, who is about to maul one of his attackers. The hunters are armed as if for warfare; two of them carry figure-of-eight shields, which the Mycenaeans may have adopted from Crete. The two other shields shown are of the rectangular type that was most commonly used by the Homeric warriors; like the figure-of-eight shields, they were suspended over the shoulders with a strap so that both arms could be left free for fighting. Inlaid with silver and gold, the dagger is a ceremonial weapon, probably of Cretan workmanship. The hunters shown on it have their waists tightly bound and wear costumes similar to those that were worn in Crete.

a raid or into battle? It was no quarrel with the Trojan spear-men that brought *me* here to fight. They have never done *me* any harm. They have never lifted cow or horse of mine, nor ravaged any crop that the deep soil of Phthia grows to feed her men; for the roaring seas and many a dark range of mountains lie between us."

As his anger mounts, Achilles reviles the king in more intemperate terms: "You drunken sot . . . with the eyes of a dog and the courage of a doe! You never have the pluck to arm yourself and go into battle with the men or to join the other captains in an ambush—you would sooner die. It pays you better to stay in camp, filching the prizes of anyone that contradicts you, and flourishing at your people's cost because they are too feeble to resist . . ."

It has been plausibly suggested that the idea of glorifying Achilles at the expense of Agamemnon—a story that was given its final form in the *Iliad*—came from northern Greece. It seems hardly likely that the court poets of Mycenae would have ever ventured to recite a tale in which their great king was so thoroughly upbraided by a comrade-in-arms of what-ever rank.

Mycenaean Greece had long known the impress of Minoan culture. But in view of the evidence we have discussed, scholarly opinion gradually moved away from Evans' belief that such places as Mycenae and Tiryns—fortified palaces with adjoining towns—were Minoan colonies, mere off-shoots of the island civilization. Indeed, by the time of the Trojan War Crete was evidently merely another Achaean kingdom. Among the troops that assisted Agamemnon at the siege of Troy, according to the *Iliad,* was a contingent from Crete, then ruled by Idomeneus, described by Homer as a grandson of Minos. Thus Minos would himself have been an Achaean king; in fact, *Minos* may have been, or have become,

a royal title rather than the name of an individual ruler.

It is widely believed that Knossos was sacked by the Mycenaeans about 1400 B.C. By that date, in any event, the mainlanders had long since learned enough about seafaring to compete with the Cretans, and over the next two cen-turies they developed a commercial empire that virtually monopolized the sea-borne trade in the Aegean and in other areas of the Mediterranean. Mycenaean pottery, obviously produced in large quantities to satisfy widely distributed markets, has been found at sites far up the Nile, in Sicily and along the shore of the Bay of Naples, and in Mace-donia and at Troy, as well as in Syria and Palestine. To implement this foreign commerce Mycenaean trading sta-tions and settlements took root and flourished on the islands of Rhodes and Cyprus, on the western shores of Asia Minor and the Levant, and elsewhere. We might gather from the records that Rhodes enjoyed an almost independent status, as it was firmly enough established as an outpost of Myce-naean authority to bring the great king of the Hittites to civil terms in the course of a dispute.

All that has been said thus far about the Mycenaeans has been gleaned from archaeological evidence, plus some con-temporary documents of other civilizations, and the later epics of Homer. When Evans first began excavating the re-mains at Knossos he thought they were the ruins of Myce-naean buildings. He also believed that such a highly civilized society would have had to rely upon a system of writing for its bookkeeping and administration. Eventually he recognized Knossos for what it was—a monument of Minoan culture, which was revealed in ever greater detail as his investi-gations progressed. Also, he discovered evidence of three writing systems, one a form of hieroglyphics, and the others the so-called Linear A and Linear B scripts, but none of

them had been deciphered at the time of his death in 1941.

Then, in 1952, a discovery was made that added an entirely new dimension to the understanding of Mycenaean civilization. A brilliant young English architect, Michael Ventris, announced that he believed he had "cracked" the Linear B script and that it represented an early form of the Greek language. For the first time it could be *proved* that the Mycenaeans were Greek; and now they would be allowed to speak for themselves. This was perhaps the greatest feat of decipherment ever achieved, even more remarkable than the decipherments of Egyptian hieroglyphs by Champollion and of cuneiform by Rawlinson and others. For unlike these earlier men, Ventris had no bilingual clues to guide him; no one has yet found identical texts written both in Linear B and in a previously known script.

It had taken Ventris sixteen years—ever since as a schoolboy he had heard Evans lecture—to break this most difficult of "codes"; for years he had been in communication with other scholars working on the same problem. They exchanged data, and as new material was published or discovered it was studied, analyzed, and compared. At first Ventris had to rely only on the tablets discovered by Evans at Knossos, few of which—one hundred sixty or so out of a total of about three thousand—had been published.

In 1939 Carl Blegen of the University of Cincinnati had begun to excavate at Pylos, in the southwestern Peloponnesus, and found a Mycenaean palace, which he and many archaeologists believe to have been that of the sage King Nestor, wise counselor and friend of the other Achaean leaders. In the palace archives Blegen came upon numerous clay tablets that had been baked (and thus accidentally preserved) in the fire that destroyed Pylos toward the end of the thirteenth century B.C. These too were written in the

Linear B script. The publication of these in 1951 further advanced Ventris' work. Still later more tablets turned up at Mycenae, also in the now familiar Linear B script. Then, in 1952, Sir John Myres published in the second volume of *Scripta Minoa* the tablets that Evans had found, and that same year Blegen found more tablets at Pylos.

With all this virgin material, Ventris and his colleagues, especially his friend and collaborator John Chadwick, were able to test the theory that forced itself on Ventris—that the documents were in some form of Greek. Up till 1952 he had assumed, with others, that they were written in some non-Greek language, a language possibly related to Etruscan; but after laborious grammatical analyses and comparative studies, he found that some tablets contained Cretan place-names, such as Knossos, Phaistos, and Tylissos; the grammatical structure of the language—as shown, for instance, in variant word-endings—was like that of Greek, but a relatively early form of the language, which seemed to bear some faint similarity to that of Homer.

Ventris was essentially a modest man, generous, open-hearted, with no scholarly axe to grind (he was not a professional philologist), and it was not until he and Chadwick had tested their theory to the full and discussed it with other researchers that they published their historic work, *Documents in Mycenaean Greek*. They had conquered, as one writer happily expressed it, "the Everest of Greek archaeology." Shortly before the publication of the book Ventris met a tragic death in a road accident; he was thirty-four years old.

Today the majority of Greek scholars, as well as specialists in Aegean archaeology, accept Ventris' decipherment, although the documents are still not easy to read and some of Ventris' conclusions may have to be modified in the light of further research. Also there are a few scholars, and eminent

Funeral masks covered the faces of some of the princes who were buried in the shaft graves at Mycenae; the one shown below, made of gold, was one of three that were discovered in the same grave. Other offerings buried with the dead included the rock crystal bowl above, which represents a duck, and the gold cup seen at right. Probably used for libations, it has handles decorated with birds, like King Nestor's cup described in the Iliad; and like the Cup of Nestor, the one shown here is "pierced with golden rivets."

ones, who have yet to be convinced that the language is in fact Greek. But assuming that the majority are right, this astonishing revelation poses an entirely new set of problems. For if the Linear B tablets found at Knossos (and they have been found nowhere else on the island) are in Greek, and if their dating of about 1400 B.C. is accepted, it means that Greek-speaking people must have been ruling at Knossos in the fifteenth century B.C. And if the Mycenaeans were at Knossos in 1400 B.C., then it can hardly have been they who destroyed the palaces at about this time. When had they come from the mainland? How long had they been on the island?

Tablets written in Linear A, as well as in an earlier hieroglyphic version of it, have been found throughout the island of Crete but nowhere else. The Linear A form apparently replaced the hieroglyphs around 1750 B.C., remained in use for some three centuries, and then gave way to Linear B. It became clear that the last was an adaptation of the Minoan script and was used to give written form to the Greek language. It uses similar symbols, but in a different way—not unlike the differences between the Greek and Roman alphabets, as Chadwick has pointed out.

The documents themselves are disappointing in that they include no literature, only lists and inventories, records kept by the palace clerks. These, however, provide fascinating details concerning the equipment and organization of Mycenaean life. Many refer to objects such as swords, tripods, chariots. A typical example, found in the Knossian armory, can be translated into English by the Ventris system: "Horse (chariots), painted crimson and with joinery work complete, supplied with reins. The bridle (?) is of leather, with fittings (?) of horn, and there is (no?) 'heel' (?)." Another series of tablets from Knossos, a muster roll, refers to an armored brigade, which in Chadwick's estimation may

A princess' gold diadem, its head-band and radiating leaves finely embossed, was another of the treasures found in a shaft grave at Mycenae.

have comprised a force of well over a hundred chariots.

Other tablets describe furnishings in a surprising variety of specialized forms—chairs, footstools, tables, fire tools, and the like—many of which would appear to have been elaborately wrought and which reflect an intricate domestic economy. Chairs, for instance, were made of ebony and ornamented with delicately carved and inlaid ivory; tables were of marble inlaid with rock crystal, gold, and ivory. And to give tangible evidence to this record of luxury and convenience, in 1955 Blegen found in the palace at Pylos a built-in bath with a place for a sponge.

The list of specialized workmen and craftsmen drawn from the inscriptions reveals a complex and highly organized society. There were seamstresses and cleaners, saddle makers or leather workers, carpenters and masons, shipbuilders and caulkers, bronzesmiths and goldsmiths, bowmakers and, of course, potters, and so on down a long line of trades and occupations, including a variety of agricultural pursuits. That there were also slave traders is indicated by the number of captive peoples, many of whom seem to have been brought from the west coast of Asia Minor, and who performed menial chores in the palaces and great houses.

There are no Mycenaean inscriptions such as those found in Egypt and Mesopotamia that proclaim the might and right of rulers and the omnipotence of the gods. Still other tablets, however, refer to people who appear to have well-known Homeric names, such as Hector, while on three tablets discovered at Pylos appear the names of several familiar Greek gods—Poseidon, Zeus, Hera, Athena, Hermes, and others. There is also, at Pylos and at Knossos, a frequent reference to *Potnia*—"Mistress" or "Our Lady"; these last inscriptions confirm what archaeologists had long suspected from the evidence on seals discovered on the mainland—that the Mycenaeans also worshiped the Minoan mother goddess.

The inscriptions give evidence of filing systems that maintained records of land, food supplies, and slaves—some called "servants of the god" and others belonging to the king. The impression one gets is of a tightly organized bureaucracy, with many scribes keeping records of land tenure, military supplies, taxation, heads of sheep, cattle, and other domesticated beasts, amounts of oil, wine, and grain, and so on. In many respects it seems quite unlike the much simpler society that Homer describes.

It is quite possible that the Minoans, and even the Mycenaeans, also wrote on papyrus, which they could have imported from Egypt, and there is a tradition of writing on palm leaves, leather, and bark. But such documents would naturally have perished; none have been found, and it is disappointing that no document in either Linear A or B has to date turned up in Egypt.

Recently the philologist Leonard Palmer has ventured a theory that the tablets found at Knossos date no earlier than 1200 B.C.; that the palace there did not go into a decline after 1400 B.C.; and that it was during the two centuries of Achaean domination between those dates that Knossos actually reached its full glory. Even the famous frescoes, including those of the bull leapers, might belong to this epoch, according to Palmer's contention. His theory cannot be discussed here in any detail; it can only be put on record with the comment that many archaeologists disagree with it. If he were to be proved right the destruction of Knossos could have occurred about the same time as the mainland palaces were destroyed. It would also follow that Homer could have been right in stating that at Agamemnon's behest, Crete was able to contribute a large expeditionary force to the Mycenaean cause at Troy. "The illustrious spearman Idomeneus led the Cretans," the *Iliad* reports; "the men from Knossos, from Gortyn of the Great Walls, from Lyktos, Miletus, chalky Lykastos, Phaistos, and Rhytion, fine cities all of them; and the other troops that had their homes in Crete of the Hundred Towns. All these were led by the great spearman Idomeneus and by Meriones, a compeer of the man-destroying war god. Eighty black ships came under their command." Despite Palmer's contention, however, it is widely believed that Evans was right and that Knossos was laid waste about 1400 B.C., not later.

At the end of the thirteenth century B.C., the great Mycenaean palaces, such as Tiryns, Pylos, and Iolkos, were burned level, never to rise again. Again and again, in examining these sites, one sees the sinister marks of fire. Iolkos, the legendary home of Jason in Thessaly, is the most mouth-watering archaeological site in Greece. This ancient city was not built high on rock, but on low-lying ground near the harbor. Successive rebuildings have produced a tell—that is, a mound created by many centuries of almost continuous occupation and successive rebuilding—with clearly stratified layers that range from a possible early level of about 2300 B.C. down through the entire Bronze Age—including, of course, the Mycenaean period (roughly from 1600 to 1200 B.C.)—to the eighth century B.C. The marks of burning are clearly visible in the side of the mound. The late Alan Wace, who found Linear B tablets at Mycenae, thought there might be a possibility of finding palace archives amid the debris at Iolkos, tablets baked by fire to an enduring hardness. (The tablets were never deliberately fired.) One hopes he was right; time alone will show. Part of the modern town of Volos sits on top of the mound, however, and would have to be demolished before the site could be thoroughly explored.

At Tiryns the evidence is even more dramatic, for there, buried beneath charred debris at the foot of the city walls, lay the skeletons of the last defenders where they fell or where their bodies were thrown. Among the tablets found by Blegen at Pylos, tablets whose preservation is due to the fire that destroyed the palace, are some that appear to suggest preparations for defense against an impending attack. Watchers are posted to guard the coast; ships' crews—"rowers"—are dispatched on naval business, significantly to a point where there were no coastal forts. At Mycenae, as elsewhere, excavations have revealed that defenses were strengthened and the water supply was protected. At Gla, on Lake Copais in Boeotia, not far from Thebes, a huge wall was built—the longest defense-work ever erected in Mycenaean Greece. Its ruins were discovered in a shattered condition; it may never have been finished. In any event, the settlement it was supposed to guard perished shortly after it was first occupied. There are no written records of this catastrophe. Only the mute stones stand witness to whatever events took place.

According to legend and tradition, the last wave of invading Greeks were the descendants of Heracles—the Heraclidae—who, meeting resistance when they returned to the Pelo-

ponnesus, conquered the land by force. To historians this is known as the invasion of the Dorians, an illiterate people who drove down from somewhere in the northwestern regions, passing through central Greece and occupying much of the Peloponnesus by the twelfth century B.C. In the words of Blegen: "The Dorian invasion, whatever its sources and however it ran its course, has left a broad gash, like a fire-scar in a mountain forest, cutting through the archaeological panorama of ancient Greek history. Many towns that flourished in the preceding Heroic Age were henceforth abandoned or declined to a state of insignificance. Even some of the great . . . strongholds sank into virtual oblivion, and the places where they had stood were lost from the view of men."

It was roughly about this time (the twelfth century B.C.) that hordes of migrants were pouring down the coast of Syria and Palestine and on to Egypt, where they were met and defeated by Ramesses III. Shortly before, the great Hittite empire in Anatolia had collapsed under the weight of hosts of invaders. There seems to have been a great stirring of peoples, tribe thrusting out tribe, each fighting for new lands. Aside from the Egyptian documents and monuments, the written records tell us little of all this; only occasionally, as in Homer, does one get a clue as to what was happening. The Trojan War, allegedly fought to avenge the honor of Menelaus, in fact may have represented a desperate attempt by the Mycenaeans—or Achaeans, as Homer calls them—to secure new lands and to control the trade routes that led to the north and to the east.

When the Mycenaean heroes won their war against Troy, they returned home, leaving no settlers at the site. But their descendants, fleeing from the domination of their Dorian overlords, eventually did settle in Asia, primarily on the coast south of Troy and on the islands nearby. One great Mycenaean city, Athens, had escaped destruction by the Dorian hordes, and it was into Athens that the Mycenaean refugees first fled before they crossed the Aegean to the new land, which came to be called Ionia. This migration from the mainland centers continued throughout the Dark Age of Greece.

The refugees brought with them an ancient tradition of song. An Ionian elegy written in the seventh century B.C. recalls the foundation of the city of Colophon centuries before by men who had fled from the Peloponnesus. "We left Pylos, the town of Neleus, and reached lovely Asia by sea. We settled in fair Colophon, in the strength of our might . . ." Neleus had been the father of King Nestor and the founder of the town of Pylos. About a century after the Trojan War, his heirs, seeking new lands, led a band of migrants across the seas from Greece to Ionia. There the Mycenaean refugees had to fight to dislodge the native inhabitants; like their forefathers, the warriors of the *Iliad*, they found themselves battling in a hostile land along the coast of Asia. When their descendants in Ionia sang of the ventures of those remote Mycenaean heroes who had fought at Troy, it might have recalled to them as well the struggles that had secured a homeland for them in Ionia.

THE LORDS
OF MYCENAE

In the *Iliad* Homer describes the Greek heroes as "dear to Zeus" or "honored like a god." This is a dim memory of the days when the Mycenaeans did honor their kings like gods and kingship was sacred; when the king's land was called *temenos,* a word used later in Greece only for the precinct of a temple; and when divine honors were paid to a king upon his burial. The gold "Mask of Agamemnon" (above), which was placed over the face of one Mycenaean ruler, testifies to the richness of such burials; if the king died abroad, a stone was interred in place of his body, so that his royal presence could continue to reside among his subjects. The ruler of Mycenae held nominal sovereignty over the other princes of the mainland, and in the *Iliad* Agamemnon is generally called "king of men." His city was the richest and most powerful of all the citadels of Greece. At the time when Agamemnon ruled, in the thirteenth century B.C., Mycenae's cultural and commercial influence reached as far as Egypt and the Levant.

THE DOMAIN
OF THE HEROES

The structure of Mycenaean society was more similar to that of the despotic kingdoms of the contemporary Near East than it was to the city-states of classical Greece. The divine king, ruling from a fortified citadel, commanded a class of landholders, whose great estates were tilled by tenants or by numerous captive slaves. They sent tribute of horses and chariots, armor and sheep to the palace of the king, and their tenants provided hides, honey, and wheat, or manufactured weapons for the royal arsenal. Riches were measured in livestock or by the great copper caldrons that were sometimes used as a unit of exchange and buried with the dead as a posthumous store of wealth. (In the *Iliad* Agamemnon gives Achilles twenty of them.) The decipherment of the Linear B tablets has given us a clear idea of the economy of Pylos and Mycenae, and of Knossos under Mycenaean rule. The tablets provide censuses of the animals owned by the king, the names of the herdsmen, and even the nicknames of some individual oxen, which have been translated as "Glossy" and "Blackie." We have lists of the women occupied in spinning and combing wool at Pylos, and the complete records of supplies brought in and out of one building at Mycenae, either a spice merchant's house or a palace annex devoted to the manufacture of perfumed oil. With their concern for recording meticulous accounts of the most trifling commercial transactions, the men whose lives are revealed in the Linear B tablets seem to bear little resemblance to the spirited heroes of the Homeric epics.

Overlooking the broad and fertile Argive plain, the citadel at Mycenae commanded a major highway into the Peloponnesus. The grave circle shown here is on the lower part of the acropolis; below it were the houses and shops of townsmen.

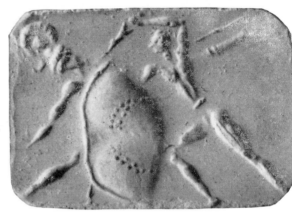

THE WAR WITH TROY

Mycenaean adventurers frequently engaged in pirate raids along the coast of Asia Minor, but their activity increased during the thirteenth century B.C.; contemporary documents record that they were a constant threat to the western borders of the Hittite kingdom. When the Hittites fell there was a power vacuum in the west, and a confederacy led by Troy and rivaling the Greeks in power may have arisen to fill it. Troy was a flourishing city and an important customer for Mycenaean products, perhaps exchanging wool and horses in return. There could have been many reasons why the Greeks besieged Troy, but it is unlikely that the abduction of Helen was the major one. If that romantic incident did occur, it may have had little to do with the Trojans; a similar tale is found in Canaanite literature, and it is probable that Helen's story was part of a cycle of poems that the Mycenaeans recited long before the time of the Trojan War. Equally ancient was another, related story that told of the siege of a stronghold by the sea. The Trojan War may have made such a deep impression that the site of these traditional stories was transferred to Troy. Despite this transfer, reminders of the original Greek stronghold by the sea still survive in the *Iliad*, and some of the Trojan princes in the poem retain Greek names, many of which appear in the Linear B tablets as the names of ordinary Mycenaean citizens.

Opposite, a Mycenaean warrior, carved of ivory, wears a boar's-tusk helmet and carries a figure-of-eight shield similar to the model shield at right.

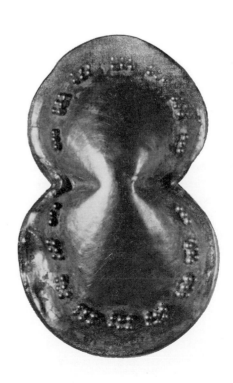

291

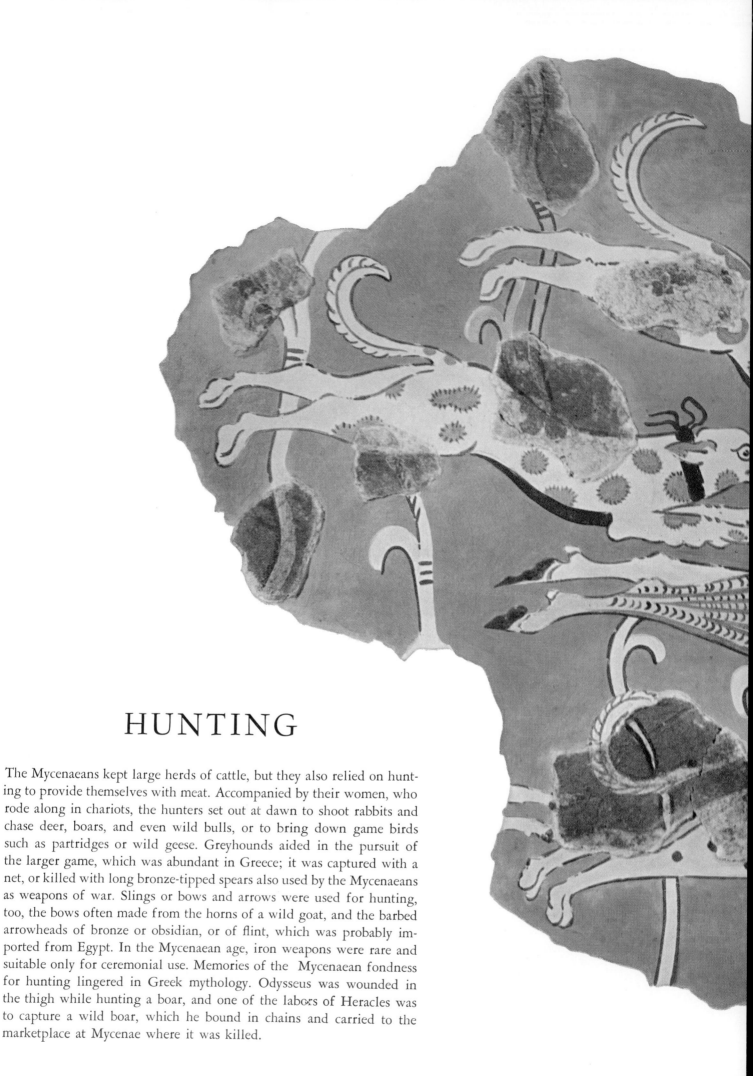

HUNTING

The Mycenaeans kept large herds of cattle, but they also relied on hunting to provide themselves with meat. Accompanied by their women, who rode along in chariots, the hunters set out at dawn to shoot rabbits and chase deer, boars, and even wild bulls, or to bring down game birds such as partridges or wild geese. Greyhounds aided in the pursuit of the larger game, which was abundant in Greece; it was captured with a net, or killed with long bronze-tipped spears also used by the Mycenaeans as weapons of war. Slings or bows and arrows were used for hunting, too, the bows often made from the horns of a wild goat, and the barbed arrowheads of bronze or obsidian, or of flint, which was probably imported from Egypt. In the Mycenaean age, iron weapons were rare and suitable only for ceremonial use. Memories of the Mycenaean fondness for hunting lingered in Greek mythology. Odysseus was wounded in the thigh while hunting a boar, and one of the labors of Heracles was to capture a wild boar, which he bound in chains and carried to the marketplace at Mycenae where it was killed.

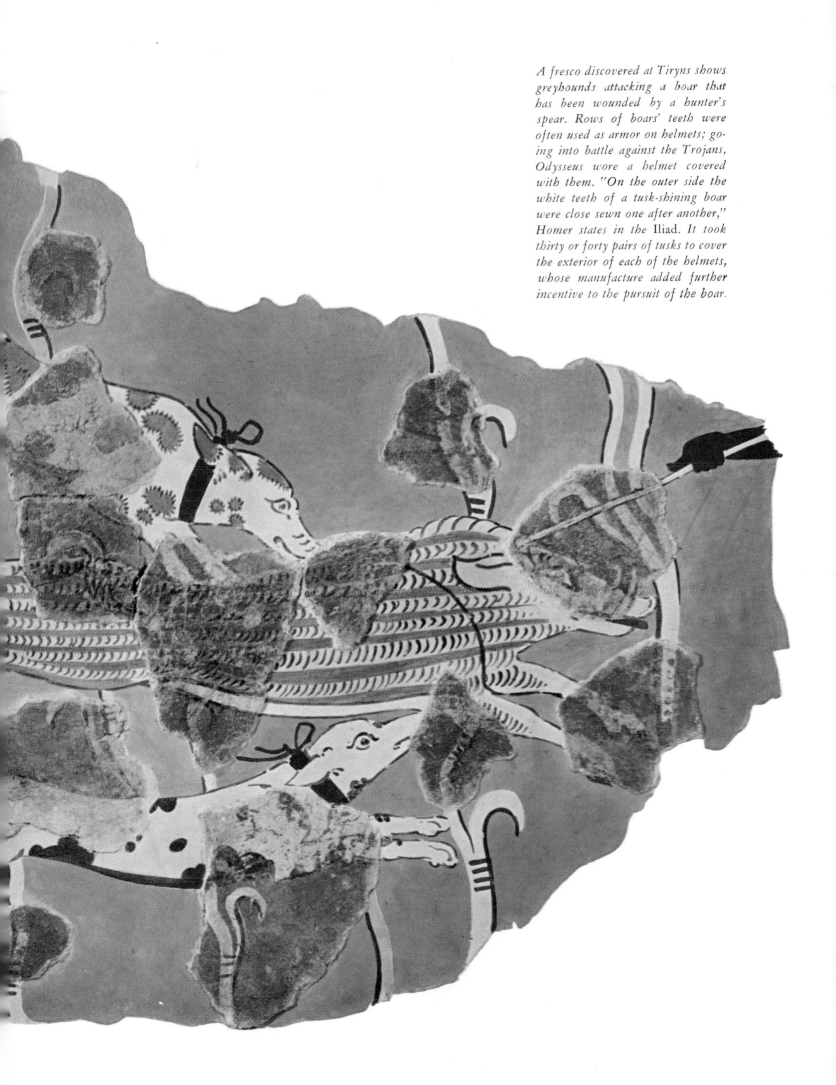

A fresco discovered at Tiryns shows greyhounds attacking a boar that has been wounded by a hunter's spear. Rows of boars' teeth were often used as armor on helmets; going into battle against the Trojans, Odysseus wore a helmet covered with them. "On the outer side the white teeth of a tusk-shining boar were close sewn one after another," Homer states in the Iliad. It took thirty or forty pairs of tusks to cover the exterior of each of the helmets, whose manufacture added further incentive to the pursuit of the boar.

AEGEAN LEGACY

The reliefs on the gold Vaphio cups represent the capture of two wild bulls, to provide animals for the Cretan bull games or to keep the beasts from roaming free about a herd of cattle. On the cup above, a trapped bull struggles to liberate himself. The other illustrations are details from the matching cup; below, a bull is being decoyed by a cow, while a herdsman, shown on the facing page, hobbles his leg with a rope.

"Many and stout, the Cretans from Knossos the city of Minos sailed on their business in a black ship to sandy Pylos, to deal with the men of the country," one of the Homeric hymns recalls. Cretan traders brought finely made daggers and golden jewelry to the people of the mainland, and eventually Minoan artisans worked there themselves, teaching their skills to the native craftsmen. The pictures on these pages illustrate two gold cups found near the town of Vaphio, which were imported from Crete by a Peloponnesian prince or made for him in the Cretan style. Mycenaean women adopted the Cretan costume and imported luxurious fabrics from Knossos. Mycenaean men, however, wore tunics, instead of the narrow-waisted garments worn in Crete. They let their beards grow, and unlike the Cretans, evidently preferred war to athletics.

When they became the leading traders of the Mediterranean, the Mycenaeans took over a position the Cretans had long maintained. Their colonists or trade representatives settled at Rhodes and Cyprus, and soon these islands too became outposts of the Minoan-Mycenaean culture, with a related language and writing, and similar styles in art. No doubt the Minoans had established trading posts on the Syrian coast; but in later times Mycenaean trade there was much more extensive than that of the Cretans had been. When the Sea Peoples invaded the Syrian coast at the end of the thirteenth century B.C. and disrupted Mycenaean trade with Asia, there was probably a severe economic depression in Greece. This may have affected the ability of the Mycenaeans to defend themselves against another wave of invaders, the Dorians, who were overrunning Greece from the north.

The Dorians conquered Mycenae, but failed to profit from its culture as the Mycenaeans had benefited from that of Crete. Much of the heritage that had been handed down from the Minoans disappeared, and even the art of writing was forgotten. The Peloponnesian citadels were so thoroughly destroyed that little Mycenaean art remained. A few relics of the ancient civilization did survive, in lands such as Attica, which the Dorians had failed to conquer, or on the Ionian coast of Asia Minor, to which many refugees had fled. Long after Mycenae's palaces and treasures had disappeared, it was in Ionia that the poet called Homer gathered together the traditional songs that celebrated the deeds of the Achaean heroes, and composed them into the epics that are Mycenae's noblest legacy.

THE LOST WORLDS OF
ANATOLIA

Anatolia was the home of the Hittites, who between three and four thousand years ago ranked as one of the great civilized powers of the ancient world. One glance at a map of Turkey will show the geographical reasons why the peninsula of Asia Minor was so important in ancient times. The shape of the country roughly resembles the head of an Assyrian lion, the shoulders of which are firmly set in Asia, the crown of the skull supporting the Black Sea, the mane overhanging the east Mediterranean and Cyprus, while the nose thrusts out boldly into the Aegean, linking Asia with eastern Europe. To change the metaphor, Anatolia is an enormous two-way land bridge between Europe and Asia, the route by which the Mycenaeans may have entered Greece and by which Alexander invaded Asia.

Few areas of comparable size anywhere in the world present such a variety of climates and landscapes. The western coast, fronting the Aegean, is typically Mediterranean, hardly distinguishable from the coast of southern Greece and the Cyclades. There are olive groves and vineyards; the climate is warm and relaxing, with dry summers and rainy winters. The southern coast, overlooking Cyprus, grows cotton and citrus fruit. Much of the Black Sea coast is semitropical, whereas the eastern mountains have an alpine climate. Someone has commented that a Swiss, a Scotsman, an Italian, a Russian, and an African would each find some part of Asia Minor where he would feel comfortable.

However, the mountainous character of much of the country is more significant to the story of Anatolia than these climatic variations. The mountains of the Taurus range loom so enormously that they seemed to divide the eastern Mediter-

On the wind-swept plains of Central Anatolia, massive masonry walls once protected Hittite cities against invaders. From the wall that guarded Alaja Huyuk, a sphinx gateway (left) still stands.

ranean world into northern and southern halves; even to the imperial Roman legions looking north from the Syrian plains they constituted an almost impassable barrier. Parts of central Anatolia are like a raging sea turned to stone; peaks and massifs rear up on every side, tumbling to the restless horizon. From the central plateau, where the Hittites lived, one looks eastward toward the towering peak of Erjiyes Dagh, almost thirteen thousand feet high and snowcapped. Beyond it the chain of the Anti-Taurus runs northeastward to merge with the highlands of Armenia. This violent landscape, fit home for mysterious gods and peoples, is utterly unlike the monotonous plains of the Tigris and Euphrates or the Indus, or the well-nurtured valley of the Nile.

The people who have lived in Asia Minor during the past seven thousand years have consequently differed widely in character. There would be little in common between, say, a Cilician living in the warm southeast and a man living near the Pontus, on the Black Sea; and even less between them and someone living on the high central plateau or a person dwelling near the shores of "windy Troy."

Anatolia remains the least-known sector of that part of the world which nourished the earliest civilizations. For some five hundred years it was the heartland of the Ottoman Empire, a closed-in territory that few Europeans were allowed to penetrate. Even after the rebellion under Ataturk, when unbelievers were shown greater tolerance, poor communications and other factors still mitigated against visits from foreigners. Greece has attracted tourists since the Renaissance and even before—indeed since Roman days. Egypt has had a tourist industry for more than fifty years. Even Babylonia has for some time been reasonably accessible to foreign scholars, although it offers few attractions to tourists. But Anatolia has remained apart until quite recently.

Perhaps this is just as well, since it may have saved

Before the Hittites came to Anatolia, people skilled in the arts lived at Alaja Huyuk. Buried with their kings in tombs dating from 2400 to 2200 B.C. were finely wrought treasures of silver, bronze, and gold which excel in craftsmanship many known Hittite artifacts. Stylized figures of stags were found in the tombs. Some stand in circular twists of bronze (left) or are enmeshed in grill-work disks; others stand alone. Most probably the object of a ritual cult, the stag was also considered sacred in lands far to the north and east of the Black Sea, and could be a guide to the origin of both the early rulers of Alaja Huyuk and the Hittites, who revered the animal as well.

archaeologically valuable remains from the ignorant, indiscriminate plundering that destroyed so much in Egypt and Mesopotamia, preserving them against a time when modern, scientific techniques would extract the maximum information from such undisturbed sites as still remain.

The discovery of the lost world of the Hittites and their neighbors vies with that of Sumer and of Crete as a fascinating archaeological story, the end of which is not yet in sight. In the case of Mesopotamia and Anatolia investigators were led first by biblical reference (though in the latter case supplemented by Egyptian and Assyrian inscriptions). But the search was confused by the fact that the Hittites of the Bible, who occupied parts of Syria, were not the Hittites who had earlier fought the Egyptians at Kadesh. The trail led the hunters by a devious route, with many doublings and some blind alleys, from an inscribed stone on the wall of a mosque in Aleppo to obscure passages in the Book of Numbers, from Egyptian temple inscriptions and the files of Akhenaten's diplomatic correspondence to the cuneiform records of the early Assyrian kings, from the plains of Syria to beyond the mighty mountains of the Taurus.

In a sense those who have read thus far in this book are in a position similar to that of scholars of half a century ago. Like them, the reader possesses certain evidence, to which more will be added in the following pages. They know, of course, about the ancient Egyptians, and are aware that for a while during the New Kingdom the Hittites were among the Egyptians' most deadly foes. They know that contemporaneously with Egypt Mesopotamia had produced a succession of civilizations—Sumerian, Akkadian, Babylonian, Assyrian—and that these people wrote in cuneiform on clay tablets. They know that the horse and chariot were introduced into Egypt about 1600 B.C. and appeared in Greece at about the same time; the Mycenaeans, Homer's "bronze-clad

Achaeans," were adept with this military weapon. And they will also recall that from about 2000 to 1700 B.C. there was a movement of Indo-European peoples into Greece, perhaps via Asia Minor, and later into the Indus Valley via Afghanistan. In 1280 B.C. the pharaoh Ramesses II signed a treaty of friendship with the Hittite king Hattusilis III, and ninety-three years later Ramesses III defeated a coalition of invaders who, forging down the coast of Syria and Palestine, had reached the very gates of Egypt. Among these Peoples of the Sea, as we have come to call them, were those the Egyptians named the Danuna, whom some identify as Homer's *Danaoi*.

Syria and Palestine, not having nurtured a major civilization up to this point in the history of the ancient world, have hardly been mentioned in the previous pages, but it is worth recalling that among the best known of the Old Testament stories is that of King David and Uriah the Hittite, whose wife David coveted; and that in the Book of Numbers it is stated that "The Amalekites dwell in the land of the south; and the Hittites, and the Jebusites, and the Amorites dwell in the mountains [of Syria]." Also, in the Second Book of Kings, when the Assyrians were besieging Samaria, the Samarians quote them as saying, "Lo, the king of Israel hath hired against us the king of the Hittites."

The statements in the foregoing paragraph may seem like a bewildering catalogue of unrelated information. They provide, however, vital clues that helped archaeologists and scholars in other fields to establish the identity of the Hittites and to retrace the complex ancient history of Anatolia. With them in mind we also can thread our way through this labyrinth of the past.

In one form or another the name of the Hittites kept cropping up again and again. In Egypt Ramesses II left huge temple reliefs illustrating and describing his battles with the "abominable Kheta," as he once termed the Hittites when

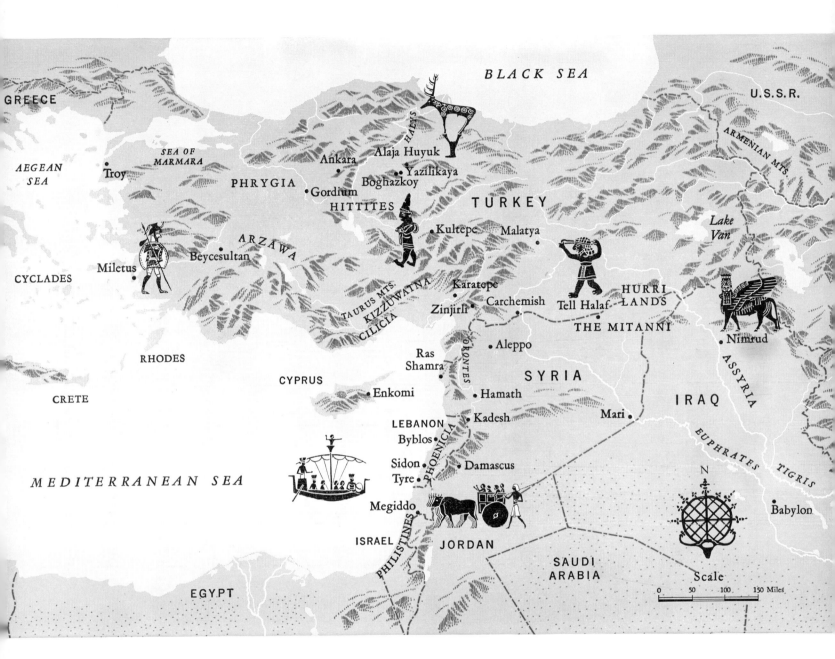

When the Hittites, in their texts, were about to shift from one of the several written languages they used to another, they occasionally announced the fact: "The singer of the Land of Hurri sings as follows," might precede a passage in Hurrian, the language of the Hittites' frequent harassers to the east. Unfortunately, many of their references to neighboring peoples are still inexplicable. A subject of great debate are the Akaiwasha, or Ahhiyawa; their name bears a persuasive linguistic likeness to the Achaeans whose pottery has been found at Miletus. The Muski, mentioned in Assyrian records, are tentatively equated with the Phrygians, who may have forced the Hittites down into northern Syria where they lingered after their empire fell. Part of this same upheaval, the Sea Peoples attacked Egypt, by sea in high-prowed boats, by land in ox-drawn carts.

The sistrum above makes a jangling sound when shaken; it may have been used for musical accompaniment to ancient religious rites in Anatolia.

they were his enemies. We see the pharaoh in his war chariot shooting arrows into the foe, and the panic-stricken Hittite soldiers, men with long noses and prognathous jaws, falling headlong into the Orontes River, near the Syrian town where the battle was fought. (As we have earlier noted, the battle was actually a standoff; the Hittites were by no means beaten in this conflict.) Again, in Mesopotamia an inscription dating from the reign of the Assyrian king Tiglath-pileser I (1100 B.C.) described how that ruler came into contact with a powerful kingdom called Great Hatti; and how later, returning from a campaign, Tiglath-pileser received homage from another king of Great Hatti. The Hittites of the Hebrews, the Kheta of the Egyptians, and the Hatti of the Assyrians, it was assumed, were all the same people. But who were they? And where did they come from? Had they a capital city, and if so, where was it?

As in Sumer and as in Crete, it was the discovery of a hitherto-unknown form of writing which first put archaeologists on the scent. In 1812 an explorer named Johann Burckhardt came upon an inscribed block of basalt at Hamath, in Syria. No one else took much notice of the discovery at the time. Later, in 1871, a similar block was found in the wall of a mosque in Aleppo. Both bore inscriptions in a form of hieroglyphic writing which resembled no known language. The worshipers at the mosque considered the stone holy, and resented any attempt by foreigners to examine it. However, copies were made and circulated, but linguists could make nothing of them. Following Burckhardt's discovery, several decades were to pass before reports began to filter through that what appeared to be similar hieroglyphs had been found engraved on rocks high in the Taurus mountains, hundreds of miles to the north.

A. H. Sayce, a well-known Assyriologist, announced in 1876 that he believed both the Hamath and Aleppo inscrip-

"The day the import of your tablet was made known to me, I provided your agents with three minas of silver for the purchase of lead. Now, if you are still my brother, let me have my money by courier." So wrote an Assyrian, probably in Assur, to one of his countrymen who was living in the thriving Assyrian trading colony outside Kultepe, a pre-Hittite settlement in central Anatolia. Their four-thousand-year-old transactions were recorded in cuneiform on clay tablets and inserted into seal-impressed clay envelopes (right). The lion-shaped vessel (shown left) is the work of Kultepe potters.

tions to be in the Hittite language, and in subsequent articles he also tentatively identified rock inscriptions at Ivriz, Boghazkoy, and Alaja Huyuk as being in Hittite. These and other sites had been visited by a number of adventurous travelers between 1834 and 1876. From the end of the eighteenth century on, more and more explorers mounted expeditions into what was still the dangerous hinterland of Anatolia. The country was difficult to travel in and at the time extremely inhospitable. Excitement grew as each explorer brought back reports of inscriptions, sculptures, and even the ruins of cities, high up in the central tableland of Anatolia.

Of such ruins the most impressive were found near Boghazkoy, an obscure village high in the mountains within the bend of the Halys River, and another at Alaja Huyuk, fifteen miles to the northeast. Here were not only inscriptions in the mysterious writing first found at Hamath, but great sculptured reliefs depicting men of somewhat similar appearance to the Kheta shown on the ancient Egyptian temple reliefs. Had the archaeologists traced the elusive Hittites to their homeland? It seemed probable, yet while the writing system remained undeciphered it could not be proved. The final investigation, which had only just begun, was to show that the Hittites were relative latecomers to Asia Minor, which had known other rich and highly developed cultures long before their time. But this is to anticipate.

In 1887 another clue turned up in far-off Egypt. It was found not by an archaeologist, but by an Egyptian peasant woman digging for *sebakh* at el Amarna, Pharaoh Akhenaten's long-deserted capital. (*Sebakh* is the name given to the crumbled mud brick of ancient cities, which the practical Arabs discovered makes a useful fertilizer.) The woman came upon large quantities of baked-clay tablets, which were eventually loaded into a sack and carried to the nearest dealer (many of them crumbled to dust during their

rough passage). The dealer recognized that the tablets bore cuneiform inscriptions, but at first officials refused to believe that these were genuine. By the time the authenticity of the tablets had been established many of them had been destroyed. Among those which remained, however, were a series of letters addressed in the Akkadian language to the pharaoh by certain of his Syrian and Palestinian vassals and city governors. With this correspondence was the famous appeal from Ribbadi, quoted earlier in this book.

There were also two letters written in an unknown language, though the word Arzawa could be made out. A Norwegian scholar suggested that one of these was from the pharaoh Amenhotep III to the king of a state called Arzawa (wherever that might be) and that the other was probably written from Arzawa to Egypt. He believed that the language belonged to the Indo-European linguistic group. The theory attracted little attention, although one fact was clear. The peasant woman had come upon a file from Akhenaten's foreign office; some of these letters were an attempt to bring home to the pharaoh the imminent threat to his Syrian dominions by a powerful foe from the north—and the enemy that was menacing Egypt was the Kheta.

Even so this discovery did little but add to the archaeologists' frustration. They already knew that the Hittites had existed; there was abundant testimony from the peoples of lands such as Egypt and Assyria. They had even found what they strongly suspected to be the actual homeland of these people. But the Kheta themselves, if that is whom the rock-cut sculptures represented, remained silent, looking down from their niches in the Anatolian mountains—stocky, hook-nosed men in conical hats, thick woolen robes, and mountaineer's boots, surrounded by tantalizing inscriptions in hieroglyphic that no one could read.

In 1880 certain cuneiform tablets had appeared in the

hands of antique dealers in Ankara, Turkey. These were the first tablets to turn up in Anatolia and had been found by peasants at a mound of ruins known as Kultepe. They were in Assyrian and proved to be valuable, but they provided meager information about the Hittites. In 1893–1894 tablets were excavated at Boghazkoy, the ancient Hattusas. These were in the same cuneiform script as the two Arzawa letters found at el Amarna, which had not yet been deciphered. A German scholar, Hugo Winckler, with the express purpose of searching for more tablets, undertook excavation at Boghazkoy. He started digging at the site in 1906.

One approaches this remote village across a wide fertile valley, but gradually the hills close in until a point is reached at which two small streams break into the plain through narrow clefts in the mountains. The gorge is deep and impressive, with steep cliffs at the sides. At the junction of the streams is the little Turkish village, consisting of but a handful of modest houses, stores, farms, and beyond them rough tracks threading the fields. Above that cluster of buildings rise the ruins of an ancient city. One sees remains of Cyclopean walls girdling a total area of some three hundred acres. Monumental gateways pierce the wall. Flanking one gateway, sculptured lions seem to roar defiance at the approaching stranger; on another, when Winckler saw it, the vigorously sculptured figure of a god strode resolutely forward, right hand clasping a battle-axe, left hand clenched, powerful muscles rippling in thigh and arm. There are power and virility in these weather-worn stone carvings, and the figures seem to shout, "Look at us. We ruled an empire once!" Below, in the valley, the gentle murmur of the streams sounds mournfully among the rocks.

This is what Winckler saw fifty-odd years ago. Nearby, he also saw the mysterious shrine of Yazilikaya, where ranks of sculptured figures, each in his tall helmet, short tunic,

and boots with upturned toes, march in procession. At the center a god and goddess confront each other. Within a secluded sanctuary another relief, carved from the living rock, shows a king embraced by a god in a tall, conical headdress. In a niche nearby the strange hieroglyphs that had baffled Sayce and others still mocked the German scholar. But Winckler had not come to marvel at these sculptures, which were now well known among archaeologists. He had come to search for more tablets. He turned his attention to the area enclosed by the great walls, and made a wide trench to the top of the citadel mound.

To his astonishment and delight he came upon what had evidently been a palace archive. Over ten thousand were discovered, all in cuneiform, including many in the mysterious language still referred to at that time as Arzawa. But besides the Arzawan tablets there were some in Akkadian, which could of course be read. Had he discovered the capital city of Arzawa or something different? The find would be of even greater interest if this were possibly the capital city of the long-sought-for Hittites.

It was true. This heap of stones on a rugged Turkish hillside had once been Hattusas, capital of the Hittite empire—capital of a power that, for a brief period at least, could meet even mighty Egypt on equal terms. The tablets in Akkadian revealed much. More interesting was that the tablets, written in what had been called Arzawan, were in fact in the Hittite language—that is to say, in a cuneiform script adapted to the Hittite language. When these were deciphered, largely by the Czech scholar Bedrich Hrozny, it became possible to learn something of Hittite life and culture. There were the names of successive Hittite rulers and chronicles of their conquests. There were legal documents, a code of law, correspondence with foreign rulers, even a copy (in Hittite) of the famous treaty between Ramesses II and the Hittite king Hattusilis III,

According to legend, an early Anatolian king, Anittas of Kussara, destroyed and cursed the city of Hattusas, saying, "I took it by storm during the night and where it had been I sowed weeds. Whosoever becomes king after me and again settles Hattusas, may the weather god of heaven strike him!" Despite the curse, one of the first nonlegendary Hittite kings established his capital there, and no doubt took his name—Hattusilis I—from the site. Kings reigned from the capital, now called Boghazkoy, for nearly five hundred years. Many gates led through its miles of fortifications. One gate was guarded by lions (left); another by the figure at right, who is probably a god.

of which another copy was inscribed on one of the Egyptian temples at Karnak. There was a religious literature, with hymns and rituals, and there were references to the peoples of Syria and Mesopotamia, and other peoples of Anatolia with whom the Hittites had been in contact.

After Winckler's discoveries the search was on for more tablets. Anatolia became an archaeological Mecca. Other Hittite sites were systematically explored, including Kultepe, where some tablets had earlier been found and where Winckler had dug. He had worked there for eight days but found very little. Yet, year after year, more tablets came on the market that could be traced back to this site. Eventually a Czechoslovak expedition led by Hrozny made a serious and determined effort to locate the source of these documents.

For a long time this team searched unavailingly in the main mound, while the innocent-seeming villagers, who knew very well where the tablets lay, watched with interest and made misleading suggestions. The villagers had, in fact, come upon the cache of tablets some years earlier and had been discreetly and profitably leaking them onto the market a few at a time. They had already watched two other expeditions vainly searching, but this time they were unlucky. Two of Hrozny's men were from the area and by questioning them he eventually was able to locate the true site, only a few hundred yards from the major mound, Kultepe. It yielded more than a thousand tablets, some in Assyro-Babylonian cuneiform, that revealed much about this ancient site.

Kultepe had controlled the trade route from central Anatolia down to northern Syria, and here Hrozny found the remains of a trading post in which Assyrian merchants had lived for generations before the rise of the Hittite empire. There were their neat houses and orderly offices, containing baked-clay tablets neatly stacked on shelves: bills of sale, contracts, receipts, accounts—all the paraphernalia of a prosperous trading community which lived in amity with the rulers of the nearby Bronze Age city. These merchants supervised the donkey caravans that moved between Anatolia and Assyria, exchanging Anatolian metals for the woolens and other textiles of the Tigris-Euphrates Valley.

Meanwhile other sites had been identified in northern Syria, where Hittite influence was apparent, such as Carchemish, on the upper Euphrates, Milid, the modern Malatya, and Hamath. A few years before the outbreak of the First World War, a British archaeologist began to excavate at Carchemish, assisted by a young Oxford graduate named T. E. Lawrence, later to become "Lawrence of Arabia." They found substantial remains of a powerful city, including a great wall of sculptures with a procession of deities and warriors celebrating some great victory.

A German expedition dug at Zinjirli, and French archaeologists at Arslantepe. Other sites, such as Sakjegozu, also yielded valuable evidence—well-planned cities with temples and palaces, and ponderous but crude works of sculpture which seemed to owe something to Assyria, yet were not Assyrian. Were these Hittite remains? Most of these north Syrian sites belonged to a period considerably after 1500 B.C. There was a clear relationship between them and the mountain strongholds in Asia Minor—which were believed to be earlier—yet they were different. The solution of this mystery came later, after other significant finds.

Much was still to be learned about pre-Hittite Anatolia. Until fairly recently it was thought that human beings had not begun to occupy Anatolia much before 3000 B.C. But as a result of numerous excavations there is now considerable evidence of human occupation, in southern and southwestern Asia Minor, as far back as 5000 B.C., almost three thousand years before the first evidence of Hittite occupation. Remains of villages have been discovered dating from the Neolithic

King Tudhaliyas is shown (right) protected by the god Sharma, in a Hittite religious sanctuary near Boghazkoy. Similar reliefs, carved on isolated outcroppings of rock scattered far from the seat of empire, may mark the ancient reaches of Hittite suzerainty in Anatolia. A few of the carved figures can be identified by accompanying royal insignia and inscriptions, often repeated on seals. On the Tarkondemos seal (left) the actual figure of a king appears; the ten cuneiform and six hieroglyphic signs constitute the first Hittite bilingual text found.

and Chalcolithic Periods. But the oldest known city to have been systematically excavated is Troy, near the Dardanelles, first dug by Schliemann over ninety years ago, and subsequently re-dug more scientifically by Carl Blegen of the University of Cincinnati. The "great" period of Troy comes in Level II, about 2400 B.C., when Troy had a monumental fortress with mansions and a high civilization with a rich and sophisticated art. The celebrated jewelry that Schliemann found, which he romantically named the Treasure of Priam, actually dates from the Early Bronze Age, over a thousand years before the traditional date of the Trojan War. Again and again the archaeologists have found at Troy the marks of fierce fire—calcined stone, vitrified bricks, and the marks of charred timber. Such a strategic position, astride the trade routes, was bound to invite attack by ambitious peoples; there were many sackings of Troy.

Not long ago, at Dorak, near the Sea of Marmara, archaeologists came upon a rich Bronze Age burial that appears to be related stylistically to Troy II, although the finds have not yet been adequately published. The graves were of a local ruler and his wife, buried in the same tomb, while nearby lay another separate tomb containing one male body, probably of another king. The king entombed with his wife was accompanied by his favorite hunting dog, food offerings, and beautifully made ceremonial weapons. These, it has been reported, were of the finest workmanship and materials; there was a scepter of pink-veined marble with a gold-encased wooden handle. Behind one body lay four ceremonial axeheads made of amber, lapis lazuli, obsidian, and nephrite, and the shaft holes were bound with gold and silver. The queen had been provided with her jewelry and a scepter with a silver-encased handle. One tomb even contained fragments of a richly colored carpet, the most ancient ever found. One of the sword blades was of iron, and there was a dagger with

a silver blade engraved with little pictures of sailing ships, about the earliest known representations of ships outside Egypt. The household treasures of these Early Bronze Age rulers included vases, jugs, and bowls of gold and silver, and a particularly beautiful drinking vessel of fluted gold.

But perhaps the most remarkable and fortunate discovery, from an archaeological viewpoint, was part of what had been a gold-encased throne. On the fragments of gold leaf was the unmistakable cartouche of the Old Kingdom Egyptian pharaoh Sahure. The throne could have been a gift, but is more likely to have been acquired through trade. It enabled the discoverers to date the grave with some confidence to about 2500 B.C. This was about five hundred years before the Hittites moved westward into Asia Minor.

An even richer find was made underneath the ruined Hittite city of Alaja Huyuk, in central Anatolia. Here, in 1935, a Turkish expedition penetrated to the deeper levels of the Hittite mound, hoping to find evidences of the pre-Hittite settlement. They found more than they had bargained for— a series of lavishly furnished tombs dating from the Early Bronze Age, about the same period as the Dorak graves. But these were much more elaborate. The method of burial recalls elements of both the Mycenaean shaft graves and the Scythian burials of a much later date. There were altogether thirteen interments, each consisting of a shaft cut into the burial mounds and covered by a roofing of logs, above which had been placed the skulls of sacrificed oxen.

As at Mycenae, the burials had not all been made at the same time. There was evidence that in at least one case a queen had preceded her husband by some years. When he died the grave was opened to admit his body. These tombs contained valuable offerings, including jewelry, toilet articles, ornaments, and weapons of high esthetic quality. Many of them were of gold and silver, and displayed a technical

In a coup d'état, *King Urhi-Teshub, whose royal seal appears at right, was forced from the throne by his uncle and banished, first to Syria and finally to an island that may have been Cyprus. Records of royal intrigue as well as the empire's relations with its provinces and lands beyond Hittite control form part of the official archive found at Buyukkale, a citadel within the capital. Included also were seal impressions, the names on which helped scholars decipher Hittite hieroglyphic texts. The strangely shaped stamp (left) may show gods and cult scenes.*

quality hardly inferior to that of the Sumerian metalwork Woolley had discovered in the Ur death pits. On the other hand the vigorous animal portraiture, in the form of bronze bulls and stags is faintly reminiscent of nomadic tribes of the Asian steppes. Other objects, of slightly later date, found at Horoztepe nearer the Black Sea, are even more strikingly similar to Scythian art than are the bronze animals.

At another site, Beycesultan, in western Anatolia, an archaeological expedition has recently unearthed the remains of a well-built city containing a palace with features recalling that of Knossos in Crete, although it is built mainly of mud brick, stone rubble, and timber. In a double shrine, probably dedicated to a male and female deity, worshipers had to make their offerings across a kind of altar shaped like the "horns of consecration" in the Knossian palace. What used to be considered the characteristic Homeric or Mycenaean palace with its broad hall with central circular hearth and pillared porch—the megaron—also has been discovered at several places in Anatolia in an earlier context than that of Mycenae, Pylos, or Tiryns. These facts may point to an Anatolian origin of both the Minoan and Mycenaean peoples, though archaeologists differ on this matter.

Nevertheless one fact appears fairly clear. All these Bronze Age settlements were relatively small communities with a ruling aristocracy drawing its wealth and military manpower from a few score thousand peasants. Trade and cultural contacts there undoubtedly were, but on the whole each king ruled from his fortified city over a limited area. Maybe he entered into alliances with neighboring princelings, married one of their daughters, and exchanged gifts and compliments, as did the Achaean nobility of the *Iliad*. There was as yet no unified state with a common social and economic system, as in Babylonia and Egypt. The physical nature of Asia Minor, divided by mountain ranges, discouraged such a development

and it required the energy and daring of the Hittites to bring about at least a temporary and partial unification.

The Hittites spoke an Indo-European language akin to Sanskrit, Greek, and most European tongues. They entered Anatolia early in the second millennium B.C., possibly in the same migratory movement that brought the Mycenaeans, or Achaeans, into Greece. Like the Mycenaeans, the ancestors of the Hittites found a Bronze Age people living in the land which they invaded. The Hittites acquired the name of the conquered territory—Hatti—in the same way that the Anglo-Saxon invaders of the British Isles took on the original name of the island, which was, of course, Britain.

Conquest and unification were a very slow process. Hittite records found at Boghazkoy state that "at first the land was small, but wherever he marched to battle he [Labarnas, an early king] subdued the lands of his enemies with might. He destroyed the lands and made them powerless, and he made the seas his frontiers."

The successor to Labarnas was Hattusilis I, in whose reign the Hittites began to move southward, beyond the Taurus, into Syria, and to the southeast, no doubt attracted by the riches of the older civilizations long established in Mesopotamia. Hattusilis I had a warlike grandson, Mursilis I, who conquered Babylon in about 1600 B.C., just around the time the Seventeenth Dynasty pharaohs were liberating Egypt from the rule of the Hyksos.

During the fifteenth century B.C. the Hittites came into conflict with the Hurrians, who had occupied an area bordering the northern Euphrates. It was at this time that the great warrior Pharaoh Tuthmosis III was leading his conquering armies into northern Syria; it was he, and not the Hittite king, who eventually crushed the Hurrians and took the pressure off the Hittite frontier. Indeed, the Hittites may well have been valued allies of the Egyptians at this point, and if

so, this would have been the first contact between the established imperial power of ancient Egypt and the newly emergent nation of the mountain dwelling people.

When an Indo-European ruling caste known as the Mitanni later established sway over the Hurrians, they entered into friendly relations with the pharaohs Amenhotep III and Amenhotep IV (Akhenaten). Egypt was going through a non-militant phase and for a time the Mitanni were the most potent power in western Asia. Once again the Mitanni-ruled Hurrians gave great trouble to the Hittites, detaching their vassal states and threatening Hatti itself. The Hittites apparently suffered assault from various directions. One of their later chronicles, which seems to refer to this period, states that ". . . the Hatti lands were sacked from beyond their borders. The enemy from Kaska came and sacked the Hatti lands and made Nenassa his frontier. From beyond the Lower Land came the enemy from Arzawa, and he too sacked the Hatti lands and made . . . [a new] frontier."

Two Hittite kings of this period, Hattusilis II and Tudhaliyas III, struggled against the formidable power of the Mitanni, but with little success. It was one of Tudhaliyas' successors, the great Suppiluliumas, who turned the tide. Suppiluliumas might be called Tuthmosis III of Hatti, a fighter, a cunning strategist, wise in the ways of war and diplomacy. However, it may have been fortunate for him that he did not have to meet the great Tuthmosis himself in battle. The Egypt to which he was opposed was peacefully concerned with its own affairs. The heretic Akhenaten was a pacifist and a dreamer, preoccupied with his religious reforms; he apparently disregarded the threats to his border lands.

After first suffering defeat at the hands of the Mitannian king, Tushratta, Suppiluliumas devised a new and daring plan. Crossing the Euphrates near Malatya, and traversing wild and dangerous country peopled by hostile tribes, he took the Mitanni in the rear. He recovered his lost provinces and sacked the Mitannian capital. Evidently shaken by this unexpected attack the king of Mittani avoided battle. Suppiluliumas had disposed of his ancient enemy. Once again the Hittite armies began to roll southward and found themselves near the frontiers of Egyptian influence. It is possible that at this stage Suppiluliumas would have been content to establish his boundary on the Orontes, in Syria, and withdraw. But one of Egypt's vassals, the king of Kadesh, came out and offered battle. His armies were destroyed in the terrifying charge of the Hittite chariotry, and Suppiluliumas, carried forward by the impetus of his advance, pressed on into the Levant. The Hittites had come far from their mountain homeland, and from that rich coastal strip between the Lebanese mountains and the Great Green Sea, the Mediterranean, they turned their gaze south toward the gates of Egypt. The time of the Hittite advance was about 1370 B.C.

The rough highlanders from beyond the Taurus, with their chariots and horses and their powerful leader, encamped in Lebanon, while the petty kings of Syria, former vassals of Egypt, came to the tent of Suppiluliumas bearing tribute. And only a few hundred miles to the south lay the greatest power on earth, with a civilization stretching back more than fifteen hundred years to a time when the ancestors of the newly mighty Hittites may have been only skin-clad barbarians living in a primitive Stone Age society.

After another thirty years of arduous campaigning, during which he had battled the Assyrians and consolidated his hold on Syria, the Hittite king, now an old man, was encamped near Carchemish, on the upper Euphrates. After an eight-day siege that great fortress surrendered, and the army was resting after its victory. Then a messenger arrived from Egypt, carrying a letter—one of the familiar baked-clay cuneiform tablets. When his secretary read the message to

"King of Heaven, Lord of Hatti," the weather god (left) officially shared the divine throne with the sun goddess, who "directed the government of Hatti" from Arinna, a local cult center. The scenes on Hittite seals above and below are thought to portray rituals but only the figure standing on the back of an animal is known to be a god.

him the old king could not at first believe it, for it purported to be from the queen of Egypt. "My husband has died," she wrote, "and I have no son, but of you it is said that you have many sons. If you would send me one of your sons, he could become my husband. I will on no account take one of my subjects and make him my husband. I am very much afraid."

This letter was found by Winckler among the archives of Hattusas, the Hittite capital. Unfortunately there were no copies of the king's replies to this and further letters from the queen, which had evidently caused her some annoyance. He seems to have been skeptical about her overtures. Her next letter reads: "Why do you say, 'They are deceiving me?' If I had a son, would I write to a foreigner to publish my distress and that of my country? You have insulted me in speaking thus. . . . My husband is dead and I have no son. I will never take one of my subjects and marry him. I have written to no one but you. Everyone says you have many sons; give me one of them that he may become my husband."

Archaeology, which all too often has to concern itself with scraps of pottery, rarely stumbles on such a human story as this. The Egyptian queen who wrote those letters was almost certainly Ankheshamen, the girl-queen of Tutankhamen, widowed when the young pharaoh died at the age of about eighteen. According to Egyptian custom the next pharaoh could only legitimize his succession by marrying the royal heiress, in this case, Ankheshamen. Surrounded by intriguing, power-hungry courtiers and politicians, such as Ay, who had been Akhenaten's chief minister, the queen looked around desperately for an escape. Hence her statement, "I will never take one of my subjects and marry him." (Ay was already an elderly man, which may have had some bearing on the reasons underlying the girl's desperation.)

While her husband's youthful body soaked for the customary one hundred days in its natron bath, before embalm-

ment and burial, she tried to bring off a coup that could defeat the intriguers who hoped to ride to power by marrying the pharaoh's heiress. She was probably not more than sixteen when she wrote those letters, and yet there is in them a feminine imperiousness worthy of Cleopatra. "You have insulted me in speaking thus. . . . Everyone says you have many sons; give me one of them. . . ."

But Suppiluliumas, when he moved, moved too late. The end of the story is tragic. When one of the sons of the Hittite king was at last sent to Egypt, he never reached Thebes; possibly he was murdered by one of Ay's agents. And the Egyptian king-lists show that the next pharaoh was Ay—the man who is depicted on the wall of Tutankhamen's burial chamber, making due offerings to the *ka* of the dead pharaoh, had himself become a god-king.

When Suppiluliumas died the Hittite empire, which stretched from Anatolia to southern Syria, was the dominant power in western Asia, and the chief rival of Egypt. Eventually, of course, the two clashed. It was in 1300 B.C. at Kadesh, on the Orontes, that the great battle we have referred to earlier took place. Here the chariotry of Ramesses II met that of the Hittites; Egypt claimed success, but it was only Ramesses' bravery and energy that enabled the Egyptians to escape a crushing defeat. Yet, in the customary manner of the pharaohs—omnipotent as they traditionally made themselves appear—he caused to be carved those colossal temple reliefs of the battle that no visitor to Thebes can escape and that proclaimed his total victory. In fact, more wall space was devoted to this battle than to any other event in the history of Egypt. Later, however, Ramesses signed a mutual defense treaty with a subsequent Hittite king, Hattusilis III, copies of which were preserved both at Karnak and at Boghazkoy. As we have also already observed, Ramesses even married a Hittite princess and was delighted with his bride.

The adversaries of the Hittites were not confined to their southern neighbors in Syria and those at the borders of the land of Hatti. There were fresh disturbances in Asia Minor as well. Among the tablets found at Boghazkoy were some letters referring to a certain man named Attarissiyas who had evidently been troubling the Hittites; he had driven one of the Hittite king's vassals from his kingdom in western Anatolia. From this correspondence it appears that the Hittite king treated the king of Akaiwasha, over whom he had no jurisdiction, as an equal. There is a reference to a city in Asia Minor called, in Hittite, Millawanda, a city outside the control of the Hittite monarch but under the indirect control of the king of Akaiwasha. The correspondence also refers to a principality called Zippasla, which was given to the displaced vassal.

Letters like these give us many still-puzzling references to the political geography of western Anatolia; scholars compare words from Hittite texts to Greek words in an effort to learn whether the two great cultures were in contact. Now the name which Homer gave to the Mycenaean Greeks was the Achaeans, linguistically a word not unlike Akaiwasha, and we know that the name of the father of Agamemnon and Menelaus—the Atridae—was Atreus, which, it has been suggested, might be compared with Attarissiyas. Millawanda was very likely the ancient Greek colony of Miletus, on the Aegean coast of Asia Minor, where a Mycenaean settlement has been unearthed. It is tempting to think that the kingdom of Akaiwasha was Mycenaean Greece itself; or was it a Mycenaean domain on the mainland of Anatolia, or, as has also been suggested by scholars, was it the island of Rhodes where the Achaean Greeks were established in considerable force? Are we stretching coincidence too far in seeking to compare a name recorded in a Hittite document to Greek names of lands and people of whom there is contemporary record? Here is another of those fascinating areas of speculation where, as has so often happened in the case of lost worlds rediscovered, archaeology and legend may prove to be in accord.

Still another cuneiform tablet records the fact that a king of Akaiwasha sent his sons to the court of the Hittite king in order to be trained in chariotry and horsemanship. We know from the *Iliad* that the chariot was the aristocratic arm of the Mycenaean Greek forces. Did they perhaps learn their craft from their neighbors in Asia Minor? The Hittites in turn, who were notable charioteers, probably took the idea of the chariot from the "horse-rearing Mitanni" of the upper Euphrates, with whom they were in contact of the course of years both in peace and war.

Among the occasional adversaries of the Hittites were the kings of Arzawa, the land referred to in the tablets found at el Amarna and, obviously, no longer to be identified with the land of Hatti. In the latter part of the fourteenth century B.C. the Hittite king Mursilis II sent a challenge to the king of Arzawa that was in effect a declaration of war. "My subjects who went over to you, when I demanded them back from you, you did not restore them to me. Up then! Let us fight, and let the storm god, my lord, decide our case!" Apparently the storm god favored Mursilis and his cause, for the campaign records state that "I, My Majesty, brought back to the royal palace [from Arzawa] 66,000 civilian captives; but what the lords, the soldiers, and the charioteers of Hattusas brought back in the way of civilian captives, oxen, and sheep—there was no counting it." But unfortunately at this time, we are unable to ascertain just where Arzawa was.

Although records tell us much of the Hittites' military exploits they tell us little about the people and the manner in which they lived. From the pictures they have left of themselves they do not appear as a particularly attractive people; they were short, stocky, broad-shouldered mountain folk, hardy and active. Both men and women wore long woolen

The toy-like fragment of a vase from Boghazkoy shows how the Hittites fortified their cities; serrated battlements strengthened both walls and high, windowed towers.

robes and stout upturned boots as a protection against the winter snows. Their principal cities somewhat resemble those of the Mycenaeans—citadels on easily defended hills, with strong walls and towers. The kings and nobles lived in relatively small palaces within the enclosing walls; other houses of merchants and farmers stood outside, but near the citadel. At Boghazkoy cattle and men were protected by an additional and more extensive outer wall.

The Hittites were certainly clever strategists, and, toughened by their life in the mountains, doughty fighters; but there is no evidence that their conquests were accompanied by the refined cruelties that the Assyrians inflicted on their defeated foes. A conquered city was given humane treatment; its people were spared, provided due tribute was paid. If the city resisted it was looted, burned, and its inhabitants made slaves; but they were apparently not mutilated or tortured. They appear to have had a rough but genuine humanity which is reflected in some of their laws that have been found. Many of these are essentially the practical, down-to-earth laws of a peasant people. For instance: "If a pig goes upon a threshing floor or a field or a garden, and the owner of the meadow, the field, or the garden smites it so that it die, he shall give it back to its owner; but if he does not give it back he becomes a thief . . . If anyone borrows and yokes an ox, a horse, a mule, or an ass and it dies, or a wolf devours it, or it goes astray, he shall pay in full value; but if he say 'by the hand of a god it died,' then he shall take the oath."

However, as in all ancient civilizations there was a clear distinction between freeman and slave, with varying conditions for the treatment of each class. The Hittite king tells his garrison commanders: "Into whatever city you return, summon forth all the people of the city. Whoever has a suit, decide it for him and satisfy him. If the slave of a man, or the maid-servant of a man has a suit, decide it for them and

satisfy them. Do not make the better case the worse or the worse case the better. *Do what is just."*

As in Egypt, there were in Anatolia a large number of local and regional religious cults; and as in Egypt these continued to exist long after the Hittite state was unified and a state religion had developed. The king was the high priest of this cult, and there exist many cuneiform tablets that give us the names and functions of the gods, and the prayers addressed to them by the royal family. There are also a number of myths and poems of religious character, but it is strange that these do not appear to refer to the principal deities of the state religion. It has been suggested that this religious literature was derived from the local cults.

In many parts of central Anatolia there are rock-cut sculptures, possibly depicting these deities. The most impressive are those at Yazilikaya (the Turkish word meaning *inscribed rock*), near Boghazkoy, which Winckler visited early in this century. Here, in a narrow cleft in the rock, gods and goddesses march in two processions toward a central point, each carrying a symbol that can be recognized although with difficulty. These sculptured reliefs reveal the curious fact that, by the thirteenth century B.C., the Hittites had apparently based their state religion on deities adopted from their once formidable enemies, the Hurrians. Among these deities some can be identified with certainty, despite the weathering of the rock over a period of some three thousand years; they include Ea, god of the Nether Sea, who originated in Sumer; Shaushka, goddess of love and fertility, derived from the Mesopotamian Ishtar; Halki, god of grain; Kushukh, the moon god; the sun god, whose name is unknown; and Hesui, who was an underworld deity.

But the most important deity to the Hittites was the weather god Teshub, who occupied a central position at Yazilikaya. His consort Hebat (or Hepit) was almost as im-

portant as he was. Teshub has some similarity to Olympian Zeus; he is often shown standing alone, grasping a symbolic bolt of lightning in one hand and an axe in the other. His sacred animal was the bull, on which he is sometimes shown standing. It is natural that the Hittites, who lived in a land subject to frequent, violent storms, should have given precedence to a god who manifested himself in thunder and lightning, as it was natural to the ancient Egyptians, living under cloudless skies, to honor Re above all other deities. On the other hand, some state deities have their equivalents in ancient religions of different lands; the fertility goddess for example can be equated with the Egyptian Hathor, the Babylonian Ishtar, and the Greek Aphrodite. There was also Telipinu, a god of agriculture and son of Teshub. One of the hymns represents the weather god as saying, "This son of mine is mighty; he harrows and plows, he irrigates the fields and makes the crops grow."

Despite the establishment of the state cult at Hattusas, one gets the impression that in Hatti the independent spirit of the people frustrated any attempt that may have been made by the systematizing theologians of Hattusas to bring the whole realm under one tidy religious system. For instance, although Teshub the weather god was supreme at Hattusas itself, at Arinna, a cult center some distance from the capital, he was merely the consort of a sun goddess, Wurusemu. Could it be that in Anatolia, as in pre-Hellenic Greece, there was conflict between an earlier religion, dominated by female deities, and a later cult in which male gods were predominant?

There is possibly an intriguing example of this in the presence of two sun deities, a god and a goddess. The Hittite king Muwatallis addresses this prayer to the sun god: "Sun god of heaven, my lord, shepherd of mankind! Thou risest, O sun god of heaven, from the sea and goest up to heaven. O sun god of heaven, my lord, daily thou sittest in judgment

upon man, dog, pig, and wild beasts of the field." Yet the sun goddess is described as "Queen of the Land of Hatti, Queen of Heaven and Earth, Mistress of the kings and queens of the Land of Hatti, directing the government of the Land of Hatti." And the husband of Wurusemu was not the sun god but the weather god Teshub.

Because of these varying godly alliances, it is difficult to gain an altogether clear picture of Hittite religion. Their state chronicles, on the other hand, were written with clarity and directness; reading the recorded statements of some of the Hittite kings is almost like listening to a verbatim report. One king, Hattusilis I, had named his nephew Labarnas as his successor, but the young prince had caused trouble. So the king assembled his fighting men and dignitaries and said to them: "Behold, I have fallen sick. The young Labarnas I had proclaimed to you, saying 'He shall sit upon the throne.' I, the king, called him my son, embraced him, exalted him, cared for him continually. But he showed himself a youth not fit to be seen; he shed no tears, he showed no pity; he was cold and heartless. I, the king, summoned him to my couch and said, 'Well! No one will in future bring up the child of his sister as a foster son! The word of the king he has not laid to his heart, but the word of his mother, that serpent, he has laid to his heart. . . . Enough! He is my son no more!'"

Then, the chronicle goes on, "His mother bellowed like an ox: 'They have torn asunder the womb in my living body! They have ruined him, and you will kill him!' 'But have I, the king, done him any evil? . . . Behold I have given my son Labarnas a house; I have given him arable land in plenty; sheep in plenty I have now given him . . . Behold Mursilis is now my son. In place of the lion the god will set up another lion. And in the hour when the call to arms goes forth, you, my servants and leading citizens, must be at hand to help my son . . .'" It is straightforward and imposing, with a

ring of personality that is lacking in the more formal records of the Egyptian and Mesopotamian rulers.

An equally vivid record describes the anger of a king when, at the siege of an enemy town, "they broke the battering ram. The king waxed wroth," the chronicle continues, "and his face was grim; 'They constantly bring me evil tidings!'" Then he blistered his inefficient officers with the words, "'May the weather god carry you away in a flood! Be not idle! Make a battering-ram in the Hurrian manner and let it be set in its place!'"

Although the Hittites appear to have borrowed much of their art, their culture, their religion, and—importantly—a convenient writing system from their more highly developed Mesopotamian neighbors, they come to life in their own right in their surviving documents, as in the furious exhortation of the king just quoted. They were a rugged, independent people —energetic, determined, probably coarse and rough, a people toughened by hardship and adversity, adventurous and brave, not afraid to march down from their mountain strongholds and challenge the older, more sophisticated peoples of Mesopotamia and Egypt.

They lived by agriculture, stock-raising, and trade, exchanging their copper, silver, and iron (Anatolia was rich in minerals) for the textiles and other goods produced in Syria and Mesopotamia. The smelting of iron in commercial quantities was to revolutionize the ancient world, and this technique is believed to have originated in Asia Minor. The metal had been known long before, but it was not until an unidentified people (perhaps the Chalybees in the Armenian mountains) discovered the secret of making it cheaply that it spread across the world.

Another letter from a Hittite king to a fellow monarch is worth quoting in this connection: "As for the good iron which you wrote about to me, good iron is not available in my seal-house [a storage place for worked iron] in Kizzuwatna. That it is a bad time for producing iron I have written. They will produce good iron, but as yet they will not have finished. When they have finished I shall send it to you. Today now I am dispatching an iron dagger blade to you."

When this letter was written, in the thirteenth century B.C., the Iron Age had not begun. The noblemen of Egypt, Babylon, and Mycenae were still using bronze weapons. In the tomb of Tutankhamen (fourteenth century B.C.) was found one of the pharaoh's most valuable possessions—a ceremonial dagger with a hilt of gold and semiprecious stones, but a blade of iron, more precious than the gold and jewels. The rest of the king's weapons were merely of bronze.

Although there were obviously iron deposits in their territory and although equally obviously they were familiar with the metal, the Hittites remained essentially a Bronze Age people. With the more general use of iron for tools and weapons the face of ancient society was changed beyond recognition. It was in the dawn of the Iron Age that the inhabitants of Asia Minor were thrown into complete confusion by waves of invading peoples who appear at the beginning of the twelfth century B.C. This was, as we have seen in earlier chapters, a time of international disturbance and unrest.

In Anatolia itself one displaced tribe caromed into the next, displacing it in turn, like billiard balls. The Hittites were swept down from the mountains into the hills and valleys of northern Syria. These lands were not totally unfamiliar to them for some of their culture had been implanted south of the Taurus during the centuries their imperial legions had battled the Mitanni, the Assyrians, and local princelings on the Syrian plains. Long before the fall of Hattusas, the populations of many of these cities included Hittite elements, along with Aramean and Hurrian, and it was perhaps then that the builders of Carchemish and Malatya, among others, had begun to borrow from Anatolian traditions. The style that resulted was a blend, however, difficult to date or to separate into its various components, and although Hittites surely settled in this north Syrian region, the only record of them we have during this murky period of history is the occasional Assyrian reference to the area as "the land of Hatti." There seems to have been enough recognizably Hittite influence—along with their hieroglyphs—to lead some experts to call these cities, unearthed by archaeologists some fifty years ago, Neo- or Syro-Hittite. There is much that is still obscure, but it has been suggested that this may offer an explanation of the biblical Hittites at a period long after the Anatolian Hittites had been dispersed. The rulers and inhabitants of such north Syrian towns may not even have been of Hittite stock, but rather peoples who had absorbed various elements of the culture of the Hittites.

We have lingered over the Hittites and their empire because of all the heterogeneous peoples who occupied Asia Minor in ancient times, their story is most fully documented; and because it was the search for the Hittites that turned the attention of archaeologists to the hitherto little-known Anatolia. Here, at what had been the center of Hittite power, a different people emerged during the centuries following 1200 B.C.—the Phrygians, a people of the Iron Age.

Apart from giving their name to the conical hat which became a symbol of revolution in eighteenth-century France, the Phrygians have best been remembered chiefly for their king, Midas of the golden touch, whose legendary avarice was used by the Greeks to adorn a moral tale. But there may have been a King Midas—probably several bearing the same name. The word *Mitas* occurs in Assyrian records, and at Gordium, the Phrygian capital where Alexander cut the Gordian knot, the University of Pennsylvania made a sensational discovery as recently as 1957. At the site, which stands near the Sangarius River, there is an artificial hill about one hundred feet high, known by tradition as the Tomb of Midas. The American archaeologists, who had already done some notable and valuable work in excavating the city, decided to investigate the tomb, using modern methods. Instead of laboriously trenching into the hill, they drilled a small hole in the top and eventually came upon the roof of what appeared to be the tomb chamber. Then, starting again at ground level, they drove a tunnel horizontally through the earth until they came upon the stone retaining walls of the rubble mound which covered the wooden tomb chamber.

And then they struck trouble. Having breached this wall, they were forced to remove the greater part of the rubble filling in order to get at the chamber, so that eventually all that was left was an empty space under a heavy earthen covering, now deprived of most of its support. It required some courage to enter, but upon doing so at the risk of being buried alive, the Pennsylvania team was rewarded by an extraordinary sight. Near the middle of the chamber, on a bed that had collapsed, lay the untouched body of a Phrygian king. In the glare of the floodlights they saw the skeleton, lying under the remains of some twenty coverlets. Against the wall

rested rich furniture adorned and inlaid with rare woods. Scores of fine copper vessels had collapsed onto the floor. The cascade of metal, we are told, almost filled the chamber, shining in the brilliant green of oxidized copper. There were massive caldrons for food, with their supporting tripods, and other articles that had lain with their owner for at least twenty-seven hundred years. But no gold—not a scrap or particle.

That might seem to dispose of the Midas legend—except, of course, there is no proof that this was Midas' sepulcher, assuming that the legendary king was a real person and not a myth. There certainly was an important Phrygian king named Midas who, according to Greek tradition, died during the Cimmerian invasion of about 680 B.C.

Our knowledge of both Phrygian and Hittite history is far from complete. One of the most puzzling problems was not solved until 1945, when archaeologists found the key to Hittite hieroglyphs—the mysterious writing noted by Burckhardt at Hamath that first put archaeologists on the trail of the Hittites. During and after the First World War the task of decipherment was left mainly to British and American scholars, while the Germans concentrated on the cuneiform version of the Hittite language. For many years there had been scant success since no bilingual clue appeared to exist. Then, in a remote, little-visited region of southeastern Anatolia, the ancient Cilicia, a local schoolmaster reported that about five hours horse-ride from the town of Kadirili lay the site of a lost city.

In the autumn of 1945 the eminent German archaeologist H. T. Bossert, and his team, made their way there, to what had been the fortress city of Karatepe. Half hidden among the brambles, they found a battered, sculptured, half-human figure, lying face down, some sculptured lions with a standing human figure and, on the crown of the hill, extensive remains of walls with strong defensive gateways. Within one of these gateways the astonished archaeologists saw a series of crude sculptured scenes—a sea battle, an orchestra, a king feasting, and various sporting and religious activities. The art was obviously very late—much later than the period of the Hittite empire, but nevertheless the Hittite hieroglyphs were there carved on one side of the gateway. And, on the other side there were inscriptions in the known alphabetic script of Phoenicia; it was soon established that the two inscriptions, each in a different language, gave an identical message. The long-sought-for bilingual had been found at last.

Even so, the Hittite hieroglyphic script has still not been completely deciphered, though now it is only a matter of time and study. Much progress has already been made by the French scholar Emmanuel Laroche, and new discoveries of Hittite hieroglyphic seals at Ras Shamra in Syria have also helped to advance these investigations.

Obviously this story cannot hope to be complete. Today discoveries are being made in Asia Minor that will throw a keener light on what has been written and, no doubt, will call for revisions of current records. We are still only at the very beginning of the problem. But Anatolia, that hitherto neglected land of rich interest, is coming into its own at last.

CROSSROADS OF ANCIENT CULTURE

Since it appeared on the Baghdad art market in 1951, the figure above has defied the efforts of archaeologists and art historians to determine its age or its origin. It embodies characteristics of various ancient cultures that flourished about the eastern Mediterranean, but can be ascribed to no single one of them. The figure's giant, curling feet recall those seen in Hittite reliefs and his sturdy footgear would have served well in rugged northern regions; yet except for a bulky, rolled belt and a cap, the figure wears no clothing. The ibex horns of his headdress are a frequently used motif in the Asian steppes to the north, but the motif appears as well in the art of Mesopotamia. His eyes, once inlaid with bone, stare with the fixed gaze typical of early Sumerian carved faces. (His beard may double as the beak of the vulture-like bird slung around his shoulders.) This trudging figure remains an enigma yet it seems to symbolize the many different currents that met and mingled in the lands of the ancient Near East.

From the pictorial reports of Ramesses III, Sea Peoples in crested helmets battle the Egyptians (below). Portrayed on a terra-cotta panel (right), Phrygian soldiers march to war.

MIGRATION
AND WAR

About three thousand years ago, a mass of migratory peoples relentlessly moved across the civilized lands of the ancient Near East, rolling through the capitals of tottering empires and crushing them on its way. In continual waves, barbarian herdsmen swept down from Europe and poured through the Caucasus from Central Asia. The Phrygians entered Anatolia, probably through Thrace, closing in on the crumbling Hittite empire. (Almost a thousand years earlier, the Hittites themselves had swarmed down from the north to occupy the land. At that same time, the northerners who were to become the Mycenaeans had entered Greece, and they too succumbed to Indo-European invaders—Dorians—at the tumultuous end of the second millennium.) Still another surge of heterogeneous migrants gathered enough momentum to descend to the very shores of Egypt; these so-called Sea Peoples did not breach the Egyptian defenses, but their pressure added to Egypt's internal problems, and the power of the mighty land of the pharaohs began to fade. About five hundred years later, descendants of these Indo-European hordes kindled the generative fire of new cultures in Persia and Greece, shifting the focus of civilization away from its birthplace in Egypt and Mesopotamia.

THEMES AND VARIATIONS

Pharaoh's soldiers, returning from a Syrian campaign, may have described to Egyptian artists the image of Astarte, the naked Syrian war goddess, on her horse, depicted above on an ostracon from Thebes. Below, a fragment of an ivory box lid from the port of Ras Shamra shows a goddess who is part Aegean and part Asian.

"Putting his right boot on his left foot and his left boot on his right foot," the Anatolian god, Telipinu, young lord of agriculture and the earth's fertility, hastily fled from his home in an apparent fit of temper. According to Hittite texts, the land languished until he returned. "Barley and . . . wheat throve no more, oxen, sheep, and humans ceased to conceive, and those who were pregnant could not bear. . . . [The gods at a feast] ate but they were not satisfied; they drank but quenched not their thirst. Then the weather god remembered . . . 'Telipinu is not in the land; he was angry and has . . . taken all good things with him.'"

The absent god, whose return would once more bestow life upon the blighted earth, was represented in the pantheon of virtually every ancient Near Eastern culture. Such deities as Osiris in Egypt, Tammuz in Mesopotamia, Adonis in Syria, and Attis in Phrygia symbolized, as did Telipinu, the regenerative force in nature. In various ways, these gods continually died or vanished and were reborn or rediscovered, often paralleling the seasonal death and rebirth of vegetation. The differences between them, however, were greater than the similarities. Telipinu's restorative powers might be invoked at any time of the year, whereas Adonis revived the land only in the spring. Osiris was reborn in the nether regions of a world where male gods predominated; Attis died a youth in a land where the host of divinities was headed by the great mother goddess. In borrowing foreign though related gods to serve as models, craftsmen often confused the deities' attributes. A Levantine ivory carver, for example, portrayed the Aegean mother goddess (left), but pictured her feeding goats, a motif symbolizing an explicitly Asian notion of the direct force of her nourishing powers; he also gave her a stool shaped like an hourglass, a form used in the Aegean only to represent a sacred altar.

Common in Crete and Syria, the winged griffin (above) also appeared in the art of the Mycenaeans, the Mitanni, and the Assyrians; this plaque, found at Megiddo, represents the work of a multi-national school of second-millennium ivory carvers. The embossed design of the silver bowl below blends Egyptian, Assyrian, and Phoenician elements.

An Egyptian portrayed traveling Asian metalworkers entering Egypt with their families.

THE REACH OF TRADE

When ancient warriors and migratory peoples moved into foreign lands, they no doubt left vivid impressions of the places from which they had come; yet over the centuries it was the traders, carrying the materials of one culture to another, who established lasting contacts between the widespread centers of civilization. This process of peaceful exchange began in prehistoric times, and by 2000 B.C. a large part of the ancient world was crossed with well-traveled land or sea routes. Before Upper and Lower Egypt were united, villagers along the Wadi Hammamat fashioned crystalline rock bracelets specifically for export, and long-distance caravans could have brought obsidian from the Aegean and juniper berries from Syria into the Nile Delta. In Mesopotamia, Sargon of Akkad, according to one source, "proudly proclaimed (that) ships from or destined for Meluhha, Makkan, and Telmun were moored in the harbor outside his capital"; these strange lands comprised a third millennium B.C. shipping circuit that stretched from the Persian Gulf across the Arabian Sea to ports of entry for the Indus Valley (Sargon's Meluhha); Makkan could have been in northeast Arabia, and Telmun, today the Gulf island called Bahrein, served as a midway market place. So organized was this commerce that tablets from Ur record partnerships, rules for investment risk, and the taking of long-term loans.

Byblos, the oldest trading center on the Levantine coast, shipped cargoes of cedarwood to Egypt in 2700 B.C. From a Byblos temple of the second millennium, the golden scabbard (left) shows a mixture of Syrian and Egyptian motifs whereas the metalworking methods, seen also on the crescent-bladed axe (right), are typically Amorite and Syrian. Later, when the Syrian traders gained a foothold in Egypt itself and shipping between the two areas by way of Cyprus was established, Syrian designs became more apparent in Egyptian art. The pitcher (above left) was found on Cyprus; in the scene depicted, one man falls into the sea as another looks at a huge jar of wine, the ship's freight.

THE ENIGMATIC
ETRUSCANS

The world of Etruria is, in some ways, more mysterious and inaccessible than that of Egypt, Mesopotamia, Crete, or Mycenae, despite the fact that it is closer to us in time than any of these others. Unfortunately, the Etruscans cannot speak to us directly through their literature. Livy was told that a few generations before his time young Romans studied the Etruscan literature as conscientiously as they later did the Greek, but except for brief inscriptions, none of this has survived. The inscriptions are in letters much like the Greek, and can be read and pronounced, but they are only imperfectly understood. No Michael Ventris has yet come forward to decipher the Etruscan language.

In the later centuries of their development the Etruscans were well known to the Greeks and the Romans, both of whom fought them and wrote about them. Partly because of this ancient hostility the information provided by Greek and Roman historians and commentators is often inaccurate and distorted. The Romans were the worse culprits, since they learned a great deal from the Etruscans, then virtually obliterated them as a separate entity, and finally slandered and vilified their memory. For impartial evidence we have to rely on the archaeological investigations of their cities and cemeteries, which are numerous, although they suffered almost two centuries of indiscriminate plundering before modern methods and skills were applied to excavation.

Ancient Etruria lay on the western side of Italy, between the Apennines and the Tyrrhenian Sea. It extended from the land about the Arno River in the north to the Tiber River in the south, and included modern Tuscany, which takes its

A terra-cotta portrait of the god Turms (opposite), who conducted the souls of the dead to the underworld, decorated the roof of an Etruscan temple at Veii; he was identical with the Greek Hermes.

name from the Etruscans. But at one period the Etruscans controlled Campania and the basin of the Po River, and had reached the northern Adriatic. Many of the most famous cities in Italy were originally Etruscan—Pisa, Arezzo, Cortona, Siena, Volterra, Orvieto, Perugia, Assisi, and others. (Rome itself was once an Etruscan center; and the islands of Elba and Corsica were also Etruscan.) But there were other towns which were either deserted or which lost their former importance with the decline of Etruscan culture and it is mainly at these, such as Veii, Tarquinia, Cerveteri, and Chiusi (the ancient forms of these names were, respectively, Tarquinii, Caere, and Clusium), that archaeologists have found rich remains.

The Etruscan country varies between fertile plains, such as those near the Campanian coast and in Tuscany below Arezzo, and steep narrow valleys which cleave the Apennines. There are only two rivers of any size, the Arno and the Tiber, and these are navigable for but short stretches. The rest are mainly *torrenti*—dry boulder-strewn gullies in summer, roaring sluices of foam in winter. Vines, olives, and wheat grow in the lowlands; cattle graze on the lower hills, and goats and sheep on the higher slopes.

Tuscany is one of the most beautiful regions in Italy, and even those who have never seen it have admired it in the works of the great Florentine painters. It is therefore difficult to imagine Etruria as a rude and desolate country. Yet just over a century ago, even though the history of the Etruscans had long been a subject of considerable investigation and speculation, the English traveler George Dennis could write of "remains of an ancient art completely unknown to the rest of the world, an object of the ignorant astonishment of peasants and . . . still neglected; in a countryside almost decimated by malaria, never crossed by the educated and intelligent traveler, the most striking monuments may rest for

Acres of circular mounds, tombs of aristocratic families, mark the site of Cerveteri, once an important port and one of the greatest of Etruscan cities. For almost a century it was ruled by the Tarquin Dynasty centered in Rome. Some of the tombs of the necropolis were almost two hundred feet in diameter; these were surrounded by smaller tombs for less august members of the family. Phallic symbols and little stone houses representing wombs were often placed in front of Etruscan tombs to signify the number and sex of the occupants.

centuries without attracting attention. . . . I am convinced that Italy has been only half explored. . . . In addition, ruins and remains are such common sights in this country that they excite no particular attention."

Where was this "ancient art" that so excited Dennis and later explorers? Mainly in tomb-sites, which were often whole underground streets of sepulchers cut out of the rock and clearly designed to look like the earthly homes of their occupants. Sometimes the burials were found by accident—a peasant plowing suddenly saw one of his draft oxen disappear into a hole in the ground, and there was a tomb—but more often they were dug for, or rather mined, by plunderers in search of salable loot, or by amateur archaeologists searching for art objects with which to enrich their collections. Even as early as the eighteenth century a wave of "Etruscomania" had swept across Europe; societies were formed for study; scholars examined ancient records and tried to decipher the Etruscan inscriptions; and the interest hardly abated over the years to come.

In time such an abundance of these treasures came to light that during the latter half of the nineteenth century, museums and private galleries overflowed with them—statues in stone, terra cotta, and bronze; painted and figured pottery and gold vessels; domestic equipment such as lamps, candelabra, and engraved mirrors; and bracelets, fibulae, rings, and pendants. Some of these objects bore a resemblance to Roman forms, and many were created with a suavity and sensuousness that showed Greek influence; but they were neither Roman nor Greek. They were oriental in feeling, but they were clearly not oriental in origin. These remarkable finds, emerging into the sunlight of Italy after lying in darkness for more than twenty-four hundred years, had belonged to the mysterious Etruscans of whom the Greeks and Romans had written.

Yet in spite of this abundant evidence and the research it stimulated, the Etruscans continue to remain an enigmatic people even to modern scholars.

We are not yet sure where they came from. Nearly all the ancient historians believed that they originated in Lydia, in Asia Minor, but most of these writers probably followed Herodotus. In the fifth century B.C. this Greek traveler described how a great famine had occurred in Lydia, and how after enduring this for many years, the Lydian king divided his people into two groups and cast lots to decide which group was to stay: "He appointed . . . his son Tyrrhenus to command the emigrants [who] . . . went down to the coast at Smyrna, where they built vessels, put aboard all their household effects, and sailed in search of a livelihood elsewhere. They passed many countries and finally reached Umbria in the north of Italy, where they settled and still live to this day. Here they changed their name from Lydians to Tyrrhenians, after the king's son Tyrrhenus, who was their leader."

Herodotus has been proved right in so many instances that one hesitates to dismiss this story as a legend. Yet from the time of Dionysius of Halicarnassus, who lived in the first century A.D. and who questioned Herodotus' explanation, scholars have been divided between those who believe the Etruscans were the descendants of an oriental people who modeled western Italy sometime after 1000 B.C., and those who claim they were an indigenous race whose culture developed on Italian soil, but who were subject to influences from the east. The dispute still goes on.

One fact, however, is certain. At the beginning of the first millennium B.C. there was nothing in Italy, or in Western Europe for that matter, worthy of the name of civilization. A primitive Bronze Age culture had existed for hundreds of years on the Italian peninsula, but nothing at all com-

GAULS

PO

Spina

Bologna

Fiesole

ARNO

Arezzo

Volterra

Cortona

Perugia

Populonia

Chiusi

Orvieto

Vetulonia

Tuscania

CORSICA

Tarquinia

Veii

Alalia

Cerveteri

Rome

Palestrina

Capua

Naples

Cumae

Pompeii

Paestum

SARDINIA

TYRRHENIAN
SEA

YUGOSLAVIA

ADRIATIC SEA

ALBANIA

ITALY

MAGNA
GRAECIA

Taranto

IONIAN
SEA

SICILY

Reggio

Agrigento

Syracuse

Carthage

TUNISIA

Scale

0   25   50   75 Miles

The Etruscan homeland lay between the Arno and the Tiber rivers; its colonies reached north to the farmlands of the Po Valley, and south to the hills around Naples. Despite Etruscan wealth and the prowess of its military forces, rival nations proved stronger. Greek colonists and Carthaginians stole away Etruscan commerce, invading Gauls overwhelmed the northern settlements, and Rome conquered city after city, destroying the nation which had fostered her culture.

parable to what had developed in the Aegean area. Then, about 1000 B.C., a wave of invaders—people who were familiar with use of iron—entered Italy from the north, overcame the indigenes, and established themselves in what is now Tuscany, and other places both to the north and to the south on the peninsula.

This culture, called Villanovan from the type-site at Villanova (a suburb of Bologna), flourished most vigorously in the area about Tarquinia, Cerveteri, and Veii, which later was the heart of Etruscan civilization. With this new development, which is characterized by cremation burial, great importance was attached to the welfare of the dead. The cinerary urns, some of which are hut-shaped, probably in imitation of Villanovan dwellings, were buried in pits and surrounded by objects intended for the afterlife; men had their bronze and iron weapons, women their bronze fibulae, bronze and amber jewels, and combs, needles, and spindles. These are interesting, but in no way rich or elaborate; on stylistic grounds they can be dated between 1000 and 750 B.C.

This period corresponds to the so-called Dark Age in Greece, between the collapse of the brilliant civilizations of Crete and Mycenae and the dawn of the classical period. After two thousand years of high achievement Egypt had begun its slow decline. But powerful new civilizations were emerging. Assyria had begun its second rise to power, which reached a peak about 750 B.C. In Asia Minor the Phrygians had established themselves in the central plateau and the Lydians had become dominant in the southwest. The peoples of the Aegean and the Mediterranean world were in a ferment. Fresh waves of invaders poured down into southern Europe. The Phoenicians of the Levant, themselves under pressure from the east, had begun to move westward, establishing their great colony at Carthage on the North African

coast and even getting a foothold in Spain. During this period the Dorian Greeks were also on the move, thrusting westward in search of new lands and trading possibilities.

Towards the end of this period, sometime in the eighth century B.C., there were dramatic changes in the Villanovan culture, changes that anticipate the splendid development of Etruscan civilization in the centuries that followed. The dead are no longer cremated; rather they are interred, first in ditch graves and later in stone-built, vaulted mausoleums covered with mounds of earth. The grave goods become richer, and different in character. There is a greater abundance of bronze objects, such as vases, helmets, and shields, which, although not the same as those used in the Aegean area, nevertheless resemble them.

The migrant Greeks could have been the intermediaries through which this eastern influence first appeared among the Villanovans. However, many of the innovations that appeared were certainly not Greek in origin. For instance, it seems hardly likely that, as has been claimed, there was any direct connection between the domed mausoleums of seventh-century Etruria and the famous tholos tombs of Mycenae. In Greece the construction of such domed tumuli had been discontinued centuries earlier, in the late Bronze Age. In Asia Minor, on the other hand, they were being built well into the Iron Age, as witnessed by the famous Tomb of Midas at Gordium. If there was a connection between developments in Etruria and regions to the east it is more likely to have been with Anatolia than with Greece.

This oriental connection, so long ago suggested by Herodotus, is indicated, though not proved by any means, by numerous other parallels. To name a few: as in the case of many Eastern peoples, Etruscan religion was a revealed religion; a god or spirit named Tages had in the remote past dictated its

Tombs were equipped with all that the dead might need in the afterlife; in one, shown opposite, household utensils were modeled in stucco on the walls. In early times the dead were cremated. Because souls were sometimes thought of as dwarflike, the ashes were placed in tiny huts like the one above, or in human-headed urns (right), which were often dressed like dolls.

principles, and these immutable laws had been written down and transmitted by the priests to succeeding generations. It was a highly ritualistic religion, and it made great use of divination by signs. Such a conception was common in the ancient East, but not among the Indo-European peoples of the West. The Etruscan name for themselves, Rasenna, is found in various forms in Asia Minor. On the island of Lemnos, in the Aegean, archaeologists discovered inscriptions in a language which is remarkably like ancient Etruscan. If the Etruscans came from Anatolia it would be natural for some of them to have occupied Lemnos, which is a few miles off the coast. As further evidence, in tomb paintings depicting the earthly life of the Etruscans, women are given an honored place. We see them banqueting with male guests and being embraced by their husbands. Sometimes the names of the female as well as the male ancestors of the deceased are mentioned in funerary inscriptions. Such was not the attitude of the Greeks toward their womenfolk, though it was a characteristic of some of the older oriental civilizations.

It seems likely that Greek influences had little to do with the earliest development of the Etruscan nation. But the story is different later. When the Etruscans finally were exposed to Greek culture, they enthusiastically adapted it to their own. Indeed one scholar has recently suggested that ". . . getting to know Homer was one of the most important experiences of the dawning Etruscan civilization . . ." The aristocrats of Etruria modeled themselves on the heroes of Mycenae, and the major Etruscan gods were closely identified with the divinities of Greece. Etruscan artists found it appropriate to decorate tombs and vases with scenes from Greek mythology, scenes which were apparently readily understood by the public, and as early as the seventh century B.C., there were Greek vase painters working in Cerveteri. The Etruscan

alphabet itself is of Greek origin, probably derived from a variant of the standard Greek alphabet used by Hellenic colonists in the town of Cumae, near Naples. In the commercial centers, such as Cumae, Greek and Etruscan merchants settled alongside each other.

Setting aside all questions of the still debatable racial origins of the Etruscans, it is a matter of overriding importance that their culture took on its distinctive form at a time when the Greeks and other migrants from the east were founding settlements and pushing their trading ventures into the western Mediterranean area. The west had much to offer these newcomers. Its lands were for the most part sparsely populated and occupied by relatively primitive peoples who were incapable of developing their own resources. There were copper and iron in Italy and elsewhere, silver in Spain, and tin in far-off Cornwall in the British Isles, to which the Phoenicians gained access.

In this struggle for raw materials, in which Greeks contested with Phoenicians, Etruria stood in a key position. The main source of Etruria's wealth and prosperity was her mineral deposits, of which other Mediterranean powers were envious. In the northern part of Etruria were the hills known today as the Colline Metallifere (Metalliferous Hills), rich in iron, zinc, tin, and copper. The gold, silver, ivory, and other precious materials that the Etruscans later imported to adorn their bodies, their homes, and eventually their tombs can only have been obtained in exchange for these valuable minerals. The Greeks, who had already founded trading colonies along the western coast of Italy, at Paestum, Cumae, Naples, and elsewhere before 600 B.C., were well aware of these riches. They had also established themselves in Sicily, southern Gaul (at Marseilles), North Africa, and even Spain, where they had little difficulty in exploiting the natural re-

The ceremonial helmet shown above, modeled after a Grecian prototype, was designed to provide protection for the warrior's cheeks and nose. The surface of both cheekpieces is finely embossed with scenes of battle.

sources of the hinterland. But in Italy they confronted an intelligent, well-organized, civilized people, both appreciative of the natural riches of the land they occupied and capable of capitalizing on them.

Etruria had resources other than metals. It had dense forests which both provided timber and sheltered abundant game; the climate was kindly, the plains fertile, and the foothills offered abundant pasturage. There were good harbors, and a long sea coast from which mariners could set out on adventurous journeys to other lands.

That the Etruscans were skillful and formidable sailors we know from the Greeks. One of their legends tells how Etruscan mariners even succeeded in capturing the Greek god Dionysus, who only escaped by changing his captors into dolphins. In these Greek stories the Etruscans appear to be ruthless pirates, as no doubt they often were. On one occasion they descended on the sanctuary of Artemis at Brauron, near Athens, possibly because it not only possessed rich treasures but was served by young priestesses. Incidents such as these did not make the Greeks love the Etruscans (and help to explain an anti-Etruscan bias in later Greek writings), but they prove what a power these pre-Roman rulers of western Italy must have been. Greece, wrote Dionysius of Halicarnassus, was "full of the name of Etruria."

Since we are concerned here with the world of the Etruscans rather than with their political history, the latter need only be briefly sketched. During the period 700 to 500 B.C., the Etruscan coastal cities, such as Cerveteri, Tarquinia, and Vetulonia, sent out fleets which sailed venturously along the coasts of Provence, Spain, and North Africa, mixing legitimate trading with profitable piracy. In so doing they encountered their chief rivals, the Greeks and the Carthaginians, whom they often fought with zest and success. For a short time Etruria dominated the western seas as the Mycenaeans had earlier dominated the Aegean.

But when the Greek colonists, having already established themselves in Sicily and southern Italy, began settling in Corsica, the Etruscans allied themselves with Carthage against the Hellenes. After a major naval battle in 540 B.C. the Greeks evacuated Corsica, but though the Etruscans had removed one danger, Carthage profited most from the victory. From then on she dominated the western Mediterranean and guarded the Straits of Gibraltar, monopolizing the Cornish tin trade. Thereafter the Etruscans were for the most part confined within the Tyrrhenian Sea.

Their landward expansion, however, was formidable. Between 550 and 500 B.C., their armies crossed the Tusco-Emilian Apennines and then began gradually subduing the Italic tribes of the Po Valley. They settled at Bologna, building a great city there, crossed over to the Adriatic, occupied Rimini and Ravenna, and established a thriving port at Spina, which became the entrepôt for valuable trade between the Greeks and the Celtic peoples beyond the Alps. Ancient Spina was, like Venice, built on piles amid a network of canals, and recent aerial photography has revealed the plan of the early city that covered some eight hundred and fifty acres. From this trade and their own exports Etruscan merchants became rich. Many Etruscan bronze and gold objects, as well as products of Greek origin, which were probably traded by the Etruscans to the people farther north, have been found in Switzerland and even Burgundy.

Southward they penetrated into Latium and Campania. The Latin tribes were weak and divided and the Etruscans had little difficulty in establishing control. They occupied the site of Rome, at that important strategic point where an easy crossing of the Tiber was guarded by the adjacent heights.

It was they who made Rome a city. Later tradition recalled that the Etruscan dynasty of the Tarquins ruled Rome between 616 and 510 B.C. and that they were the last kings of ancient Rome before the founding of the Roman Republic. Before they were overthrown, Tyrrhenian soothsayers predicted that Rome would one day be "the head of all Italy," and their predictions came to pass.

Etruria was never an empire united under a strong central government, but rather a loose federation of city-states each under its chief or lord, the *lucumon*. The lucumones were priest-kings, who ruled their native cities as chief judge and commander of the army. But their religious functions were equally important. On certain ritual occasions they appeared before the people riding in a chariot, drawn by white horses, and dressed as the god Tinia, king of the heavens. Like the god's, their own faces were colored vermilion, and they wore long cloaks ornamented with stars. No doubt many of the most impressive early tombs that have been discovered were intended for the burial of lucumones.

Eventually the Etruscan monarchies were superseded by oligarchies, although the process was a gradual one. In Tarquinia and Cerveteri, kingship was abolished around 500 B.C., but in Veii it lingered on for decades more. Within the Etruscan league, which linked the major towns in a loose confederation, varying systems of government could exist side by side. There were twelve cities in the League, headed by a chief magistrate of the Etruscan nation, who was elected annually, but the confederation was never enabled to provide individual cities with reliable military protection against Rome.

Although they may have been less gifted as artists and innovators, the Romans had one vital quality that the Etruscans lacked—the capacity not only to rule but to win and retain the loyalty of the ruled. They also learned how to maintain

power at the center and to create a unified state that, as it expanded, did not break under stress. The Etruscan cities, though they fought bravely and often successfully against Rome, never managed to unite in effective common action against her. When Rome began her march to power, she annexed first one and then another piece of Etruscan territory. Then in the fourth century B.C. a new threat appeared from the north when the wild, semi-barbaric Gauls swept down into Italy.

At first the Etruscans fought the Gauls, later they tried to make allies of them against Rome, but the Romans, after suffering defeat and seeing their city burned by the invaders, eventually paid the Gauls to leave, as the Etruscans also had done. By that time the glory of Etruria was over, and not long afterward she had become, like the other Italian peoples, merely part of the Roman Republic.

The Romans learned, borrowed, and inherited much from their Etruscan neighbors and overlords before eliminating them as a cultural and political entity. Among other things, Etruscan elements survived in the trappings and insignia of office. The Roman toga originated as an Etruscan ceremonial garment and the sign of the fasces was originally carried by the Etruscan lictors when they marched in procession before their rulers; the bound rods of the fasces were for scourging, and the axe was a symbol of kingly power. The robe of office of the Etruscan rulers was purple, a color which Romans adopted for a similar purpose and which, indeed, is still today an emblem of royalty. Together with these symbols the Romans also inherited the military "triumphs" that followed a victory, and probably the gladiatorial shows and animal fights that gratified the lust for blood exhibited by Roman crowds in later days.

With this expansion of Roman power and influence Etruscan customs were overlaid by Roman. We can judge what

sort of people the Etruscans were only by their earlier remains and by allusions to them in the later literature of other peoples. The latter, as we have earlier noted, were often prejudiced. In the fourth century B.C. the Greek historian Theopompus wrote, "The Etruscans raise all children born without knowing to whom they belong . . . It is not shameful to the Etruscans to be seen not only preparing 'to do the thing,' but also performing it. They are so far from considering this a disgrace that should, while the master of the house is making love, someone call on him, the visitor is told that he is doing this or that particular thing with no hesitation in specifying exactly which thing." The same charming narrative goes on to describe how, "When friends or relatives gather, this is their conduct: after they have finished drinking and are preparing to sleep, the slaves bring to them, while the lamps are still lighted, first prostitutes, by and by pretty young boys, then even the women married to those who took part in the festivities. They all engage in making love, some watching one another, some isolating themselves by means of rattan screens set up around the couches, each couple wrapped in one cover."

There is some archaeological evidence to support this statement. The Etruscans did depict scenes of uninhibited pleasure on the walls of their tombs. The later Romans too had no scruples about painting orgiastic scenes on the walls of their villas, as at Pompeii. Unfortunately, since the Etruscans themselves have left us no memoirs to modify this picture of depravity as detailed in varying forms by Arnobius, Aristotle, and Plautus, we must either accept them or rely purely on the facts revealed by archaeology.

It would be disingenuous to ignore such stories altogether, since they have obtained wide currency. Theopompus may have had a weakness for romantic and exaggerated stories, yet

Part lion, part serpent, and part goat, the chimaera (left) was a frightening creature derived from Greek mythology, like the gorgon shown above. Also Greek in origin but considerably less alarming, are the figures at right, in a terra-cotta group that represents a satyr abducting a maenad.

most Greek writers stress the Etruscans' fondness for and indulgence in luxury—a point amply confirmed by the sumptuous paraphernalia that accompanied them to their graves. As the tombs reveal, they were a life-loving people charged with such vigor as the Greeks had reason to complain of.

One sees the earlier Etruscans as sunburned sailors straining at the oars, while the sea foam crashes over the bulwarks and the lookout sights yet another island to explore or plunder; or marching smartly along their military roads in the triple formation of light, medium, and heavy infantry which the Romans copied in their legions. Their system of roads was as fine as anything achieved in Tuscany by the Romans centuries later—roads engineered to carry heavy traffic, well-drained, and laid out with tunnels and cuts. The lean and muscular armed warriors of grim and inscrutable visage, so familiar in early bronze and terra-cotta figures that have survived, as well as their resplendent and formidable chariots (such as the fine example, with its heavily embossed decorations, in the Metropolitan Museum of Art in New York) speak eloquently for their military prowess.

One sees these early Etruscans mining copper and iron, trading with the barbarians of the north, and exchanging their raw materials for the exotic products of the East that they valued so highly, or for the gold and silver that their craftsmen fashioned into exquisite jewelry and ornaments. One sees their great fortified towns, mostly on hilltops— cities such as Volterra, which still retains part of its Etruscan walls, including the famous Porta dell' Arco. These cities were usually laid out on a gridiron plan with two main intersecting thoroughfares, a system that the Romans also imitated in their military camps as well as in their cities. At the foundation of Rome, according to Plutarch, Romulus brought in Etruscans. The men from Tuscany "prescribed all the details

in accordance with certain sacred ordinances and writings, and taught them to him as in a religious rite. A circular trench was dug . . . and in this were deposited first fruits of all things, the use of which was sanctioned by custom as good and by nature as necessary; and finally, every man brought a small portion of the soil of his native land and these were cast in among the first fruits and mingled with them. They call this trench, as they do the heavens, by the name of *mundus*. Then taking this as a center, they marked out the city in a circle round it."

This shaft, at the center of each Etruscan city, led directly to the underworld. It was covered by a great stone, called by the Romans "the stone of souls," which was lifted up only on the days on which the dead were allowed to ascend among the living, or at the time when the first fruits were deposited underneath it as a harvest offering to the gods. The two main streets of the town crossed at this spot, dividing the area within the walls into quarters. This gridiron plan of the streets had a specific religious meaning; it reflected very closely the Etruscan view of the universe.

The Etruscans believed that the heavens above them were divided up into quarters, each of which had an occult significance. In the north, at the very summit of the sky dwelt the king of the gods, Tinia. The east side of the heavens, on his left hand, was propitious. The west side, on his right, was less favorable, and the northwest corner of the heavens was the least fortunate of all, casting an especially malignant influence. Diviners further divided the heavens into sixteenths and assigned a meaning to each portion. Thus, it is no wonder that the Etruscans considered it necessary to search the heavens so carefully for omens.

Etruscan *haruspices*, or expert diviners, could read portents in thunderstorms and in the flight of birds, and find

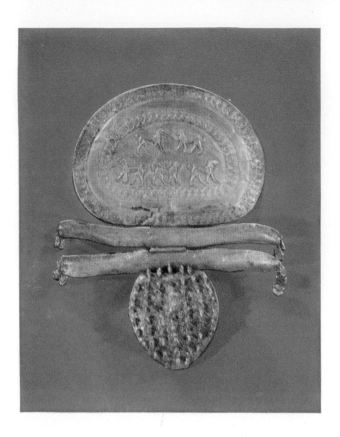

Discovered within the tomb of a princess, the dress pin reproduced at left is made of gold, and decorated with the figures of five lions shown within a border of intertwined flowers. Its lower half is adorned with rows of winged lions, and with representations of ducks, beautifully modeled in gold. Upon the surface of the pin, thousands of tiny granules of gold are fused together to fashion the designs. This was a difficult technique in which the Etruscan goldsmiths excelled; it is also used to make the beard of the horned river god, Achelous, who is shown on the facing page. Achelous was one of the many gods whom the Etruscans borrowed from Greece. The god Tinia (opposite) was indigenous to Etruria, but assumed many of the attributes of Zeus. Like Zeus, Tinia was the ruler of the heavens and the head of the pantheon. The bronze statuette on the facing page shows him wearing a coronet with seven rays, and holding the remains of a thunderbolt in his right hand.

significance in the direction from which lightning came; they could foresee the future by examining the liver of a sheep which had been sacrificed especially for this purpose. At Piacenza, a bronze model of a liver was found. Like the heavens, it was divided up into sections, or "houses," each of which was the residence of a particular god. This, it has been suggested, was a memory-aid for the haruspices; if they found an abnormality in part of the liver they were examining, they had only to refer to the bronze model to discover which divinity was concerned. The liver was chosen to represent the heavens because it was believed to be the seat of life.

The haruspices formed a special class, whose skill in the art of divination was the envy of other ancient nations. After the fall of Etruria, they continued to be honored in Rome, and were frequently called upon to read omens for the emperors. Even as late as A.D. 408, when Rome was threatened with attack by a Visigoth army under Alaric, Pope Innocent I allowed them to try to conjure up lightning in an attempt to predict the future. (The future was bleak; the barbarians soon sacked the city.) It was only official members of the college of haruspices who could correctly interpret the intricate laws of divination, which had been inscribed in the ancient ritual books of Etruria and transmitted from generation to generation.

Besides the haruspices, there were other priests who officiated at religious ceremonies in the temples. The word *temple* itself is of Etruscan origin. It originally denoted that part of the heavens from which the diviner gathered his omens. The temples of Etruria were earthly counterparts of this sacred zone of heaven. Each temple was divided into three sections, one for each of the major gods of the Etruscan trinity; the building faced to the south, so that the image of Tinia could stand at the northern end of the sanctuary, the way the god himself lived at the northern end of the sky. The temple which the Tarquins constructed atop the capitol at Rome was similarly divided into three parts, and throughout their history the Romans followed this form whenever they built a capitoline temple within a newly founded city.

The Etruscans' houses, with a portico leading to a pillared courtyard from which frescoed rooms opened, were also copied by the Romans when they too had acquired a strong taste for luxurious living. Visitors to Pompeii and other Roman sites can see houses not unlike those in which the Etruscans lived and whose plan was reflected in Etruscan tombs. Even the Roman habit of dining from small, low tables while reclining on couches (a custom also known to the Greeks) was derived from Etruria. Such couches and banqueting scenes are depicted on the walls of Etruscan tombs as well as in the sarcophagi sculptures.

Music and the dance played a prominent role in Etruscan life. Aristotle is claimed to have said that the Tyrrhenians fought, kneaded dough, and beat their slaves to the sound of the flute. Other ancient writers tell us that music provided an inevitable accompaniment to sacrifices, banquets, boxing matches, and solemn ceremonies, and that the Etruscans even used music to aid them in snaring wild pigs and stags. Their painted tomb scenes of dancing to music have an abandon and frenetic ecstasy never approached in either Greek or Roman art. As D. H. Lawrence expressed it: "This sense of vigorous, strong-bodied liveliness is characteristic of the Etruscans, and is somehow beyond art. You cannot think of art, but only of life itself, as if this were the very life of the Etruscans, dancing in their coloured wraps with massive yet exuberant naked limbs, ruddy from the air and the sea-light, dancing and fluting along through the little olive-trees, out in the fresh day."

The same spirit of warm, exhilarant life appears in the hunting scenes, especially in the idyllic fresco in the Tomb of Hunting and Fishing at Tarquinia. This has a delightful freshness and informality that is lacking in similar scenes from Egypt. A youth leans over the prow of a boat and drops his line, while a dolphin playfully leaps nearby. The oarsman is taking things easy in the stern, while other youths in the boat gesticulate to him. Overhead startled birds rise in hurried flight. There is no scene in any ancient fresco more enchanting than this; one can see what Lawrence means.

And yet there was another, darker side to the Etruscan character, an apparent fascination with pain, cruelty, and death particularly noticeable during the later and more decadent period of their history. Virtually all ancient authorities agree in describing the Etruscans as a highly religious people, in the sense that virtually every aspect of their life was prescribed by ritual regulations, from the founding of cities to burial of the dead. Unlike the Greeks, whose faith was liberally laced with skepticism and humor, the Etruscan mind was disciplined by strict and fearful regard for the divine powers and a constant anxiety lest by neglect of omens, signs, and rites these powers should be offended.

The Greeks also used divination, but their philosophic spirit prevented them from allowing their lives to be completely dominated by religious doctrine or practice. The Romans later also adopted certain Etruscan religious customs, including divination by the examination of entrails, but they too distinguished between secular and religious matters. The Etruscans did not. Their minds appear to have been imprisoned within a rigid framework of doctrine, which had been revealed to their ancestors and which was immutable. This doctrine was not concerned with problems of ethical or moral conduct. The correct interpretation of signs and the due observance of the appropriate rites were apparently, to the Etruscans, ends in themselves.

The Etruscans had numerous gods, some of whom were adopted Hellenic deities, but the principal triad consisted of Tinia, Uni, and Menerva, whose Roman analogues were Jupiter, Juno, and Minerva. But there were also demons, spirits of horror and death, and as the centuries passed these were depicted more and more frequently in the tombs. One of them, the sinister Charun, who obviously took his name from the Greek ferryman of the Styx, had a horse's ears and a beaked nose, and was armed with a large mallet. With a body the color of decaying flesh he seems a veritable embodiment of a scene of human sacrifice, the figure of Charun was shown towering over the victim, his demon's face painted an eerie blue, and holding an enormous hammer in his hand.

After the fifth century B.C. Etruscan funerary paintings emphasize scenes of massacre, torture, and violent death. The grimmest of these pictures depict what appear to have been the ritual "sports" that accompanied Etruscan funeral ceremonies. One wall painting shows a battle to the death between two Etruscan gladiators; another the sacrifice of the Trojan captives who were killed at the tomb of Patroclus by Achilles. Some have suggested that such horrors may only depict the sufferings of the damned in an Etruscan hell, but as Etruscan religion does not appear to have contained any doctrine of sin and punishment this is unlikely. It is probably true, however, that such scenes represented ritual performances in accordance with the Etruscan religious doctrine, unlike the later pointless and brutal spectacles that were staged in the days of imperial Rome.

Curiosity about pain, violence, and death, always present in the darker recesses of the human mind, may have been magnified by the Etruscans until it developed into a morbid obsession. What caused this we cannot be certain, but it may have been a succession of military defeats, reinforcing a belief already impressed by Etruscan religion that as in the life of man, so in that of peoples there is birth, maturity, and death. In one of the Etruscan religious documents, the *Libri fatales* (the books of destiny), which is known from Roman writings, human life is given a span of twelve times seven years (seven often occurs as a sacred number in primitive religion). The Etruscans also believed that their nation had a life of ten *saecula* (a variable period of eighty to one hundred and twenty years), after which it would disappear. Perhaps, as the Etruscan hegemony gradually collapsed under the alternate hammerblows of Romans and Gauls, the Etruscans saw in this the inexorable workings of destiny. No doubt, as the time ordained for the death of their nation drew closer, Etruscan soldiers went out to war with little heart for battle, little expectation of victory. This fatalism may be why, during the period of their decline, the Etruscans laid increasing emphasis on the more somber aspects of their religion. It may be so, but we do not know.

Certainly from the earliest times they had been deeply concerned for the welfare of their dead, burying them in tombs of increasing richness and beauty, decorating the walls with painted frescoes, and equipping these mausoleums—which, like those of ancient Egypt, were Houses of Eternity —with everything the dead would need in the afterlife. But after the fifth century B.C. the gay scenes of hunting and feasting and dancing become fewer, and are replaced by more solemn subjects such as those described above. The sculptured figures on the sarcophagi also change, becoming soft, flabby, and indolent; they loll on cushions, and hold wine cups, while on their faces is a curious expression, neither wholly joyous nor wholly melancholic, but an expression resigned, detached, and enigmatic.

By 250 B.C. Etruria was part of the Roman political system, though for a time it still retained its individual character. One hundred years later, throughout the land funeral inscriptions were being written in Latin, and by the time of Christ the Etruscan language had died out, except among the country people. Roman cities rose on the sites of such Etruscan towns as Tarquinia, Perugia, and Arezzo, to be replaced in turn by medieval and modern buildings. Some Etruscan towns were deserted and never reoccupied, and even these were plundered of their stone, so that today little survives. But the cemeteries—the huge underground cities of the dead at Cerveteri, Tarquinia, Vulci, and many other sites —remain. Though thousands of tombs have been ransacked and their precious wall paintings left to decay, others are still intact. As recently as 1957, the Italian archaeologist Carlo M. Lerici began using electronic methods to detect tomb sites, and then examined still-buried tombs by boring a narrow hole in the roof, lowering an automatic camera that could be revolved around 360 degrees, and photographing the interiors. In this way he discovered the first painted and decorated tombs found at Tarquinia since 1892; one of these contained a lively depiction of various athletes leaping, running, and tossing the discus. At Vulci a large tomb was discovered containing an elaborate sarcophagus with scenes of different character carved in high relief—a massacre of maidens watched by a male and a female deity. No doubt more tombs will be found, of which a few may yet remain intact. Etruscology is now as precise a discipline as other branches of archaeology, and new scientific methods have replaced the careless plundering of former years.

We may one day succeed in understanding the Etruscan language, though all known examples are short inscriptions, mostly funerary; the longest, a religious document, is of only fifteen hundred words. Possibly the long-debated question of Etruscan origins may finally be settled. Until these problems are solved, and perhaps even after they are, the Etruscans themselves will retain their mystery. We can enjoy their vital, exuberant art, admire the craftsmanship of their jewelers, metalworkers, sculptors, and painters. But they themselves continue to remain apart from us. Across twenty-five centuries their sensitive, worldly faces regard us with ironical amusement, half-smiling, as if they held some secret. They remain one of the great enigmas of history.

THE FORCES
OF DESTINY

The Etruscans celebrated the end of a year, not its beginning. As the year drew to a close, representatives of the
Etruscan League gathered at the central shrine of the nation, where a priest hammered an iron nail into a wall
within the temple of Fortune, to mark the inexorable passage of time. Each nation, like each man, was ordained to
live a certain length of time. Etruria was destined to survive for ten *saecula,* each roughly a century long; any
omen—a plague of mice, an earthquake, a rain of blood—
might announce the end of a *saeculum.* Priests studied the
omens to discover their meaning, and searched for ways to
appease the gods and postpone the nation's fate. But if the
end were ordained, neither priests nor Etruria's fiercest soldiers such as the one shown above, could avert it. Even
the gods of the Etruscan pantheon did not have ultimate
control. Above them were other gods, whose name, sex, and
character were unknown, and it was they who advised Tinia,
the ruler of heaven, when to unloose the final thunderbolt.

The gravestone at left shows a woman riding to the underworld in a chariot. Mirrors, through which the dead could travel between this world and the next, were often placed in tombs; like souls, their reflections are both alive and intangible. The mirror below shows a soothsayer examining the liver of a sacrificed beast for omens.

SHADES OF THE DEAD

A terra-cotta sarcophagus found at Cerveteri shows an Etruscan aristocrat and his wife reclining together on a couch as if attending a banquet in the life hereafter.

According to Etruscan belief, each man was destined to a life span of seventy years. If he read the omens correctly, and made the proper sacrifices to placate the gods, he might postpone his fate a little longer, until the age of eighty-four; but then he was finally doomed. Even if his body survived, his soul would be taken away from him, for no man could defy fate after that age. Upon the death of an aristocrat, a great banquet took place within his tomb, a feast at which the corpse sat in attendance, along with its friends and grieving relatives. The blood of animals and humans was sacrificed to reinvigorate the body whose vitality had departed. Careful efforts were taken to ensure that the dead remained comfortable within the tombs, for their souls lived on there; these precautions also served to keep them from coming back to haunt the living. Three times a year the souls of the dead were allowed to return to earth, however, when priests lifted up a stone which marked the place where the two main streets crossed at the center of each Etruscan city. This stone covered a shaft leading to the underworld where the shades of the dead made their home.

ETRUSCAN
SOCIETY

In the early years of Etruscan history no great class differences existed; only acrobats and slaves were considered inferior. Eventually, the primitive equality that the Etruscans had enjoyed under a monarchy disappeared as oligarchies gained control of the Tuscan cities. They were supported by priests, aristocrats themselves, who interpreted the omens in such a way as to maintain their class in power. Below the ranks of the freemen—peasants and city people—were the slaves, either war captives or descendants of Italic tribes defeated by the Etruscan armies. As the population of Etruria grew, colonists emigrated to the fertile valley of the Po, or south to Campania; there land was divided up into farms for them in perfectly demarcated squares. Easing of population pressures failed to free Etruria from class strife, which was widespread at this time in Mediterannean lands. In the third century, the lower classes revolted, seized the government for a time, and abolished laws against intermarriage with the aristocracy.

Wearing the broad-brimmed hat characteristic of his class, an Etruscan peasant (below) walks behind his team of yoked oxen. A votive offering, this charming model is one of the few Etruscan bronzes that represent a scene of rural life. The terra-cotta figure reproduced above shows a young girl plaiting her hair. The women of Etruria enjoyed a great deal of freedom; unlike their contemporaries in Greece, they were allowed to participate in public life.

As sea birds fly overhead, a group of youths sail on a fishing expedition. One leans over the prow, fishing with a handline; before him, a dolphin leaps out of the sea. An eye is painted on the prow of the boat as a good-luck symbol.

MUSIC
AND
DANCE

The Etruscans danced in order to appeal to their deities, to elicit the favor of the gods of war or expiate the sins that had brought down plague upon them. At festivals and religious ceremonies, and at funeral games as well, both male and female members of the guilds of dancers performed to the sound of stringed instruments and the shrill notes of the double flute. The flute was the characteristic musical instrument in Etruria; it was also played as accompaniment to ordinary acts of daily life, such as baking bread and hunting game. The Etruscan word for dancer was *hister,* from which our word *histrionic* comes; the Romans borrowed the word from Tuscan dancers, who were the first performers seen in Rome. Throughout the ancient world the Etruscans were renowned for their devotion to music. The Greeks attributed to them the invention of the trumpet, an instrument that was probably exported from Etruria to the other Mediterranean lands.

Many representations of dancers illustrate the Etruscan love of pleasure. The red figured vase shown opposite, which dates from the fifth century B.C., *shows a company of youths dancing. The animated couple on the engraved mirror-back above are probably performers too, although in antiquity it was rare for dancers to embrace. One of the best known and best preserved of all Etruscan tomb paintings appears at right. The musician at the center plays on the double flute, and one of his companions holds a lyre. Their dance may be taking place in a sacred laurel grove.*

The tomb fresco above shows two powerful wrestlers struggling against each other during a ritual contest for the dead. The three bowls standing beside them may be the winner's prize. The two priests at left are referees; one of them carries a lituus, or curved staff, to signify his office. At right is an athlete, from the recently discovered Tomb of the Olympiad, who prepares to throw the discus.

FUNERAL GAMES

The brutal gladiatorial contests that delighted the crowds of imperial Rome were a heritage from the Etruscans, who arranged bloody battles between men to celebrate the funerals of important persons, believing that the blood that was spilled would invigorate the souls of the dead. Such contests were often represented on the walls of tombs; one, whose brutality may be typical, pits a gladiator whose only weapon is a fierce dog against another contestant, made blind by a sack placed over his head and armed only with a club. Throughout Roman history, these contests betrayed their Etruscan origin. It remained the custom for gladiators who were killed during combat to be dragged from the arena by men wearing the mask of an Etruscan demon of the underworld.

341

THE FALL OF VEII

When the Romans conquered the neighboring city of Veii in 396 B.C., it marked the beginning of the lingering decline of Etruscan power in Italy. A few miles south of Veii, Rome blocked the way between that city and the sea; as it grew to maturity, there was constant warfare between the two towns. According to one account, Veii was finally vanquished when the enemy soldiers dug a tunnel under its walls into the town's main sanctuary and sprang forth from beneath the temple floor during a religious ceremony, like demons from the underworld. The image of the goddess Uni (Juno) was escorted to Rome by a company of the most handsome youths in the Roman army. Veii was destroyed and its site abandoned.

Once it had begun, the Roman advance was relentless. None of the other Etruscan cities had come to Veii's aid, but even when they did join each other in a common defense, their league was no match for Rome. By 250 B.C. Rome was the master of Etruria. Roman soldiers were garrisoned within the Etruscan towns and intermarried freely with the local population. Roman colonists settled in the Tuscan countryside or built new towns to supplant the old Etruscan centers as Florence did Fiesole. By the second century A.D. even in the remotest reaches of Etruria the native language had died out, and the world of the Etruscans survived only in memory.

A pair of winged horses harnessed to the chariot of a god adorned the pediment of a temple at Tarquinia. When the Romans sacked Etruscan temples, they ignored such sculptures and carried off the cult images. According to Livy, the Romans made war "more with the land than with men"; they burned and pillaged, and at the end of the fourth century B.C. Tarquinia sued for peace. Rome granted a forty-year truce, but received the right to march its armies through Tarquinian territories to war against the other Etruscan cities.

VOICES FROM THE PAST

In a few fortunate instances, contemporary accounts of civilizations that were later to disappear have survived in the works of travelers or historians who had the opportunity to observe them before they vanished. Other records of lost worlds occur parenthetically in the writings of early authors, sometimes in a paragraph or two introduced into a discussion of another subject. Sometimes these accounts are biased, or based on hearsay, but often they supplement or confirm what archaeologists have learned from field research. On the following pages appear a number of selections taken from some of the works that restore these last civilizations to us.

ON EGYPT: About Egypt itself I shall have a great deal more to relate because of the number of remarkable things which the country contains, and because of the fact that more monuments which beggar description are to be found there than anywhere else in the world. That is reason enough for my dwelling on it at greater length. Not only is the Egyptian climate peculiar to that country, and the Nile different in its behavior from other rivers elsewhere, but the Egyptians themselves in their manners and customs seem to have reversed the ordinary practices of mankind. For instance, women attend market and are employed in trade, while men stay at home and do the weaving. In weaving the normal way is to work the threads of the weft upward, but the Egyptians work them downward. Men in Egypt carry loads on their heads, women on their shoulders; women pass water standing up, men sitting down. To ease themselves they go indoors, but eat outside in the streets, on the theory that what is unseemly but necessary should be done in private, and what is not unseemly should be done openly. No woman holds priestly office, either in the service of goddess or god; only men are priests in both cases. Sons are under no compulsion to support their parents if they do not wish to do so, but daughters must, whether they wish it or not. Elsewhere priests grow their hair long; in Egypt they shave their heads. In other nations the relatives of the deceased in time of mourning cut their hair, but the Egyptians, who shave at all other times, mark a death by letting the hair grow both on head and chin. They live with their animals—unlike the rest of the world, who live apart from them. Other men live on wheat and barley, but any Egyptian who does so is blamed for it, their bread being made from spelt, or *Zea* as some call it. Dough they knead with their feet, but clay with their hands—and even handle dung. They practice circumcision, while men of other nations—except those who have learnt from Egypt—leave their private parts as nature made them. Men in Egypt have two garments each, women only one. The ordinary practice at sea is to make sheets fast to ring-bolts fitted outboard; the Egyptians fit them inboard. In writing or calculating, instead of going, like the Greeks, from left to right, the Egyptians go from right to left—and obstinately maintain that theirs is the dexterous method, ours being left-handed and awkward. They have two sorts of writing, the sacred and the common.

His narration of the wars between the Persians and the Greeks gave the Greek historian Herodotus a chance to astonish his audience with an account of the marvels that he had seen and heard of in his extensive travels. Quite aptly, Herodotus has been called both "the father of history" and "the father of lies." In his book, myth and gossip are mingled indiscriminately with historical reports of considerable value and vivid descriptions of life and customs among the peoples of the East.

344

They are religious to excess, beyond any other nation in the world, and here are some of the customs which illustrate the fact: they drink from brazen cups which they scour every day—everyone, without exception. They wear linen clothes which they make a special point of continually washing. They circumcise themselves for cleanliness' sake, preferring to be clean rather than comely. The priests shave their bodies all over every other day to guard against the presence of lice, or anything else equally unpleasant, while they are about their religious duties; the priests, too, wear linen only, and shoes made from the papyrus plant—these materials, for dress and shoes, being the only ones allowed them. They bathe in cold water twice a day and twice every night—and observe innumerable other ceremonies besides. Their life, however, is not by any means all hardship, for they enjoy advantages, too; for instance, they are free from all personal expense, having bread made for them out of the sacred grain, and a plentiful daily supply of goose meat and beef, with wine in addition. Fish they are forbidden to touch; and as for beans, they cannot even bear to look at them, because they imagine they are unclean (in point of fact the Egyptians never sow beans, and even if any happen to grow wild, they will not eat them, either raw or boiled). They do not have a single priest for each god, but a number, of which one is chief priest, and when a chief priest dies his son is appointed to succeed him. Bulls are considered the property of the god Epaphus—or Apis—and are therefore tested in the following way: a priest appointed for the purpose examines the animal, and if he finds even a single black hair upon him, pronounces him unclean; he goes over him with the greatest care, first making him stand up, then lie on his back, after which he pulls out his tongue to see if that, too, is "clean" according to the recognized marks—what those are I will explain later. He also inspects the tail to make sure the hair on it grows properly; then, if the animal passes all these tests successfully, the priest marks him by twisting round his horns a band of papyrus which he seals with wax and stamps with his signet ring. The bull is finally taken away, and the penalty is death for anybody who sacrifices an animal which has not been marked in this manner. The method of sacrifice is as follows: they take the beast (one of those marked with the seal) to the appropriate altar and light a fire; then, after pouring a libation of wine and invoking the god by name, they slaughter it, cut off its head, and flay the carcase. The head is loaded with curses and taken away—if there happen to be Greek traders in the market, it is sold to them; if not, it is thrown into the river. The curses they pronounce take the form of a prayer that any disaster which threatens either themselves or their country may be diverted and fall upon the severed head of the beast. Both the libation and the practice of cutting off the heads of sacrificial beasts are common to all Egyptians in all their sacrifices, and the latter explains why it is that no Egyptian will use the head of any sort of animal for food. The methods of disemboweling and burning are various, and I will describe the one which is followed in the worship of the goddess whom they consider the greatest and honor with the most important festival. In this case, when they have flayed the bull, they first pray and then take its paunch out whole, leaving the intestines and fat inside the body; next they cut off the legs, shoulders, neck, and rump, and stuff the carcase with loaves of bread, honey, raisins, figs, frankincense, myrrh, and other aromatic substances; finally, they pour a quantity of oil over the carcase and burn it. They always fast before a sacrifice, and while the fire is consuming it they beat their breasts. That part of the ceremony done, they serve a meal out of the portions left over.

All Egyptians use bulls and bull-calves for sacrifice, if they have passed the test for "cleanness"; but they are forbidden to sacrifice cows, on the ground that they are sacred to Isis. The statues of Isis show a female figure with cow's horns, like the Greek representations of Io, and of all animals cows are universally held by the Egyptians in the greatest reverence. This is the reason why no Egyptian, man or woman, will kiss a Greek, or use a Greek knife, spit, or caldron, or even eat the flesh of a bull known to be clean, if it has been cut with a Greek knife.

THE BUILDING OF THE PYRAMIDS: Up to the time of Rhampsinitus, Egypt was excellently governed and very prosperous; but his successor Cheops (to continue the account which the priests gave me) brought the country into all sorts of misery. He closed all the temples, then, not content with excluding his subjects from the practice of their religion, compelled them without exception to labor as slaves for his own advantage. Some were forced to drag blocks of stone from the quarries in the Arabian hills to the Nile, where they were ferried across and taken over by others, who hauled them to the Libyan hills. The work went on in three-monthly shifts, a hundred thousand men in a shift. It took ten years of this oppressive slave-labor to build the track along which the blocks were hauled—a work, in my opinion, of hardly less magnitude than the pyramid itself, for it is five furlongs in length, sixty feet wide, forty-eight feet high at its highest point, and constructed of polished stone blocks decorated with carvings of animals. To build it took, as I said, ten years—including the underground sepulchral chambers on the hill where the pyramids stand; a cut was made from the Nile, so that the water from it turned the site of these into an island. To build the pyramid itself took twenty years; it is square at the base, its height (eight hundred feet) equal to the length of each side; it is of polished stone blocks beautifully fitted, none of the blocks being less than thirty feet long. The method employed was to build it in tiers, or steps, if you prefer the word—something like battlements running up the slope of a hill; when the base was complete, the blocks for the first tier above it were lifted from ground level by cranes or sheerlegs, made of short timbers; on this first tier there was another lifting-crane, which raised the blocks a stage higher, then yet another which raised them higher still. Each tier, or story, had its crane—or it may be that they used the same one, which, being easy to carry, they shifted up from stage to stage as soon as its load was dropped into place. Both methods are mentioned, so I give them both here. The finishing-off of the pyramid was begun at the top and continued downwards, ending with the lowest parts nearest the ground. An inscription is cut upon it in Egyptian characters recording the amount spent on radishes, onions, and leeks for the laborers, and I remember distinctly that the interpreter who read me the inscription said the sum was sixteen hundred talents of silver. If this is true, how much must have been spent in addition on bread and clothing for the laborers during all those years the building was going on—not to mention the time it took (not a little, I should think) to quarry and haul the stone, and to construct the underground chamber?

But no crime was too great for Cheops: when he was short of money, he sent his daughter to a bawdy-house with instructions to charge a certain sum—they did not tell me how much. This she actually did, adding to it a further transaction of her own; for with the intention of leaving something to be remembered by after her death, she asked each of her customers to give her a block of stone, and of these stones (the story goes) was built the middle pyramid of the three which stand in front of the great pyramid. It is a hundred and fifty feet square.

Cheops reigned for fifty years, according to the Egyptians' account, and was succeeded after his death by his brother Chephren. Chephren was no better than his predecessor; his rule was equally oppressive, and, like Cheops, he built a pyramid, but of a smaller size (I measured both of them myself). It has no underground chambers, and no channel was dug, as in the case of Cheops' pyramid, to bring to it the water from the Nile. The cutting of the canal, as I have already said, makes the site of the pyramid of Cheops into an island, and there his body is supposed to be. The pyramid of Chephren lies close to the great pyramid of Cheops; it is forty feet lower than the latter, but otherwise of the same dimensions; its lower course is of the colored stone of Ethiopia. Both these pyramids stand on the same hill, which is about a hundred feet in height. Chephren reigned for fifty-six years—so the Egyptians reckon a period of a hundred and six years, all told, during which the temples were never opened for worship and the country was reduced in every way to the greatest misery. The Egyptians can hardly bring themselves to mention the names of Cheops and Chephren, so great is their hatred of them; they even call the pyramids after Philitis, a shepherd who . . . fed his flocks in the neighborhood.

The next king of Egypt after Chephren was Mycerinus, the son of Cheops. Mycerinus, reversing his father's policy of which he did not approve, reopened the temples and allowed his subjects, who had been brought into such abject slavery, to resume the practice of their religion and their normal work. Of all kings who ruled in Egypt he had the greatest reputation for justice in the decision of legal causes, and for this the Egyptians give him higher praise than any other monarch; for apart from the general equity of his judgments, he used to compensate out of his own property any man who was dissatisfied with the result of his suit, and so leave him with nothing to complain of. . . .

He, too, left a pyramid, built square, with its lower half of Ethiopian stone; it is much smaller than his father's, each side at the base being only about two hundred eighty feet long.

ANIMALS, SACRED AND FORBIDDEN: Some Egyptians reverence the crocodile as a sacred beast, others do not, but treat it as an enemy. The strongest belief in its sanctity is to be found in Thebes and around Lake Moeris; in these places they keep one particular crocodile, which they tame, putting rings made of glass or gold into its ears and bracelets round its front feet, and giving it special food and ceremonial offerings. In fact, while these creatures are alive they treat them with every kindness, and when they die, embalm them and bury them in sacred tombs. On the other hand, in the neighborhood of Elephantine crocodiles are not considered sacred animals at all, but are eaten. . . .

The hippopotamus is held sacred in the district of Papremis, but not elsewhere. This animal has four legs, cloven hoofs like an ox, a snub nose, a horse's mane and tail, conspicuous tusks, a voice like a horse's neigh, and is about the size of a very large ox. Its hide is so thick and tough that when dried it can be made into spear-shafts. . . .

Pigs are considered unclean. If anyone touches a pig accidentally in passing, he will at once plunge into the river, clothes and all, to wash himself; and swineherds, though of pure Egyptian blood, are the only people in the country who never enter a temple, nor is there any inter-marriage with them and the rest of the community, swineherds marrying their daughters and taking their wives only from amongst themselves.

EGYPTIAN TRADITION: The Egyptians who live in the cultivated parts of the country, by their practice of keeping records of the past, have made themselves much the best historians of any nation of which I have had experience. . . . The Egyptians keep to their native customs and never adopt any from abroad.

THE LAND BETWEEN THE RIVERS: The rainfall of Assyria is slight and provides enough moisture only to burst the seed and start the root grow-ing, but to swell the grain and bring it to maturity artificial irrigation is used, not, as in Egypt, by the natural flooding of the river, but by labor-ers working hand-pumps. Like Egypt, the whole country is intersected by dikes; the largest of them has to be crossed in boats and runs in a southeasterly direction from the Euphrates until it joins another river, the Tigris, on which Nineveh was built. As a grain-bearing country Assyria is the richest in the world. No attempt is made there to grow figs, grapes, or olives or any other fruit trees, but so great is the fertility of the grain fields that they normally produce crops of two hundredfold, and in an exceptional year as much as three hundredfold. The blades of wheat and barley are at least three inches wide. As for millet and sesame, I will not say to what an astonishing size they grow, though I know well enough; but I also know that people who have not been to Babylonia have refused to believe even what I have said already about its fertility. The only oil these people use is made from sesame; date palms grow everywhere, mostly of the fruit-bearing kind, and the fruit supplies them with food, wine, and honey. The method of cultivation is the same as for figs, par-ticularly in regard to the practice of taking the fruit of what the Greeks call the "male" palm and tying it into the "female" or date-bearing tree, to allow the gall-fly to enter the fruit and ripen it and prevent it from drop-ping off . . . the male palms have the gall-fly in their fruit, like wild figs.

I will next describe the thing which surprised me most of all in this country, after Babylon itself: I mean the boats which ply down the Euphrates to the city. These boats are circular in shape and made of hide;

they build them in Armenia to the northward of Assyria, where they cut withies to make the frames and then stretch skins taut on the underside for the body of the craft; they are not fined-off or tapered in any way at bow or stern, but quite round like a shield. The men fill them with straw, put the cargo on board—mostly wine in palm-wood casks—and let the current take them downstream. They are controlled by two men; each has a paddle which he works standing up, one in front drawing his paddle toward him, the other behind giving it a backward thrust. The boats vary a great deal in size; some are very big, the biggest of all having a capacity of some fourteen tons. Every boat carries a live donkey—the larger ones several—and when they reach Babylon and the cargoes have been offered for sale, the boats are broken up, the frames and straw disposed of, and the hides loaded on the donkeys' backs for the return journey overland to Armenia. It is quite impossible to paddle the boats upstream because of the strength of the current, and that is why they are constructed of hide instead of wood. Back in Armenia with their donkeys, the men build another lot of boats to the same design.

THE ZIGGURAT AT BABYLON: The temple is a square building, two furlongs each way, with bronze gates, and was still in existence in my time; it has a solid central tower, one furlong square, with a second erected on top of it and then a third, and so on up to eight. All eight towers can be climbed by a spiral way running round the outside, and about halfway up there are seats for those who make the ascent to rest on. On the summit of the topmost tower stands a great temple with a fine large couch in it, richly covered, and a golden table beside it. The shrine contains no image, and no one spends the night there except (if we may believe the Chaldaeans who are the priests of Bel) one Assyrian woman, all alone, whoever it may be that the god has chosen. The Chaldaeans also say—though I do not believe them—that the god enters the temple in person and takes his rest upon the bed.

BABYLONIAN CUSTOMS: The dress of the Babylonians consists of a linen tunic reaching to the feet with a woolen one over it, and a short white cloak on top; they have their own fashion in shoes, which resemble the slippers one sees in Boeotia. They grow their hair long, wear turbans, and perfume themselves all over; everyone owns a seal and a walking stick specially made for him, with a device carved on the top of it, an apple or rose or lily or eagle or something of the sort; for it is not the custom to have a stick without some such ornament. I will say no more about dress and so forth, but will go on to describe some of their practices. The most ingenious in my opinion is a custom which, I understand, they share with the Eneti in Illyria. In every village once a year all the girls of marriageable age used to be collected together in one place, while the men stood round them in a circle; an auctioneer then called each one in turn to stand up and offered her for sale, beginning with the best looking and going on to the second best as soon as the first had been sold for a good price. Marriage was the object of the transaction. The rich men who wanted wives bid against each other for the prettiest girls, while the humbler folk, who had no use for good looks in a wife, were actually paid to take the ugly ones, for when the auctioneer had got through all the pretty girls he would call upon the plainest, or even perhaps a crippled one, to stand up, and then ask who was willing to take the least money to marry her—and she was knocked down to whoever accepted the smallest sum. The money came from the sale of the beauties, who in this way provided dowries for their ugly or misshapen sisters. It was illegal for a man to marry his daughter to anyone he happened to fancy, and no one could take home a girl he had bought without first finding a backer to guarantee his intention of marrying her. In cases of disagreement between husband and wife the law allowed the return of the purchase money. Anyone who wished could come even from a different village to buy a wife.

This admirable practice has now fallen into disuse and they have of late years hit upon another scheme, namely the prostitution of all girls of the lower classes, to provide some relief from the poverty which followed upon the conquest with its attendant hardship and general ruin.

Next in ingenuity to the old marriage custom is their treatment of disease. They have no doctors, but bring their invalids out into the street, where anyone who comes along offers the sufferer advice on his complaint, either from personal experience or observation of a similar complaint in others. Anyone will stop by the sick man's side and suggest remedies which he has himself proved successful in whatever the trouble may be, or which he has known to succeed with other people. Nobody is allowed to pass a sick person in silence; but everyone must ask him what is the matter. They bury their dead in honey, and their dirges for the dead are like the Egyptian ones. When a Babylonian has had intercourse with his wife, he sits over incense to fumigate himself, with his wife opposite doing the same, and at daybreak they both have a bath. Before they have washed they will not touch any household utensil.

There is one custom amongst these people which is wholly shameful: every woman who is a native of the country must once in her life go and sit in the temple of Aphrodite and there give herself to a strange man. Many of the rich women, who are too proud to mix with the rest, drive to the temple in covered carriages with a whole host of servants following behind, and there wait; most, however, sit in the precinct of the temple with a band of plaited string round their heads—and a great crowd they are, what with some sitting there, others arriving, others going away— and through them all gangways are marked off running in every direction for the men to pass along and make their choice. Once a woman has taken her seat she is not allowed to go home until a man has thrown a silver coin into her lap and taken her outside to lie with her. As he throws the coin, the man has to say, "In the name of the goddess Mylitta"—that being the Assyrian name for Aphrodite. The value of the coin is of no consequence; once thrown it becomes sacred, and the law forbids that it should ever be refused. The woman has no privilege of choice—she must go with the first man who throws her the money. When she has lain with him, her duty to the goddess is discharged and she may go home, after which it will be impossible to seduce her by any offer, however large. Tall, handsome women soon manage to get home again, but the ugly ones stay a long time before they can fulfill the condition which the law demands, some of them, indeed, as much as three or four years.

EGYPT'S POPULATION AND WEALTH: In density of population it far surpassed of old all known regions of the inhabited world, and even in our own day is thought to be second to none other; for in ancient times it had over eighteen thousand important villages and cities, as can be seen entered in their sacred records, while under Ptolemy son of Lagus these were reckoned at over thirty thousand, this great number continuing down to our own time. The total population was . . . about seven million and the number has remained no less down to our day. . . .

Since the Nile has a gentle current, carries down a great quantity of all kinds of earth, and, furthermore, gathers in stagnant pools in low places, marshes are formed which abound in every kind of plant. For tubers of every flavor grow in them and fruits and vegetables which grow on stalks, of a nature peculiar to the country, supplying an abundance sufficient to render the poor and the sick among the inhabitants self-sustaining. For not only do they afford a varied diet, ready at hand and abundant for all who need it, but they also furnish not a few of the other things which contribute to the necessities of life; the lotus, for instance, grows in great profusion, and from it the Egyptians make a bread which is able to satisfy the physical needs of the body . . .

In accordance with the marriage customs of the Egyptians the priests have but one wife, but any other man takes as many as he may determine; and the Egyptians are required to raise all their children in order to increase the population, on the ground that large numbers are the greatest factor in increasing the prosperity of both country and cities. Nor do they hold any child a bastard, even though he was born of a slave mother; for they have taken the general position that the father is the sole author of procreation and that the mother only supplies the fetus with nourishment and a place to live, and they call the trees which bear fruit "male" and those which do not "female," exactly opposite to the Greek usage. They feed their children in a sort of happy-go-lucky fashion that in its inexpensiveness quite surpasses belief; for they serve them with stews made of any stuff that is ready to hand and cheap, and give them such stalks of the *byblos* plant as can be roasted in the coals, and the roots and stems of marsh plants . . . And since most of the children are reared without shoes or clothing because of the mildness of the climate of the country, the entire expense incurred by the parents of a child until it comes to maturity is not more than twenty drachmas. These are the leading reasons why Egypt has such an extraordinarily large population, and it is because of this fact that she possesses a vast number of great monuments.

HERODOTUS: Now as for the stories invented by Herodotus and certain writers on Egyptian affairs, who deliberately preferred to the truth the telling of marvelous tales and the invention of myths for the delectation of their readers, these we shall omit, and we shall set forth only what appears in the written records of the priests of Egypt and has passed our careful scrutiny.

A MONUMENT OF RAMESSES II: Ten stades from the first tombs . . . in which, according to tradition, are buried the concubines of Zeus, stands a monument of the king known as Osymandyas. . . . beside the entrance are three statues, each of a single block of black stone from Syene, of which one, that is seated, is the largest of any in Egypt, the foot measuring over seven cubits, while the other two at the knees of this, the one on the right and the other on the left, daughter and mother respectively, are smaller than the one first mentioned. And it is not merely for its size that this work merits approbation, but it is also marvelous by reason of its artistic quality and excellent because of the nature of the stone, since in a block of so great a size there is not a single crack or blemish to be seen. The inscription upon it runs: "King of Kings am I, Osymandyas. If anyone would know how great I am and where I lie, let him surpass one of my works."

THE PYRAMIDS: It is generally agreed that these monuments far surpass all other constructions in Egypt, not only in their massiveness and cost but also in the skill displayed by their builders. And they say that the architects of the monuments are more deserving of admiration than the kings who furnished the means for their execution; for in bringing their plans to completion the former called upon their individual souls and their zeal for honor, but the latter only used the wealth which they had inherited and the grievous toil of other men.

ROBBERY IN EGYPT: The Egyptian law dealing with thieves was also a very peculiar one. For it bade any who chose to follow this occupation to enter their names with the Chief of Thieves and by agreement to bring to him immediately the stolen articles, while any who had been robbed filed with him in like manner a list of all the missing articles, stating the place, the day, and the hour of the loss. And since by this method all lost articles were readily found, the owner who had lost anything had only to pay one-fourth of its value in order to recover just what belonged to him. For as it was impossible to keep all mankind from stealing, the lawgiver devised a scheme whereby every article lost would be recovered upon payment of a small ransom.

GOLD MINING: At the extremity of Egypt and in the contiguous territory of both Arabia and Ethiopia there lies a region which contains many large gold mines, where the gold is secured in great quantities with much suffering and at great expense. For the earth . . . contains seams and veins of a marble which is unusually white and in brilliancy surpasses everything else . . . and here the overseers of the labor in the mines recover the gold with the aid of a multitude of workers. For the kings of Egypt gather together and condemn to the mining of the gold such as have been found guilty of some crime and captives of war, as well as those who have been accused unjustly and thrown into prison because of their anger, and not only such persons but occasionally all their relatives as well, by this means, not only inflicting punishment upon those found guilty, but also securing at the same time great revenues from their labors. And those who have been condemned in this way—and they are a great multitude and are all bound in chains—work at their task unceasingly both by day and throughout the entire night, enjoying no respite and being carefully cut off from any means of escape; since guards of foreign soldiers who speak a language different from theirs stand watch over them, so that not a man, either by conversation or by some contact of a friendly nature, is able to corrupt one of his keepers. The gold-bearing earth which is hardest they first burn with a hot fire, and when they have crumbled it in this way they continue the working of it by hand; and the soft rock which can yield to moderate effort is crushed with a sledge by myriads of unfortunate wretches. And the entire operations are in charge of a skilled worker . . .

THE ETRUSCANS: It remains for us now to speak of the Tyrrhenians. This people, excelling as they did in manly vigor, in ancient times possessed great territory and founded many notable cities. Likewise, because they also availed themselves of powerful naval forces and were masters of the sea over a long period, they caused the sea along Italy to be named Tyrrhenian after them; and because they also perfected the organization of land forces, they were the inventors of the *salpinx,* as it is called, a discovery of the greatest usefulness for war and named after them the "Tyrrhenian trumpet." They were also the authors of that dignity which surrounds rulers, providing their rulers with lictors and an ivory stool and a toga with a purple band; and in connection with their houses they invented the peristyle, a useful device for avoiding the confusion connected with the attending throngs; and these things were adopted for the most part by the Romans, who added to their embellishments and transferred them to their own political institutions. Letters and the teaching about Nature and the gods they also brought to greater perfection, and they elaborated the art of divination by thunder and lightning more than all other men; and it is for this reason that the people who rule practically the entire inhabited world show honor to these men even to this day and employ them as interpreters of the omens of Zeus as they appear in thunder and lightning.

The land the Tyrrhenians inhabit bears every crop, and from the intensive cultivation of it they enjoy no lack of fruits, not only sufficient for their sustenance but contributing to abundant enjoyment and luxury. For example, twice each day they spread costly tables and upon them everything that is appropriate to excessive luxury, providing gay-colored couches and having ready at hand a multitude of silver drinking cups of every description and servants-in-waiting in no small number; and these attendants are some of them of exceeding comeliness and others are arrayed in clothing more costly than befits the station of a slave. Their dwellings are of every description and of individuality, those not only of their magistrates but of the majority of the free men as well. And, speaking generally, they have now renounced the spirit which was emulated by their forebears from ancient times, and passing their lives as they do in drinking bouts and unmanly amusements, it is easily understood how they have lost the glory in warfare which their fathers possessed. Not the least of the things which have contributed to their luxury is the fertility of the land; for since it bears every product of the soil and is altogether fertile, the Tyrrhenians lay up great stores of every kind of fruit. In general, indeed, Tyrrhenia, being altogether fertile, lies in extended open fields and is traversed at intervals by areas which rise up like hills and yet are fit for tillage; and it enjoys moderate rainfall not only in the winter season but in the summer as well.

GREECE'S EARLIEST INHABITANTS: . . . it is evident that the country now called Hellas had in ancient times no settled population; on the contrary, migrations were of frequent occurrence, the several tribes readily abandoning their homes under the pressure of superior numbers. Without commerce, without freedom of communication either by land or sea, cultivating no more of their territory than the exigencies of life required, destitute of capital, never planting their land (for they could not tell when an invader might not come and take it all away, and when he did come they had no walls to stop him), thinking that the necessities of daily sustenance could be supplied at one place as well as another, they cared little for shifting their habitation, and consequently neither built large cities nor attained to any other form of greatness. The richest soils were always most subject to this change of masters; such as the district now called Thessaly, Boeotia, most of the Peloponnesus, Arcadia excepted, and the most fertile parts of the rest of Hellas. The goodness of the land favored the aggrandizement of particular individuals, and thus created faction which proved a fertile source of ruin. It also invited invasion. Accordingly Attica, from the poverty of its soil enjoying from a very remote period freedom from faction, never changed its inhabitants. And here is no inconsiderable exemplification of my assertion, that the migrations were the cause of there being no correspondent growth in other parts. The most powerful victims of war or faction from the rest of Hellas took refuge with the Athenians as a safe retreat; and at an early period, becoming naturalized, swelled the already large population of the city to such a height that Attica became at last too small to hold them, and they had to send out colonies to Ionia.

THE POWER OF MYCENAE: Now Mycenae may have been a small place, and many of the towns of that age [the time of Agamemnon] may appear comparatively insignificant, but no exact observer would therefore feel justified in rejecting the estimate given by the poets and by tradition of the magnitude of the armament. For I suppose if Lacedaemon were to become desolate and the temples and the foundations of the public buildings were left, that as time went on there would be a strong disposition with posterity to refuse to accept her fame as a true exponent of her power. And yet they occupy two-fifths of the Peloponnesus and lead the whole, not to speak of their numerous allies without. Still, as the city is neither built in a compact form nor adorned with magnificent temples and public edifices, but composed of villages after the old fashion of Hellas, there would be an impression of inadequacy. Whereas, if Athens were to suffer the same misfortune, I suppose that any inference from the appearance presented to the eye would make her power to have been twice as great as it is. We have therefore no right to be skeptical, nor to content ourselves with an inspection of a town to the exclusion of a consideration of its power; but we may safely conclude that the armament in question surpassed all before it, as it fell short of modern efforts; if we can here also accept the testimony of Homer's poems, in which, without allowing for the exaggeration which a poet would feel himself licensed to employ, we can see that it was far from equalling ours. He has represented it as consisting of twelve hundred vessels . . .

PIRACY: For in early times the Hellenes and the barbarians of the coast and islands, as communication by sea became more common, were tempted to turn pirates, under the conduct of their most powerful men; the motives being to serve their own cupidity and to support the needy. They would fall upon a town unprotected by walls, and consisting of a mere collection of villages, and would plunder it; indeed, this came to be the main source of their livelihood, no disgrace being yet attached to such an achievement, but even some glory. An illustration of this is furnished by the honor with which some of the inhabitants of the continent still regard a successful marauder, and by the question we find the old poets everywhere representing the people as asking of voyagers—"Are they pirates?"—as if those who are asked the question would have no idea of disclaiming the imputation, or their interrogators of reproaching them for it.

That ancient guidebook, Pausanias' Description of Greece, *has been criticized for its pedestrian style and for its reliance on outdated descriptions, taken from earlier books, complaints familiar to modern authors who attempt a similar task. Yet Pausanias' book, written in the second century* A.D., *was as reliable as many of the guidebooks of today. Like Baedeker, the Greek traveler gave a detailed account of the routes leading through each region, and supplemented it with observations, both philosophical and critical, on the sights and monuments of art that could be seen along the way.*

THE FOUNDING OF MYCENAE AND ITS DESTRUCTION: Ascending to Tretus, and again going along the road to Argos, you see on the left the ruins of Mycenae. The Greeks are aware that the founder of Mycenae was Perseus, so I will narrate the cause of its foundation and the reason why the Argives afterward laid Mycenae waste. . . .

For on its site the cap (*myces*) fell from [Perseus'] scabbard, and he regarded this as a sign to found a city. I have also heard the following account. He was thirsty, and the thought occurred to him to pick up a mushroom (*myces*) from the ground. Drinking with joy water that flowed from it, he gave to the place the name of Mycenae. Homer in the *Odyssey* mentions a woman Mycene in the following verse: "Tyro and Alcmene and the fair-crowned lady Mycene." She is said to have been the daughter of Inachus . . . they say that this lady has given her name to the city. . . .

It was jealousy which caused the Argives to destroy Mycenae. For at the time of the Persian invasion the Argives made no move, but the Mycenaeans sent eighty men to Thermopylae who shared in the achievement of the Lacedaemonians. This eagerness for distinction brought ruin upon them by exasperating the Argives.

THE FALL OF ANCIENT CITIES: . . . I know that heaven is always willing something new, and likewise that all things, strong or weak, increasing or decreasing, are being changed by Fortune, who drives them with imperious necessity according to her whim. For Mycenae, the leader of the Greeks in the Trojan War, and Nineveh, where was the royal palace of the Assyrians, are utterly ruined and desolate; while Boeotian Thebes, once deemed worthy to be the head of the Greek people, why, its name includes only the acropolis and its few inhabitants. Of the opulent places in the ancient world, Egyptian Thebes and Minyan Orchomenos are now less prosperous than a private individual of moderate means, while Delos, once the common market of Greece, has no Delian inhabitant, but only the men sent by the Athenians to guard the sanctuary. At Babylon the sanctuary of Belus still is left, but of the Babylon that was the greatest city of its time under the sun nothing remains but the wall. The case of Tiryns in the Argolid is the same. These places have been reduced by heaven to nothing.

A few references to the Etruscans appear in the works of Pliny the Elder and the Greek historian Dionysius of Halicarnassus. In his Roman Antiquities, *written around the time of Christ, Dionysius discussed the origin of the Etruscans, foreshadowing an argument that is raging among scholars today. Pliny's* Natural History, *according to the author's estimation, incorporated twenty thousand facts about nature and its relationship to mankind. Among them was a section on lightning and thunder and the interpretation of its significance by the Etruscan soothsayers.*

PLINY, THE INTERPRETATION OF THUNDER BY THE ETRUSCANS: The Tuscan writers hold the view that there are nine gods who send thunderbolts, and that these are of eleven kinds, because Jupiter hurls three varieties. Only two of these deities have been retained by the Romans, who attribute thunderbolts in the daytime to Jupiter and those in the night to Summanus, the latter being naturally rare because the sky at night is colder. Tuscany believes that some also burst out of the ground, which it calls "low bolts," and that these are rendered exceptionally direful and accursed by the season of winter, though all the bolts that they believe of earthly origin are not the ordinary ones and do not come from the stars but from the nearer and more disordered element: a clear proof of this being that all those coming from the upper heaven deliver slanting blows, whereas these which they call earthly strike straight. And those that fall from the nearer elements are supposed to come out of the earth because they leave no traces as a result of their rebound, although that is the principle not of a downward blow but of a slanting one. Those who pursue these enquiries with more subtlety think that these bolts come from the planet Saturn, just as the inflammatory ones come from Mars, as, for instance, when Bolsena, the richest town in Tuscany, was entirely burnt up by a thunderbolt. Also the first ones that occur after a man sets up house for himself are called "family meteors," as foretelling his fortune for the whole of his life. However, people think that private meteors, except those that occur either at a man's first marriage or on his birthday, do not prophesy beyond ten years, nor public ones beyond the thirtieth year, except those occurring at the colonization of a town.

DIONYSIUS, ETRUSCAN ORIGINS: As regards these Tyrrhenians, some declare them to be natives of Italy, but others call them foreigners. Those who make them a native race say that their name was given them from the forts, which they were the first of the inhabitants of this country to build; for covered buildings enclosed by walls are called by the Tyrrhenians as well as by the Greeks *tyrseis* or "towers."

But those who relate a legendary tale about their having come from a foreign land say that Tyrrhenus, who was the leader of the colony, gave his name to the nation, and that he was a Lydian by birth . . .

And I do not believe, either, that the Tyrrhenians were a colony of the Lydians; for they do not use the same language as the latter, nor can it be alleged that, though they no longer speak a similar tongue, they still retain some other indications of their mother country. For they neither worship the same gods as the Lydians nor make use of similar laws or institutions, but in these very respects they differ more from the Lydians than from the Pelasgians. Indeed, those probably come nearest to the truth who declare that the nation migrated from nowhere else, but was native to the country, since it is found to be a very ancient nation and to agree with no other either in its language or in its manner of living. And there is no reason why the Greeks should not have called them by this name, both from their living in towers and from the name of one of their rulers. The Romans, however, give them other names: from the country they once inhabited, named Etruria, they call them Etruscans . . .

The most valuable account of life in Cambodia during the years in which the Khmer empire was still flourishing was written by a Chinese, Chou Ta-kuan, who had been sent to Angkor on a diplomatic mission from the court of Timur Khan at Peiping. A contemporary of Marco Polo, Chou Ta-kuan was considerably less awed by foreign sights than the Venetian traveler was. Despite the splendor and wealth of Angkor Thom, the Khmers were still "southern barbarians" to him, and his report on their customs and country, though lively, is somewhat patronizing.

ANGKOR THOM: Six or seven miles of walls surround the city, which may be entered by five gates, each of which has two side gates. Two gates open onto the east; and the others have only one. Just outside the walls there is a broad moat, beyond which there are causeways with enormous bridges. On both sides of the bridges there are fifty-four stone divinities, looking like generals, terrible and gigantic. All five gates are alike. The bridges have stone parapets, carved in the form of nine-headed serpents; and the fifty-four divinities hold the serpent in their hands as though to prevent it from escaping. Above the gates there are five heads of Buddha in stone, the faces turned toward the four cardinal points. That in the center is decorated in gold. Stone elephants are carved on both sides of the gate.

The walls are constructed entirely of stone blocks, piled on top of each other to a height of about twenty-four feet. They are carefully fitted and no wild grass appears in the niches. There are no battlements; and certain places on the walls are sown with a species of plant. The inner side of the walls forms a ramp . . . at the height of which there are large gates, closed at night and open in the morning. Criminals who have had their toes cut off are not allowed to pass by the gatekeepers.

The walls form a perfect square, at the corners of which rise four stone towers. Marking the center of the kingdom is a tower of gold, surrounded by more than twenty stone towers and hundreds of stone cells. On the east side two golden lions flank a golden bridge, and eight Buddhas of gold are placed at the foot of stone cells.

About a third of a mile north of the golden tower there is a bronze tower, even higher, from which the view is magnificent. At the foot there are ten or more small stone houses. Still another third of a mile farther north is the residence of the king, where another golden tower exists in his sleeping apartments. It is all these wonders which we think have inspired merchants to speak glowingly of "rich and noble Cambodia" . . .

CLOTHING: Everyone, even the prince, men and women alike, wear their hair in a chignon and are bare shouldered. They simply wrap a piece of cloth around their loins over which they drape another larger one when they go outdoors. The type of material depended on rank; and some that the prince wears are worth three or four ounces of gold. Such material, of course, is the most beautiful in color and workmanship. Although linen is woven here, a highly regarded variety comes in quantity from Siam and Champa, and the most prized of all, of especially fine and delicate workmanship, comes from India.

Floral patterns, woven into the cloth, are reserved for the prince. He wears a crown of gold like those on the head of Vajradhara, and when he doesn't wear the crown, his chignon is wrapped with garlands of flowers, perfumed with a kind of jasmine. His neck is hung with nearly three pounds of huge pearls. On his wrists and ankles he wears bracelets, and on his fingers he wears gold rings set with cat's eyes. The soles of his bare feet and his palms are stained with a red drug. Outside, he carries a golden sword in his hand.

Ordinary women dye the soles of their feet and their palms, but men would not dare. Fabrics with a pattern of thinly scattered flowers may be worn by great nobles and princes; and the palace attendants' clothes are unique in having two clusters of floral design. Among the ordinary people, women only are permitted to wear such clothes, but if a newly arrived Chinese happened to wear a pattern with two clusters of floral design, his ignorance of the rules would excuse him from condemnation.

CAMBODIAN WOMEN: Women in this country are said to be very lascivious. No sooner have they given birth than one or two days later they sleep with their husbands. They abandon their husbands if the latter grow cold, and if he goes far away, they may stay faithful for a few nights, but soon they are sure to ask, "How can I sleep alone? I am made of flesh and blood!" That's how depraved they are! But I have heard that a few are faithful, too.

Women here age very quickly; probably because they marry and have children before they are old enough. At twenty or thirty, they look like Chinese women of forty and fifty. . . . It would be characteristic of parents who have a daughter to make this prayer: "May you be desired by men, may your hand in marriage be asked by a hundred thousand husbands!" At a certain age, the girls are deflowered ceremoniously by Buddhist or Taoist priests. This ceremony is performed on daughters of the rich between the ages of seven and nine, and on the daughters of the poor by the age of eleven.

When a woman marries, cloth is usually given . . . Marriage often occurs between a man and his former mistress to no one's . . . shame.

THE INHABITANTS: The king has five wives, one for his apartment and one for each point of the compass. As for concubines and palace girls, I have heard mentioned that there may be as many as three to five thousand, divided into various classes, but they rarely come out. The times when I saw the king, he came out with his first wife and sat at the golden window of his private apartments. The palace women ranged themselves below the window waiting their turn to look. . . . Any family blessed with a beautiful daughter brings her to the palace.

There are female palace attendants of lower status, and they number at least one or two thousand. They all are married and live among the people. But they shave the front part of their hair in the fashion of northern people and place there a vermilion mark, as well as one on each temple. This is their distinctive mark. They have access to the palace as ordinary women do not, and they are always passing to and fro on the roads near the palace. These palace women also wear hairpins, combs, and hair ornaments, as well as bracelets and gold rings.

JUSTICE: The king listens to all legal disputes, even minor ones. In cases of a major crime, the criminal is placed in a ditch outside the west gate, and earth and stones are heaped on top of him, and this is the end. Smaller crimes are sometimes punished by toes, fingers, or nose being cut off. Debauchery and gambling are not forbidden . . .

If a corpse is found in the streets, it is dragged by ropes to some waste area outside the city, but no real investigation is made. Whoever catches a robber may himself imprison and forcibly question him.

THE MAYA OF YUCATAN: The Indians of Yucatan are a race of pleasing appearance and of tall stature, robust and very strong, but generally bowlegged, since in their childhood their mothers carry them from one place to another astride on their hips. . . . They did not grow beards, and they said that their mothers burned their faces in their childhood with hot cloths, so as to keep the beard from growing; but now they grow beards, though very rough, like horsehair. . . .

The Indian women of Yucatan are generally better looking than Spanish women and larger and well made, for they do not have such large loins as the black women. . . . They are not white but of a yellowish brown color, caused more by the sun and by their constant bathing than from their nature. They do not make up their faces as our nation does and they consider this immodest. . . . They wore their hair very long, they made of it and still make of it a very elegant headdress with the hair divided into two parts, and they plaited their hair for another kind of coiffure. The careful mothers devote themselves to looking after the hair of the young girls who are ready to be married with so much attention, that I have seen many Indian women with as well cared-for hair as that of careful Spanish women. They dress the hair of the little girls, until they reach a certain size, in four or two horns, which are very becoming to them. . . . [The men] tattooed their bodies, and the more they do this, the more brave and valiant are they considered, as tattooing is accompanied with great suffering, and is done in this way. Those who do the work first painted the part which they wish with color and afterward they delicately cut in the paintings, and so with the blood and coloring matter the marks remain in the body. This work is done a little at a time on account of the extreme pain, and afterward also they were quite sick with it, since the designs festered and matter formed. In spite of all this they made fun of those who were not tattooed. . . .

They bathed frequently without taking the trouble to hide their nakedness from the women, except what the hand could cover.

They were great lovers of perfumes, and for this they used bouquets of flowers and odoriferous herbs, arranged with great care.

CHICHEN ITZA: Chichen Itza, then, is a very fine site, ten leagues from Izamal, and eleven from Vallodolid, in which, as the old men of the Indians say, three lords who were brothers ruled, who as they remember to have heard from their ancestors came to that country from the west, and brought together in those localities a great population of towns and peoples; whom they governed in great peace and justice for some years. They were devoted worshipers of their god; and so they erected many and magnificent buildings, and especially one, which was the largest, of which I will here give a sketch, as I drew it when I was there, so that it can be better understood. . . . This building had around it, and still has today, many other well built and large buildings and the ground between it and them covered with cement, so that there are even traces of the cemented places, so hard is the mortar of which they make them there. At some distance in front of the staircase on the north, there were two small stages of hewn stone, with four staircases paved on the top, where . . . farces were represented and comedies for the pleasure of the public.

THE
LAND
OF THE
KHMERS

Deep in the jungles of central Cambodia stands the vast temple city of Angkor Thom, with its dazzling towers and richly sculptured walls, its rows of columns and carved figures and serenely smiling Buddhas. Although it was abandoned to the jungle only five hundred years ago, it recalls an age that is millenniums away from us in spirit, for its builders were inspired by religious and magical impulses similar to those that raised the lofty ziggurat of Marduk at Babylon and the temple of Amen-Re, king of gods, at Thebes. When Angkor Thom was built, Europeans were constructing cities of quite a different kind, dominated by cathedrals such as Chartres, Cologne, and Salisbury, but still essentially secular, like cities of today. But on the other side of the world at the same period, among a Cambodian race known as the Khmers, the spirit that had animated the most ancient civilizations was still alive, and an entire city of faith, whose import and purpose might have been understandable to Ramesses and Nebuchadnezzar, rose high above the jungles of Cambodia.

This is not to suggest that there was any direct contact between the civilizations of the ancient Near East and that of Cambodia (although scholars can trace the diffusion of ideas throughout the Asiatic world). By the time that Angkor Thom was built at the turn of the thirteenth century A.D., these cultures were separated by thousands of miles and thousands of years. Their art, religion, and social customs had developed along distinct and separate lines. But in both areas, as in so many ancient places, a similar sequence of events produced comparable results: a fertile land and an industrious people created wealth; an emerging social order organized

The roots of banyan and silk-cotton trees, as if poured from above, still hold many Khmer shrines in their grasp; the ensnared temple **ruin at left** *was once a small shrine outside the Khmer capital.*

labor, skill, and craftsmanship and channeled the economic potential of the country into relatively few hands. Pre-eminence was given, as always, to a highly complex religion in which the gods were worshiped through a process of magic and ritual that only the educated and powerful understood. The kings were venerated as incarnations of the gods; and they were accepted as such by millions of people, who wore out their lives in the endless labor of constructing and adorning the temples and tombs of their divine rulers.

The awesome monuments raised by that labor can still be seen. Visitors accustomed to the splendors of Egypt, Greece, and Rome stand in bewildered silence before the vast temples, lakes, and terraces at Angkor Thom and the neighboring Angkor Wat. Even today when a modern aircraft deposits the casual tourist within a short distance of the ruins, their impact is overwhelming. How much more wonderful they must have seemed to the French explorer Henri Mouhot when he came upon them just over one hundred years ago, in what was then one of the most remote countries of the world. To him the ruins of Angkor Wat were "far more grandiose than anything built in the heyday of Greek or Roman art . . ."

What was even more astonishing to Mouhot was to discover such glory buried in the tropical jungle, among people with only a vague memory of its former significance. When Mouhot asked them who built the temples and the miles of walls that rose here and there amid the choking vegetation, he received various polite but puzzling replies:

"They built themselves."

"We owe these buildings to the Leper King."

"It is the work of giants" (as the Dorian Greeks had long before said of the ruins of Mycenae).

"It is the work of the King-of-the-Angels, my Lord."

Returning later to the site, the awed explorer looked across

a vast artificial moat, more than six hundred feet wide, upon a panorama filled with walls and towers, terrace upon terrace, all reflected in the calm surface of the moat. Those walls were over two miles in circumference. Inside them, within a cloistered gallery, a sculptured relief extended for almost half a mile, covered with portraits of gods, warriors, and kings, with scenes from ancient Hindu religious epics and representations of incidents and personages from the contemporary history of the Khmers. These reliefs surrounded the main part of the temple, which was approached by staircases that rivaled those of Versailles in grandeur.

Mouhot did not know that he had come upon the temple-tomb of Angkor Wat, perhaps the finest achievement of the Khmer civilization, which for centuries had flourished so brilliantly in Cambodia—a civilization that found its noblest expression in art and in architecture.

The beautifully ornamented gallery of Angkor Wat, a splendid monument in itself, surrounded a colossal stone structure that was surmounted by five towers. This was the main temple at the very center of the shrine; around it the whole vast complex had been built. Its towers once surveyed a rich and carefully planned landscape—palaces and roadways, canals and artificial lakes, and the rice fields, where the Cambodian peasants bent to their daily tasks.

From this point, in former times, one could also have seen other temples in the immediate area, along the banks of the ancient canals that cross the countryside. Now these buildings are hidden to the eye, lost amid the heavy foliage; some, despite efforts toward restoration, are still at death grips with enormous vines and tree roots powerful enough to break stone. Doorways, heavy with decoration, have been toppled by the intrusive vegetation, and stone carvings that once gleamed new and bright in the Cambodian sunshine have

acquired a patina of moss and lichen until they are almost unnoticeable on the forest floor.

The results of this titanic struggle between stone and the living jungle can be observed in every part of Angkor by the modern tourist, but at least he can comfort himself with an assurance that great and lasting efforts have been made to preserve these unique monuments and isolate them from the overwhelming jungle that surrounds them. Mouhot had no such assurance, and it is largely due to the interest his writings aroused that the French authorities, who ruled Cambodia at the time, exerted themselves to save the ruins of Angkor Wat and the even larger royal capital of Angkor Thom.

Mouhot himself died of a tropical fever contracted in Cambodia, never knowing, perhaps, the full significance of his discovery. He had written: ". . . to obtain any idea of its splendor one must imagine the most beautiful creations of architecture transported into the depths of the forests in one of the most remote countries of the world . . . incomparable ruins, the only remaining signs, alas, of a lost race, whose very name, like those of the great men, rulers, and artists who adorned it, seems destined to remain forever hidden among the rubbish and dust . . ."

If Mouhot could return today, he would be both surprised and gratified to find out how much of the civilization has been reconstructed on the basis of archaeological research. Thanks mainly to the work of his countrymen, the forgotten world of the Khmers has emerged again into the light. Scholars have pieced together evidence from many sources: from the numerous inscriptions and reliefs carved on temples throughout the area; from reports that were written by ancient travelers, Indian, Arab, and Chinese, who visited Cambodia or lived there; and from folk traditions and anthropological research. Restoration of the monuments has from the first been

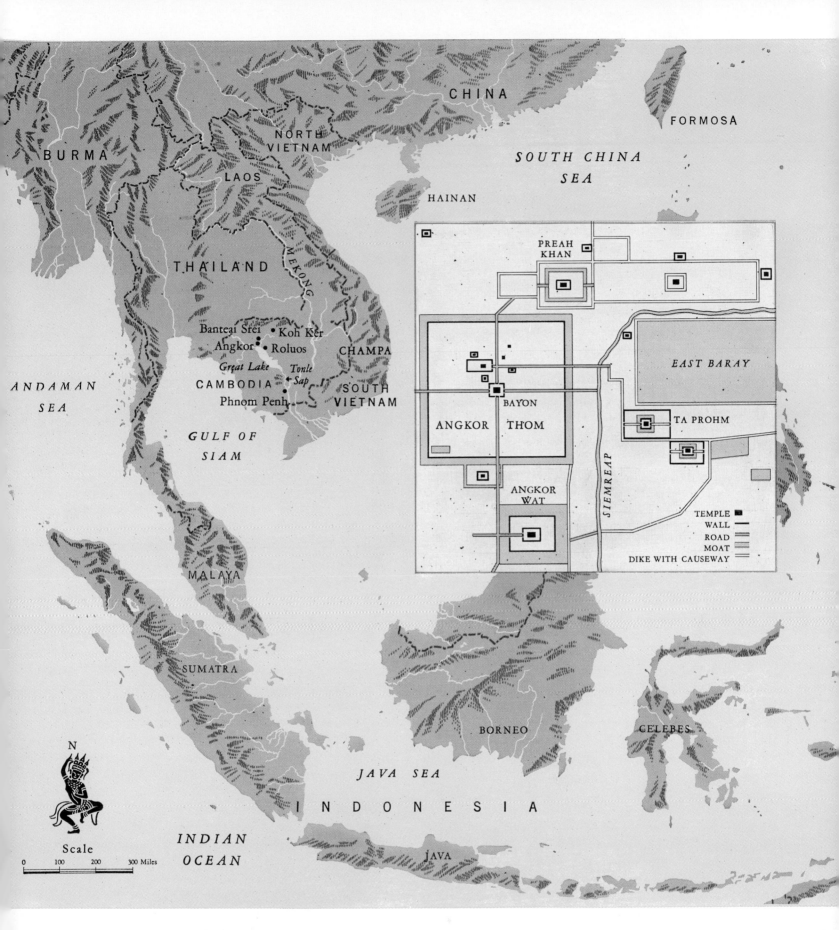

CHINA

FORMOSA

BURMA

NORTH
VIETNAM

LAOS

SOUTH CHINA
SEA

HAINAN

THAILAND

MEKONG

Banteai Srei • Koh Ker
Angkor • • Roluos
CHAMPA
Great Lake
Tonle
Sap
SOUTH
VIETNAM
CAMBODIA
Phnom Penh

ANDAMAN
SEA

GULF OF
SIAM

MALAYA

SUMATRA

N

Scale
0   100   200   300 Miles

INDIAN
OCEAN

JAVA SEA

INDONESIA

BORNEO

CELEBES

JAVA

PREAH
KHAN

EAST BARAY

ANGKOR THOM

BAYON

TA PROHM

SIEMREAP

ANGKOR
WAT

TEMPLE
WALL
ROAD
MOAT
DIKE WITH CAUSEWAY

*One of the first Khmer kings moved his capital five times for security against
invasion. In addition to that early building activity, every monarch was obligated
to construct a temple complex when he took the throne; the custom of building
shrines was also popular among members of the court. Because of these various
motivations to build Cambodia was covered with temples, cities, and systems of
moats and canals. The most continuously occupied and rebuilt state center was at
Angkor, where both the city Angkor Thom and the temple Angkor Wat stand.
The land between the region's clustered temples was interlaced with waterways.*

carried out with the techniques of modern archaeology.

The result is an astonishing picture of a great civilization flourishing in southeast Asia at a time when the area was virtually unknown to Europeans, of Khmer techniques of agriculture, irrigation, hydraulic engineering, architecture, sculpture, and metalwork that equal and occasionally surpass those of the world's other great ancient civilizations.

Yet the ordinary European or American, confronted for the first time with the products of Khmer civilization, may be struck by their alien character; mixed with admiration for their beauty, he feels a sense of mystery, a lack of kinship. Even Mouhot, European that he was, perhaps unwittingly chose the term *grandiose* in comparing Angkor with Greek and Roman art. One could put several dozen Greek temples and the imperial palaces of Rome into the Angkor group and leave room for other monuments. But for Europeans Angkor is quite unlike the Parthenon, the palace at Knossos, or the temple at Karnak. With all these, even those most remote from us in time and spirit, we can feel some sense of kinship because their creators helped to mold our own civilization. With Angkor we cannot experience so close a tie.

The enormous and mysterious structures that rise above the Cambodian jungle overwhelm us by their sheer size, and dazzle the mind with the complexity of their ground plans, too great for the eye to encompass. Their intricate decoration is filled with art motifs unfamiliar to men born in the Western world. Their reliefs, depicting exotic myths and the events of unknown times, are carved with more naturalism than those of other cultures that are further from us in time, and yet they seem infinitely more remote. Why?

Possibly because the Khmer civilization, like others that arose in southeast Asia, drew its historical inspiration from India, which until recently also remained separate from Western culture. The Khmer gods were those of India: Brahma, Vishnu, Siva, and later on, Buddha, as well as the myriad lesser deities of Indian religious tradition.

The Khmer mythology came from India, derived directly from that of the Hindus and Buddhists. Even the towering pyramidal structure of Khmer temples was Hindu in origin, symbolizing the mountain that was the legendary home of the gods. The approaches to many of these temples are flanked by stone figures that depict a Hindu creation myth, the Churning of the Sea of Milk, out of which arose the Ambrosia of Life. Side by side with these Brahmanic myths occur those associated with Buddha, who had never claimed to be a god, although his followers developed a divine mythology about him. The classic, enigmatic faces of Buddhas appear in countless places at Angkor Thom, carved sometimes in giant scale, as on the four-faced towers of the Bayon, the central temple of the city. Yet, Indian-influenced though it was, the civilization created by the ancient Khmers was to become uniquely their own.

By the beginning of the Christian era, Hindu civilization as we know it, with its Brahmanic religion, its law, literature, architecture, and sculpture, had not only penetrated all of India, but had been carried eastward and southward to what are now Burma, Thailand, Malaya, and the Indonesian islands. In some of these countries hybrid cultures, part Indian, part indigenous, had grown up, several of which were to erect lasting monuments. The temple cities of Anuradhapura and Polonnaruva in Ceylon, and Pagan in Burma, and the Barabudur in Java are among the impressive remains of these ancient cultures.

It was during this formative period from the first to the sixth centuries A.D. that the Khmer kingdom began its rise. At this time, the area now comprising Thailand, Cambodia,

and southern Vietnam belonged to several races, including those speaking the Mon-Khmer group of languages still used in parts of Burma and Cambodia. Cambodia formed part of a powerful state (called Funan by the Chinese) that was strongly influenced by India's culture and by its spiritual ideals. By about A.D. 550 a Khmer prince had seized control of the entire country of Funan, of which Chenla, the Khmer homeland, formed but one part. From this time onward, Chinese historians no longer write of Funan but of the land known as Chenla, kingdom of Bhavavarman, the man who became the first great ruler of the Khmer people.

During the next three centuries there were successive and, in the main, successful attempts by the Khmer kings to aggrandize their power. Their names, strange to our ears, such as Mahendravarman and Isanavarman, are of importance to scholars but of small interest to lay readers; little is known about the personal lives of most of the monarchs, for their chronicles are primarily records of war and conquests and wrangles over the succession to the throne.

Occasionally these dry chronicles are illuminated by a legend. One, related by a ninth-century Arab traveler to the Orient, tells how the Khmers became subject for a period to the ruler of the neighboring island of Java.

A young king, newly ascended to the Khmer throne, was jealous of Javanese power. "I have one desire, which I would like to satisfy," he announced, ". . . I wish to see before me on a plate the head of the Maharajah, King of Zabag (Java). . . . The statement passed from mouth to mouth until it came to the knowledge of the Maharajah." To avenge this insult, he made secret preparations to invade the country of his enemy, but disguised his real intentions by pretending only to be taking a trip among his islands. He landed by surprise and took the young king prisoner. Bringing him captive

before his throne, he said to him: "You have manifested the desire to see before you my head on a plate . . . I am going to apply to you the treatment you wished to apply to me and I will then return to my country, without taking anything belonging to Khmer, either of great or small value." And after that, "The Kings of the Khmer, every morning on rising, turn the face in the direction of Zabag, incline themselves to the earth and humiliate themselves before the Maharajah to render him homage."

Then, in the eighth century A.D., a new king, Jayavarman II, came to the throne and declared his independence of Java; he ruled for sixty years, establishing so strong a foundation for the Khmer empire that it grew and prospered for centuries thereafter. It was during Jayavarman's reign that the name Kambuja, from which the modern word Cambodia is derived, came into common use.

The king's first preoccupation was to find a suitable place for his capital, one which would not be vulnerable to foreign attack. He experimented with several sites before deciding on the summit of a mountain called Phnom Kulen close to the site on which Angkor later rose. There he induced a Brahman "skilled in magic science" to perform a ceremony designed to rid Kambuja forever of foreign danger and establish her as an independent state. This ceremony endowed the king with the creative energy of Siva, the Hindu god who is both creator and destroyer. From this time on, the king of the Khmers was considered divine and was worshiped as a deity, the link between mankind and the spirits of nature. This concept of divine kingship, which underlay all ideas of religion and government in Cambodia, was what gave the civilization of the Khmers its distinctive form.

The identification of the king with the forces of nature is illustrated by a Cambodian legend, which relates that in later

times Khmer kings kept a tall golden tower in their sleeping apartments at Angkor into which they were obliged to retire for a time each night. Here was said to exist the spirit of the kingdom, a nine-headed serpent that appeared in the form of a woman; only after the king entered the tower and united with the spirit was he allowed to visit with his wives. If the divine spirit failed to appear, or the king neglected to keep his appointment, a disaster was said to threaten the kingdom.

Throughout much of Cambodian history the king's divine power was represented by a linga, a sacred stone pillar shaped like a phallus, that symbolized the creative power of Siva. What may appear to us as a mere theological abstraction involved the Khmers in titanic works of architecture, for each king felt impelled by religious custom to house the royal linga in larger and larger temples, dedicated to himself as the god. When Jayavarman's successors inherited his divine title, they embarked upon ambitious building programs supported by the great natural wealth of the country and by tribute from their vassals. The original mountain capital had been abandoned when conditions became safer, and to the north of the Tonle Sap, the great lake of Cambodia, sacred cities and temples arose, consecrated to the cult of god-kings.

A group of priests, a horde of lesser dignitaries, and whole villages were dedicated to the maintenance of these temples and to the religious ceremonies centered about them. Later, when Buddhism became the official religion at Angkor, the figure of a bodhisattva came to personify the divine king, as the linga had done earlier. The great carved heads of the Bayon temple at Angkor Thom which are generally thought to depict the monarch Jayavarman VII (who ruled from A.D. 1181 to 1215) are a magnificent fusion of royal portraiture with the representation of a compassionate Buddhist divinity, who had reached Nirvana but postponed

his own entry into this heavenly state of non-being in order that he might aid the rest of mankind.

It is to these syncretistic cults that we owe the sacred city of Angkor Thom, built in its present form at the end of the twelfth century, and the nearby temple-tomb of Angkor Wat, which was erected by the king Suryavarman II in the first part of the same century. At the time that the monuments at Angkor were built, the wealth and power of the Khmer kingdom were at their height. In Europe, during the same period, there were few nations that could have rivaled Cambodia. Suryavarman constructed temples throughout the land and in regions of Laos and Thailand under his control; his tomb of Angkor Wat is universally considered the most beautiful of all Khmer buildings. But it was during the reign of Jayavarman VII, the last great Khmer king, that the civilization of the Khmers flourished most splendidly. Jayavarman was a zealous religious reformer who established Buddhism as the dominant religion in Cambodia; Angkor Thom and many other shrines throughout the kingdom still commemorate his devotion. His vast building program made his reign the most productive period in the history of Khmer art, and under his leadership Cambodia became the strongest state in southeast Asia.

The Khmers had never been freed from the necessity of waging foreign wars. The most frequent were with the neighboring Indochinese kingdom of Champa, with which Cambodia long maintained an uneasy balance of power. Indeed, Khmer history is primarily a record of wars, most of them unimportant, against the peoples of Champa, Burma, Thailand, and Laos. When Jayavarman came to the throne, the Chams, who had recently sacked Angkor, were expelled from Cambodia, and Khmer armies overran parts of Thailand, Burma, and Malaya. Jayavarman even claimed sovereignty over Java. But his empire was an insecure one. Although

Hinduism and Buddhism lived side by side in ancient Cambodia, providing the mystical formulas by which ruling Khmer monarchs were deified as Vishnu, Siva, or Buddha. Nevertheless, indigenous Cambodian legends survived, such as the story of the leper king. According to one version, the ruler was contaminated by drops of serpent blood which spattered upon him as he wrestled with a giant snake. The relief from the Bayon at right apparently depicts this struggle. Hindu mythology often casts the serpent in a more benign role. The relief from Angkor Wat at left portrays the Hindu legend of the Churning of the Sea of Milk; the serpent helps Vishnu procure immortality for the Khmers in the form of ambrosia from the milky sea.

Cambodia was usually able to maintain a formidable army, led by officers who rode into battle mounted on elephants, the Khmer monarchs never succeeded in controlling the lands beyond their own frontiers for any extended period of time.

A remarkable and comprehensive account of Khmer life a century after the reign of Jayavarman VII has come down to us, written by a Chinese envoy to Angkor named Chou Ta-kuan. Through his somewhat supercilious eyes, for to him all non-Chinese were barbarians, we can see the sculptured reliefs of Angkor come to life and take on human flesh. In a famous passage, Chou Ta-kuan describes a royal procession: ". . . the king appears, standing on an elephant and holding the precious sword in his hand. The tusks of his elephant are sheathed in gold, and the other elephants mill around him while troops protect him. He is escorted by more than twenty white parasols, decorated with gold and with gold handles. If the king is traveling to a nearby spot, he may simply use a golden palanquin carried by palace girls. Most of the time the king leaves the palace to visit a small gold pagoda with a gold statue of Buddha in front of it. Those who see the king must prostrate themselves, touching their foreheads to the ground . . . they would be punished if they failed to do so."

Perhaps the most enchanting of all these pictures is that drawn by the same Chinese envoy when he describes the appearance of the king at a small window of the palace to hear the petitions of his subjects: "Twice a day, for the affairs of government, the king holds an audience. There are no fixed laws and those who come to consult, officials and ordinary people, must sit on the ground and wait for him to appear. After awhile, distant music can be heard from the direction of the palace . . . Moments later, the curtain is lifted by the slender fingers of two palace girls, and the king appears standing at the window of gold with his sword in

his hand. People and ministers join their hands and touch their foreheads to the ground and may only raise them when the music ceases. Where the king sits is the royal lion skin—a hereditary treasure. When the audience is terminated, the king leaves, and the two girls let the curtain fall. Everyone rises. So one sees that though this may be a kingdom of barbarians they know full well the meaning of royalty . . ."

Life in Cambodia in the thirteenth century was probably little different from what it is today. Then, as now, the people around the great cities lived by agriculture and fishing. The great lake of Cambodia, the Tonle Sap, is a natural reservoir, accommodating the rise of the Mekong, that long and powerful river that flows down from the mountains of southern China and spans the Indochinese peninsula. The lake abounds with fish, and when its waters are low, an enormous food supply is readily available. Fed by monsoon rains, the river was diverted in a thousand ways through the flat and fertile plains of Cambodia, where broad fields of rice, millet, and innumerable other crops were capable of supporting a considerable population, one so large that a ninth-century Arab traveler was inspired to write that "There is no country which possesses a more numerous population than the Khmer." The knowledge of the art of irrigation had come early to Cambodia, and the Khmers became expert at building huge water catchments—dams and canals—as well as pleasure lakes and temple moats. Impressive remains of such hydraulic works still survive.

Along with their cereal crops, the people of Angkor tended groves of banana, orange, and pomegranate trees and other tropical fruits. They gathered aromatic wood from aloe, storax, and sandalwood trees. There was a commercial trade oddly enough in rhinoceros horns, probably used for an aphrodisiac, and in blue kingfisher feathers, which were gath-

Many Angkorean temples were reconstructed by a method known as anastylosis. Banteai Srei was the first Khmer shrine restored by this technique, which begins with extensive photography of a ruined monument, followed by the dismantling of whatever part of it still stands. When the foundations are traced out and every fragment identified, the building is put back together, stone by stone, like a giant jigsaw puzzle. The relief at right once ornamented a Banteai Srei entranceway, but the portal itself had disappeared long before reconstruction began. As a result, the carved stones were sent to a museum in France. They depict the story of a damsel sent by the gods to divert two demons who were disrupting world order.

ered by Khmer hunters, who waited silently in the thickets beside forest pools in order to trap the birds.

The land, another Chinese observer wrote, "encloses great marshes, with a climate so hot that one never sees snow or ice. The soil there engenders pestilential exhalations and swarms of venomous insects." In this climate, the Khmers often contracted leprosy, which Chou Ta-kuan blandly attributes to the fact that they indulged too frequently in love-making and in bathing directly thereafter. Chou Ta-kuan's record of the tradition that "a former king contracted leprosy, which is why people do not scorn lepers . . ." is an interesting confirmation of one of the answers which Mouhot received when he asked who had built the temples of Angkor, and was told that it was the Leper King.

Wildlife was prolific throughout the land; elephants, tigers, and rhinoceroses were common, and crocodiles infested the rivers. Snakes no doubt abounded; as in so many other ancient cultures, they had been both feared and worshiped from ancient times. Symbols and representations of the *naga* (the Sanskrit word for snake) are one of the most characteristic of Khmer art motifs.

Chinese travelers speak of the valuable minerals of Cambodia, as well as its abundant wildlife. Gold, silver, copper, and tin are mentioned, and pearls, ivory, coral, and glass were offered as tribute. Gold seems to have come from the rivers of southern Laos, and iron was found in the Cambodian mountains, but some of the other minerals may have been imported. Chou Ta-kuan, who may have visited Cambodia as a commercial attaché, goes into great detail about which products of the land might be profitably exported.

Such was the physical environment of the land of the Khmers. But what did the people look like, and how did the ordinary person live? To Chou Ta-kuan, of course, all Cam-

bodians looked alike. They were the same everywhere, he claimed, "on islands in the sea, or on the busiest streets." He did manage to distinguish the aristocrats, however. In the noble homes some of the men and women were "as white as jade," because they never went out in the sun.

The houses of the nobles were of a different size and character than those of the ordinary people, and a person's rank could immediately be determined by the size and grandeur of his dwelling. The king's palace was roofed with lead tiles, those of the nobles with clay, and the common people's houses with thatch. Costumes also indicated rank and many of the legends of Cambodia are concerned with these social distinctions. (Khmer society seems to have consisted of a number of different groups each somewhat isolated from the rest by variations in rank and ritual practice.) A charming Chinese story, dating from a pre-Khmer period, describes how the Cambodians were persuaded to adopt the characteristic costume worn by aristocrats in earliest times.

At the beginning, Funan had for a sovereign a woman named Lin-yeh (Willow-leaf). Willow-leaf was celebrated for her beauty and strength. She clad herself "only in sunbeams," and so appeared to a young man named Hun T'ien who arrived suddenly by ship. The young queen and her followers promptly attacked the ship, but Hun T'ien possessed a divine bow and arrow with which he pierced the queen's ship from side to side. Willow-leaf surrendered and soon after married the young man. Hun T'ien appears to have been something of a prig, however; he was shocked by his bride's nakedness, which he regarded as a sign of barbarism. He designed a costume for the queen and her subjects consisting of a "fold of cloth, with a hole through which she passed her head, and made her do her hair up in a knot."

Another Chinese writer of the same period, some three

centuries before the Khmer period, confirms this by saying: "The sons of the well-to-do families wear sarongs of brocade . . . the women pull a piece of cloth over the head." He continued: "The people of Funan make rings and bracelets of gold and vessels of silver. They cut down trees to build their houses . . . when the king goes out, he rides an elephant. For amusement the people have cockfights . . . they have no prisons. In cases of dispute, they throw rings or eggs into boiling water," and only the innocent could remove them.

Such trials by ordeal were common, and at Angkor, Chou Ta-kuan reported, there were two towers on top of which disputing parties sat. "He who is guilty does not fail to sicken; either he gets ulcers, or he catches a cold or a malignant fever. The innocent party remains quite healthy."

In the early Cambodian state of Chenla it was "the custom of the inhabitants to go about always armored and under arms," another Chinese traveler, Ma Tuan-lin, noted. "The least quarrel entails bloody combats. . . . The men are small and black but many women are white. All roll up their hair in a chignon and wear ear-pendants. They are of a lively and robust temperament. . . . They make ablutions each morning, clean their teeth with little pieces of poplar wood and do not fail to read or recite their prayers . . ." These customs undoubtedly survived in Cambodia in later times.

The life of the court was centered about the person of the king; he was, according to one Khmer inscription, "the repository of all virtues," so superior to other beings that he remained "unmoved by the delights of kingship which drive other monarchs mad with joy." Hundreds of courtiers surrounded him, generals and judges, captains of the royal elephants, household officials and priests, and even several special attendants charged with the task of carrying his supply of betel nuts. Besides the queen consort, the other royal wives,

and "a thousand young princesses, like to the goddess of beauty," the monarch was attended by concubines and dancing girls, and a bodyguard consisting exclusively of devoted ladies, skilled in martial exercises.

Not all officials were allowed to approach the king, for the number of civil servants required to administer the complex governmental structure of Cambodia was too large to permit such easy intercourse. "Like ourselves," Chou Ta-kuan reported, "this country has counselors, generals, astronomers, etc., and below them all sorts of minor officials. Their names are different, that is all. Nobles are usually chosen for the posts, or those who have offered their daughters as royal concubines. Insignia and the number of attendants are dependent on rank. The highest dignitaries use palanquins with gold shafts and four parasols with gold handles; the next have the same palanquin, but only one or two parasols. Lesser dignitaries have silver shafts on their palanquins, or simply a silver handled parasol. The parasols are made of a red Chinese taffeta, and their fringes hang down to the ground."

This horde of government officials was mainly devoted to the administration of the land, which may have been owned by the king and distributed to its occupants by royal grant. Strong central control was required to maintain the dikes and irrigation canals that gave Cambodia its fertility and allowed it to support so large a population. (This became evident when the Khmer empire collapsed; with no central government to regulate the irrigation system, the land was neglected and became impoverished.) Kings were as concerned with extending the irrigation network as they were with building temples. Inscriptions laud monarchs who "by raising holy barrage . . . made the water to flow where before there was little or none . . . a reservoir beautiful as the moon to refresh mankind and drown the insolence of other kings."

Moss and creeping vines now clothe the carved figures that adorn the ruined walls of Angkorean temples. A devata, or female deity, is portrayed in relief at left, and the meditating figures at right are believed to represent attendants of Buddha. Sacred spirits were embodied as well in free-standing statues that were placed inside the shrines. On special occasions the sanctuary idols are said to have been carried in processions and their torsos were either gilded and bejeweled or "clad entirely in silk." The splendor of such an event can be judged by the possessions of a single sanctuary, which were said to include 35 diamonds, 40,620 pearls, 512 beds of silk, and 967 Chinese veils; for one festival, 165,744 candles were burned.

Between the class of officials, with its parasols and palanquins, and the mass of ordinary people who tended the soil, there was an immense distance. The irrigation system eased the peasants' life, but their labor still was hard, and their possessions were meager. Chou Ta-kuan catalogues their goods. "Ordinary people have a house," he writes, "but no table, bench, basin, or bucket. They simply use a clay pot for cooking rice and besides that a clay frying pan for preparing the sauce. They bury three stones to make the hearth and use the shell of a coconut for a ladle. . . . To serve the sauce, they use leaves from trees, of which they make little cups which, even when full of liquid, let nothing spill over. . . . The homes of the nobles or the rich have for each person silver or even gold containers."

The elaborately beautiful dress of the men and women depicted on the Angkor reliefs was almost surely confined to the ruling aristocracy. Certainly women of rank no longer wore the mere "fold of cloth with a hole in it" prescribed for Willow-leaf. All classes of women, however, even the king's wives, went about barefoot.

At Angkor women controlled much of the commercial life. "In this country," Chou Ta-kuan marvels, "it is the women who do the trading." His own countrymen were quick to take full advantage of that fact. "If a Chinese first thing upon arriving here takes a wife, it is, among other things, to profit from her commercial aptitudes. Each day the market opens at six and closes at noon. There are no little shops in which people live, but they use a sort of straw mat which they spread out on the ground. Each has his own spot. I have heard tell that a person pays the authorities to rent his spot. In the smaller transactions, the payment is rice, cereals, and Chinese objects; next are cloth goods; and for the large transactions gold or silver is used."

Rich or poor, all the women of the city of Angkor, including those of noble birth, periodically gathered together in enormous numbers to bathe in the nearby river. Describing the scene, Chou Ta-kuan gives the impression of great hilarity, in which the women "have no shame about leaving their clothes on the river bank and going into the water." He adds, with a straight face, that the Chinese in Cambodia, in their leisure time, amuse themselves by watching.

But there was a more sober side to Khmer life in the time of Chou Ta-kuan. For many centuries, the Cambodian kings had been able to satisfy their mania for building, but eventually they exhausted the nation's resources; the frequent wars they waged against neighboring lands resulted in a depopulation of the countryside. By A.D. 1296, when the Chinese envoy visited Angkor, the Khmer empire was already beginning to disintegrate. "In the recent wars with the Siamese," he writes, "the countryside was completely devastated."

Under the Mongol kings of China, most notably Kublai Khan, most of the states of Indochina had been forced to acknowledge the Chinese as their overlords; indeed, Chou Ta-kuan had come to Angkor attached to a diplomatic mission that was attempting to establish his nation's influence in Cambodia. Threatened by the Chinese and attacked by the warlike Thai tribesmen who were immigrating into the region, the Khmer were unable to maintain their dominant position in Indochina. Finally, in the fifteenth century, when a raid by the Siamese coincided with the death of the Cambodian king and the defection of many powerful nobles and priests, the city of Angkor was abandoned. It is true, however, that Cambodia remained a force in the southeastern part of Asia for several centuries more.

But long before Angkor itself was abandoned the great age of Cambodian civilization had already come to an end. Why?

Warfare and the craze for construction are not the only explanations. Perhaps, as has been suggested, the Khmer people, now converted to Buddhism, with its disregard of human endeavor, would no longer continue to build splendid monuments one after another. Certainly no building had been erected at Angkor for two centuries before its fall. After the reign of Jayavarman VII, the god-king no longer commanded the devotion necessary to construct enormous temples in his honor, and it appears that the people in some cases mutilated their temples so that they would not have to devote their lives to temple maintenance. The ardor had disappeared, leaving a tired and bewildered people, who at least found ease in the mild religion of Buddha, devoted to poverty, peace of soul, and social tranquillity. As the French scholar Louis Finot has observed about Buddhism: "The Khmer people accepted [such a religion], one may believe, without repugnance, and willingly laid down the crushing burden of their glory."

Sculpture and architecture are practically all we have by which to judge the glory of the Khmer achievement. But the myriad carved reliefs of Angkor and the vast temple complexes are testimony enough. Perhaps no other group of buildings in the world boasts such richness of sculptural decoration, complexity of planning, and sheer size. They are the culmination of a long tradition in Khmer architecture, which developed out of constructions of timber, brick, and stone built long before the time that the monuments at Angkor were begun. The earliest buildings being entirely of wood have, of course, disappeared, but in a few places "primitive Khmer" structures still survive, mainly remains of brick-built shrines faced with stone. Later, after the beginning of the ninth century A.D., magnificent stone-built temples were erected at a number of places that preceded Angkor Thom as the capital of the kingdom.

These temples were the homes of the gods, and were embellished accordingly with figures of dancing girls whose performances amused the gods, statues of guardian deities, and hundreds of garlands, carved in stone, that recalled the flowers that had traditionally been offered upon the altars. Though modeled in stone, much of this decoration was as delicately carved as the wooden ornamentation upon the earliest Khmer temples, which indeed it was supposed to imitate.

Within the temple rested the ashes of the god-king for whom the building had been erected, and sometimes those of certain favored officials as well. At Angkor Wat, the entrance door faces the west, the direction in which the sun sets, the direction of the dead in Khmer as well as in Egyptian tradition. But Angkor Wat and the other Khmer temples are equally noteworthy for their representations of life. The dancing girls, or *apsaras,* with their ornate headdresses, who dance in groups of twos and threes along the whole length of the walls of Angkor Wat; the elephants and warriors within the Bayon; the scenes that depict a woman in childbirth or a dwarf sounding a gong, make it apparent that the interests of the Khmers were not confined to other-worldly pursuits, as one might have imagined from their religion.

Yet there is an other-worldly aura to the art of the Khmers, and not only because of its exoticism to Western eyes. To those who believed in the concept of reincarnation, the body was unimportant; in Cambodia sometimes it was cremated after death and sometimes merely left to rot. It was the soul that counted. Even in the highly naturalistic reliefs, in which one can almost see the faces of peasants who labor in the Cambodian fields today, there is a harmonious repose suggesting that artists were trying to portray the soul as well as the body.

The years when Angkor Wat was built mark the classic age of Khmer art. A few decades later, when Jayavarman VII constructed Angkor Thom, "Angkor the Great," architecture was dominated by a mania for colossal size and extravagant display, although sculpture was often more naturalistic than it had been in earlier times. At Angkor Thom Jayavarman erected an enormous temple, the Bayon, topped with fifty or more towers each of which had its four sides modeled in the shape of a gigantic face, to represent the king himself either as Buddha or as the bodhisattva Lokesvara. Enormous stone faces were everywhere in the Bayon, so that the very buildings themselves seemed to be alive. Outside the gates of Angkor Thom stood other figures—rows of giants, carved of stone and holding an enormous serpent in their arms. The serpent's body began at the north gate, and when the site was viewed from a distance, seemed to extend into the town, coil itself around the central tower, and emerge from the opposite gate. The gates themselves were massive, and were supported by the figures of elephants, each of which had three heads and three trunks reaching to the ground. On one terrace within the town, a procession of elephants carved along the walls extended for fifteen hundred feet.

At Angkor Thom, the Khmer sculptors and architects improvised with a freedom that had been denied to them in building the earlier shrine of Angkor Wat. The buildings themselves, despite their lively ornamentation, have a monumentality almost brutal in its impact. But, like some of the late temples at Karnak in Egypt, they were built in a slipshod way, without the careful craftsmanship that had marked the classic periods of both civilizations. Angkor had become decadent, and its kings, increasingly alienated from the nation which surrounded them, were to become imprisoned by their own religion, and dominated by a priestly caste, as the rulers of Egypt had been two millenniums before.

There are no epic poems, hymns, personal letters, or legal codes that have come down to us from Angkor. Although the palaces of Nebuchadnezzar and Ramesses II are now mere mounds of crumbling brick, we know more about the thoughts of the people who built them than we do about the Khmers. Scholars can show us lapidary inscriptions in Khmer or Sanskrit, but these turn out to be little more than complex official chronicles and religious odes, vivid occasionally but difficult to penetrate. There are no papyri, no baked-clay tablets like those that put us in direct touch with the schoolboys or lovers or merchants of Egypt and Mesopotamia. No beautiful Khmer princess calls out to us across the centuries, "You have many sons . . . send me one that he may be my husband . . ."

At Angkor we must rely on the hundreds of carved reliefs, and most impressive of all, on those endless, empty, stone-flagged avenues under the forest trees, stone staircases sweeping to the sky, stone faces wearing their tranquil smiles; and always, as a background, the croaking of frogs in the moat, the chatter of monkeys, and the flapping and crying of startled birds, their brilliant colors flashing in the sunlight before they are gone to mingle indistinguishably with the color of the jungle. One is left alone with only the scent of the forest and the echo of one's own footsteps on the interminable pavements.

Above, a thousand tons of intricately carved masonry stand poised against the sky. The light stings the eyes, and one looks down again to where the stone figures of a king and his courtiers disport themselves at a palace festival. Such ancient life is all around—the life of the Khmers who walked these pavements centuries ago. Warriors in chariots and on foot, spears and shields upraised, engage their enemies and lead their captives. The stone writhes with the movement of struggling figures. A squatting man, with the face of a monkey, gazes from his pedestal. Warships clash in naval battle, fish swim endlessly across the carved panels. Fishermen drop their nets into the Tonle Sap, and peasant women sit in the market place, while youths play at gambling games.

Entering another courtyard, however, one is in the presence of an ineffable ideal, more than human, the unattainable; a god-king seated with half-closed eyes and praying hands has sloughed off all earthly desires, all that only ends in agony and frustration. He has achieved Nirvana, which is the state of non-being. Not far away, as if to console those who are left behind, are carved the bare-breasted semi-divine dancing figures, symbols of a primitive and more ancient religion, their arms upraised, fingers outstretched in the same ritual movements which still beckon and entice in the dances of Southeast Asia to the present day.

SPIRIT OF ANGKOR

The bronze Cambodian figure above, holding a builder's tool on his shoulder, is said to represent the "celestial architect." He embodies the divinely inspired impulse to build that drove the Khmers to raise temple after temple in the jungles of Cambodia, as if building were in itself an act of piety. Their temple-cities symbolized the order of the universe; at the center of each miniature cosmos stood the god-king's shrine, which was the "navel of the earth and the gateway of heaven." There the essence of the deified monarch met with the gods to gain their favor for his mortal subjects. Although founded in mysticism, the Khmers' continual construction program greatly improved the land and made it prosper. For wherever new buildings arose, canals were cleared and reservoirs were created around them; highways were cut through the jungle, and virgin fields were granted to the farmers. It is said that custom may have required newly enthroned kings to build the life-giving waterworks even before they began their temples.

THE GREAT NAGA

The serpent, or *naga*, was supreme among the animal spirits of ancient Cambodia. Snake deities were thought to dwell in the earth and to embody the spirit of the soil as well as the life-giving terrestrial waters. Khmer monarchs claimed their descent from the legendary *naga*-king's daughter, who married an Indian prince exiled from his home. To provide a dowry for the bride, the king of the *naga* swallowed the waters that covered the soil of Cambodia and gave the newly-wed couple the land.

A primitive animism remained the people's religion in Cambodia even after the state cult was formulated, first from Hinduism and later from Buddhism; these imported faiths alternated with each other as the official religion, according to the spiritual disposition of the reigning monarch. Within this Indian legacy, new *naga* legends came to Cambodia, and it is from these, rather than indigenous myths, that the most often depicted serpent motifs were taken.

In a story about the Buddha's enlightenment, it is said that during the mild season Buddha sat in a state of blissful revelation beneath the Tree of Muchalinda, the Serpent King. From his home in the soil, the giant cobra realized that the meditating savior would not notice the strangely violent storm then clouding the heavens; he emerged from the earth and coiled himself around the entranced figure, spreading a hood above him to shield him from the seven-day storm. Together the snake and the savior became the Muchalinda Buddha and represent the union of antagonistic forces; Buddha, as the spirit freed from the material bonds of life through revelation, is joined with Muchalinda, the spirit of earthly bondage in the life-death cycle. The serpent is also central to the Hindu legend, the Churning of the Sea of Milk. In this myth, the great *naga* is named Vasuki; coiled several times around Mount Mandara, which is supported by the god Vishnu, the snake is pulled from one side by eighty-eight gods, and from the other by ninety-two demons; as he is tugged back and forth, he turns the mountain that is in the cosmic sea and from it churns ambrosia, the drink of immortality. Khmer monarchs are often pictured as Vishnu, and ambrosia represents the welfare they promise their subjects.

The image of the Muchalinda Buddha (left) has lost the protective serpent hood that once framed the statue; mottled with mosslike lichen, the figure sits upon the giant snake coils.

Causeways leading into Khmer cities were often balustraded with huge snakes held by demons and gods; demons are distinguished by their downturned mouths and round eyes, gods by their gentle smiles and almond-shaped eyes. The naga *balustrade above ornaments an approach to Angkor Thom. The serpent railing could portray the legendary snake that forms a magic rainbow bridgeway from the earth to the home of the gods or depict the popular myth of the Churning of the Sea of Milk.* OVERLEAF: *Together with the mania for building, waging war may have eventually exhausted the country of the Khmers, whose kings, according to one inscription, "so delighted in battle . . . [that] the dust of their armies blotted out the sun." In a scene from one of the many Bayon reliefs, camp followers bring the provisions necessary to sustain the troops in the field.*

CITADEL
OF WOMEN

Temple inscriptions from periods of comparative peace in Khmer history tell us that "Brahmans celebrated for their wisdom and penetrating éclat" crowded the royal court. "Scholars occupied the first charges of the State . . . their daughters were queens." In such ages of learning the Khmers honored their women as much for intellectual achievement as for grace and beauty. Women are known to have held high political posts and to have served as jurists; they were lauded by contemporary Chinese writers for their knowledge of government and skill in science. According to an inscription, one woman "acquired a high position [and] the first of the royal masters, the most eminent savants, rendered homage" to her.

The ornate temple of Banteai Srei, known as the "citadel of women," was commissioned during one of these intellectual eras by a royal adviser who was "first in the knowledge of the Buddha, medicine, and astronomy"; the official's accomplished sister also inscribed a monument in the shrine to Siva. But as if to acknowledge the Khmers' frankly sensuous nature, glowing pink sandstone *apsaras,* or celestial dancers, adorn the temple walls; they are said to be the most voluptuous *apsaras* figures in all Khmer art.

Guarded by monkeys and mythical monsters, the doorways leading to the shrines of Banteai Srei (right) are less than five feet high. The miniature temple complex is characterized by elaborate ornamentation, such as is seen in the detail of the sanctuary façade at right and the foliage that frames the apsaras *shown at left.*

THE BUDDHA KING

Before he became king, Jayavarman VII had embraced the mild and humane doctrines of Buddhism. He was apparently dedicated to the avoidance of bloodshed, for when his father died and a relative contested his claim to rule Cambodia around A.D. 1170, he seems to have chosen to go into exile rather than to endanger the peace of his country in a struggle against the usurper. Temple inscriptions record that during Jayavarman's absence Cambodia "plunged into a sea of misfortunes." The throne was seized by a second usurper, and in this period devastating foreign invasions bloodied the land. The Chams, militant neighbors of the Khmers, sailed up Cambodia's rivers to the capital city itself, sacked and razed the ill-defended site, and slew the ruling monarch.

This devastation evidently roused Jayavarman from his religious pursuits, for he soon returned to "draw the earth out of this sea of misfortune into which it was plunged," and "founding himself in the law, [he] killed in combat the enemy chief with a hundred million arrows to protect the earth." Once enthroned, however, this savior king—who was worshiped as a compassionate Buddha and whose "loving care for the good of mankind" was said to be virtually limitless—launched a self-glorifying building program that seems to have bordered on megalomania. During Jayavarman VII's reign, the Cambodians constructed nearly half of the major Khmer monuments ever built. Temples rose in dedication to the king and members of the royal family; the slaving builders were no doubt grateful for the hospitals and pilgrims' inns Jayavarman commissioned, but when the Buddha-king died, he left a country sapped beyond recovery. The civilization survived for several hundred years, but the Khmers' creative need to build was never exercised again.

Considered a monarch of only minor importance until about 1900, Jayavarman VII (above) is now believed to have been the greatest of all Khmer kings. Some suggest he was also the legendary Leper King, who turned to Buddhism for relief from his affliction. He crowned Angkor Thom with the Bayon (right), from which his own image, deified as Buddha, looks out across the land in seemingly countless portrayals. The Bayon relief below may show laboring artisans.
OVERLEAF: *Even Jayavarman's monuments could not equal the almost supernatural beauty of Angkor Wat, the supreme example of the Khmer temple-mountain as the meeting place of kings and gods and the deities' earthly home.*

THE
RIDDLE
OF THE
MAYA

The mysteries that surround the story of the Maya are in many respects as inexplicable today as they appeared when the remains of their once flourishing civilization were first rediscovered in the tropical rain forests of Middle America. Archaeologists cannot yet explain, for example, why the Maya suddenly and unaccountably abandoned the ancient home of their culture, after nearly a thousand years of continuous cultural development and intellectual achievement.

It is equally perplexing that among all the early civilizations discussed in this book, the Maya alone, so far as can be determined, failed to develop truly urban centers, with their concomitant secular concerns, at any time during the period of their greatest glory. Indeed, more consistently than any other civilized people of the past, the Maya were guided by exclusively religious considerations; their heaviest labor and most refined thought were alike dedicated to their gods, and it was only when long years of relative cultural isolation ended that secularism, borne by alien influence, began to play a significant role in Maya life.

In spite of the rare genius of the Maya, they have appealed less to the popular imagination than some of the other pre-Columbian cultures that were at the peak of their development when the first white man reached the Americas and whose resistance to the Spaniards has become a part of the epic literature of the New World. At the time of the conquest, however, the great age of the Maya was but a dim memory, distorted by the decadent remnants of Maya tradition that survived in the hybrid settlements in the Yucatan.

For the next several centuries, the finest Maya monuments lay undisturbed and all but forgotten beneath a cover of

The compelling ancient portrait shown opposite represents an idealized classic Maya profile. Modeled in stucco and marked with traces of red paint, it was found in a tomb at Palenque.

jungle growth. Late in the eighteenth century the process of rediscovery was tentatively begun. Like most other lost worlds, the Maya attracted its share of earnest but often incompetent investigators who, in their enthusiasm, frequently destroyed the very materials upon which archaeologists depend for their reconstruction of the past. It was with the published reports of the American John Lloyd Stephens that serious interest turned to the subject of Maya archaeology.

What has emerged from the persistent research of generations of scholars is a picture—still far from complete—of a brilliant civilization, which was based, like neighboring and related Indian cultures, upon the most rudimentary agrarian economy, but which was distinguished from them by a highly developed system of writing, certain architectural refinements, and a genius for mathematics and astronomy.

It is just one further puzzling aspect of the Maya experience that their civilization should have taken root and flowered in the low-lying rain forests of Central America and surrounding regions. This so-called heartland region of Maya culture includes the Peten District of Guatemala as well as sections of Mexico and British Honduras. For the most part it is an inhospitable territory, which is covered over by dank marshlands and dense rain forests with trees that often grow to towering heights; although rivers flow through the region travel there even now is difficult except when one can fly from airstrip to airstrip. The climate, especially during the rainy season, is excessively hot and humid.

It was here in this jungle world, during what is generally referred to as their classic period—roughly between A.D. 300 and A.D. 900—that the Maya built their great ceremonial centers, without the help of such elementary devices as metal tools, wheeled vehicles, or beasts of burden. These are often called cities, but their function was probably more like that of a cathedral close. Around such centers, with their

The Maya classic age flowered from about A.D. 300 to 900. The term classic in general applies to a stage of development when the Maya were building structures employing the corbeled vault, when stelae and altars were often raised, and when hieroglyphic inscriptions were carved. Centuries before these cultural components matured, pre-classic Maya-speaking communities existed in the western Guatemala highlands. Centers like Kaminaljuyu were clearly influenced by Mexican cultures, but they may also have been the source of certain classic Maya characteristics. The Kaminaljuyu figure at the left may date from before 1500 B.C.

vast plazas and courts and their towering pyramid-temples, rising in one case more than two hundred feet into the sky, the Maya cleared enough of the forest to plant their crops and build their homes. At the bases of the temples they raised huge stelae which can still be seen at Tikal, Quirigua, Uaxactun, Copan, and scores of other places—sacred monoliths intricately carved with hieroglyphic inscriptions and depictions of fantastically garbed human figures. It is said that in some areas the descendants of the early Maya still burn incense before these stone monuments.

We do not know to what extent the Maya themselves were responsible for many of the most characteristic features of their classic culture. Various students have speculated on how much of what is often considered Maya may in fact owe its origin to the influences which were widespread throughout Middle America during the formative period of their culture. The ideas of temples or massive sacred structures, jaguar and serpent worship, monumental art, and the theocratic structure of Maya society could well have stemmed from a source also parental to other cultures in the region. For the Maya shared these features of their civilization with neighboring Indian civilizations, such as the Zapotec, and the Olmec or La Venta cultures, whose beginnings are also obscure.

These were but a few among hundreds of more or less separate American Indian nations or tribes whose ultimate origin must be sought in Asia. Sometime between 15,000 and 10,000 B.C., although some authorities favor an even earlier date, their remote ancestors had crossed over the Bering Straits from northeastern Asia into Alaska and began emigrating southward. These migrant hunters were roaming over North America before 9000 B.C., as we know from their bones and weapons and from the remains of the animals they killed. They used a device called a spearthrower, which is still used today by the Eskimo, the Australian aborigine, and

other primitive people; they could fashion fine stone points, which have been found in a number of places, and use them to kill such large beasts as mammoths and bisons. As early as 10,000 B.C. mammoths were being killed by spears in the valley of Mexico.

It must have taken the descendants of these migrants a very long time to drift southward into Central and South America. Even when they did eventually arrive in Middle America after centuries of wandering they were still at a very low stage of development. From about 6000 to 5000 B.C., when they had begun to settle down in a few chosen places, only a few groups had begun to learn the rudiments of agriculture. But very gradually they began to turn more and more to the gathering of food plants. Stratified debris in the dry interiors of cave sites in Mexico and elsewhere document the slow but all-important domestication of corn, beans, and squash, the fundamentals of Indian life. The security provided by these staples in turn underlay the emergence of village living, a development believed to have occurred in Middle America about 2000 B.C.

It is obvious that these early settlers did not bring with them to America skills such as those developed by the peoples of the Near East, who had not begun working metals and erecting substantial buildings until about the fourth millennium B.C. There could possibly have been links with the earlier paleolithic cultures of Europe and Asia; but aside from such remote and undefinable influences, Maya civilization assumed its distinctive form in the complete isolation of its New World home. It flourished most abundantly during those centuries when medieval Europe knew its darkest days. When the Spanish conquistadores first set foot on the American continent, they saw only the withered bloom of this once hardy and magnificent growth.

During what archaeologists call the formative or archaic

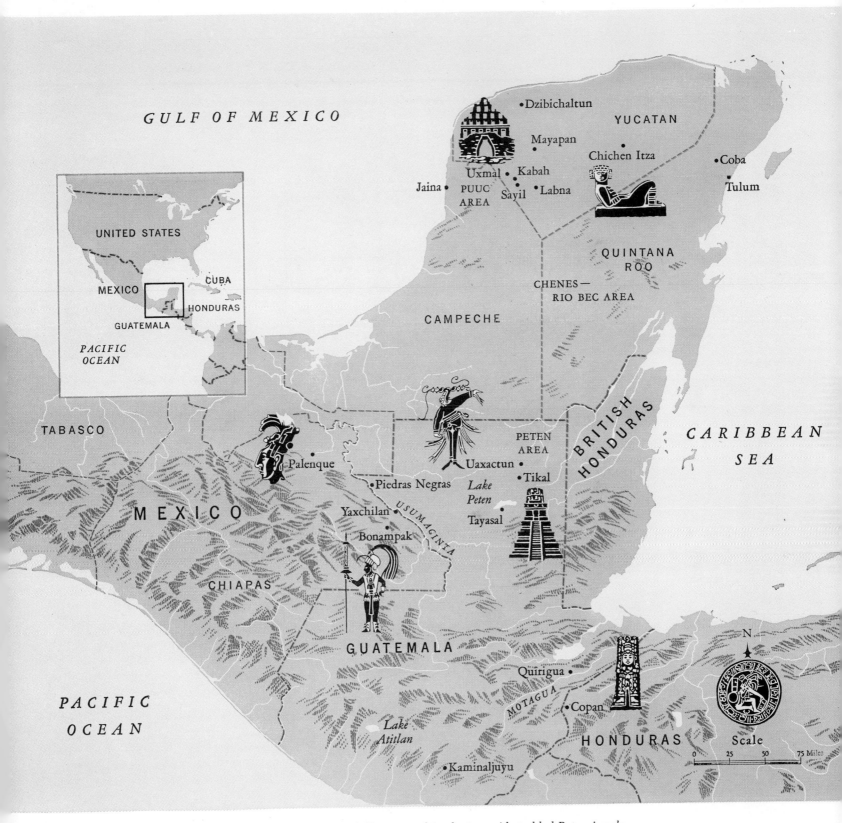

GULF OF MEXICO

UNITED STATES

CUBA

MEXICO

HONDURAS

GUATEMALA

PACIFIC
OCEAN

• Dzibichaltun

YUCATAN

Mayapan

Chichen Itza

• Coba

Uxmal • Kabah

Jaina • PUUC   • Sayil   • Labna
        AREA

• Tulum

QUINTANA
ROO

CHENES —
RIO BEC AREA

CAMPECHE

TABASCO

PETEN
AREA

BRITISH
HONDURAS

CARIBBEAN
SEA

• Palenque

Uaxactun •

• Piedras Negras   Lake
                     Peten   • Tikal

M E X I C O

Yaxchilan •

USUMACINTA

• Tayasal

• Bonampak

CHIAPAS

GUATEMALA

N

Quirigua •

MOTAGUA
• Copan

Scale

Lake
Atitlan

HONDURAS

0   25   50   75 Miles

PACIFIC
OCEAN

• Kaminaljuyu

*Classic Maya culture was carefully nurtured in the pyramid-studded Peten jungle.
Regional variations developed to the south in Copan, to the west along the
Usumacinta River, and to the north in the Puuc and Chenes-Rio Bec regions. Long
after the classic centers were inexplicably deserted and while inter-city strife was
decimating the post-classic communities in the Yucatan, a Maya-speaking tribe
called the Itza is said to have migrated south from the peninsula and settled
on Lake Peten-Itza, in the nearly vacant heartland of the classic world. This last
stronghold of the Maya legacy did not surrender to the Spanish until the close
of the seventeenth century, nearly two hundred years after Cortez visited the lake.*

period, between 1500 B.C. and A.D. 300, the Maya were evolving beyond the level of primitive village life. They had mastered the cultivation of maize, cotton, agave, and other plants, and learned to make fine pottery and baskets, and to spin fibers to weave into cloth for garments. Late in this period one finds evidence of embryonic pyramid-temples with carvings and impressive staircases leading to the summit. These are indications that the primitive farmer-hunters who lived there before 500 B.C. belonged to the same race as those who raised the monumental pyramids, temples, and paved courts of Palenque, Tikal, and other sites a few centuries later. This need not surprise us, since the ancestors of the Egyptian pyramid-builders were undoubtedly the predynastic peoples who had been burying their dead in little pit graves near the Nile just a short time before Egypt began its astonishing development in the fourth millennium B.C.

To clear land for planting, the Maya cut down trees with their stone axes or killed them by girdling their trunks, and burned the dead timber as well as the tangled underbrush. (This burning was considered a highly sacred act and the priests chose the date for the ceremony with great care.) After several sowings among the dead, fire-blackened stumps of felled trees, the soil became exhausted and weed-choked and the farmers moved to a new plot in the forest and repeated the process. A measure of the difficulties that the Maya must have had to face has been witnessed by modern archaeologists, who on returning to excavated sites after a period of only a few years find them densely overgrown.

The principal crop of the Maya farmer was maize; indeed it was the foundation of his economy, and the plant itself was worshiped as a god. The Maya probably had greater reverence for this god than for all the other deities to whom the priests made sacrifice in the temples. These divinities comprised an extraordinarily complex pantheon. It incorporated a variety of gods derived from the simple nature spirits worshiped by the earliest Maya; their character had been elaborated over centuries of development by the priesthood, who may have required an increasingly intricate theology in which to couch their predictions of the future. Gods with contradictory attributes could very conveniently be used by priests whose predictions no doubt frequently proved to have been inaccurate, or at least wrong in some detail.

Many Maya gods exerted both good and bad influences. The rain god, for example, sent life-giving waters but also brought the dampness that rotted the crops and the hail that broke the stalks. Some deities could operate in both the underworld and the heavens, and responsibility for one phenomenon could belong simultaneously to two quite different gods. According to the late Maya scholar, Sylvanus G. Morley, who has described the Maya pantheon in great detail, many divinities were four gods in one, their aspects associated with a different point of the compass and a different color. (The four sacred shades in this connection were red, yellow, black, and white—significantly, the colors of different kinds of corn.) The god Chac was such a four-in-one deity. He was the actual rain god, but by association, as Morley suggested, he was at the same time lord of the wind, thunder, and lightning. In one of his four manifestations he was called Ekib Chac—the Black Man—Chac of the West.

Among the many Maya deities the most benevolent divinity was Itzamna, the aged god associated with the sun. He was apparently the chief divinity of the pantheon but he did not maintain his importance in post-classic times as did the Maya rain deities. Medicine, books, and writing were among his spheres of influence. Ixtab, the goddess of suicide, was another benevolent deity, since death by one's own hand insured a place in the Maya paradise. Hanging was especially laudable and Ixtab, sometimes called the goddess of the gal-

The Maya played a game of ball according to rules that varied with the shape of the court. At Copan (left), round stones, similar to the one shown at right, marked the court and were laid flush with the playing alley. Team members may have had fixed positions. They wore protective girdles and knee and arm guards; they also held handstones to steady themselves when they lunged for the small, rubber ball, which could be hit with hips, elbows, and thighs. The game had ritual significance and the stakes were often high; it is said that the winner could demand spectators' finery, but carvings at Chichen Itza suggest that a player was sacrificed at the end of the game.

lows, appears in one surviving document hanging from the sky with a noose around her neck. According to one early Spanish account, the Maya also believed that men who were killed in war and women who died while giving birth were guaranteed a place in the eternal Maya heaven, where all was abundance and no one worked. In Mitnal, the Maya hell, there was no food, warmth, or cessation of torment.

Strangely enough, Ixchel, the goddess of pregnancy, the inventor of weaving, and the wife of Itzamna, was predominantly a malevolent deity, who is pictured in another document as an old and ugly woman, surrounded with death symbols and identified with the destruction of the world by floods. The god of death was called Ah Puch. When pictured, he resembles in part a bloated corpse or a fleshless figure; the owl, Moan bird, and dog which are frequently depicted with him had sinister significance as well. There was also a god of violent death who doubled as a god of war and figured in human sacrifice. Ek Chuah, "the black war captain," was still another malevolent deity who is said to have aided Ixchel when that goddess deluged the land; but he, too, had a benevolent side and when his better nature was in force, he protected traveling merchants and the precious cacao from destruction.

Maya religion has often confounded those who have attempted to understand it. Despite the inevitable frustrations in trying to interpret what was an occult discipline even to the Maya, scholars have learned much in the past half century, studying the sculptures and frescoes and the texts inscribed on numerous monuments; the invaluable descriptions of life in sixteenth-century Yucatan by the Spanish bishop, Diego de Landa; and the famed Maya codices, or books. These three remaining codices are in Paris, Dresden, and Madrid and are named after these cities. Each book is made of a long strip of bark cloth that is folded accordion-fashion

to form a number of pages; the surfaces were sized with a thin wash of stucco and painted with representations of the Maya divinities and with religious texts. Although Maya hieroglyphics are not yet completely deciphered, scholars have concluded that these texts are largely divinatory in content, reckoning the good and evil aspects of the gods who governed each day and their effects upon all the activities in the lives of the Maya people.

The ordinary laborer and field worker would have had no more understanding of the complexities of theology than the Sumerian working on the temple estate of Inanna or the Egyptian fellah reaping grain for the god Amen-Re; he would have felt nearer to the deities of the fruitful earth which gave him life. But he accepted what the priest-rulers told him—that the gods must have temples for sacrifice and have their needs regularly supplied. So, throughout a period of more than one thousand years, generation after generation labored in the tropical heat of Middle America, felling trees, quarrying stone, hauling it to the temple site, sliding the cut blocks into position in quantities of lime mortar, layer upon layer; then building, at the top of the pyramid, the shrine or temple with its few dark, damp rooms which the priests alone could enter. They made the great ball courts, too—sacred enclosures in which a ceremonial game was played by Maya youths. No one knows exactly how or why this game was played, except that a rubber ball was used, and that the contestants were only permitted to strike it with the hips, thighs, and elbows—never with the hands or feet. The cult of this sacred ball game was widespread among civilizations of the New World, and it survived up to the time of the Spanish conquest throughout the Americas.

What most remarkably distinguished the civilization of the Maya from all others—ancient or contemporary, in Europe or Asia or the neighboring regions of America—was

Maya priests painted their bodies a sacred blue color; black was the color warriors used, according to Spanish chronicles. They also report that months of fasting were followed by rites of purification, when both priest and layman washed specially prepared soot from their bodies to symbolize the cleansing of evil. Thus the black figures (right), on an extended design from the famous Chama vase, could represent either soot-covered priests before a ceremonial bath, or warriors. The figures on the Uaxactun vase at left have a more recognizably "priestly" air.

an obsession with the passage of time. Maya intellectual life was almost entirely devoted to the problem of measuring its flow. For to the Maya time was the philosophical and spiritual basis of the universe. Unless this is first understood and accepted any consideration of Maya society and culture will tell us little. According to their unique view, history was repeated in endlessly recurrent cycles, and complete understanding of these provided an explanation of the present and a forecast of the future. In control of this cyclical pattern were the gods, good and evil, who operated within a complex chronological as well as theological system. In devising the sacred time counts Maya priests became calendrical experts as well as intermediaries between man and his gods.

To the Maya, each day was a deity, who carried the weight of time upon his back, the way an Indian porter carries a load along a mountain trail. Time was a never-ending, cyclical procession of day gods, night gods, week gods, month gods, and year gods moving from the darkness of the past into the darkness of the future.

The Maya calendar consisted of two separate counts, one an approximate solar year, the other mainly ceremonial. The solar year, called the *tun,* was comprised of three hundred sixty-five days. It was made up of eighteen divisions of twenty days each as well as one malevolent five day period. Running concurrently with this so-called solar year was the ceremonial year, only two hundred sixty days long, made up of thirteen day numbers and twenty named days. The solar years and the ceremonial periods were combined to form a larger unit of fifty-two years, the calendar round, a period somewhat equivalent to our century. Still another measure, the "long count," totaled the number of days that had elapsed on any given date, according to the Maya priests, since the beginning of Maya time.

To measure the passage of time, the Maya studied the cycles of the sun and the moon, and of the planet Venus, although they were unaware of the true significance of what they observed. To them the earth was flat, and the sun and the stars moved around it. But they noted the recurrent cycles so closely that they were able to make remarkably accurate records of them.

In later times the most significant and sacred period of time was the *katun,* a period of twenty solar years. Each katun was governed by a particular divinity. There were thirteen of these, and after thirteen katuns had elapsed, the cycle began over again, so that after approximately two hundred fifty-six years the influence of the patron god of each katun reasserted itself. The events that had occurred two and a half centuries earlier were bound to be repeated once more. Several katuns brought favorable times; most of these divisions of time were less propitious.

The cycles of the Maya calendars, as scholars interpret them, interlocked with each other like the meshing cogs of wheels of different sizes; an important part of the priest's duties was to know which particular cogs—or gods—were in mesh at any moment of time, past, present or future. To determine the influences at work on any specific day, the priest-mathematicians at times made calculations millions of years into the past, in one case four hundred million years.

The revolutions of the sun and planets cannot be reduced to round figures, a fact which made the reckonings of their cycles difficult. We know, for instance, that the solar or tropical year is approximately 365.2422 days in length, the sidereal year is a trifle under 365.2564 days, and the revolution of Venus is not 585 days but 583.92. The Maya, over centuries of record keeping, learned this too, though they had no way of expressing fractions or decimals. Yet somehow they managed to bring these awkward figures into harmonious relationship with their artificial almanacs. They did this, not by

using leap years, as we do, but by keeping accurate records so as to be able to determine, when needed, the discrepancy between the true solar year and their year of 365 days. If the reader has not become fogged by these figures he will appreciate the achievement of the Maya in predicting solar eclipses so accurately that their forecasts compare well with the calculations of modern astronomers. (One scholar who has enormously expanded our understanding of Maya calendrics and enabled us to make this comparison is the noted Maya authority, J. Eric S. Thompson.)

All this prodigious intellectual effort may seem to us an exercise in futility. What was its value? The Egyptians, Babylonians, and other peoples of the ancient Near East had also learned to calculate the movements of heavenly bodies with varying degrees of exactitude; but they put their mathematical knowledge to different practical uses. They measured the seasonal variations in flooding; they divided and allocated their lands; they determined crop yields and sizes of herds; they used their arithmetical skills to keep business accounts. The Maya did not need to apply their mathematical abilities to any of those problems of daily life, for in their world the concept of individual property with its accompanying need for land valuation, measurement division, and taxation of wealth hardly existed; there were no annual floods needing measurement and control.

However, for the Maya to apply mathematics to the study of time was deemed to be of the greatest practical value; for every Maya farmer was told that his welfare, and that of his family, his crops, and his possessions—everything on which he depended—lay at the mercy of the deities who in their eternal rounds controlled the natural forces, deities whose aid he must invoke and whose demands he must satisfy. Ultimately, he must have known, he depended upon his priest, who alone could interpret the future for him and intercede

with the gods if the omens were inauspicious. Only they could say which particular combination of good and evil influences operated at any particular moment of time.

The calendrics of the Maya may possibly have had a historical purpose—the recording of the reigns of the priest-rulers. Until very recently, only the calendric portion of the texts inscribed on stelae and building stones could be read and it was natural to suppose that the whole text was just as impersonal as these portions of it. However, new studies have made it evident that certain sections of such inscriptions refer to the accession of rulers, presumably the figures who are represented on the stelae. Another part of the texts may refer to the rulers' birth dates or to the dates of their initiation into training for the priesthood. In the light of this fresh evidence, it now seems that some of the figures portrayed are women—women who may have been wives or mothers of rulers, or perhaps even regents; at least they were aristocratic and consequential figures in Maya society. The presence of dynasties at various Maya centers is gradually being recognized. No longer can a monument be assumed to portray a priest in the guise of a god, with an impersonal text referring purely to the passage of time. It can be hoped that further investigation and study of these matters will reduce some of the mystery that still shrouds the Maya world.

A major problem confronting the archaeologist has been to correlate the Maya calendrical system with our own, to translate Maya dates into the equivalent dates of our own Gregorian calendar. We know that the date of the Spanish conquest of Merida, the capital of Yucatan, is 1541. The corresponding Maya date is given as the end of Katun 13 Ahau. But without an independent reference it would be difficult to anchor this date in relation to our time, for it recurs every 256 years in the Maya calendar.

With the advent of the radiocarbon, or carbon 14, method

The long-nosed creature above, pecked into an inside temple wall at Tikal, may have been the work of religious neophytes, momentarily diverted from their training.

of dating, archaeologists have acquired a new tool for investigating such problems. This remarkable technique utilizes the fact that a small fixed percent of the carbon that is found in all living matter occurs in the form of the isotope carbon 14, instead of the normal form of the element, carbon 12. After the death of the organic material involved, however, the carbon 14 slowly loses its two extra electrons and deteriorates at a known rate to nitrogen 14. About fifty-seven hundred years after a tree has been cut down, its wood will only contain half its original amount of carbon 14; after approximately fifty-seven hundred years more, the amount of that isotope will have again decreased by half.

Archaeologists carefully collect pieces of charcoal from construction fills, and wooden beams from temples and tombs, measure the percentage of carbon 14 that they still contain, and compare this figure with the amount known to exist in living matter. From the difference between the two amounts, scientists can calculate the time that has elapsed since trees were felled for use in the construction. At the classic Maya site of Tikal, there are wooden lintels on which the date of construction has been carved. Some of them, when radiocarbon dated, seem to confirm a dating system called the Spinden correlation, a chronology which places the Maya classic period about two hundred fifty years earlier than the more widely accepted Goodman-Thompson correlation. This latter system has been upheld by other radiocarbon dates and appears to best fit historical and archaeological evidence. It fixes the classic era—known from inscriptions to have lasted at least six hundred years—from about the fourth to the tenth centuries A.D.

Exactly what did such sites as Copan, Palenque, Uxmal, Tikal, and Uaxactun look like during this great florescence of Maya culture? At Tikal, archaeologists have found evidence of nearly three thousand buildings within an area less than

Several typically classic Maya motifs appear on a detail from a Tikal lintel (left), one of the few wooden panels to survive the attack of termites and the jungle climate. The horizontal interwoven bands reproduce a pattern the Maya commonly used in making mats. The mat-weave as a symbol, however, is a sign of authority; "he who sits at the head of the mat" is designated leader. The weave here decorates a throne. The three pendant plaques and the human head form a motif frequent in lowland classic Maya art. Also found amid the temple ruins at Tikal, the bowl lid at right is strongly Mexican in style.

seven square miles. To the east and west of a spacious ceremonial arena at the heart of this architectural complex were the towering, sacred pyramids; these solid rubble and masonry structures served to raise tiny, one-to-three-room temples nearer the heavens. To the north, on a platform that rose in several levels beyond a great array of vertical stone stelae, a cluster of somewhat smaller temple-capped pyramids reached skyward. On a higher platform to the south of the main court were nearly a score of low-lying, multi-chambered structures we call "palaces," although their function is unknown; and beyond them were still other temples and palaces on raised platforms. At some sites these large ceremonial buildings, connected with each other by causeways, were often so situated that they formed a giant sundial, or they were located according to the position of the stars. Thousands of other buildings, mapped but still unexcavated, must have existed at Tikal. Within the temple or ceremonial precincts are more than two hundred stelae and drum-shaped stone altars, some of them elaborately carved. What appears on the surface of the site is merely the end product of a thousand years of growth; beneath these visible remains are the floors and buried walls of other buildings.

In their architecture the Maya never mastered the true arch; but for their ceremonial buildings they, virtually alone among the Middle American Indians, used the corbeled vault. This device, in which each course of masonry overlaps the one beneath until two confronting walls can be bridged at their topmost level by laying on a capstone, called for a studied understanding of the problems of stress and strain in construction. The engineering skill demonstrated by such performances was also evident in the broad highways that traversed the jungles and crossed the swampy terrain and the lakes that separated centers of activity.

There must be thousands of sites like these, large and small, in Guatemala and on the Yucatan peninsula. Whether they were purely religious centers, populated solely by priests and sustained by the peasants who farmed and dwelt in the surrounding countryside, or whether they could have been cities—truly urban—with markets, artisans, an administrative system, and a large and varied population made up of all social classes, poses a very important question that has not yet been fully or finally answered by archaeologists. Other questions still tantalize scholars who have studied the Maya: What were the bonds between priest and farmer? What sustained this civilization for over a thousand years? And what factors eventually and abruptly terminated its classic phase?

The stupendous amount of construction and renovation at every major Maya center has been well documented by archaeologists. The conclusion is inescapable—religion was the primary motivation for all that was built. Peasants labored year after year to erect the brilliant white stucco buildings demanded by their theocratic overlords. The peasants' toil provided the setting in which the priests enacted their rites. The priestly caste in turn provided assurances for the future—predictions about all aspects of life and the sacrifices necessary to propitiate the deities. Classic Maya civilization appears to have been a product of the brilliance of a few priests and the labor of the millions who lived under their control.

What we know of Maya life and the structure of Maya society within this broad theocratic framework is derived largely from Maya and Spanish accounts of the late postclassic period in Yucatan, which is distinguished from the classic era by the intrusion of full-scale warfare and widespread human sacrifice. It is more than likely, however, that the class system was essentially the same in the earlier era. According to Morley, the *halach uinic,* or true man, was foremost amid a host of official functionaries. He performed both secular and sacred duties, and as chief ruler in one of

the Maya city-states—which apparently comprised a loose confederation—he regularly received tributes from the common people settled around the ceremonial center from which he reigned. Below him were the myriad priests who conducted specific portions of the ceremonial rites. One of these functionaries was the *nacom;* it was his duty to remove the hearts of sacrificial victims and because of his bloody office, de Landa reported, the people held him in low regard. The priests who spoke the divine prophecies were called *chilanes;* they were so highly esteemed that the Maya would not let their feet touch the ground when they moved among the rank and file, who carried them upon their shoulders or in litters.

Membership in the priestly hierarchy was hereditary; sons succeeded their fathers, if at an early age they showed "an inclination for this profession." There was also a hereditary nobility, again headed by the halach uinic. In this capacity he was supported by lesser chiefs, called *batabs,* who dwelt in the small communities surrounding the ceremonial center. Each batab may have controlled a small force of warriors but one of his major duties was to keep on schedule the flow of tributes required by the halach uinic. Morley's list of suitable gifts included the fruits of the field, salt, meat, and dried fish, copal incense which the Maya called *pom,* cacao beans—frequently used as currency—jade and coral beads, and shells. Hunting and fishing expeditions to provide offerings were communal undertakings and the Maya often roasted deer flesh directly after a hunt to keep it from spoiling before they returned home to present it to their lords.

Maya economy depended upon the large segment of the population that was made up of the farmers. But it was the laborers and the artisans with only limited equipment—the Maya used only wood and stone tools—who performed prodigies. Quite apart from the construction and decoration of monumental buildings, enormous patience and skill were devoted to the creation of objects on the smallest scale. Figurines and ornaments were exquisitely fashioned of jade, their hard substance often covered with intricate patterns carved in low relief. Painting, so splendidly represented by the few murals that have been discovered, was finely applied to polychrome pottery. This art was widely practiced during the classic period, to the immense benefit of archaeologists searching for revealing evidence. The weaving of sisal fiber, cotton, and feathers into serviceable garments and ceremonial robes was undertaken by the women as a holy duty. Virtually nothing of their handiwork has survived, but it is represented in paintings and carvings and the Spaniards wrote of it in their contemporary reports.

At the lowest level of society were slaves, most probably neighboring villagers taken in raids who were kept in some kind of servitude if they were not subjected to the sacrificial knife. On stelae such captive figures are shown bound with cord and crouching in cowering postures.

A luminous portrayal of nearly all these levels of classic Maya society was discovered not long ago upon the walls of three small temple rooms deep in the forest of Chiapas. In 1946 native chicle gatherers led archaeologists to the site— soon after named Bonampak ("painted walls"). If we interpret the content of these unique Maya murals correctly—the hieroglyphic inscriptions painted on them have not yet been translated—we see the halach uinic, his wife, and their child, probably the heir apparent, surveying and participating in a sumptuous ceremonial event. They are attended by lesser priests and nobles. The scenes are filled with warriors and masked god-impersonators, dancers and musicians, endless priestly functionaries, and bound prisoners; it is possible that some of the latter are sacrificial victims but these representations may be intended to portray slaves since their hands are shown dripping blood, and a red hand print, made with

blood or perhaps paint, is thought to signify slave status.

The story the murals tell seems to begin with a raid led by the halach uinic; in the tangle of warriors one can distinguish the enemy by his coarse and stringy hair. Scenes follow in which priests and other performers dress and line up for a final ceremonial dance. Many figures stand about in animated conversation and a small bloodletting ceremony takes place among what appear to be members of the ruling family. Before the dance, the prisoners captured in the raid are arraigned before the halach uinic, his attendants, and his wife. One of the prisoners may have been sacrificed during the wild dance upon the pyramid steps that climaxes the story.

In these paintings as well as on sculptured stelae, the splendid dress of the upper classes is clearly portrayed. All Maya wore basically the same garments—loincloths for the men, sack-like dresses for the women—but in the higher ranks of society the stuffs used were richer and more ornately contrived. Priests' raiments were heavily encrusted with beads and shells; their headdresses, worked upon high wooden frames in the shape of animals or the faces of gods, were the most elaborate of all Maya accouterments. No other single document so colorfully and suggestively recreates a scene of Maya life in its classic phase as the splendid panorama painted at Bonampak. It dates from about A.D. 800, the year of Charlemagne's coronation in faraway Rome, and it pictures Maya culture at its zenith.

Yet despite this record in addition to the great body of information provided by decades of excavation and study, most scholars would still concede that in large areas of study the story of the civilization of the Maya remains an enigma.

Valuable discoveries continue to be made, however. In the archaeology of the Maya region, as elsewhere, excavation can be slow and frustrating. It is a day-to-day matter of collecting and recording masses of information with the hope that once the data is put into the proper chronological perspective, a clearer picture will be revealed of the development of the Maya way of life. This work of discovery is conducted for the most part in a logical, businesslike, even tedious manner. But the unsuspected, the incredible can always emerge with the next blow of the excavator's pick.

In 1949 the Mexican archaeologist Alberto Ruz, after clearing the floor within the Temple of the Inscriptions at Palenque, one of the most lovely Maya sites, found that one large floor slab had finger-holes in its surface, apparently put there to facilitate lifting. When the great slab was raised, it disclosed a vaulted staircase that descended at a forty-five degree angle into the rubble-packed interior of the temple's pyramid base. Over the next few seasons the Mexican expedition slowly worked its way down through the rubble that filled the stairway. A landing was reached; then the stairway reversed itself and continued down in the opposite direction. At the eighteenth step down, at a depth of about sixty feet below the temple room floor, a crude wall blocked the way. When the excavators removed the rubble before it, they found an offering of seashells and pottery, beads, and a pearl, contained in a large stone vessel. Proceeding farther in the passageway Ruz encountered a large, vertically set slab of stone. At its base he discovered the skeletal remains of six individuals who had been buried without offerings, ". . . beneath small stones and lime . . . the most precious gift the Maya priests could offer on that dramatic occasion when they closed their sacred place," as Ruz described his discovery. The offering and the skeletons were unmistakable clues that something extraordinary, like nothing yet found, lay ahead.

When a great stone slab was carefully removed, what faced Ruz in the light of his lamp was a sight that even the most optimistic members of the expedition could hardly have anticipated. He saw a vaulted chamber, almost thirty feet long,

Sites clustered in the hilly country of western Yucatan, known as the Puuc, are characterized by a distinctive architectural style. Labna (above) famed for its corbeled archway, displays the typically Puuc use of columnar decoration, as does the ruin shown at right.

its walls displaying the figures of nine richly garbed personages modeled in stucco relief, and at the center a magnificently sculptured rectangular slab covered with remains of jadeite mosaic human heads and slate pendants. The examination of this chamber, some seventy-five feet beneath the floor of the temple, occupied Ruz and his colleagues for many months. The top of this slab was carved to represent a young man, dead, lying upon a macabre mask of an earth monster and surrounded by Maya symbols of life and death. Its sides were carved with a hieroglyphic text indicating a date of around A.D. 700. This five-ton slab proved to be a "sepulchral stone" covering the lid of a great stone sarcophagus.

Within was the skeleton of the priest-ruler for whom the elaborate crypt had been prepared. Laid out on his back, he was adorned with an incredible array of jewelry. Around his face were the fragments of a mosaic death mask made of some two hundred pieces of jadeite (shown on page 411 as it has been restored). Along with it were jadeite earplugs, a diadem, pendants, and pearls. About his neck and arms were a collar and bracelets of jadeite beads and each finger had a jadeite ring. Jadeite figurines were strewn about his legs. The red shroud in which he had been interred had disintegrated, leaving a colored deposit on the skeleton and the offerings.

There seems little doubt that the Temple of the Inscriptions had been built over this richly furnished crypt; the Maya did not tunnel down into the pyramid in order to construct the tomb. In other words, the death or anticipation of the death of a very important priest-ruler had prompted the building of the temple. Thousands had long labored to raise this stupendous monument—a fact that immediately brings to mind the parallel of the mortuary pyramids of the Nile.

This rich burial took place barely a hundred years before the classic Maya culture began its mysterious decline and Palenque, like the other sites in the central region, fell into

decay. During the ninth century A.D., some one remarkable event or some combination of events must have occurred that was capable of shaking the very foundations of Maya culture, for throughout the century, the great cities or cult centers were gradually deserted—a few of them, it seems, almost overnight. Buildings clearly still in the course of construction were abandoned. This does not mean that all the Maya left the region at once, although there may have been mass migrations to other areas. But certainly in this century, the Maya no longer lived according to the rather rigid pattern that marked their classic age. People still entered the great ceremonial precincts and continued to worship and sacrifice among the untended temples. Archaeological investigation seems to indicate that some people even came to occupy the "palaces" and bury their dead in these structures; but no new stelae rose in the sacred courtyards and eventually these last inhabitants disappeared. The Tikals and Copans were left to the rain forests and to the roots of the jungle vines.

The abrupt ending of ceremonial activity over so wide an area, and after so many centuries of continued performance, cannot adequately be attributed either to some spreading disease or to a natural calamity. Could it have been the consequence of war? Throughout the millennium that marks their growth and flowering, the Maya remained essentially a pacific people. Their contacts with their neighbors in Mexico and the highlands of Guatemala were largely commercial. Unlike most of the cities built by other ancient civilizations, Maya centers were rarely protected by defensive walls. They apparently never engaged in major wars, and such surprise attacks as they made from time to time on bordering villages were probably designed primarily to obtain prisoners for their sacrifices to the gods.

Did the stability and order of a thousand years vanish so rapidly because of overpopulation and soil depletion, politi-

Framed by a fantastic headdress, the terra-cotta face at the left may be the portrait of an important Maya woman.

cal divisiveness, a wave of social unrest emanating from Mexico, or cultural exhaustion brought about simply from having done the same things in the same ways for too long? Were the priests liquidated in center after center or did they for some incomprehensible reason emigrate to some distant settlements voluntarily or because they were expelled by a peasant uprising? And finally, what happened to the great population, numbering in the millions, that had lived and thrived for so long in the rain forests of northern Guatemala and the surrounding country?

Answers to these questions still elude us but we know that as the jungle grew back over those long-established centers in the central region, the cultural focus of Maya life shifted northward, particularly to the area now comprised by the modern Mexican state of Yucatan. Maya sites in Yucatan had been occupied in classic times, among them Chichen Itza and Uxmal, but they had also been abandoned during the disturbances that brought the classic age to an end. By A.D. 1000 a new people, either Mexicans or Maya tribes strongly influenced by Mexican life, invaded the area and settled at a site to which they gave their tribal name, the Itza. Called Chichen Itza, the site name means "at the mouth (*chi*) of the well (*chen*) of the Itza." It is located in the northern region of the Yucatan peninsula, where deep natural wells often lie just below the crusty limestone surface of the earth. One of two such wells or *cenotes* at Chichen Itza functioned as the center of a great sacrificial cult; according to its ritual, live victims as well as precious objects were cast into its murky waters. Although the cult is not fully documented until this Mexican period, the sacred cenote may have been the destination of a heavily traveled pilgrimage route from the central area in classic times. Perhaps this influenced the Itza in their choice of sites, but whatever their policy was, the Itza managed to rule from their great center at Chichen

Itza, referred to as the Mecca of the Maya world, and it flourished most splendidly in the following two centuries.

The intruders or newcomers were quite unlike the pacific Maya of the classic period. They were warriors imbued with the same belligerent spirit that was to inspire the Aztecs in the years to come. According to legend, the Itza had been led into Yucatan by Quetzalcoatl, the Mexican "feathered snake" whom the Maya called Kukulcan. We cannot tell whether he was a man or a god; Maya tradition supports either possibility, but in any case the feathered serpent became a dominant theme in the art of Chichen Itza.

The immigrants brought with them new ideas of architecture and a new sculptural style which were in some instances grafted onto the classic buildings still standing at Chichen Itza. They constructed new temples with great staircases flanked by balustrades made in the form of feathered serpents to represent Quetzalcoatl. Other monumental stone serpents supported the lintels of the doorways. Prowling jaguars and eagles clutching the hearts of sacrificial victims decorated the façades of buildings. Extending alongside the ceremonial structures were great galleries with seemingly endless rows of columns covered with vaulted roofs. In important places rested the peculiar reclining human figures, called chacmools, that are so characteristic of Chichen Itza sculpture. Many of these traits point to the influence of the Toltec Indians, whose center was at Tula, near modern Mexico City —indeed this phase of Maya history has been called Toltec.

The military orders that sprang up during this period were also derived from the Toltecs. Most prominent among them were the Jaguars and the Eagles, whose symbols are visible upon many of the buildings at Chichen Itza. These ceremonial orders were organized solely for the purpose of making war. Their members raided other centers to acquire victims who were sacrificed in bloody ritual.

Even after A.D. 1200, when the leadership of the Maya passed from Chichen Itza to the center of Mayapan, warriors remained in control. More and more the priests came to abandon their intellectual exercises and devoted themselves to the gory human sacrifice to which the militant orders owed their existence. The priests at Mayapan no longer served as the intermediaries between the ordinary man and the forces of the universe. Indeed many of the four thousand structures within the city walls are residences with attached family shrines, giving evidence that religion was becoming more personal and less an experience mediated by priests.

Even in these times, however, the Maya were still imbued with the belief in moderation that characterized their classic ancestors. Their late writings described the Itza as foreigners and deplored their bloody customs. The excesses and barbarities of the Itza invaders offended them. A Maya chronicler wrote: "Their hearts are submerged in sin. Their hearts are dead in their carnal sins. They are frequent backsliders, the principal ones who spread sin, Nacxit Xuchit in the carnal sin of his companions . . . They are the unrestrained lewd ones of the day . . . They are the rogues of the world."

The theme of human sacrifice is increasingly important during this period of Mexican influence in Yucatan. How important such sacrifice had been during classic times is hard to assess. The incomparable frescoes of Bonampak portray in extraordinary detail a raid for gaining prisoners. Another shows a ceremonial dance in which the body of a sacrificial victim is apparently being rolled down the pyramid steps. At Piedras Negras, a beautiful late classic stele shows an individual, his back arched over a support and his chest split open, with symbolic vegetation issuing from the gaping wound from which his heart had been ripped. Another picture within a Tikal temple (a graffito that may be postclassic in date) shows an individual hurling a spear at a victim tied to a frame. At classic sites there are offering burials of heads and of headless corpses.

But it was under Mexican influence that human sacrifice became unmistakably institutionalized in Yucatan. Bishop Diego de Landa, the great chronicler of life in Yucatan at the time of the Spanish conquest, writes vividly of a sacrifice: "Besides the festivals in which they sacrificed persons in accordance with their solemnity, the priest or *Chilan,* on account of some misfortune or necessity, ordered them to sacrifice human beings, and everyone contributed to this, that slaves should be bought, or some in their devotion gave their little children, who were made much of, and feasted up to the day . . . they led them from town to town with dancing, while the priests, chilans, and other officers fasted. And when the day arrived, they all came together in the court of the temple, and if the victim was to be sacrificed with arrows, they stripped him naked, and anointed his body with a blue color, and put a *coroza* [loosely, a headdress] on his head. When they had reached the victim, all armed with bows and arrows, [they] danced a solemn dance with him around the stake, and while dancing they put him up on it and bound him to it . . . . The foul priest in vestments went up and wounded the victim with an arrow in the parts of shame, whether it was a man or woman, and drew blood and came down and annointed the faces of the idol with it. And making a certain sign to the dancers, they began one after another to shoot, as they passed rapidly before him, still dancing, at his heart, which had been marked beforehand with a white mark. And in this way they made his whole chest one point like a hedgehog of arrows. If the heart of the victim was to be taken out, they led him with a great show and company of people into the court of the temple, and having smeared him with blue and put on a *coroza,* they brought him up to the round altar, which was the place of sacrifice, and after the priest and his officials had anointed the stone with a blue color, and by purifying the temple drove out the evil spirit, the *chacs* [assistants to the priests, not the rain gods with the same name earlier mentioned] seized the poor victim, and placed him very quickly on his back upon that stone, and all four held him by the legs and arms, so that they divided him in the middle.

"At this came the executioner, the nacom, with a knife of stone, and struck him with great skill and cruelty a blow between the ribs of his left side under the nipple, and he at once plunged his hand in there and seized the heart like a raging tiger and snatched it out alive and, having placed it upon a plate, he gave it to the priest, who went very quickly and anointed the faces of the idols with that fresh blood. Sometimes they made this sacrifice on the stone and high altar of the temple, and then they threw the body, now dead, rolling down the steps. The officials below took it and flayed it whole, taking off all the skin with the exception of the feet and hands, and the priest, all bare, covered himself, stripped naked as he was, with that skin, and the others danced with him. And this was considered as a thing of great solemnity amongst them. The custom was usually to bury in the court of the temple those whom they had sacrificed, or else they ate

them, dividing him up among those who had arrived (first) and the lords, and the hands, feet, and head were reserved for the priest and his officials, and they considered those who were sacrificed as holy. If the victims were slaves captured in war, their master took their bones, to use them as a trophy in their dances as tokens of victory. Sometimes they threw living victims into the well of Chichen Itza, believing that they would come out on the third day [with a prophecy from the gods], although they never appeared again."

Landa's description of the important cenote ritual, although biased and gathered second-hand from informants, is corroborated by depictions of such sacrifices found at Chichen Itza as well as the dredging operations there, which have yielded a great treasure of objects in gold, copper, jadeite, and other materials and the bones of a great many people who had been cast as sacrificial victims into its depths.

The Maya in later times were sanctimoniously prone to lay the blame for excess on others, first on their Mexican overlords, and later their Spanish conquerors. "Before the coming of the mighty men and Spaniards," one Maya scribe had written, "there was no robbery by violence, there was no greed and striking down one's fellow man in his blood, at the cost of the poor man, at the expense of the food of each and everyone." The scribe adds, "It was the beginning of tribute, the beginning of church dues, the beginning of strife with purse-snatching, the beginning of strife with guns . . ." But there is every reason to believe that the Maya themselves throughout their history looked upon human blood, and its sacrifice to the gods, as sublime. Set against this gory strain in the make-up of the Maya people was one of puritanism, balance, and self-control.

In one case at least these traits saved a Spanish zealot his life, although he richly deserved to lose it. Long after the Mexican intruders had been absorbed by the Maya (the era in which Maya and Itza became virtually synonymous), and the Spanish invaders had conquered and subjugated most of what had been Maya territory, one remote citadel of Maya culture held out in northern Guatemala at a place called Tayasal, south of the long-deserted classic center of Tikal. Two of the "mighty men and Spaniards," albeit men of God, entered Tayasal on one of many expeditions there in an attempt to convert the pagan natives. According to Morley, they found the Itza worshiping an image of a horse, carved after the death of a lamed animal the Spaniard Cortez had left with them; the fathers were so incensed at the Itza's idolatrous behavior that they smashed the sacred idol of the infidels. The missionaries were nevertheless allowed to leave Tayasal in peace.

These last holdouts against the conquistadores were not always so charitable. For nearly two hundred years, the Itza had waged bloody battles against the soldiers and the priests of the new faith, even though the Itza leader, Canek, is said to have anticipated a time of dramatic change, when the old gods would no longer demand his people's loyalty. These last Maya at Tayasal in fact believed that Katun 8 Ahau, the katun of change, had arrived when they ultimately submitted to their Spanish conquerors.

THE WORLD OF
THE CLASSIC MAYA

According to a Maya legend, the gods created man several times, first of mud, then of wood, and in the version that finally pleased them, they made man out of maize. Corn for planting, like the life substance itself, was considered a gift of the gods who had, at man's urging, rescued the grain from beneath a great mountain so that it could be cultivated. Maize was the basis of ancient Maya life; it was eaten at each meal, and in time, the Maya deified the crop. Thus, with devotion as well as hard work, they hacked their fields out of the heavy jungle. They attended every stage of the corn's growth with ritual sacrifice, and the Maya's field was said to be more dear to him than his family. During the months the crops did not demand care, Maya labored on priest-directed building programs; it was as if the act of building could itself propitiate the gods. An image of the corn god (above) sometimes looked down from structures already completed; his benign visage no doubt assured the Maya that their efforts were appreciated by the deity they most revered.

CEREMONIAL CENTERS

The Maya did not live in their stone cities, although priests and specially skilled artisans may have lived on the immediate fringes. Even a center the size of Tikal—the largest and probably the oldest Maya site—was used almost exclusively for priestly rites and ritual pageantry. The people settled near their fields, scattered outside the carefully planned ceremonial centers, and except to put up a new temple or pave a causeway, they came in only to watch the sacred spectacles and perhaps to trade—feathers for beads, sea shells for cacao beans. The people probably gathered in the great courts while grotesquely masked men impersonating gods, and musicians with drums and huge wooden trumpets, formed colorful lines along low stone platforms. When a sacrifice was made on the summit of a pyramid, priests in brilliantly beaded loincloths and towering headdresses of quetzal feathers may have danced on the pyramid steps, their motions encircled by the swirl of the long green plumes. No ceremony was complete without ritual drunkenness; priest and farmer alike probably drank bowls of *balche,* the Maya intoxicant fermented from honey and the bark of the *balche* tree. Everywhere in the city, the green of jade ornaments must have glowed through a haze of smoking copal incense.

An incense burner with the face of the Maya old god (right) was found in an early Tikal burial. Wrinkled and nearly toothless, this earth god was thought to cause earthquakes when he stirred in his subterranean home. As incense burned in his belly, smoke poured from his gaping jaw. He holds an effigy head; human thigh bones form the legs of his chair. The temples of Tikal (above) are today barely visible in a sea of jungle.

RITUALIZED
DESTRUCTION

The Maya methodically destroyed and buried many ceremonial buildings and the carved stone monuments that stood before them. At Uaxactun, a temple center about fifteen miles north of Tikal, buildings in faultless condition were covered over with terraced platforms and upon them more structures were raised. At Tikal part of a stele was carried up into a temple from the court below; there its carved faces were carefully scraped away, it was burned, and finally buried beneath the temple walls that were torn down as if to complete a ceremony.

Why these sacred structures could no longer be used is not fully understood; the Maya often built over them after entombing a man of high rank (probably their priest-leader) and experts suggest that when such a theocrat died, his people may have ceremonially "killed" and buried a temple and stele associated with his reign. (To archaeologists the phrase *killed object* in general refers to a deliberately damaged tomb offering; in the ancient world it was thought that such an object, when ritually broken, released its spirit to travel with the deceased in the afterworld.)

Maya hieroglyphs form the eyebrows of the fuchsite figure shown above, found in a ceremonial cache at Uaxactun. The incised folded hands and bare head, however, are not characteristic of Maya art, recalling instead the style of the Olmecs, a neighboring culture that preceded the classic Maya and may have contributed to their development.

The plate above was ritually "killed" before it was placed in a Uaxactun burial sometime after A.D. 600. Note the "kill hole" in the center.
The man, who may be a dancer, is far less formal than the figures
conversing (left) in a copy of one of the earliest Maya murals,
discovered on the wall of an intentionally buried building at Uaxactun.
One of the many Maya ceremonies may be in progress but proof must
wait until the hieroglyphic inscriptions between the gesticulating figures
are completely understood. The mural was painted around A.D. 400.

UNITY
AND
REGIONALISM

A pervading reverence for the passage of time unified the classic Maya world. Periods comparable to our days, months, and years were worshiped everywhere as divinities; even the names and numbers which identified them were deified. The priest-ruler in this role of sacred astronomer endlessly scanned the heavens, for in the cycles of celestial bodies he read the eternal round of the gods. The main purpose was magico-religious, to discover in advance the combined effect of the deities who controlled the coming period. Some combinations augured well for the Maya, most did not, and with esoteric computations or sacrifices, the priests tried to re-arrange or cajole the divine influences into harmony. After centuries of faithful astrological observation, calculations became so refined that the Maya calendar was in some instances truer to the astronomical year than our own Gregorian count.

The center of Maya astronomy may have been Copan, the most southern classic site; astronomer-priests from distant cities perhaps traveled there to compare their findings. (When a new calculation of the solar year's length was completed at Copan about A.D. 700, an altar was dedicated on which sixteen figures, thought to be visiting priests, are carved; each man sits cross-legged over an unusual glyph which may name his distant home.) But while time worship, like the uniform deification of maize, bound Maya everywhere together, many of the self-sustaining and autonomous ceremonial centers were characterized by a strongly individual style of sculpture and architecture, despite the identical ritual functions for which they were all designed. Even Tikal and Uaxactun—so close that their suburbs of thatched huts mingled—were strikingly different from one another. Tikal's pyramids, for example, were among the tallest New World structures of the time—one towers over two hundred feet above the jungle floor—whereas at Uaxactun, within five hours walking distance, buildings were scarcely a third as high.

Copan's sculptors gave the center a part of its unique appearance; they carved stelae figures in such deep relief that they emerged from the stone as almost free-standing statues, rarely found elsewhere in the Maya world. Inscribed with time counts, and possibly dynastic records, the stelae stand in the great court at Copan (right).

BLOOD FOR THE GODS

The Maya bargained for the favor of their gods with human blood. If their priests forecast ill-fated days, the Maya willingly mutilated their bodies to obtain the precious offering, for they believed the gods valued human blood highly and in exchange for it might send better days. Throughout the Maya and Mexican worlds, for example, the sun god was thought to depend on blood for nourishment; when he passed through the underworld each night in order to reach the east by dawn, his body was turned bone-thin by his trip in the land of the dead. To make their sacrifices, the Maya pierced their bodies with fish spines and sting ray barbs, collecting the blood that fell on bark paper, which they placed before their idols. If this failed to affect an evil prophecy, they resorted to human sacrifice (and although they were not a war-like people, they sometimes raided nearby centers to provide an ample number of victims). Captives were held breast upward over a stone. With a flint knife called "the hand of god," a priest split open the bared chest and cut out the beating heart, which was carried to an idol and placed in its bloodstained mouth.

Victims taken in a raid (detail right) are ceremonially bled in the scene above and wait in terror to hear what part they will play in the final sacrificial dance (not shown). The man in front of them may already have been sacrificed to the gods. Above him, the figure in the short jaguar tunic is probably the secular and religious leader the Maya called halach uinic. Priests flank him, and the woman (with a fan) may be his wife. The murals were painted about A.D. 800 at the site discovered and named Bonampak in 1946. Watercolor copies of two scenes are shown here.

MASKS
AND PROFILES

To beautify themselves, the Maya often notched their teeth and filled them with discs of jade and metallic rock; they pierced their ears to insert enormous jade plugs, and they tattooed patterns on their faces and bodies. Both men and women anointed themselves with a perfumed red salve. They fixed small bits of pitch in their children's hair for it was hoped that the strands, dangling before their eyes, would make them cross-eyed. The Maya also flattened their foreheads by binding infants' skulls between two boards for several days.

This self-styled profile was especially characteristic of the area around Palenque, a site that marks the western edge of the classic Maya world. There the idealized faces appear on low-relief, inscribed plaques which cover temple and palace walls. The classic profile also distinguishes a death mask (above right), found in the most unusual Maya burial of the period. Until 1951, Maya pyramids were thought to serve primarily as supports for the temples, but with the discovery of a secret stairway which cut down through the pyramid under Palenque's Temple of the Inscriptions, an additional purpose was apparent; the stairway led to an elaborate crypt, built before the pyramid was erected and held in readiness for a Maya of great rank. After the entombment, the pyramid probably became a funerary monument to the man buried in splendor beneath it.

OVERLEAF: *When the noted explorer John Lloyd Stephens first saw the city of Uxmal, he said it was "in picturesque effect . . . almost equal to the ruins of Thebes"; at dusk it was "a work of enchantment."*

Mists often come down from the hills behind Palenque and rest upon the delicate filigree roof combs of the site's small and graceful temples, such as the Temple of the Cross (facing page). From a huge hieroglyphic plaque found in Palenque's palace-like structure, the detail below shows two figures with idealized Maya profiles. The mask above was worked in jade mosaic.

Geometric masks with bizarrely bending noses confront each other from the corners of classic Maya buildings at Chichen Itza (left). The structures they ornament continued to be used when militant invaders took over the site. They built the colonnaded Temple of the Warriors (right) and used characteristically Mexican columns in the shape of feathered serpents on the entrance to the Temple of Kukulcan (shadowed foreground). Kukulcan was the Maya name for the Mexican god, Quetzalcoatl (feathered serpent); legendary leader of the invaders, he was the city's patron god.

BATTLE OF CULTURES

"Rascals . . . tricksters . . . foreigners who speak our language brokenly"; so Maya chronicles described the men who conquered Chichen Itza, a Maya center on the Yucatan peninsula that was invaded shortly after the great classic centers to the south were abandoned. Exactly who these "foreigners" were remains a mystery, but in the post-classic city that flourished on this site, two cultures—Maya and Mexican—merged. Much of what was built in the newer part of the city remarkably duplicates architectural and ornamental motifs found at Tula, the distant home of the militant Mexican Toltecs.

Hundreds of years before, even the jungle-protected Peten heartland had been penetrated by influences from the valley of Mexico. Around A.D. 400, a stele was erected at Tikal; on it, the honored figure is carved in the classic Maya style and represents a typical Maya theocrat. He is flanked by two figures adorned in the style of Teotihuacan—the dominant power in central Mexico before the Toltecs—and they may perhaps portray visiting dignitaries from that distant city. No heads of state stand together in the later carvings at Chichen Itza however; humbled before Mexican warriors the Maya are portrayed with their left hands raised to their right shoulders in the traditional Middle American pose of surrender.

Figures like the one below from Chichen Itza are rarely found at other Maya sites, although similar statues have been recovered elsewhere in Central America and Mexico. They consistently look sharply over one shoulder and hold bowls upon their stomachs, possibly to receive ritual offerings. OVERLEAF: Marked by wrinkles and the nearly toothless grin of the Maya old god, this inscrutable face peers from the encroaching jungle like a guardian of secrets the past forever holds.

415

ACKNOWLEDGMENTS AND INDEX

ACKNOWLEDGMENTS

The editors wish particularly to acknowledge their indebtedness to Bernard Bothmer of the Brooklyn Museum and Robert H. Dyson, Jr., of the University Museum of Philadelphia for their invaluable advice. The editors are also grateful to William R. Coe of the University Museum and George Montgomery of the Asia Society for their assistance. We wish to thank the following persons and institutions for their generous co-operation in advising and guiding us and for their assistance in making available pictorial material in their collections.

American Museum of Natural History, New York
    Dr. Gordon Ekholm
    Walter A. Fairservis, Jr.
American Research Center in Egypt, Inc., Cairo
    Nicholas B. Millet
Archaeological Museum, Herakleion
Ashmolean Museum, Oxford
    Department of Antiquities
    Griffith Institute
Asia Society, New York
    George Montgomery
Bibliothèque de l'Arsenal, Paris
    Jacques Guignard
British Museum, London
    Dr. R. D. Barnett
    Miss Macpharlane
    C. Burland
Alan Doré
Editions Gallimard, Paris
    Albert Beuret
Editions Ides et Calendes, Neuchâtel, Switzerland
Explorer's Club, New York
    Roy Owen
Faber and Faber Ltd., London
Hirmer Verlag, Munich
    Mrs. Aldegund Drees
Dr. Jotham Johnson, New York University
Miss Helen Keiser, Baghdad
Prof. George Kiebler, Yale University
Prof. M. E. L. Mallowan, London
Metropolitan Museum of Art, New York
    William Hayes
    Vaughn Crawford
    Miss Lillian Green
    Joseph Noble
    Mrs. Margaret Nolan
    Mrs. Edward S. McGill
Dr. H. W. Muller, Munich
Musée Guimet, Paris
    Phillippe Stern
Musée du Louvre, Paris
    André Parrot
Musée du Petit-Palais, Paris
    Mme. Suzanne Kahn
Museum of Fine Arts, Boston
    William Stevenson Smith, Curator
      of the Egyptian Department
    Miss Joan Rassiear
    Miss Elizabeth P. Riegal
National Museum, New Delhi
    Dr. Grace Morley, Director
    Shri C. Sivaramamurti, Keeper
Oriental Institute, University of Chicago
    Dr. A. Leo Oppenheim
    Dr. R. C. Haines
    Mrs. John Switalski
John Papadimitriou, Director of Antiquities, Athens
Peabody Museum, Harvard University, Cambridge
    Dr. John Otis Brew
    Dr. Tatania Proskouriakoff
    Mrs. Katherine B. Edsall

Pierpont Morgan Library, New York
    Frederick B. Adams, Jr.
Miss Josephine Powell, Rome
Mrs. Margaret Robinson, New York
Miss Margaret Scherer, New York
Semitic Museum, Harvard University
    Dr. Otto Edzard
Silvana Editoriale d'Arte, Milan
Soprintendenza alle Antichità dell' Etruria Meridionale, Rome
    Dr. Mario Moretti
Soprintendenza alle Antichità Egittologia, Turin
    Prof. Ernesto Scamuzzi
Staatliche Museen zu Berlin
    Dr. S. J. Wenig
    D. W. Muller, Komm. Direktor
    Dr. Gerhard Meyer
State Pushkin Museum of Fine Arts, Moscow
    Mme. Raisa Cherinova
Thames and Hudson Ltd., London
    Walter and Eva Neurath
    Trevor Craker
Time, Inc., New York
    Miss Dorothy L. Smith
University Museum, University of Pennsylvania, Philadelphia
    Mrs. Caroline Dosker

Grateful acknowledgment is made for permission to quote from the following works:

Carl Blegen, "Excavations at Pylos 1939," *American Journal of Archaeology*, Vol. XLIII, No. 4, 1939. J. H. Breasted, *Development of Religion and Thought in Ancient Egypt*, Charles Scribner's Sons, New York. D. G. Bridson, *The Quest of Gilgamesh*, British Broadcasting Corporation, London. Lawrence Palmer Briggs, "The Ancient Khmer Empire," *American Philosophical Society Transactions*, Vol. XLI, Pt. 1, 1951. Bernard Broslier & Jacques Arthaud, *The Arts and Civilization of Angkor*, trans. by Eric Ernshaw Smith, Frederick A. Praeger Inc., N. Y. C. W. Ceram, *The Secret of the Hittites*, Alfred A. Knopf Inc., N. Y. John Chadwick, *The Decipherment of Linear B*, Cambridge University Press, N. Y. Albert Champdor, *Babylon*, G. P. Putnam's Sons, N. Y. Edward Chiera, *They Wrote on Clay*, University of Chicago Press, copyright 1938 by The University of Chicago. Chou Ta-kuan, *Mémoires sur les Coutumes du Cambodge*, French trans. by Paul Pelliot, Librairie d'Amérique et d'Orient, Paris; original English trans. by George Montgomery, adapted by the editors of *Horizon. Diodorus Siculus*, Vols. I and II; Dionysius of Halicarnassus, *The Roman Antiquities;* passages reprinted by permission of the publishers from the Loeb Classical Library, Cambridge, Mass.: Harvard University Press. I. E. S. Edwards, *The Pyramids of Egypt*, Penguin Books Ltd., Harmondsworth, Middlesex, England. Adolf Erman, *The Literature of the Ancient Egyptians*, Methuen and Co. Ltd., London (spelling of names revised by permission of the publisher). Sir Arthur Evans, *The Palace of Minos at Knossos*, reprinted 1963 by Agathon Press Inc., N. Y. Joan Evans, *Time and Chance*, Longmans, Green and Co. Ltd., London. Henri Frankfort, *Ancient Egyptian Religion*, Columbia University Press, N. Y.; *The Art and Architecture of the Ancient Orient*, Penguin Books Ltd.; *Kingship and the Gods*, University of Chicago Press, copyright 1948 by The University of Chicago. Sir Alan Gardiner, *Egypt of the Pharaohs*, The Clarendon Press, Oxford. Gustave Glotz, *Aegean Civilization*, Routledge and Kegan Paul Ltd., London. O. R. Gurney, *The Hittites*, Penguin Books Ltd. *Herodotus: The Histories*, trans. by Aubrey de Selincourt, Penguin Books Ltd. (by permission of David Higham Associates Ltd., London). Alain Hus, *The Etruscans*, trans. by Jeanne Unger Duell, Grove Press Inc., N. Y. E. O. James, *The Ancient Gods*, G. P. Putnam's Sons. Robert Koldewey, *Excavations at Babylon*, trans. by Agnes S.

Johns, Macmillan and Co., London. Samuel Noah Kramer, *History Begins at Sumer*, The Falcon's Wing Press, Indian Hills, Colorado. *Landa's Relacion de las Cosas de Yucatan*, ed. by Alfred M. Tozzer, Peabody Museum, Harvard University, Cambridge, Mass. D. H. Lawrence, *Etruscan Places*, by permission of The Viking Press Inc., all rights reserved. Miriam Lichtheim, "The Songs of Harpers," *Journal of Near Eastern Studies*, Vol. IV, No. 3, 1945, The University of Chicago. Seton Lloyd, *Early Anatolia*, Penguin Books, Ltd. Daniel David Luckenbill, *Ancient Records of Assyria and Babylonia*, by permission of The University of Chicago Press, copyright 1926 by The University of Chicago. Henry Frederick Lutz, *Selected Sumerian and Babylonian Texts*, The University Museum, University of Pennsylvania, Philadelphia. Svend Aage Pallis, *The Antiquity of Iraq*, Ejnar Munksgaard A/S, Copenhagen. Pausanias, *Description of Greece*, passages reprinted by permission of the publishers from the Loeb Classical Library, Cambridge, Mass.: Harvard University Press. J. D. S. Pendlebury, *The Archaeology of Crete*, Methuen and Co. Ltd. Pliny, *Natural History*, passages reprinted by permission of the publishers from the Loeb Classical Library, Cambridge, Mass.: Harvard University Press. James B. Pritchard, ed., *Ancient Near Eastern Texts Relating to the Old Testament*, copyright 1955 by Princeton University Press, Princeton. E. V. Rieu, trans., *The Iliad* and *The Odyssey*, Penguin Books Ltd. Sir Osbert Sitwell, *Escape With Me*, Macmillan and Co., London (by permission of David Higham Associates Ltd.). George Steindorff and Keith C. Seele, *When Egypt Ruled the East*, University of Chicago Press, copyright 1942 and 1957 by The University of Chicago. Dirk J. Struik, *A Concise History of Mathematics*, copyright 1948 by Dover Publications Inc., published by Dover Publications Inc., New York 14, N. Y. at $1.75, passage reprinted through permission of the publisher. Ralph L. Roys, *The Book of Chilam Balam of Chumayel*, Carnegie Institution of Washington, Washington, D. C. Thucydides, *History of the Peloponnesian War*, trans. by Richard Crawley, revised by R. Feetham, Everyman's Library, passages reprinted by permission of E. P. Dutton and Co. Inc., N. Y. Alan Wace, *Mycenae: An Archaeological History and Guide*, copyright 1949 by Princeton University Press. Sir Mortimer Wheeler, *Early India and Pakistan*, Frederick A. Praeger Inc. H. E. Winlock, *Models of Daily Life in Ancient Egypt*, The Metropolitan Museum of Art, N. Y.

PICTURE CREDITS

The source of each picture is listed below. Its title or description appears after the page number, which is in boldface type, and is followed by the original location, where possible, and the present location. Photographic credits appear in parentheses. Where two or more pictures appear on one page, the references are separated by dashes.

The following abbreviations are used:

AMH—Archaeological Museum in Herakleion

AP—Archives Photographiques

Baghdad—Iraq Museum, Baghdad

BM—British Museum, London

BN—Bibliothèque Nationale, Paris

Cairo—Egyptian Museum, Cairo

FM—Foto Marburg

Guatemala—Museo Nacional de Arqueologia, Guatemala

Hirmer—Hirmer Verlag, Munich

India—National Museum of India, New Delhi

Louvre—Musée du Louvre, Paris

Mexico—Museo Nacional de Antropologia, Mexico

MFA—Museum of Fine Arts, Boston

MMA—Metropolitan Museum of Art, New York

NAMA—National Archaeological Museum in Athens

Orinst—Oriental Institute, University of Chicago

Pakistan—National Museum of Pakistan, Karachi

TV—Tel-Vigneau

UMP—University Museum, University of Pennsylvania, Philadelphia

VG—Museo di Villa Giulia, Rome

FRONT MATTER—Jacket: (Eliot Elisofon). Back jacket: Egyptian tile of Nubian. Collection of E. Kofler-Truniger, Lucerne—Etruscan pendant. Louvre—Khmer sculpture of Jayavarman VII Phnom Penh (Baugey-Multiphoto)—Cretan goddess. Herakleion (Powell). Cover design from a photograph by George Holton of a relief of hieroglyphics at Edfu. Title page: Head of an Elamite. MMA—Gudea. MMA—Apollo from Veii. VG (Scala)—Hatshepsut, reconstructed. MMA—Copyright page: Phoenician statuette. Louvre (AP)—INTRODUCTION—7 Rosetta Stone. (BM)

MYTH AND REALITY

16 Tapestry cartoon, "The Anger of Achilles" by Rubens. (Museum Boymans-van Beuningen, Rotterdam)—The Trojan horse. Detail. Français 22552. (BN) 17 Abduction of Helen. Nouv. Acq. Fr. 24920. (BN) 18-19 "The Rape of Europa" by Titian. Isabella Stewart Gardner Museum 20-21 "Theseus and Ariadne" by Piero di Cosimo. Musée des Beaux Arts, Marseilles (Giraudon) 20 Attic amphora. (MMA) 22 "Horatio at the Bridge" by George Pencz. BM—"Horatio Cocles" by Marcantonio. (MMA) 23 Death of Lucretia. Ms. 5193. (Bibliothèque de l'Arsenal)—Lucretia by Parmigianino. Museo Nazionale, Naples (Alinari)—Tarquin and Lucretia by Cagnacci. Galleria di San Luca, Rome (Anderson) 24 Building the Tower of Babel. Add. Ms. 18850. (BM) 25 Merchants of Babylon lamenting. The Douce Apocalypse. Ms. Douce 180. Bodleian Library, Oxford (Courtesy Faber & Faber)—Drawing of Nebuchadnezzar by William Blake. (The Tate Gallery, London) 26 Tapestry of Semiramis. Honolulu Academy of Arts 27 "The Feast of Balthazar" by V. M. Bigari. Pinacoteca Nazionale, Bologna (Giraudon) 28 Ivory relief of Joseph distributing corn in Egypt from the Maximian Cathedral. Archepiscopal Museum, Ravenna (Anderson)—Ivory relief of Moses slaying the Egyptian. Museo Civico Cristiano, Brescia (Anderson)—Joseph in Egypt. Panel from bronze doors by Ghiberti. Baptistery, Florence (Brogi) 29 Hebrews in the desert. Ms. Fr. 247. (BN) 30-31 Death of Osiris by Pinturicchio. Detail. Ceiling of Borgia Apartments, Vatican 31 Elephant obelisk. Francesco de Colonna, *Hyperotomachia Poliphili* (MMA)

Kingdom of the Pharaohs · I
THE FLOWERING OF EGYPT

32 Sphinx. Giza (Hassia) 34 Pyramids. Giza (George Holton—Photo Researchers) 36 Palette. Louvre (AP) 36-37 Palette. Detail. Louvre (AP) 37 Knife. Louvre

(Giraudon) 38 Animals relief. Saqqara (Hassia)—Fishing relief. Saqqara (Sameh) 39 Herdsmen relief. Saqqara (Hassia)—Painting of marsh life. Detail. BM (Hassia) 40 Drawing of macehead of the "Scorpion King." W. S. Smith, *Egyptian Sculpture and Painting in the Old Kingdom*, Boston, 1949. Original in Ashmolean Museum, Oxford 40-41 Narmer palette. Detail. Cairo (FM) 41 Narmer palette. Cairo (Hassia) 42 The Gayer Anderson cat. Roman period (BM)—Toueris. Cairo (FM)—Anubis. Cairo (MMA) 43 Painted wooden stele. Louvre 44-45 Papyrus. Cairo (Hassia) 46 Step Pyramid. Saqqara (Hirmer) 47 Disk. Cairo (John G. Ross)—Djoser relief. Saqqara (Hirmer) 48-49 Delinquent tax-payers relief. Saqqara (Orinst) 49 Herdsman relief. Meir (FM)—Force-feeding fowl relief. Berlin (Grantz-Giraudon) 50 Mycerinus and queen. (MFA)—Ankhhaf. MFA (Barney Burstein) 51 Cheops. Cairo (Walter Sanders, courtesy *Life*) 52 Drawing. C. R. Lepsius, *Denkmaeler aus Aegypten und Aethiopien*. Berlin, 1849-1859 52-53 Bartering relief. Saqqara (Sameh) 53 Thief relief. Saqqara (Sameh) 54 Statuette of children. (Orinst) 55 Relief of dancers. Saqqara (Sameh) 57 Chephren. Cairo (James Whitmore, courtesy *Life*) 58 Painting from Tomb of Horemheb. Saqqara (Duncan Edwards-FPG) 59 Predynastic bird-headed figurine. (Brooklyn Museum) 60-61 Mourners relief. State Pushkin Museum of Fine Arts, Moscow (courtesy Bernard Bothmer) 62 Relief from sarcophagus. Cairo (Hassia) 62-63 Papyrus of Ani. BM

Kingdom of the Pharaohs · II
ANARCHY AND RECOVERY

64 Copper statue of Pepi I (caption refers to the second pharaoh of that name rather than the subject illustrated). Cairo (Hirmer) 66 Yacht of Meketre. Detail. MMA 66-67 Yacht of Meketre. MMA 68 Painting of garden. Sheik Abd el Qurna. (Hassia) 69 Painting of Apu's garden. Thebes. Copy (MMA) 70 Pectoral. (MMA) 71 Collar. MMA—Head of a woman. Cairo (Walter Sanders, courtesy *Life*)—Bracelet. Cairo (MMA) 73 Sesostris III. (MMA) 74 Seneb and wife. Cairo (James Whitmore, courtesy *Life*)—Ka-aper. Cairo (FM) 75 Scribe. Louvre (Eliot Elisofon, courtesy *Life*)—Rehotep and Nofret. Cairo (James Whitmore, courtesy *Life*) 76-77 Model of Meketre inspecting cattle. Cairo (Hassia) 78-79 Painting of harvest. Sheik Abd el Qurna. (Hassia) 78 Herdsmen relief. Saqqara (Sameh) 79 Donkeys relief. Saqqara (Hirmer) 80 Carpenters relief. Saqqara (Sameh)—Sculptors relief. Cairo (Hassia) 80-81 Painting of workmen. Thebes (MMA) 81 Statuette of lady making beer. Cairo (Sameh)—Men chopping relief. Saqqara (Sameh) 82 Painting of musicians. Sheik Abd el Qurna (Walter Sanders, courtesy *Life*) 83 Painting of banquet. BM 84 Papyrus of lady applying lip rouge. (Museo Egizio, Turin)—Ostracon of girl with lotus. (Berlin)—Relief from sarcophagus of lady Kawit. Cairo (Hassia) 84-85 Cosmetic spoon. Louvre (Giraudon) 85 Mirror. (MFA)—Unfinished head. Cairo (Egyptian Exploration Society) 86 Ostracon (MMA) 86-87 Painting. Sheik Abd el Qurna (Hassia)

Kingdom of the Pharaohs · III
GLORY AND DECLINE

88 Akhenaten. Berlin (F. L. Kennett) 90 Tile. (MMA)—Ahmose I axehead. Cairo (MMA) 91 Ostracon. (MMA)—Chariot. Museo Archeologico, Florence

(Alinari) 92 Hypostyle Hall. Karnak (Hirmer)—Capital from Temple of Ptah. Karnak (Roger-Viollet) 93 Temple of Amen, Mut, and Khonsu. Luxor (Duncan Edwards-FPG) 94 Tiles from Palace of Ramesses III. Medinet Habu. Collection of E. Kofler-Truniger, Lucerne 95 Painting of Syrians. MMA 96 Craftsmen relief. Cairo (Hassia) 97 Blind harpist relief. Leiden (F. L. Kennett) 98 Portrait of Senenmut from his tomb. Deir el Bahri. (MMA)—Horemheb relief. Leiden (F. L. Kennett) 99 Scarab. (MMA)—Queen Teye. Berlin 100-101 Painted wooden stele. Cairo (Hassia) 101 Sphinx. (Brooklyn Museum) 102 Ostracon of cat, rat, and child. (Orinst)—Comic papyrus of game. (BM) 102-3 Ostracon of bulls. (MMA) 103 Ostracon of acrobat. Museo Egizio, Turin (Courtesy A. Mekhitarian)—Ostracon of girl blowing fire. (Aegyptologisches Institut, University of Leipzig) 105 Amenhotep III. (Brooklyn Museum) 106 Drawing. L'Illustration, Histoire de la Marine, Paris, 1942 106-7 Temple at Deir el Bahri (Duncan Edwards-FPG) 107 Hatshepsut. MMA 108 Painting of Tuthmosis III before Amen. Cairo—Painting of Syrian tribute bearers. BM 108-9 Tuthmosis III relief, Temple of Amen. Karnak (Hirmer) 109 Gold Amen. MMA 110-11 Warriors. Cairo (AP) 112-13 Panel of painted coffer. Cairo (Walter Sanders, ·courtesy Life) 114 Nefretiti. Berlin 115 Akhenaten and Nefretiti relief. Berlin (F. L. Kennett)—Statuette (Gulbenkian Collection, Durham University)—Amenhotep III relief. (BM) 116 Headrest. Cairo (MMA)—Lion. Cairo (Hassia) 117 Coffin. Cairo (Hirmer)—Pectoral. Cairo (MMA)—Horse blinders. Cairo 118 Colossi built by Amenhotep III. Thebes (Walter Sanders, courtesy Life) 119 Ramesseum. Thebes (Walter Sanders, courtesy Life)

Land Between the Rivers · I
SUMER: DAWN OF CIVILIZATION

120 Figure from Nippur. (Orinst, courtesy Joint Nippur Expedition and Life) 122 Ziggurat. Ur (Frank Scherschel, courtesy Life) 124-25 Dairy Frieze from al 'Ubaid. Baghdad (Frank Scherschel, courtesy Life) 126 Female head from Uruk. Baghdad (courtesy Helen Keiser) 127 Vase from Uruk. Baghdad (Frank Scherschel, courtesy Life) 128 War "Standard" from Ur. Detail. (BM) 129 The Hoffman Tablet. Collection of the General Theological Seminary, N. Y. (MMA)—Seal impression of boat from Uruk. (Berlin)—Seal impression of offering bearer. Louvre (TV) 130 Helmet from Ur. Baghdad (courtesy Thames & Hudson) 131 Necklace from Ur. (BM)—Headdress from Ur. (BM) 132 Map from southern Babylonia. (BM) 132-33 Stele of the Vultures from Lagash. Details. Louvre (TV) 134 Stele of Naram-sin from Susa. Louvre 135 Seal impression. (The Pierpont Morgan Library)—Foundation figurine from Lagash. Louvre (TV) 137 Gypsum head from Bismaya. (Orinst) 138-39 Ur. (Frank Scherschel, courtesy Life) 140 Temple plan. P. Delougaz, Pre-Sargonid Temples of the Diyala Region, 1942 (Orinst) 140-41 Figurines from Tell Asmar. Baghdad and (Orinst) 142 Bull's head from Ur. UMP (Lee Boltin) 143 Goat and tree from Ur. (BM) 144 Head of Sargon(?) from Nineveh. Baghdad (Schneider-Lengyel, courtesy Gallimard) 145 Stele of the Vultures from Lagash. Detail. Louvre (TV) 146-47 Peace "Standard" from Ur. (BM) 148 Lamp cover from Lagash. Louvre (TV)—Plaque of Dudu from Lagash. Louvre (TV) 149 Gudea. Lagash (MMA) 150 Sumerian king list. Ashmolean Museum, Oxford (courtesy Views of the Biblical World, International Publishing Co.) 151 Commemorative stele of Urnammu from Ur. Detail (UMP)

Land Between the Rivers · II
THE AGE OF HAMMURABI

152 Terra-cotta head of divinity from Lagash. Louvre (TV) 154 Dudu the scribe from Lagash. Baghdad (Frank Scherschel, courtesy Life) 155 Tablet from Sippar. (MMA)—School benches from Mari. (Mission Archéologique de Mari) 156 Lady with spindle from Susa. Louvre (AP)—Woman suckling child from Lagash. (Louvre) 157 Double statuette from Nippur. (Orinst, courtesy Joint Expedition to Nippur) 158 Worshiper from offering stand from Khafaje. Baghdad (Frank Scherschel, courtesy Life) 158-59 Plaque of Sit-Shamsi from Susa. Louvre (Giraudon) 159 Wrestlers supporting double vase from Tell Agrab. Baghdad (Orinst) 161 Head of Hammurabi(?) from Susa. Louvre (TV) 162-63 Investiture of king of Mari. Copy of painting from Mari. Louvre 164 Palace. Mari (Aviation Française du Levant)—Warrior from Mari. Aleppo Museum (Mission Archéologique de Mari) 165 Goddess with flowing vase from Mari. Aleppo Museum (Mission Archéologique de Mari)—Offering bearer from Mari. Aleppo Museum (Mission Archéologique de Mari) 166 Stele of Hammurabi from Susa. Detail. Louvre (Giraudon) 167 Awil-nannar or Hammurabi from Larsa. Louvre 169 Female. (Louvre)—Man with monkeys. (Louvre)—Couple. (MMA)—Craftsman. (Louvre)—Men picking fruit. Fragment. (Yale Babylonian Collection)—Man riding bull. (Orinst)—Armed men. Louvre (AP) 170 Top of silver toilet box from Ur. UMP (Lee Boltin)—Bronze lion from Temple of Dagan. Mari. Louvre 171 Rein ring from Ur. BM (Frank Scherschel, courtesy Life) 172 Gold hero and bulls. Louvre—Inlaid soundbox of harp from Ur. Detail. (UMP)—Early dynastic plaque from Nippur. Detail. (Orinst, courtesy Joint Expedition to Nippur) 173 Assyrian relief of hero and cub from Khorsabad. Detail. Louvre (TV) 174 Statue of Queen Napir-asu from Susa. Louvre (TV) 175 Axehead from Choga Zambil. Louvre—Head of Elamite. (MMA)

Land Between the Rivers · III
KINGS OF THE WORLD

176 Winged bull from Khorsabad. Louvre (TV) 178 Black Obelisk from Nimrud. (BM) 179 Attack relief from Nineveh. (MMA) 180-81 Flight across river relief from Nimrud. (BM) 182 Musicians relief from Nineveh. Louvre (TV) 183 Assurbanipal feasting relief from Nineveh. (BM) 184-85 Neo-Babylonian seal and impression. Pierpont Morgan Library (Lee Boltin) 187 Assurnasirpal II. (BM) 188 Destruction of Hamanu relief. (BM) 189 Assyrian pursuing Arabs relief. BM (Werner Forman) 190-91 Campaign of Shalmaneser III bronze relief (BM) 192 Mede and horses relief. (MMA) 193 Captives relief. Louvre (TV) 194-95 Lion hunt relief. (BM) 195 Wounded lioness relief. (BM) 196-97 Assurbanipal shooting relief. BM (Werner Forman) 198-99 Sacrifice relief. BM 200 Assurbanipal in chariot relief. Louvre (Giraudon) 201 Transporting logs relief. Louvre (FM) 202 Terra-cotta mask of Humbaba. (BM) 202-3 Genius relief. Louvre (TV) 203 Four-faced god with foot on ram. (Orinst)—Plaque of god killing demon. Baghdad (Orinst) 204 Fly whisk. (MMA)—Cow and calf. Baghdad (courtesy M. E. L. Mallowan)—Woman at window. Baghdad (courtesy M. E. L. Mallowan) 205 Ivory cheekpiece from horse's caparison. (MMA)—Gold-leafed, inlaid, ivory plaque of lion mauling Negro. (BM) 206 Marduk relief from Ishtar Gate at Babylon. (Mella-Viollet) 206-7 West gate of Babylon. (Mella-Viollet)

THE VALLEY OF THE INDUS

Photographs are by Frances Mortimer-Rapho Guillumette, unless otherwise noted. 208 Stone bust from Mohenjo-daro. NMP (J. Powell) 210 Seal impression from Mohenjo-daro. NMI 212 Seal impression of elephant from Mohenjo-daro. NMI—Seal impression of bull from Mohenjo-daro. NMI 213 Seal impression of deity from Mohenjo-daro. NMI 214 Laughing man from Mohenjo-daro. NMP 215 Cart from Chanhudaro. (MFA) 216 Mohenjo-daro. 217 Platform. Harappa (Patellani-Pix)—Well. Mohenjo-daro 219 Female figurine from Mohenjo-daro. NMP 220 Bull from Mohenjo-daro. NMI—Monkey from Mohenjo-daro. NMP 221 Seal impression of tiger from Mohenjo-daro. NMI 222 Pot from Baluchistan. American Museum of Natural History. (Lee Boltin) 223 Dancer from Mohenjo-daro, two views. (NMI)

ROMANCE OF REDISCOVERY

227 Pyramid interior. Description de l'Egypte, Paris, 1809-26, Vol. V—Frontispiece. Ibid., Vol. I 228-29 C. R. Lepsius, Denkmaeler aus Aegypten und Aethiopien, Berlin, 1859-60 230 Yazilikaya. Charles Texier, Description de l'Asie Mineure, Paris, 1839-49, Vol. I—Tomb interior at Tarquinia. Guiseppe Micale, L'Italia avanti il dominio dei Romani, Firenze, 1821 231 Tulum ruins. Frederick Catherwood, Views of Ancient Monuments in Central America, Chiapas and Yucatan, London, 1844 (Reserve Division, New York Public Library) 232 Portrait of Belzoni. G. B. Belzoni, Narrative of the Operations and Recent Discoveries within the Pyramids, Temples, Tombs, and Excavations in Egypt and Nubia, London, 1820—Belzoni's Exhibit. (Percival Collection, BM) 232-33 Transporting winged bull. Sir Austen Henry Layard, Nineveh and its Remains, New York, 1849, Vol. II 233 Discovery of bull. Ibid., Vol. I —Khmer exhibit. Louis Delaporte, Voyage au Cambodge, Paris, 1880 234-35 Reconstruction of the palace at Nimrud. Sir Austen Henry Layard, Second Series of the Monuments of Nineveh, London, 1853 236 "Babylonian Marriage Market" by Edwin Long. (Council of the Royal Holloway College) 236-37 "Seventh Plague of Egypt" by John Martin. (MFA) 238-39 "Death of Sardanapalus" by Eugène Delacroix. Louvre

CRETE:
THE ISLAND OF MINOS

240 Horns of consecration. Knossos (Lessing-Magnum) 242 Bull's-head rhyton from Knossos. AMH (Hassia) 244 North Portico, palace of Knossos. (Harissiadis) 245 Throne Room, palace of Knossos. (Robert E. Ginna) 246-47 Exterior and interior, palace of Knossos. (both Hirmer) 248 Vase from Phaistos. AMH (Hassia)—Fresco of "La Parisienne" from Knossos. AMH (J. Powell) 249 Macehead from Mallia. AMH (Hirmer) 250 Seal impression from Knossos. AMH (Hirmer) 250-51 Harvester Vase from Hagia Triada. Detail. AMH (Hassia) 251 Statuette from Tylissos. AMH (Hirmer) 252 Gold pendant from Mallia. AMH (J. Powell) 253 Fresco from Knossos, copy. Original in AMH (Hassia) 254 Bath-sarcophagus from Pachyammos. AMH (Hassia)—Chieftain's Cup from Hagia Triada. AMH (Hassia) 255 Snake pot. AMH (Hassia)—House plaque from Knossos. AMH

(J. Powell) 256 Goddess from Knossos. AMH (J. Powell) 257 Gold ring with dancing women from Isopata. AMH (J. Powell) 258 Goddess from Knossos. AMH (Hassia) 259 Group of women and lyre player from Palaikastro. AMH (Hassia)—Female worshiper from Piskokephalo. AMH (Hassia) 260-61 Sarcophagus painting from Hagia Triada. AMH (J. Powell) 263 Double axe from a cave near Knossos. (MFA) 264-65 Hagia Triada (J. Powell) 266-67 Ivory acrobat from Knossos. AMH (Hassia) 267 Seal impression of two acrobats from Knossos district. (Ashmolean Museum, Oxford)—Seal impression of bull drinking, possibly from Priene. (Ashmolean Museum, Oxford)—Statuette of acrobat and bull. (E. G. Spencer-Churchill Collection, Gloucester) 268-69 Restored fresco from Knossos. AMH (Hirmer) 270-71 Audience fresco from Knossos, copy. (Ashmolean Museum, Oxford) 271 Seal impression from Avdon near Lyttos. (Ashmolean Museum, Oxford)—Priest-King fresco from Knossos, restored. AMH (Hassia) 272 Dolphins fresco. Knossos. (Hassia)—Vase from Palaikastro. AMH (J. Lavaud) 273 Mallia. (Descharnes)

MYCENAE: HOME OF THE HEROES

Unless otherwise noted, all objects are from the site of Mycenae. 274 Lion gate. Mycenae (Robert E. Ginna) 276 Tholos tomb. Pylos (Hirmer) 277 Rampart. Mycenae (Henle-Monkmeyer) 278 Vase. NAMA—Ivory plaque from Spata. NAMA (Hirmer) 279 Octopus ornament. NAMA (Hirmer) 280-81 Dagger blade. Detail. NAMA (Hirmer) 282 Ivory triad. NAMA (Hirmer)—Seal. NAMA 283 Gold signet ring from Tiryns. NAMA (Hirmer) 284 Rock crystal dish. NAMA—Mask. NAMA—Cup. (NAMA) 285 Diadem. NAMA 287 Mask. NAMA (J. Powell) 288-89 Grave circle. Mycenae (Viollon-Rapho-Guillumette) 290 Ivory warrior from Delos. Delos Museum (French School at Athens) 291 Vase. (NAMA)—Seal impression. NAMA (Giraudon)—Miniature gold shield from Pylos. NAMA (University of Cincinnati) 292-93 Fresco from Tiryns. NAMA 294-95 Cups from Vaphio. NAMA—Cup II. Details. (Hirmer)

THE LOST WORLDS OF ANATOLIA

296 Alaja Huyuk. (Yan) 298 Stag. Ankara (Yan) 300 Sistrum. (MMA)—Lion vessel from Kultepe. Ankara (J. Powell) 301 Tablet from Kultepe. Ankara (Turkish Embassy, London) 302 Lion gate. Boghazkoy. (J. Powell) 303 Gate figure from Boghazkoy. Ankara (Hirmer) 304 Tarkondemos seal. (Ashmolean Museum, Oxford)—Rock relief. Yazilikaya (J. Powell) 305 Five-sided stamp. (Ashmolean Museum, Oxford)—Urhi-Teshub's seal, impression. Ankara 306 Relief. Yazilikaya (J. Powell) 307 Weather god stele from Babylon. Archaeological Museums of Istanbul (Yan)—Gold ring, impression. (Ashmolean Museum, Oxford)—Tyszkiewice seal, impression. (MFA) 308 Relief of acrobats from Alaja Huyuk. Ankara (Hirmer) 308-9 Hunting relief from Malatya. Ankara (Hirmer)—Vase fragment from Boghazkoy. Ankara (Hirmer) 310 Drawing of battle at Deper. Original on Ramesseum, Thebes. W. Wreszinski, *Atlas zur altaegyptischen Kulturgeschichte*, Leipzig, 1923-36

311 Marriage stele from Abu Simbel. (Orinst)—Egyptian relief of Hittite heads. (State Museum, Berlin) 313 Statuette. Guennol Collection, Brooklyn Museum (Charles Uht) 314 Line drawing of Egyptian relief of Sea Peoples. Original at Medinet Habu. *Oriental Institute Publications*, Chicago, 1930, Vol. 8 314-15 Terracotta relief of Phrygian warriors from near Boghazkoy. Ankara (J. Powell) 316 Astarte ostracon, probably from Thebes. (State Museum, Berlin)—Mother goddess ivory from Minet el Beida. Louvre (AP) 317 Winged griffin ivory from Meggido. (Orinst)—Etruscan bowl from Palestrina, Italy. (Sop. Antichità Etruria Meridionale) 318 Egyptian painting of Syrian traders, copy. Original at Beni Hasan. C. R. Lepsius, *Denkmaeler aus Aegypten und Aethiopien*, Berlin, 1849-59 —Knife scabbard from Byblos. National Museum, Beirut (Thames & Hudson) 319 Vase from Cyprus. BM—Double axe from Byblos. National Museum, Beirut (Thames & Hudson)

THE ENIGMATIC ETRUSCANS

320 Turms from Veii. VG (Scala) 322 Cerveteri cemetary. (Marilyn Silverstone-Nancy Palmer) 324 Tomb of Stucco Reliefs. Cerveteri (Alinari) 325 Hut urn. VG (David Lees)—Human-headed urn. Castiglione del Lago. Museo Archeologico, Florence (Dimitri Kessel) 326 Bronze and silver helmet from Todi. VG (David Lees)—Chariot panel from Monteleone. (MMA) 327 Warrior. Musei Civici, Perugia (Dimitri Kessel, courtesy *Life*) 328 Chimera from Arezzo. Museo Archeologico, Florence 329 Gorgon from Veii. VG (Scala)—Satyr and maenad from Satricum. VG (Dimitri Kessel, courtesy *Life*) 330 Pin from Cerveteri. Museo Etrusco del Vaticana (Dimitri Kessel, courtesy *Life*)—Achelous pendant. Louvre 331 Tinia. (Fitzwilliam Museum, Cambridge) 333 Warrior. VG (Dimitri Kessel, courtesy *Life*) 334-35 Sarcophagus from Cerveteri. VG (*Arte Etrusca*, Silvana Editoriale d'Arte) 335 Stele from Bologna. Museo Civico, Bologna (Giraudon)—Mirror from Vulci. Museo Etrusco del Vaticana 336 Girl plaiting hair from Solaia. Museo Archeologico, Florence (Franceschi)—Plowing group from Arezzo. VG (Pallottino and Hurlimann, *The Art of the Etruscans*, Thames and Hudson) 337 Painting from Tomb of Hunting and Fishing. Tarquinia (*Arte Etrusca*, Silvana Editoriale d'Arte) 338 Vase from Campagnano. VG (Dimitri Kessel, courtesy *Life*) 339 Mirror. Antikensammlungen, Munich (Sudre)—Painting from Tomb of the Leopards. Tarquinia (Alinari) 340-41 Painting from Tomb of the Augurs. Tarquinia (David Lees) 340 Painting from Tomb of the Olympiad. Tarquinia (Fondazione Lerici-Politecnico di Milano) 342-43 Winged horses from Tarquinia. Museo Nazionale, Tarquinia (*Arte Etrusca*, Silvana Editoriale d'Arte).

THE LAND OF THE KHMERS

360 Jungle ruins. (Eliot Elisofon, courtesy *Life*) 362 Angkor Wat. (Eliot Elisofon, courtesy *Life*) 364 Cock fight relief. Bayon (Cauchetier) 365 Cooking relief. Bayon (Viollet) 366 Churning of the Sea of Milk relief. Angkor Wat (Serrailler-Rapho Guillumette) 367 Leper King relief. Bayon (Cauchetier) 368-69 Demons relief from Banteai Srei. Musée Guimet (Giraudon) 370 Devata. (Ernst Haas-Magnum) 371 Four worshipers. (Ernst Haas-Magnum) 373 Visvakarman. Collection of Dr. and Mrs. Samuel Eilenberg 374 Muchalinda

Buddha. Bayon (Ezra Stoller) 375 Naga balustrade. Angkor Thom (Eliot Elisofon, courtesy *Life*) 376-77 Camp followers relief. Bayon (Cauchetier) 378 Apsaras. Banteai Srei (Cauchetier) 379 Banteai Srei. (Serrailler-Rapho Guillumette) 380 Statue from Angkor Thom. Musée National, Phnom Penh (Baugey-Multiphoto)—Artisans relief. Bayon (Viollet) 381 Bayon. (George Holton-Photo Researchers) 382-83 Angkor Wat. (Ernst Haas-Magnum).

THE RIDDLE OF THE MAYA

384 Stucco head from Palenque, Mexico (Irmgard Groth Kimball) 386 Figure fragment from Kaminaljuyu, Guatemala (UMP) 388 Ball court. Copan (Irmgard Groth Kimball) 389 Ball court marker from Chinkultic, Chiapas, Mexico (Norman Carver) 390 Vase from Uaxactun, Guatemala (UMP) 391 Extended design from vase from Chama (UMP). *Maya Pottery in the Museum and Other Collections*, ed. by G. B. Gordon, Philadelphia, 1925 392 Graffito from Tikal. (Fritz Goro, courtesy *Life*)—Lintel from Tikal. (George Holton-Photo Researchers) 393 Pot lid from Tikal. (William R. Coe, UMP) 394-95 Plaque from Piedras Negras. (Peabody Museum, Harvard University) 395 Blood offering relief from Yaxchilan. (BM) 396 Labna. (Ezra Stoller) 397 Puuc architectural detail. (Norman Carver) 398 Terra-cotta head from Xutilha, Peten, Guatemala. (Fritz Goro, courtesy *Life*)—Priest terra cotta. Jaina style. Mexico (Irmgard Groth Kimball) 399 Figurine whistle. Jaina style. Robert Woods Bliss Collection, National Gallery of Art, Washington (Nickolas Muray) 401 Corn god from Copan. (BM) 402 Tikal. (Fritz Goro, courtesy *Life*) 403 Incense burner from Tikal. (William R. Coe, UMP) 404 Fuchsite figure from Uaxactun, Guatemala (Dimitri Kessel, courtesy *Life*)—Fresco, water-color copy. Uaxactun (Courtesy Peabody Museum, Harvard University and Carnegie Institution of Washington) 405 Plate from Uaxactun. Guatemala (UMP) 406-7 Copan. (Dimitri Kessel, courtesy *Life*) 408-9 Mural from Bonampak, water-color copies. (Peabody Museum, Harvard University and Carnegie Institution of Washington) 410 Palenque. (Norman Carver) 411 Mask. Mexico (Irmgard Groth Kimball)—Plaque from Palenque. (Villaret) 412-13 Uxmal. (Norman Carver) 414 Architectural detail. Chichen Itza (George Holton—Photo Researchers) 415 Temple of Warriors, view from Castillo. (Norman Carver)—Figure from Chichen Itza. Museo Nacional, Mexico (Irmgard Groth Kimball) 416 Head at Copan. (George Holton—Photo Researchers).

COLOR PHOTOGRAPHY: New York, Herbert Loebel, Frank Lerner, Lee Boltin, John Ross, Oliver Baker Associates; London, Zoltan Wegner; Paris, Claude Michaelides, M. Chuzeville, Bibliothèque Nationale (Service Photographique), Luc Joubert; Cairo, Costa Alifrangis; Berlin, Walter Steinkopf; Lucerne, Joseph Koch; Zurich, Walter Dräyer; Athens, D. A. Harrissiadis. All maps prepared by David Greenspan.

INDEX

NOTE: Page numbers in italics indicate that the subject is illustrated. Usually the italicized page number refers to the page on which the picture caption appears.

R

RAMESSES II, 12, 90, 92, 95, 97, 102, 103, 104, *118*, 225, 298, 302, 307, 310, *311*, 351-52, 361, 372
RAMESSES III, 97, 102, 118, 286, 298, 314
RAMESSEUM, *118*, 310
RASENNA, 325
RAS SHAMRA, SYRIA, 312, 316
RAVENNA, ITALY, 326
RAVI RIVER, 210
RAWLINSON, SIR HENRY, 283
RE, 43, 46, 57, *59*, 63, 67, 98, 107, 310
RED SEA, *28*, 56
RE-HARAKHTE, *43*
REHOTEP, *75*
REISNER, GEORGE, 49
REKHMIRE, 247
RELIGION
  Anatolian, 306, 309-10
  In ancient Near East, 316
  Assyrian, 202-3
  Babylonian, 136, 159-60, 186, 202-3
  Cretan, 242, 250-51, 260-61, 263
  Egyptian, 37, 40, 42, 43, 45, 46-48, 50-51, 57-63, 66-67, 94-96, 103-4, 115
  Etruscan, 321, 324-25, 329-30, 331-32, 333, 335, 339, 340, 341
  Greek (classical), 251, 258
  Greek (pre-Hellenic), 310
  Hittite, *306, 307*, 309-10
  In Indus Valley, 212, 214, 219, 220
  Khmer, 364, 366, 371, 372, 375
  Maya, 385, 388-89, 390-91, 393-94, 396, 401, 402, 404, 406, 408
  Mesopotamian, 165, 166, 186
  Mycenaean, 283
  Sumerian, 122, 129-30, 131, 140
RHADAMANTHUS, 241, 260
RHIND PAPYRUS, 56
RHODES, 257, 282, 294, 308
RIBBADI, 96-97, 301
RICH, CLAUDIUS JAMES, 225
RIG-VEDA, 209-10, 218
RIMINI, ITALY, 326
ROMANCE OF TROY, 15
ROME, ANCIENT, 8, 16, 226, 322, 326, 327, 329, 330, 339, 341, 356
  Conquers Etruscans, 13, 323, 328, 342
  Etruscan influence on, 328
ROME, ITALY, 93, 99, 321, 361, 395
ROMULUS, 329
ROSETTA STONE, 7
RUBENS, PETER PAUL
  Cartoon by, for tapestry, *16*
RUSSIA, 183
RUZ, ALBERTO, 396-97

S

SADLER'S WELLS, 232
SAHNI, R. B. D. R., 210
SAHURE, 67, 304
SAKJEGOZU, TURKEY, 303
SAMARIA, 179, 192, 205, 298
SAMMURAMAT, 15, .182
SANSKRIT, 305, 372
SAQQARA, EGYPT
  Mastabas at, 42, 65
  Step Pyramid at, 12, 44-45, *46*
SARDANAPALUS, 226, *237*
SARGON, 6, 7, 9, 12, 132, 133-35, 137, *145*, 175, 318
SARGON II, 179, 180, 205
SARPEDON, 241, 260
SATHATHORYNET, 72
SAUL, 10
SAYCE, ARCHIBALD H., 300 302
SCHLIEMANN, HEINRICH, 226, 242, 244, 245, 246, 248, 249, 275-79 *passim*, 280, 304
SCULPTURE
  Assyrian, 182-83
  Egyptian, 44, 67, 69
  Etruscan, *324*, 332
  Hittite, 302, *304*, 306, *308, 309*
  In Indus Valley, *209*, 214, 215, 217-18
  Khmer, 371-72
  Maya, 406
  Mesopotamian, 135
  Mycenaean, *275*, 279-80
  Sumerian, 135, 149
SCYROS, 15
SCYTHIA, 305
SEAGER, RICHARD, 247
SEA PEOPLES, 10, 12, 13, 298, 299, *314*
SEKENENRE, 89-90, 102-3
SEKHEMKHET, 66
SELEUCID DYNASTY, 186
SEMIRAMIS, 15, *26*, 182
SENEB, *74*
SENENMUT, *98*
SENNACHERIB, 6, 179, 180, 201
  Palace of, 179, 180, 225
SESOSTRIS I, 67, 69, 70
SESOSTRIS II, 67, 72
SESOSTRIS III, 67, 69, 72, *73*
SETH, 47, 93
SETHI, 97, 103
  Temple of, 41, *229*
  Tomb of, 99, 102
SEVILLE, SPAIN, 231
SHAKESPEARE, WILLIAM, 15, 104
SHALMANESER III, 179
  Black Obelisk of, *178*
SHAMASH, *166*
SHARMA, *304*
SHAUSHKA, 309
SHELLEY, PERCY BYSSHE, 226

SHEPHERD KINGS. *See* Hyksos
SHESHONQ, 104
SHINAR, LAND OF, 125, 126
SHIRAZ, IRAN, 225
SHISHAK, 104
SHU, *45*, 47, *117*
SHURUPPAK (Fara), IRAQ, 129, 156
SIAM. *See* Thailand
SICILY, 256, 282, 325, 326
SIDON, 10, 13, 192
SIENA, ITALY, 321
SIMLA, INDIA, 209, 212
SIMYRA, 97
SIN, 186
SINAI PENINSULA, 36, 65, 69, 100
SIND, PAKISTAN, 211, 213
SINUHE, 69-70
SIVA, 213, 215, 364-67 *passim*, 378
SMITH, GEORGE, 225
SMYRNA, TURKEY, 322
SNOFRU, 42, 54, 56, 69
SODOM, 7
SOLOMON, 10, 104
  Temple of, 158
SOMALILAND. *See* Punt
SOPHOCLES, 278, 279
SOUTHEAST ASIA
  Map, *363*
SOUTHERN VIETNAM, 365
SPAIN, 9, 272, 325, 326
SPARTA, GREECE, 277, 278, 279
SPHINX, *33*
SPINA, ITALY, 326
STEPHENS, JOHN LLOYD, 231, 385
  Quoted, 226, 411
STRUIK, DIRK J., 157
STYX, 332
SWEDEN, 245
SWITZERLAND, 326
SUDAN, 33, 38
SUMER, 14, 121-51, 166, 172, 182, 186, 206, 212, 214, 216, 218, 298, 300, 309
  Agriculture, *125*
  Architecture, 39, 126, 133
  Art, *132, 143, 148*, 175
  Astronomy, 124
  Burial customs, 130-32
  Chariots, *128*
  Chronology, 12
  City-states, 12, 128, 129, 133, 137, 145
  Crafts, 132
  Creation myth, 121-22
  Decline, 136, 151
  Earliest known civilization, 8-9
  And Elam, 175
  And Indus Valley, 215
  Influence, 9, 123, 128, 133, 175
  Invasions of, 135, 136, 148
  King list, *150*
  Law and justice, 153
  Literature, 131, 134, 136, 155, 157

  Map, *123*
  Mathematics, 124
  Medicine, 158
  Metalwork, *130, 131*, 143
  Pottery, 175
  Religion, 122, 129-30, 131, 140
  Revival, 136, *151*
  Sculpture, 135, *149*
  Society, 128-29, 130
  Stele of the Vultures, *132, 133*, 135
  Trade, 136
  Under Sargon, 12, 133-35, 145
  Writing, 124, 126, 127, *129*, 137
  Ziggurats, 12, 129, 140
SUPPILULIUMAS, 306-7
SURYAVARMAN II, 362, 366
SUSA (Shush), IRAN, 148, 153, 175
SUTKAGEN-DOR, PAKISTAN, 209
SYRIA, 9, 10, 13, 34, 36, 69, 70, 89, 92, 96, 135, 179, 183, 185, 256, 257, 258, 282, 286, 298, 299, 303, 305-8 *passim*, 310, 311, 316, 318
  Art, 136, 317, *319*
  Metalwork, *319*

T

TAGES, 324
TAMMUZ, 316
TANIS, EGYPT, 104
TARQUIN DYNASTY, 13, 23, 322, 327, 330
TARQUINIA, ITALY, 321, 324, 326, 327, 331, 332, 343
TARQUINII. *See* Tarquinia
TASIAN CULTURE, 37
TAYASAL, GUATEMALA, 400
TEFNUT, 47
TELEMACHUS, 277
TELIPINU, 310, 316
TELL AGRAB, IRAQ, 159
TELL ASMAR, IRAQ. *See* Eshnunna
TELL HALAF CULTURE, 125, 155, 186
TELL OBU HARMAL, IRAQ, 153
TELMUN, 185, 215, 218
TEOTIHUACAN, MEXICO, 386, 415
TETI, 52
TESHUB, 309-10
TEYE, 99
THAILAND, 357, 364, 366
THEBES, EGYPT, 35, 67, 71, 89, 90, 92, 93, 97, 98-99, 103, 104, 106, 307, 316, 347, 355, 361, 411
  Necropolis at, 99, 100, *101*
THEBES, GREECE, 279, 286, 355
THEODORIC THE GREAT, 15